1972

THE ABILITIES OF MAN

THE
ABILITIES OF MAN

THEIR NATURE AND MEASUREMENT

BY

C. SPEARMAN

AMS PRESS
NEW YORK

Reprinted from the edition of 1932, London
First AMS EDITION published 1970
Manufactured in the United States of America

International Standard Book Number: 0-404-06174-5

Library of Congress Catalog Card Number: 73-121291

AMS PRESS, INC.
NEW YORK, N.Y. 10003

FOREWORD

THIS work is the product of many hands and much patience. The lines of investigation were suggested—and even extensive beginnings made to follow them up—over twenty years ago. Since, there have been carried out a long train of laborious researches, each bringing, as it were, a single stone upon a preconceived unitary plan. And here, in this volume, at last, every stone is fitted into its place to build up the common edifice.

The joint authors of these researches have been my colleagues and collaborators, Dr. Aveling, Miss Bones, Prof. Burt, Mrs. Goulston, Dr. Wynn Jones, Prof. Krueger, Dr. Hart, Prof. Holzinger, Miss Peyer, and Mr. Philpott. No less have participated my sometime students, notably Dr. Abelson, Dr. Allen, Mr. Bradley, Mr. Edwards, Prof. Gopalaswami, Dr. Hamid, Mr. Hanlin, Mr. Hargeaves, Mr. Kay, Dr. Lankes, Dr. Magson, Dr. McCrae, Mr. Laycock, Dr. McQueen, Mr. Perera, Dr. Phillips, Dr. Saxby, Dr. Sleight, Dr. Slocombe, Prof. Strasheim, Dr. Webb, Dr. Wild, and Dr. Wohlgemuth.

Much has also been contributed by those who have so kindly read over and given advice about the present book. An unforgettable debt for many hours devoted to this purpose—notwithstanding urgent claims elsewhere—is due to Dr. Aveling. And the same may be said of Dr. Ballard, who, with much self-sacrifice, has examined the work throughout and made numerous suggestions of great value. To Prof. Holzinger, I owe, besides many shrewd and stimulating comments on the text, the vital service of checking the whole mathematical appendix. To Dr. Stead, further, thanks must be rendered for several remarks that have been useful. Last but not least to record are the services of Mr. Humphreys, who has very kindly supplied the work with an Index.

Besides all the preceding investigations done in, or connected with, our own laboratory, all possible use has also been made of the immense mass of research that during this quarter of a century has been executed farther afield. But here, frankly, the results have been disappointing. An extraordinarily small proportion of this otherwise excellent work has been devoted to the problems which, as we shall see, are really fundamental ; the work appears to have been suffering from lack of theoretical inspiration.

The present volume is the second of the series promised three years ago, the first having been an account of the general laws of cognition,[1] whilst this one presents the application of these laws to individual differences of ability. A third volume, it is hoped, will soon follow, giving a critical review of the chief general psychologies prevalent at the present day.

C. SPEARMAN.

UNIVERSITY COLLEGE,
    UNIVERSITY OF LONDON, 1926.

---

[1] *The Nature of " Intelligence " and the Principles of Cognition*, 1923 (Macmillan).

NOTE TO SECOND IMPRESSION

IN launching this new impression of *The Abilities of Man*, I would first venture to re-iterate the kinds of reader to whom it may be commended. It is meant for those who are interested in knowing the natures and degrees of the abilities of different persons ; and also the variations of the same person at different times or under different conditions. It is for those who believe that the knowledge of these abilities is of primary importance, not only for education, mental health, and commercial industry, but even for general human welfare and happiness. It is for those who, on such grounds, are willing to read a book that may demand as much mental effort as do crossword puzzles or detective stories. Finally, it might perhaps do something for those who are still talking of " intelligence " ; who imagine that they can estimate this and even measure it ; who on the strength of such estimates and measurement lightly dispose of children's lives—and all this without even knowing what they mean by the very word !

Besides such indications of the possible utility of the book, a few lines may be in order about its validity. How far has the evidence obtained during the short period since its original publication tended to verify this ? We seem entitled to answer, In an extraordinary degree.

The most drastic instances of this corroboration have come from those authors who at first were inclined to be sceptical. For these, on actually experimenting themselves, have obtained results in excellent agreement with what had been got by our own school previously.

Some such cases, it is true, have been troublesome. The difficulty has not so much arisen from the authors' very human failure to mention that their results were only repetitions of what had been obtained before. It has lain rather in their being so bent on maintaining their independence of our doctrine, that they have represented this doctrine itself in an untrue manner.

Very different has been the policy of other critics ; those whose attitude has not been subjective but objective. These, whenever they have come upon any new trail of better promise than what they had been following previously, have turned to it frankly and effectively. In this way it has come about that our school and that of Professor Thorndike, formerly regarded as antitheses to each other, have now entered into cordial collaboration. As another eminent instance of how original misunderstanding has been converted into mutual appreciation, may be cited the recent work of Dr. W. Brown.[1]

There is yet another class of critics to be taken into account. It consists of those who for long years judiciously suspended their judgment, awaiting patiently and impartially until the evidence should accumulate enough to warrant a definite decision. Such men are the real arbiters of science. Outstanding instances in the present case have been Dr. Myers and Professor Nunn. Both have now given their verdicts, and these have been decisively in accordance with the present volume.[2]

In view of such general confirmation, the changes needed in this impression would seem reducible to the following few. A revision of the paragraph on verbal group factors (p. 237). The addition of a more effective procedure for measuring specific factors (p. xviii.). And—with shame be it said—the correction of very numerous misprints.

[1] See meeting of Brit. Ass., 1931.

[2] See Myers' Report of Committee on Vocational Tests, 1930-1, Brit. Ass.; Nunn's Education, its Data, and First Principles, Edition 1930.

TABLE OF CONTENTS

PART I

THE RIVAL DOCTRINES

CHAPTER I

THE PROBLEM

To begin with, a few lines may be useful to mark out the topic which we are going to consider, and to indicate how this fits into the general order of things.

A person is aware of himself as existing in the midst of an external world—or at least, so it seems to him. He not only perceives this world and himself, but also thinks about both. As a single word to include the processes of both the perceiving and the thinking, modern psychology employs " cognition."

But what he thus perceives and thinks about the world and himself, as also about the relations between the two, excites in him activities and states of another kind, such as appetites, aversions, impulses, decisions, voluntary actions, pleasure, sorrow, and so forth. All these, to distinguish them from the cognitive processes, are called " conative " and " affective," that is to say, striving and feeling.

Take as an example the following description from *Oliver Twist* :

" So you wanted to get away, my dear, did you ? " said the Jew, taking up a jagged and knotted club which lay in a corner of the fireplace ; " Eh ? " Oliver made no reply. But he watched the Jew's motions, and breathed quickly. "Wanted to get assistance; called for the police; did you?" sneered the Jew, catching the boy by the arm. "We'll cure you of that, my young master." The Jew inflicted a smart blow on Oliver's shoulders with the club; and was raising it for a second, when the girl, rushing forward, wrested it from his hand. She flung it into the fire with a force that brought some of the glowing coals whirling out into the room. "I won't stand by and see it done, Fagin," cried the girl. "You've got the boy, and what more would you have? Let him be—let him be—or I shall put that mark on some of you that will bring me to the gallows before my time."

Here is a typical picture of human mental life in one of its most acute phases. Observe how readily and naturally it agrees with the foregoing classification of processes. Fagin sees Oliver, remembers his attempt to escape, thinks of punishing him, notices his club, marks the boy shrinking away and breathing quickly, perceives him stagger under the blow, hears his agonized whimper, foresees his better obedience in the future, and has the idea of enforcing the lesson with a second blow—all this and suchlike it is that the term "cognition" has been coined to include. But Fagin also becomes angry at what the boy has done, entertains a desire to punish him, relishes the anticipation of his writhing in pain, seizes voluntarily the club and actually uses it—all such processes as these characteristically involve conation and affection.

Now, the present volume is primarily concerned with a person's ability to "cognise." And we must at once demur—it is the chief reason for prefixing this little chapter—to an objection rather in vogue at the present day, which, if admitted, would cut the ground from beneath our feet. This consists in asserting that the processes of cognition cannot possibly be treated apart from those of conation and affection, seeing that all these are but inseparable aspects in the instincts and behaviour of a single individual, who himself, as the very name implies, is essentially indivisible.

To this protest—borrowed from metaphysics—we may reply that certainly an individual cannot be broken up into independent pieces. But no less certainly the various *aspects* of his behaviour can and must be submitted to separate consideration. Every science whatever, physical no less than psychological, is obliged to dissect its subject-matter, to deal with the different aspects of it in succession, and finally to bring each of these into relation with all the rest. Only by first dividing can the scientist eventually conquer.

In general, a person's total cognitive ability may be regarded as an instrument or *organ* at the disposal of *any* of his conative activities. It is this organ, then, that we are principally about to examine, and with especial reference to its variations of efficiency from one individual to another. The conative activities will only be brought within our scope to the extent that is needful to explain the working of the organ. But even this much will involve treating these activities in a far more fundamental manner than is usual in books on human ability.

CHAPTER II

MONARCHIC DOCTRINE : " INTELLIGENCE."

PRESENT DOMINANCE OF THIS DOCTRINE

Universal acceptance in popular usage. In considering the scientific doctrines on human ability, exceptionally great importance must be attributed to the popular view of the matter.   For this view has become ossified into current language, and thus has come to constitute a rigid shell within which the layman and the expert alike seem to be fixedly encased.

Now, paramount among the lay beliefs is that which assumes mental ability to lie under the sovereign rule of one great power named " intelligence."   In distinction from other doctrines which will be discussed in later chapters,

4

this credence in a single ruling power may be characterised as " monarchic." [1]

Judgments about intelligence conceived in this manner are made everywhere and by everyone—for the most part with much fluency and confidence. In degrees of it we habitually rate all the persons with whom we come into contact. Nothing else than such degrees do we mean when we call one man " clever," " bright," " sharp," or " brainy," whereas another is said to be " stupid," " dull," and so forth.

Such estimates are formed with peculiar abundance and emphasis in the sphere of education. From the kindergarten up to the university, the pupil is continually being subjected to ratings of this nature, whether set forth in official reports, or reserved for private guidance. But hardly less prominent is the part played by similar estimates in connection with industry. Hardly an employee is selected —from the office boy up to the general-manager—but that the chief motive (as regards ability) consists in an opinion as to whether he is or not intelligent.

Here, then, is an outstanding fact by which even the expert psychologist does not and cannot escape being profoundly influenced ; all the more so, perhaps, when this influence remains subconscious. Any doctrine put forward will sooner or later be faced by the choice between docilely accepting this popular belief so firmly entrenched in current speech, or else hardily attempting to tilt against it.

Introduction into science by biologists. This ascendancy of popular over scientific psychology has in its support, not only the prestige always attaching to the *vox populi*, but even, it would seem, a priority of authorship. For at least as far back as the fifteenth century, we find that estimates

---

[1] This term should not be confused with the " uni-focal " used in a previous work. The latter term was not so much a psychological as a statistical characteristic. It denoted a particular arrangement of a table of correlations. Such an arrangement, it may at once be added, is that which would harmonize, not with the doctrine expounded in the present chapter but rather that set forth in ch. vi.

were commonly made in ordinary life about a man's " intelligyens." Whereas in the systematic psychology of modern times, the concept does not seem to have attained to prominence earlier than the work of Herbert Spencer. By him, as might have been expected, it was brought in for the purposes of biology, at the period when this latter was being immensely stimulated by the then novel theory of evolution. Life was taken by Spencer to consist essentially in " the continuous adjustment of internal relations to external relations " ; and to " intelligence " it was that he credited the making of such adjustments in so far as these are mental.[1]

This work of Spencer was truly a surprising achievement. Besides having deep foundations in a theory whose scope envisaged the whole universe, it could boast of a fullness of elaboration, and above all a preciseness of expression, compared with which the greater part of the biological psychology now current is apt to appear nebulous and superficial.

From Spencer, who took into consideration animals in general, it was but a short step to those authors who were interested in differentiating the human from the lower species. The essential distinction between the respective powers of these two was now declared to lie in the fact that man alone is gifted with the prerogative of being intelligent. In order to explain how, nevertheless, the lower animals manage their affairs in such an effective manner as they undoubtedly do, the further power of " instinct " was brought forward as their endowment instead. Man also, indeed, was credited with some of this instinctive kind of knowing, but only for employment in such actions as had (with the human species) become mere routine. For new and individual emergencies he has recourse, it was said, to his sovereign power of intelligence.

In truth, however, the preceding doctrine was not so much a novelty as a revival. It really represented the most ancient of all known views about cognitive ability. After

[1] *Principles of Psychology*, 2nd ed., 1870, pt. iv.

long ages of neglect, it had now been rummaged out of the psychological lumber-room and hastily furbished up to meet the latest scientific requirements.

Adoption for mental tests. High as was this status attained by the concept of intelligence in biological territory, it later on became quite eclipsed by the reputation which the concept won for itself in the domain of mental tests. During a prolonged incubatory period, these had been cultivated in the seclusion of several psychological laboratories. Then, suddenly, Binet transformed such theoretical work into live practice. The success was astounding. Teachers found in tests of intelligence something that they could handle ; and the public got what it believed it could understand.

In a very few years there followed the tremendous feat of testing the intelligence of nearly two million men in the American Army. And even this, unsurpassable as a single event, was eventually outdone by the cumulative amount of testing effected in schools, universities, and other institutions.

The brilliant outlook. But the whole total of what has actually been accomplished seems as nothing compared with what looms in the not distant future, or has even already begun to be set on foot. How high the hopes are running may perhaps be illustrated by the following passage from a writer of well deserved authority :

> " Two extraordinarily important tasks confront our nation ; the protection and improvement of the moral, mental, and physical quality of its people and the reshaping of its industrial system so that it shall promote justice and encourage creative and productive workmanship." [1]

These are the opening words of a recent book on the results to be obtained through the tests of intelligence ; such tests are taken to supply an instrument capable of largely aiding the " two extraordinarily important tasks."

Nor can these hopes easily be accused of exaggeration,

[1] *American Intelligence*, by C. Brigham, 1923 ; foreword by R. Yerkes.

when we consider that an accurate measurement of every one's intelligence would seem to herald the feasibility of selecting the better endowed persons for admission into citizenship—and even for the right of having offspring. And whilst in this manner a suitable selection secures a continual rise in the intellectual status of the people taken in mass, the same power of measuring intelligence should also make possible a proper treatment of each individual ; to each can be given an appropriate education, and thereafter a fitting place in the state—just that which he or she demonstrably deserves. Class hatred, nourished upon preferences that are believed to be unmerited, would seem at last within reach of eradication ; perfect justice is about to combine with maximum efficiency.

RISE OF DOUBT AND CRITICISM

Repeated recourse to symposia. Curiously jarring with all these signs and messages of the happy new era, however, there has been sounded in certain places a note of solicitude, of suspicion, and even of downright hostility. Still more strange is it that such scepticism towards the testing of intelligence, instead of quietly subsiding under the influence of its apparently so victorious career, would seem on the contrary to be always gathering more and more force.

Some hint of the impending trouble had already begun to manifest itself with the biological psychologists. These found their " intelligence " and its supplementary " instinct " unexpectedly hard to fit into any acceptable general theory. The most fundamental questions remained obstinately unsettled. Are the two ways of knowing distinct from each other ? Has every intelligent action an instinctive basis ? Is every instinctive action determined also by intelligence ? Of such embarrassing problems there would seem to be an unlimited number.

In a resolute effort to clear up the situation, recourse was had to a symposium of several pre-eminent British authorities. And as was inevitable from such an assembly, many thoughts were uttered of high interest and suggestiveness. But in respect of the main purpose, the result can hardly be regarded as other than disappointing. On not one of the disputed matters does any approach seem to have been made towards better mutual understanding.[1]

Some years later, even greater embarrassment was felt, now among the mental testers in America. To meet it, another symposium was convoked ; here no less than fourteen leading authorities took part. But this time the task undertaken was far more restricted. Instead of attempting to settle the relations of intelligence to instinct—or to anything else—all efforts were concentrated upon describing its own nature. As before, such a distinguished gathering could not fail to beget many an observation bearing the stamp of brilliancy. But as for the essential aim, that of supplying the psychology of intelligence with a generally acceptable analysis, there appears to have been no success obtained. Each speaker gave his own opinion ; almost all of these turned out to differ widely ; and reconciliation between them was not even attempted.[2]

Eventually, yet another symposium on intelligence was called together, this time at Oxford in 1923.[3] But the situation became even more perplexed than at the previous meeting. For then the problem had only been as to the nature of the single thing, intelligence. But now there appeared in the field many different " intelligences," each presenting as hard a problem of its own !

Increasingly serious attacks. Alongside of all such symptoms of hesitation and anxiety, there has also arisen a more actively destructive criticism. Already, in 1912, Kirkpatrick had ventured to say :

> " I do not believe that the Binet tests or any other tests likely to be devised within the century will serve as a reliable measure." [4]

[1] *Brit. J. Psych.* iii. 1910.   [2] *Journ. Educ. Psychol.* 1921.
[3] International Congress of Psychology, 1923.
[4] *Journ. Educ. Psychol.* 1912.

And ten years later, this voice crying in isolation suddenly swelled into a chorus. Thus Trabue, who had himself been among the most active constructors of mental tests, veered round towards scepticism. He told of a woman who, although making a very bad record with the tests, nevertheless became

> " the housekeeper at one of the finest Fifth Avenue hotels, where she successfully directed the work of a corps of approximately 50 maids, three carpenters, two decorators, and a plumber." [1]

By this achievement on her part he was moved to conclude as follows :

> " In spite of the evidence of the tests, I insist that she is intelligent."

A different but no less damaging line of criticism was about the same time adopted by Viteles. He complained that

> although the current tests " are all called tests of ' general intelligence ' . . . the mental ability measured by each is not the same." [2]

Another assault was headed by Woodworth, who declared that the tests really touch neither the lower nor the higher ranges of intelligent behaviour.[3]

Still more recently the critical voices have continued to multiply and the tone has become even more hostile. Bishop protests that

> " The common practice of calling these tests intelligence tests will in many cases involve most serious error." [4]

Porteus picks out the three most important and widely adopted conclusions obtained by means of the tests up to the present date, and proceeds to declare that, one and all,

> " these conclusions run counter to everything that commonsense tells us." [5]

[1] *Journ. Educ. Research*, 1922.   [2] *Journ. Appl. Psychol.* 1922.
[3] *Psychology*, 1921.   [4] *Journ. Educ. Research*, 1924.
[5] *Journ. Appl. Psychol.* 1924.

And openly disdainful is the verdict of W. Lippmann :

" Psychologists have never agreed on a definition (of intelligence). . . . The intelligence tester cannot confront each child with the thousand and one situations arising in a home, a workshop, a farm, an office, or in politics, that call for the exercise of these capacities which in a summary fashion we call intelligence. He proceeds, therefore, to guess at the more abstract mental abilities which come into play again and again. By this rough process the intelligence tester gradually makes up his mind that situations in real life call for memory, definition, ingenuity, and so on. He then invents puzzles, which can be employed quickly and with little apparatus, that will according to his best guess test memory, ingenuity, definition and the rest. . . . The tester himself guesses at a large number of tests which he hopes and believes are tests of intelligence. . . . These puzzles may test intelligence, and they may not. They may test an aspect of intelligence. Nobody knows." [1]

Briefer, but even more caustic, is the summing-up of Peters, who dismisses the vast work hitherto done on the matter with the following comment :

" The problem of intelligence, touch it wherever we may, remains still only a problem." [2]

In view of all this condemnation of the tests by persons who are really competent, there seems no need to cite here the late adverse comments that they have evoked from the House of Parliament.

THE WORD " INTELLIGENCE " CANKERED WITH EQUIVOCALITY

Present prevailing chaos. Now, what, if anything, has really gone wrong ? Much of the criticism we have been

[1] *The New Republic*, Oct. 25, 1922.   [2] *Zeit. f. Psychol.* lxxxix. 1922.

quoting may be vague and contradictory ; it may suggest a disgruntled mood, rather than reasonable objections. But through it all—continually waxing in both clearness and emphasis—runs at least one theme that cannot be overlooked ; this urges from many standpoints that the very concept of " intelligence " is unsatisfactory.

Let us, then, submit this concept to some examination. And for this purpose, we shall not have to plunge into any profound arguments—as was done at the symposia—but may content ourselves with simply asking what the word " intelligence " is really intended to mean.

Take, to begin with, that very wide class of mental operations that are commonly included under the heading of memory. Is or is not this intended to come within the meaning of the word ? To our confusion, half of the authorities say yes, but the other half no. And this contradiction not only pervades the theoretical discussions, but equally so the practical framing of the tests. In the famous American Army set, as also in such standardized sets as those of Otis, of the Presseys, of the Illinois University, etc., all memorizing is excluded. But in other sets that likewise stand in highest repute—from Binet's earliest to Thorndike's latest—it is expressly introduced. Not even one and the same constructor of tests appears to maintain any uniformity in this respect. Thus Thorndike, although he admits memorizing into the tests which he has made for the purposes of matriculation, still leaves for it no place in the " National" series for which also he seems to be more or less responsible. Terman, again, retains memorizing in his tests for individuals taken singly, but excludes it from those which he has designed for groups. Binet, despite his free acceptance of memory in his test-scale, nevertheless explicitly says that it is really not intelligence but only the " great simulator " of this.[1] Nor is the consistency better on turning from the expert psychologist to the " plain man." With one breath he will say, " How intelligent of you to remember that " ;

[1] *Année Psych.* xi. 1905, 195-7.

with the next, he will excuse a lapse as not being one of intelligence but merely of memory.

Nor is this all. Rivalling even memory in scope are the operations usually attributed to the " imagination." Shall or shall not these, then, be taken to fall within the domain that is to be assigned to intelligence ? Few psychologists appear to face this obvious question at all. But two of the leaders, Stern [1] and Claparède,[2] do with their customary thoroughness deal with it ; and they both declare that this power lies not inside but outside the domain. Yet many other eminent psychologists adopt the contrary view, both in theory and in practice. For example, the test-scale of Yerkes—which has substantially the same composition as that of Binet—contains out of twenty components six that are expressly assigned by their author to " imagination." [3]

The list of such contradictory interpretations of the word intelligence can be extended indefinitely. Take the case of language. In the eyes of some writers, the great part played by this in current tests is only right and proper, on the ground of language being just that wherein human intelligence is most specifically manifested. Yet other writers, on the contrary, are always complaining of the influence of language in the tests as being irrelevant and disturbing. Or take the power of attention. Is this wholly, or partly, or not at all the same as intelligence ? All three views are widely held in current literature. Take even motor ability. By many experts this is unhesitatingly rejected from the scope of intelligence. Yet others as confidently declare that the power of co-ordinating movements has just as much right to be called intelligent as that of co-ordinating ideas.

Surely, however, the strangest fact has yet to be mentioned. If such terms as " intelligence " or " intellect " have—by right of general usage and long history—secured for themselves any unalienable core of meaning at all, this

---

[1] *Die Intelligenz der Kinder und der Jugendlichen*, 1922.

[2] *Scientia*, 1917, xxii.

[3] *A Point Scale for Measuring Mental Ability*, 1915.

certainly lies in their being opposed to and contrasted with mere sensation.   Yet even this last piece of seemingly solid ground for the word is beginning to tremble.   Already Binet wrote :

> " A sensation, a perception, are intellectual manifestations as much as reasoning is." [1]

And such a view continues to find advocates.   Thus, Haggerty declares that :

> " Intelligence " is " a practical concept connoting a group of complex processes traditionally defined in systematic psychologies as sensation, perception, association, memory, imagination, discrimination, judgment and reasoning." [2]

Chaos itself can go no farther !   The disagreement between different testers—indeed, even between the doctrine and the practice of the selfsame tester—has reached its apogee.   If they still tolerate each other's proceedings, this is only rendered possible by the ostrich-like policy of not looking facts in the face.   In truth, " intelligence " has become a mere vocal sound, a word with so many meanings that finally it has none.   The warning of Ballard would seem to have been justified only too well.[3]   The present devotion to the term recalls unpleasantly the old saying of Hobbes :

> " Words are wise men's counters, but they are the money of fools."

In a similar vein J. S. Mill writes :

> " The tendency has always been strong to believe that whatever receives a name must be an entity or being, having an independent existence of its own. And if no real entity answering to the name could be found, men did not for that reason suppose that none existed, but imagined that it was something peculiarly abstruse and mysterious."

[1] *Année Psych.* xi. 1905, 195-7.   [2] *Journ. Educ. Psych.* xii. 1921.
[3] *Mental Tests*, 1920, p. 23.

May not a prudent ear be turned to the humorous advice of J. Hart ? :

> " We shall have to give over the fun of arguing words and begin to face facts. Our intellectual joust is over ; it is time to plant some beans." [1]

Recourse to obscurantism. Not a few authors, however, seem almost deliberately adverse to any such remedial measure. Test results and numerical tables are further accumulated ; consequent action affecting the welfare of thousands of persons is proposed, and even taken, on the ground of—nobody knows what !

From such a mere obstinacy or blindness to the facts of the case, it is a relief to turn to the following passage where at any rate they are frankly challenged :

> " The tests ought to be conceived in such a fashion that they should address themselves as much as possible to pure Intelligence." Nevertheless the author continues that " it is not necessary to make an analysis to see if one test studies especially the power of attention, another the spirit of observation, or a third the spirit of combination. . . . The knowledge of the essence of intelligence is naturally a thing that merits profound research ; I nevertheless believe that the technique of the examination would not profit by it." [2]

But to announce in this way that the testing can be done just as well without knowing what has to be tested is surely, to say the least of it, a paradox.

Perhaps at bottom his meaning is much the same as that of the following passage by Terman :

> " To demand that one who would measure intelligence should first present a complete definition of it, is quite unreasonable." [3]

This time—as might have been expected from such a careful worker—a serious reason is brought forward in elucidation

---

[1] *The Survey*, June 15, 1924.　　[2] Bobertag, *Année Psych.* xvii. 1912.
[3] *The Measurement of Intelligence*, 1916, pp. 42-44.

and support. He compares the case with that of electricity. This, as everyone knows, has been investigated with conspicuous success and even measured with great accuracy, although its real nature was during most of the time conceived in a very erroneous manner ; indeed, even now, we have only some dubious speculation about it. So also the " intelligence "—Terman's argument runs—can well be investigated and measured before its real nature is known.

But here lies a danger of confounding two widely different things. First, there is the inward nature of the electricity ; and then there are its outward manifestations, such as the movements of a galvanometer. The former, no doubt, need not necessarily be known ; but certainly the latter must be. Sorry would be the plight of the physicist if he had to measure an electric current without ever settling which of several galvanometers before him was really in circuit with it. Analogously, we may perhaps dispense with knowing the " pure essence " of intelligence ; but assuredly we cannot test it without having decided which mental operations belong to its domain. Popularly and roughly expressed, we must needs know, if not *what*, at any rate *which*, it is.[1]

But even this much does not appear to have been done. So long as we have not agreed whether intelligence is intended to include memory, or imagination, or attention, or sensation, or anything else, we remain as impotent as the physicist who does not know which of the galvanometers to take into account. Small wonder, then, that Wallin, on investigating three widely adopted tests of this so-called intelligence, discovers them really to

> " measure qualities which are so different as to be practically incommensurable." [2]

Plea that the current procedure " works." There is another remarkable attempt at excuse to be considered,

---

[1] The same fact was expressed in other words by the present author as long ago as 1904 (*Am. Journ. Psych.* xv.) by saying that the intelligence must be measured in an " objective " manner. The case was already here compared with that of electricity.

[2] *Journ. Educ. Psych.* 1923, xiv.

which has some kinship to the preceding one. It urges that, no matter how blundering may be all efforts to supply the word intelligence with a definite meaning, still in practice the testing of it " works."

But how can it properly be said to have worked, so long as we do not know what sort of mental operations it ought to measure or even has been intended to measure ? The tests do, indeed, often show fair conformity with the estimates framed by teachers. But this is no great marvel, seeing that the tests have been specially selected with this view.

" The psychologist has recently given up the compilation of mental tests out of elements which his ' common sense ' told him were good measures of mental ability." He has abandoned this " in favour of a blind groping after agreement with estimates." [1]

Granting, then, that the tests have some connection or other with whatever makes a child shine at his school work— which might, for all we know, be something as trivial as mere keenness to show off !—are we on such a basis as this going to hallmark the child for life as having this very wonderful " intelligence," or to brand him as not having it ? Better than this would seem to be that the psychologist should go back to his " common sense " again.

ATTEMPTED REMEDY BY DEFINITION

Definitions distinguished from mere statements. The way to mend matters might seem obvious enough. If the word has become so disastrously equivocal, why not simply supply it with a definition ? Indeed, one might easily think that this has been done many times already. The symposia themselves could be taken to have furnished a whole treasury of definitions.

But let us pause and consider the nature of any genuine definition of a **word**, distinguishing this in particular from mere statements about the thing. Above all, the definition

---

[1] Wilson, Welsh, Gulliksen, *Journ. Appl. Psych.* 1924,

must unequivocally include the whole scope of the word and nothing but the scope. Take as example "neuron." To say that this serves the purpose of integrating bodily reactions is only a statement about the thing. To add that it typically consists of a minute body with short threadlike branches is still but a statement, though of the particular sort called description. But to lay down that it is a nerve-cell with all its processes, axon, and dendrites[1] is to give a genuine definition of the word, by virtue of which alone the preceding two statements are invested with any meaning at all. This last kind of proposition, then, is what we need for intelligence. Has anything like *this* ever been supplied at the symposia or elsewhere?

Favourite definition on a biological basis. Looking round for some proposition to fulfil the requirement, the one which seems likely to win for itself far the largest number of votes comes from Spencer and his modern biological followers, especially Stern and Claparède. Here, intelligence is said to be that mental power which produces "conscious adaptation to new situations."

Now, so long as this saying is only taken in the sense of a "statement about" intelligence, we may be confident —from the very names of their authors—that it admits of being interpreted in a valuable manner. But may it, furthermore, be taken to supply our present necessity, that of a genuine unequivocal definition?

To this question the answer cannot but be in the negative; the proposition would be equivocal through and through. Consider first the key word in it, "adaptation." With Spencer, this signified the furtherance of racial life. But with Stern it seems to have become the fulfilment of purpose. Other writers employ it in even more disparate senses, such as the discovery of truth. So too "situation" is sometimes made to mean the entire surroundings of a person as they really are, but sometimes only his very limited and fallible perceptions and thoughts about them. Even when restricted

---

[1] Starling, *Principles of Human Physiology*, 1912, p. 338.

to the latter sense, the word may still be interpreted in varying manners. Thus, Stern seems to understand by it any task with which a person may be confronted, so that it must of course include all tests he has to undergo. But Porteus, adopting another and not less natural sense of the word, has been able to urge that the power to deal with new situations is just what the current tests do *not* call into exercise.

Even supposing that some good fairy were to conjure away the ambiguousness of this definition, it would still only tell us what purpose intelligence serves, not what it is. For no general agreement exists as to what kind of mental operation really does produce " adaptation." Almost the sole detailed effort to settle this point was that made originally by Spencer ; and he concluded in favour of associative reproduction. But Stern and Claparède appear to have in view almost anything rather than this. In truth, possibly no kind of operation ought to be held exclusively responsible. Mind and body alike have evolved under conditions of survival which must have led to much adaptability in general. But what constituent of either mind or body has actually achieved this end, and how perfectly or imperfectly it does so, these are points not to be assumed *a priori* but ascertained by laborious investigation. There may perhaps be scope for operations of *every* kind.

On the whole, then, what superficially looked like an almost unanimous acceptance of this biological definition has shown itself to be at bottom little more than verbal jugglery. Psychologists have " found a formula " with which everyone can agree—provided that each interprets it differently !

Pedagogical and kindred definitions. There has been another much favoured attempt at defining intelligence, this time not so much in biological as in pedagogical interest. The power is said to consist in educability, or the capacity to learn. But this time we can be very brief—for almost all the preceding considerations about the biological view occur here over again.

According to the dictionary, " to learn " means " to acquire skill or knowledge." But this fairly intelligible meaning of the word is far from being adhered to by those who are using it to define intelligence. Their writings often imply that just the acquirement of skill, and even the absorption of knowledge, does *not* belong to it.

Moreover, we must here again ask, What mental processes do produce skill or knowledge ? On this point, as in the previous case, opinions are very discrepant. And perhaps the truth is that in learning, just as before in adaptation, every sort of mental process finds some or other useful work to do. In short, although to call intelligence the capacity to learn may perhaps supply a valuable " statement about " it, nevertheless as an attempt to furnish it with a definition such a proceeding can only render the confusion worse.

There are several further modern versions of "intelligence" to which similar comments apply. Among the most notable are the following : " The power of good responses from the point of view of truth " (Thorndike). " The ability to act effectively under given conditions " (Buckingham). " That which can be judged by the degree of incompleteness of the alternatives in the trial and error life of the individual " (Thurstone). " A biological mechanism by which the effects of a complexity of stimuli are brought together and given a somewhat unified effect in behaviour " (Jos. Peterson). Here must also be classed the important attempt of Ebbinghaus, followed by Ziehen, de Sanctis, and others, to characterize intelligence as the power of " combination." So, too, its treatment by Bergson and Wildon Carr. Many of these may make most valuable " statements about " it ; but as definitions they would plunge us back again in the old paralyzing equivocality.

Recent favour for " shape-psychology." There is another important recent doctrine, which we must not overlook. During the last twenty or thirty years the chief psychologists in all German-writing countries have been devoting themselves to the consideration of what are variously named "shapes" (Gestalten), "forms," "complexes," "structures" and " wholes." At last one brilliant little band of these authors—out of many no less eminent but still neglected— has managed to attract notice abroad. How does all this work—much of it very fine—stand in relation to our present problem, the concept of intelligence ?

The reply must be that here, as elsewhere, the concept has wrought only confusion. According to one school, with Meinong and Benussi as leaders, the activity of intelligence is just that to which all perception of shape must primarily be credited. But another school, that of Wertheimer, Köhler, and Koffka, has based its doctrine of shape-perception on the very ground that this is *not* attributable to intelligence.[1] But as neither the one nor the other school ever says what this word intelligence is intended by them to mean, the controversy has remained unprofitable. In the end, it appears to have got bogged in a quarrel as to whether relations " exist " or " subsist ", a distinction which, for psychological purposes, may be ranked with that between Tweedledum and Tweedledee.[2]

The call back to Scholasticism. Contrasting with all these attempts to use the word intelligence in some characteristically modern signification, is that which harks back to the usage of the mediaeval Schoolmen. Foremost in this movement, naturally, is the neo-scholastic school itself, which in late years has made extraordinary strides towards becoming better appreciated. Here, intelligence is defined as the operation of thinking in abstract or universal terms.[3] Such thinking has usually, but not always, been taken to fall into the following three specific manifestations—conception, judgment, and reasoning.

As an instance of return, even among experimentalists,

---

[1] Koffka, *Die Grundlagen der psychischen Entwicklung*, 1921, p. 101. Köhler, *Brit. Journ. Psych.* 1924.

[2] The recent interesting variation of this doctrine by Dr. Hazlitt has, unfortunately, reached the present writer too late for discussion here.

[3] The distinction between these two has much theoretical but little practical importance.

towards this time-honoured view may be cited the statement of Terman that—

> " An individual is intelligent in proportion as he is able to carry on abstract thinking." [1]

Now, if ever a concept can fairly lay claim to the title of intelligence, surely it is this one, so faithfully preserved for so many centuries by the Schoolmen. To the labour of these it is that the name really owes its prestige (which the other schools are now trying to annex for themselves). And in addition to possessing such titular right, this ancient doctrine even lends itself moderately well to the hard task of furnishing a definition ; its criterion, abstractness, although not so free from being ambiguous as might be desired, is at any rate far freer than any such notions as adaptability, educability, and so forth.

DOUBT AS TO POSSIBILITY OF MEASUREMENT

A further and worse difficulty. But even now, we are far from out of the wood. Bravely suppose all the preceding obstacles to have been somehow conjured away—let the word intelligence be interpreted in congruence with the best of psychological doctrines, let it be defined in some fashion that really precludes ambiguousness, and let this purified rendering of it be compliantly accepted by every leading authority—still even in this ideal case, we have not yet passed the worst part of the road which has to be traversed before establishing the current doctrine that confronts us in the present chapter.

For up to this point, we have only examined the matter from its qualitative aspect. There remains its aspect of quantity, particularly as involved in any test or measurement. In order to support effectively the monarchic doctrine, the intelligence must not only be definite in nature, but also single in function ; it must constitute a genuine " behaviour-unit."

[1] *Journ. Educ. Psych.* 1921, xii.

But where is the evidence for this ? Very competent psychologists, notably Whipple [1] and Colvin,[2] tell us just the contrary ; they report that what we measure by the current mental tests includes many different functions more or less uncorrelated with each other. The obtaining of a high total score in these tests, they say,

> "fails to get anywhere in our real inquiry as to just which ones of the various mental functions are possessed by the extraordinarily heightened efficiency. Is it memory span, or capacity for concentrated attention, or ability to handle symbols, or apprehension of abstract relations, or acute perceptive capacity, or lively imagination, or originality, or breadth of associative tendencies, or speed of learning, or what, that demarcates such a child from other children ? "

With different authors, the intelligence is analysed on different lines ; but the consequence that several measurements are requisite remains unaffected. Thus, Abramson demands that, for testing purposes, the intelligence should be divided up into such separate powers as " abstraction," " critical sense," " invention," and " recognition." [3]
Especially interesting in this respect is the interpretation of intelligence as the power of adaptation. Stern himself explicitly analyses this into many different kinds. When he throws all together under the name of intelligence, his aim is only classification ; he is far too clear-sighted to suppose that thereby he necessarily obtains a single ability measurable by a single value. Similar perhaps is the position of Claparède, when he divides the adaptation into three steps, viz. the posing of a question, the invention of a hypothesis, and the ensuing verification. To explain each of these he postulates a different mental power.[4]

---

[1] *21st Year Book*, National Society for the Study of Education, 1922.
[2] *Ibidem.*   [3] *Année Psych.* 1920, xxii.
[4] *Scientia*, 1917, xxii.   Also Intern. Congress of Psych. 1923.

Even the Scholastic doctrine of intelligence, as we have seen, divides up its manifestations into three sorts : conception, judgment, and reasoning. Each, then, would appear to require its own measurement.

What, finally, shall we say of Binet ?   He wrote (as late as 1909) that—

> " the mental faculties of each subject are independent and unequal ; with a little memory there may be associated much judgment. . . .   Our mental tests, always special in their scope, are each appropriate to the analysis of a single faculty." [1]

Why did not he then, why do not his avowed followers, measure (for each year of age) each of these independent faculties, memory, judgment, etc., one by one ?   To have made no attempt in this direction seems inconceivably illogical.

CONCLUSION

On the whole, the chronicle of the modern " intelligence " has been dramatic.   The first act shows it rapidly rising to a dazzling eminence.   But in the second, there begin to be heard notes of criticism, which soon swell into an insistent hostile chorus.   The most enthusiastic advocates of the intelligence become doubtful of it themselves.   From having naïvely assumed that its nature is straightway conveyed by its name, they now set out to discover what this nature really is.   In the last act, the truth stands revealed, that the name really has no definite meaning at all ; it shows itself to be nothing more than a hypostatized word, applied indiscriminately to all sorts of things.

Moreover, even on supposing that some cure could be invented for this blight of equivocality, there has been found a further and even worse objection to the monarchic doctrine. For this takes the intelligence to constitute a unitary function or single behaviour-unit, measurable by a single value. Whereas really, there seems to be no escape from regarding

[1] *Les Idées modernes sur les enfants*, p. 117.

it as divisible into several different functions more or less uncorrelated with each other, and therefore each needing a measurement of its own.

Such an admission would appear to break up the very foundations of both theory and practice as now largely current.   If, then, the great edifice of mental testing with all its fair promises is not to collapse like a house of cards, at least some other doctrinal support seems needed for it than is supplied by the current concept of a monarchic " intelligence."

CHAPTER III

OLIGARCHIC DOCTRINE : FORMAL FACULTIES.

GENERAL NATURE OF THE DOCTRINE

Assumption of a few great powers; "Profiles." The preceding chapter has led us from the doctrine of one single sovereign power to that of several different powers (abilities, capacities, levels, or however else they may be named). Typical instances are " judgment," " memory," " invention," " attention." Each of these is taken to constitute a separate function or behaviour-unit on its own account. Accordingly, each allows and requires its own separate measurement.

This view seems—despite its contradicting the previous one—to be in some sort advocated or implied almost universally. Whenever any person's ability comes up for examination, notice is sure to be directed towards such single traits as his " judgment," etc. We may observe this throughout ordinary life, from the most exhaustive biography down to the most casual conversation. And as for the expert psychologists, these have embodied this view in the construction of elaborate mental " profiles." Here, each trait receives its own measurement ; the values obtained are plotted on paper and then joined together by a line— the " profile "—which thus graphically depicts the person's general mental make-up. The doctrine, in comparison with the preceding one, may be termed " oligarchic." [1]

A gigantic instance in practice. To this almost unanimous theory, however, the actual practice in mental testing presents a curious contrast. Great as may be the zeal and detail with which such separate powers are advocated, still the carrying of the measurements into execution remains comparatively rare. The " profiles " so invitingly prepared remain undrawn.

But in a certain number of cases, and these of the highest importance, this oligarchic doctrine has been translated into actual practice. One instance has been supplied by an immense railway system. This business—said to be the largest employer of labour in the world—is reported to have used for the last four years a psychotechnic testing institute, which extends its sway over the entire railway service ; every prospective employee has to submit himself to the tests conducted there. These have no reference to any sovereign " intelligence." Instead, one test is assigned to each of the following nine powers: " combination " ; " fixation " ; " concentration " ; " observation " ; " reckoning " ; " distractibility " ; " speed " ; " dexterity " ; and " quick grasp."

In this one practical application alone, such enormous human interests are involved, as should stir the most dogmatic among us to a fresh and serious scrutiny of the matter.

HISTORICAL ORIGIN AND DEVELOPMENT

Problem of Plato and his solution. The most effective beginning of the inquiry would appear to lie along historical

---

[1] In a previous work, which examined this view with special regard to its significance for correlational tables, it was characterised as " multifocal."

lines. For this doctrine, so widely prevalent to-day, has a very ancient origin ; it is, in fact, by an ironical turn of fate, nothing less than an intensification of that old " faculty-psychology " from which we so often congratulate ourselves upon having nowadays become emancipated.

These faculties seem to have been born of the discovery that the senses are illusive. The earliest thinkers of whom we possess trustworthy accounts were perturbed by such facts as that the same wind can feel warm to one person but cool to another, or that a stick half immersed in water will look bent to the eyes whereas other evidence cogently proves it to be straight.

The solution to these paradoxes was found by Plato and others to consist in taking the mind to have two separate powers, capacities, or faculties (for these terms have been nearly synonymous). First, there is that of Sense ($\alpha\check{\iota}\sigma\theta\eta\sigma\iota\varsigma$), which produces only appearance and cannot be trusted ; and then there is that of the Intellect ($\nu o\hat{v}\varsigma$), which affords knowledge of reality and—in itself—is infallible. As for the " Intelligence," this was only a grammatical variant of the " Intellect " ; the latter term was used to denote the permanent mental power, whereas the former—being the present participle—naturally meant the actual putting of this power into use.

Subsequent variations of doctrine. To these original twin faculties of Sense and Intellect was not long afterwards added by many writers a third, that of Memory ; and later on, this addition appears to have been accepted by at least half of the leading authorities. A further addition—admitted by rather fewer—was that of the so-called Imagination or Invention. These four neatly supplemented one another, so as together to furnish a seemingly exhaustive account of human cognition.

Nevertheless two more were frequently introduced, and indeed were already in vogue before the fall of the Roman Empire. The one was the faculty of Speech ; the other, that of Attention. Lastly may be mentioned the faculty of

Movement, which obtained a prominent position with Aristotle and the Schoolmen, but for a long period afterwards failed to attract much psychological notice.

Any further increase in the number of faculties beyond these seven has, in general, only been attained by subdividing some or other of these. The Sense readily broke up into as many different mental powers as there are different sense organs. The Intellect (as already mentioned) was analysed into the three stages of conception, judgment, and reasoning. The Memory was split into reproductive ($\mu\nu\acute{\eta}\mu\eta$) and reconstructive ($\grave{a}\nu\acute{a}\mu\nu\eta\sigma\iota\varsigma$). The Imagination fell into " active " and " passive."

And here we may for a moment glance back at the preceding chapter. The gross equivocality there found to ruin the concept of " intelligence "—and in consequence to bring the gravest trouble upon modern psychology and mental testing—this equivocality is now at last explained. For the different powers between which this concept equivocates are in point of fact the seven historical faculties just enumerated. As usually happens, all these ideas of original thinkers percolated eventually down even to " the plain man " ; but in the course of reaching him, what had originally been distinct views became inextricably confused together.

Application to individual differences. Throughout the earlier part of this historical development of the doctrine of faculties, few if any writers were much concerned with the problem which interests us mainly at present, that of the differences between individuals. The purpose for which these faculties were first devised, and for a long time almost exclusively employed, had not been to portray the aspects in which men differ, but rather those which characterise them all alike. This was especially the case with the Intellect ; such a faculty was assigned to man ; to the lower animals it was denied. As for one individual man having it in greater or less degree than another, this was a standpoint alien to these early thinkers.

An exception, indeed, occurred with respect to Memory.

This does appear to have been regarded from the beginning as a unitary power wherein people exhibit large differences. Already Plato, for example, writes of a man having " a naturally good memory." [1]   Aristotle follows suit, entering into more detail and some adventurous physiology :

> " Neither very quick-witted nor very slow people seem to have good memories ; in the one class there is too much fluidity, in the other too much density. . . . Dwarfs and those who have a greater development in the upper parts of the body have poorer memories than those of the opposite type, because they have too great weight pressing upon the organ of consciousness. . . . Children are dwarf-like in type." [2]

Even here, we must remember that it was just memory which the earliest writers did *not* take to be a genuine faculty (in the sense of one of the parts of the psyche, μόρια τῆς ψυχῆς).

The real beginning of the faculties as explaining individual differences would appear not to have derived from professed psychologists, but from laymen.   The parting of these two ways, erudite and popular, seems to have occurred as early as the Renaissance.   Alongside of the Latin tomes wherein the laboriously acquired academic learning found expression, there now sprang up in the modern languages an abundant literature of more facile origin.   Here, the " intelligence " ceased to be regarded as an all-or-none endowment ; although still wholly denied to the lower animals, it was no longer credited in perfection to every human being, but became susceptible of degrees.   Much the same turn was taken, and even earlier, by the faculty of imagination ; one person was said to possess much of it, others little.

In this discrepancy arising between the erudite and the popular views, the advantage—following the general trend of the Renaissance—soon inclined to the popular side. Even the most learned writers began to take the faculties as

[1] *Republic.*   [2] *De Memoria,* 450 b and 453 b, trans. by Ross.

differentiating one individual from another. With Ch. Wolf, for example, a psychologist in highest repute, the intellect explicitly admitted of grades varying from person to person.[1] So did imagination and memory, as also the power of sensory perception.[2]

With later authorities, the doctrine of individual differences became most prominent in respect of sensory perception. Especially notable was Beneke, a disciple of Herbart, who greatly developed his master's teaching. Without abating any of its original theoretical profundity, he turned it to abundant practical applications and most of all to the study of individual differences. According to him, there exist certain ground-systems (*Grundsysteme*), which furnish these differences with their ultimate basis ; and one such ground-system is constituted by each of the senses, visual, auditory, tactile, gustatory, and olfactory. To these he adds some " vital " senses, which derive from the muscular, the digestive, and the sexual organs respectively.

Such an allotment of one faculty to each sense was easily extended from the domain of sensory perception to that of sensory images. Most influential here seems to have been Charcot, who ranged human persons into different classes according as their imagery is predominantly visual, auditory, or kinesthetic. His most striking clinical case was that of a merchant who had always placed entire reliance upon his images of the visual kind. One day, he was suddenly deprived of these by a nervous disorder, which nevertheless did not affect his visual percepts. The privation, although thus confined to the images and sparing the percepts, still sufficed, it was said, to reduce him to an extraordinary state of impotence in daily life. For instance, in spite of being still able to see the streets quite distinctly, he now became unable to find his way about them. This would never have happened, Charcot declared, had his images previously been not visual but auditory or kinesthetic.

Soon afterwards there followed the interesting investiga-

---

[1] *Psychologia empirica*, 1732, para. 277.   [2] *Ibidem*, para. 480.

tions of visual and auditory imagery by Fechner and Galton, which were supplemented by the graphic description that Stricker gave of his own almost exclusively kinesthetic way of representing objects. Soon the doctrine of sensory faculties gained wide acceptance, particularly in the medical and the educational professions ; mankind was divided up into the eye-, the ear-, and the muscle-minded. Radical reforms were projected to suit this state of affairs. It was even proposed to break up the school classes into sections, each being confined to the children employing one and the same sense.

The faculties preferred at the present day. From this historical excursion let us pass on to the faculties as they are being advocated in current literature. The following is a little statistical summary which shows which of them are now finding the most general support. It is an analysis obtained from 33 prominent publications on the subject :

Faculty.	Number of times advocated.	Original source.
Sensory perception - - -	15	
Intellect - - - -	16	
Memory - - - - -	19	Taken over
Imagination - - - -	11	from ancient
Attention - - - -	10	psychology.
Language - - - -	3	
Movement - - - -	6	
Various - - - - -	16	New.

A few comments on the literature from which these figures have been derived will perhaps aid towards understanding how the faculties are being at present conceived. We will take each in turn.

The sensory perception, which heads the list, appears in these cases to be sometimes thrown together into one single faculty, as occurs when a test is proposed for the power of " keen perception." But more often, some particular kind is picked out to constitute a power by itself. An example is the alleged capacity for "the analysis of visual form." But such further sub-division seems never to be carried through systematically. The particular kind of perception singled out is left by itself, all the other kinds being simply disregarded. This compares very unfavourably with the older work of Beneke.

Although the second place has been given to the " intellect," this word itself occurs seldom, and even seems to be deliberately avoided by most of the writers. But frequent usage is made of the term by which this intellect has always been essentially characterised, namely, the power of abstraction. Much the same class of operations, too, would appear to be often meant under such expressions as " superior ideation " and even simply " thought." Still more commonly, however, not the entire ancient intellect (conception, judgment, and reasoning) is advanced as a faculty, but only one of these three constituents; the other two are in such cases left out of account.

Turning to " memory " this in our cases is sometimes made to include the power of association, but at other times the two are kept distinct. Further separations not infrequently made are those between the immediate and the delayed kinds of remembrance ; between the conceptual and the imaginal kinds ; or between recognition and recall. But here again some or other subdivisions are put forward regardless of the others and without any attempt at system.

Next in order of frequency comes " imagination," which is here taken to include " invention," since the two terms seem in these writings to have been used synonymously. Attempts to split this up do not occur. The most striking feature about its treatment is the proneness to invest it with extravagant value. It has been taken as pre-eminently creative, and thence has come to be identified with " genius." Some enthusiasts have gone so far as to declare that this creative faculty—unlike intelligence or talent—is emancipated from the laws of heredity ; it is said to pertain to the very person himself, as distinguished from the mere

C

" psychoplasm " which has descended to him from his ancestors.[1]

" Attention " is in our cases usually taken to be a single faculty ; but sometimes sub-divisions are introduced. The chief difficulty lies in its ambiguousness.

About the faculty of " language," the surprise is that its advocates should have been so few. This seems attributable to the fact that our statistical record was restricted to cases where the doctrine of faculties was very explicit. If we had also included those cases where the doctrine seemed to be implicit, then language would have occupied a far more prominent position.

As for " movement," this is often depicted as a single faculty, receiving then such names as " motor control " or " manual dexterity." But at other times, here again, some special domain is carved out, such as the power of " kinesthetic discrimination " or that of " quick responsive action."

Finally, we arrive at those current faculties which do not obviously derive from the ancient seven, but instead indicate more or less originality. As instances may be quoted the following :   " censorship " ;   " foresight " ;   " keenness in noticing resemblance " ; the power to " break up a complex and properly evaluate and relate its parts " ; the ability to " re-arrange a bit of mental content in a new and prescribed way." Characteristic of all these is that in them the already noticed lack of system reaches its highest degree. They have almost always been put forward to meet some special emergency. Despite their being novel, no attempt is made to demonstrate, or even to discuss, their psychological foundation and significance. Their very authors do not consistently emphasize them from one writing to another. Small wonder, then, that in general nobody else takes any notice of them.

[1] *Psychological Principles*, Ward, 1918, p. 450 ff.

CRITICISM

Some usual but unimportant objections. After this account of the doctrine of faculties, both as it arose anciently and as it stands to-day, let us proceed to examine the stability of its foundations.

For the present purpose, we may waive all criticisms that could be brought against any particular version of it. These would only involve matters of detail. Their amendment might be expected to arrive in due course.

Nor can the charge of ambiguousness, elsewhere so damaging, be urged with much force in the present case. For the faculties are often furnished with definitions that appear to be tolerable enough.

There is, indeed, a double-barrelled accusation that has been brought against the faculties since at least the days of Malebranche ; they have been declared to make a pretence of supplying an explanation whilst really being meaningless ; and above all, they have been charged with contradicting the most essential character of the mind, its unity. To enter into either of these two points would take us too far afield. But elsewhere the writer hopes to show that both of these accusations are really groundless.

The vital point : correlation. But now comes the crux of the whole matter. It is similar to that which proved fatal to the preceding claims to measure " intelligence." For this showed itself to have several more or less independent components, and therefore to need a separate measure for each. But what was thus said of the supposed monarchic intelligence can no less pertinently be asked of each of the oligarchic faculties. Take, for instance, judgment. This, too, seems to break up into several different kinds. Judgment for politics would appear to be one thing ; that for sports, another ; that for telepathy, yet a third ; and so forth. Is not then, here also, a separate measurement needed for each kind ? Our answer must again be that all different kinds certainly require separate measurements, unless they can be shown to be perfectly inter-dependent, so that the person who excels in any one kind does so to just the same extent in all the others. Once more, the vital point is the degree of inter-dependence, or, as it is commonly called, the amount of correlation.[1]

The evidence, theoretical, casual, and experimental. Now, one argument that has commonly been urged in support of the faculties does not derive from observation but from theory. It is that the judgment or other faculty must be regarded as a single mental tool, whilst the objects judged are only so many different materials upon which this can be employed. Analogies are brought from ordinary life, as for instance that one and the same font of type will equally well print either the catechism or else a French novel. Why, it is said, should not the selfsame power of judgment deal equally well with politics, sports, or anything else ?

But such an argument is not convincing. As plausibly, it could be turned round in the contrary direction. The type used for the catechism will certainly not serve to print *all* other things, as, say, pictures.

Quitting these *a priori* flights and turning to actual observation, this is supplied to some extent even by casual experience. Long ago Herbart wrote :

" Memory and imagination agree in that their superior strength is usually limited in every man to particular

[1] Obviously, this problem in the sphere of individual differences is akin to that which is well known in the sphere of education under the title of formal training. Between the two, however, there is an important distinction. In the case of the individual differences, the point is as to whether the possession (presumably innate) of any ability involves the possession of all the other abilities which fall within the same facult;. In the case of education, the point is whether the *acquirement* of any ability involves that of the others also. The former kind of correlation might conceivably exist without the latter kind. Take as analogous to the different abilities lying within the same faculty several fields situated in the same neighbourhood. The latter will more likely than not closely resemble each other in chemical constitution of the soil. Hence, an analysis of the constitution of one among them will supply a fairly reliable test for the remainder. But quite idle, of course, would be the manuring of one field in the hope that thereby the others would grow correspondingly productive.

kinds of objects. . . . He who easily remembers the technical expressions of a science that interests him often has a bad memory for the novelties of town." Again, lunatics, he says, frequently show their imagination to be diseased in respect of some " fixed idea," whilst retaining " a very healthy activity, indeed, often the exaltation of genius, for everything not concerned with the fixed idea. . . . The marvel of these things vanishes on discarding the hypothesis of mental faculties." [1]

Volkmann, following him, declared that every idea has a memory and imagination of its own. In modern times, no less emphatic have been the writings of Thorndike :

> " The science of education should at once rid itself of its conception of the mind as a sort of machine, different parts of which sense, perceive, discriminate, imagine, remember, conceive, associate, reason about, desire, choose, form habits, attend to. . . . There is no power of sense discrimination to be delicate or coarse. . . . There are only the connections between separate sense stimuli and our separate senses and judgments thereof. . . . There is no memory to hold in a uniformly tight and loose grip the experiences of the past. There are only the particular connections between particular mental events and others." [2]

Such denials of functional unity appear to have a direct bearing on that very case where the doctrine of faculties led to such extraordinarily momentous actual practice, that is, the testing of all employees in a great railway system. For example, among the faculties thus tested was that of " concentrating attention." The actual test consisted in making the subject look over a list of numbers and tick off those which occurred in another list. The question, then, is as to whether the person who can most successfully perform this feat of ticking off numbers for a minute or two will also be the

[1] *Lehrbuch z. Psychologie,* 1834, § 10. [2] *Educational Psychology,* 1903.

most capable of attending to the duties that occur throughout the management of a locomotive. This question as to whether attention constitutes such a behaviour-unit has already been answered in the negative very long ago by Wolf. As an example, he quoted a poet who could not bring himself to attend to anything except verses or what might be conducive towards versifying. Another instance given by him was that of an erudite person who attended most keenly to whatever was concerned with his study, but was hopelessly inadvertent about all domestic affairs, matters of business, and personal toilet.[1]

From all this merely casual observation, however, let us turn to the more cogent evidence of competently conducted experiment. But here again the answer would seem to be negative. Sherman, for instance, using a test specially framed to measure attention, has found that the best performers are often those who in school or at home had showed themselves conspicuously *in*attentive.[2] Another investigator, Marcus, employed the very procedure of ticking off numbers that was applied to the railway employees ; he found that its correlation, even with work that outwardly seemed very similar, was really but little above zero.[3]

Look where we may, then, the doctrine that the faculties constitute unitary functions appears everywhere to have broken down. Even when a faculty is quite acceptable in the sense of indicating a mere *class* of mental abilities, it cannot be taken without further evidence as implying any *correlation* between these, as would be indispensable for the purpose of measuring them all by any single test.

Source of the error. One curious feature about these formal faculties has yet to be mentioned. The doctrine loses every battle—so to speak—but always wins the war. It will bend to the slightest breath of criticism ; but not the most violent storm can break it. The attacks made long ago by the Herbartians appeared to be irresistible : no serious defence was even attempted. Yet the sole permanent

[1] *Psychologia Empirica.*   [2] *Journ. Appl. Psych.* 1923.   [3] *Ibidem,* 1920.

effect of these attacks was only to banish the word " faculty," leaving the doctrine represented by this word to escape scot free. As much may be said for the onslaught of Thorndike. His audience easily agreed with him—and thereafter went on making just the same unwarranted assumptions as before.

In such cases of tenacious though tacit resistance to amendment of view, the cause always lies in some insidious temptation to go astray. And something of this sort seems to occur in the present case. The main trouble has too deep a root in philosophy to be dealt with here in any adequate manner. But we venture to touch upon it to the extent of pointing out a common though usually unspoken assumption; this is that, in perceiving or thinking, the mind supplies the activity, whereas the objects exist on their own account. When, for instance, a man sees a tree, only the operation of seeing is credited to himself : the tree is taken to be an object presented by his environment. A facile corollary of this assumption is to suppose that no change in the nature of the objects can make any difference in the nature of the mental activity involved. But really the whole assumption with its corollary is rooted in error ; the truth is that all objects which are perceived or thought of become, by virtue of this very fact, what is called " immanent " in the mind ; to this extent, they themselves become constituents of the mental activity. As for the objects as they exist in reality apart from the mind cognizing them, these are called " trans-cendent," and to deal with them is no business of psychology, but of philosophy. The doctrine of faculties is, then, based upon an almost irresistible tendency to confuse together the " immanent " and the " transcendent " objects.

There is another source of the error, one which can be detected without such digging down into philosophical depths. It consists in the old illusion whereby words are taken as real coin instead of mere counters. Having fashioned for ourselves such a name as, say, judgment, then —because the name remains the same—we fall into the belief that we are treating of an entity always the same.

Yet a third influence working in this direction appears to be the logical fallacy known as *a dicto secundum quid ad dictum simpliciter*. Anglicized, this means that everything may be regarded, either as existing simply, or else as subject to some qualification ; people often jump unwittingly from the one over to the other. In the classical instance, the fallacy runs as follows :

> " You eat raw meat. For you eat what you bought yesterday, and what you bought yesterday was raw meat."

Analogously in our case of faculties :

> " You can test the power of attention. For you can test the ticking-off of numbers, and this ticking-off is done by the power of attention."

Summing up, the " oligarchic " doctrine, which takes ability to fall into some few great faculties each functioning in a unitary manner ; which would claim to measure each faculty by a single value ; which puts together a set of such measurements into the so-called mental " profiles " ; which on the strength of these would dispose of the fate of thousands of persons—this doctrine would seem on closer scrutiny to be wholly devoid of foundation.

CHAPTER IV

OLIGARCHIC DOCTRINE : TYPES

CURRENT ADVOCACY

General nature of the doctrine. The next doctrine to be examined is much less widely prevalent, at any rate among those psychologists who work experimentally and aim at obtaining measurements. Nevertheless—in some of its varieties, at any rate—it appears to have really received a much more thorough, and even scientific, development. Its general nature is again " oligarchic," in that it takes ability to be ruled by some few great powers or tendencies. But these latter are no longer definitely founded upon what has been called the " form " of the mental operation. Their basis is not so much qualitative as quantitative. The essential reference is to some grade or degree that may characterise mental operations of any form.

It must be admitted, indeed, that the transition from the doctrine considered in the last chapter is only gradual, not clear-cut. But this in most cases is due to nothing more than obscurity and ambiguity of expression.

Usually, we are here dealing with those individual differences to which the name of " types " has often been applied.

Trait of perseveration. Of great suggestive value has been the work of G. E. Müller on what he called perseveration. This he defined to be the tendency which every idea has, after having once occurred, " to remount into consciousness spontaneously." [1]

The phenomena actually recorded by him derive only from his experiments in memorizing syllables. But so impressed does he seem to have been that—contrary to his usual cautiousness—he ventures to generalize over the whole region of thought and even action. He writes :

> " Consistency of thought and action that extends beyond the immediately given is based to an essential degree upon perseveration. . . . It is easy to see that individuals with strong perseveration will not be rightly placed in a vocation which needs a quick and frequent change of attention or a rapid disposal of numerous and quite different businesses." [2]

Subjective and objective types. In the same year, the announcement was made of a notable pair of antitypes, under the respective names of " subjective " and " objective." These had been discovered by W. Stern during his long and fine investigations in the domain of testimony (*Aussage*).

The subjective type is manifested in :

> " the tendency of his description (of pictures) to give above all things himself, to bring to expression his personal relations to the things, his temperamental, volitional, and imaginative reactions to them."

As regards the opposite or " objective " type,

> " characteristic for these persons is the tendency of their descriptions to have a cool matter-of-fact (*sachlich*) nature, to seek to be just to the object as such." [3]

---

[1] *Gedächtnis*, Müller and Pilzecker, 1900, ch. iii.
[2] *Ibidem.*   [3] *Die Intelligenz der Kinder*, 1922.

Among the numerous writers who have written subsequently upon these two antitypes at length and in an interesting way may specially be mentioned Baerwald,[1] Klages,[2] Kurella,[3] and Partridge.[4]

Primary and secondary functions. Two years later appeared a very notable publication by Otto Gross.[5] This time the field of discovery was pathological, the observations being derived from the two most prevalent features of insanity, viz. melancholia and mania. Characteristic of these two states he finds to be the " deep-narrow " and the " shallow-broad " types of mental make-up.

The deep-narrow type displays, he says :

> " difficulty in apprehending and elaborating outer stimuli, especially if numerous and disparate ; embarrassment and unpracticalness : dissolution of the spiritual personality into single large systems of ideas, which is each in itself closely connected, highly developed, and deeply rooted, but which are defectively associated between each other ; long lasting emotions ; tendency to exaggerate feeling-toned ideas ; emotional irrationality." [6]

As for the shallow-broad type, this is said to be—

> " manifested in a prompt apprehension and instant utilization of outer impressions ; presence of mind, cunning and courage. But defective power to build up large systems of ideas, especially in ethical and social respects ; inability to be profound ; strong unstable emotions ; levelling of feeling-toned ideas ; emotional irrationality." [7]

Translated into physiological terms, the shallow and the deep types are said to arise respectively out of the propor-

[1] *Zur Psychologie der Vorstellungstypen*, 1916.
[2] *Prinzipien der Charakterologie*, 1910.
[3] *Die Intellektuellen und die Gesellschaft*, 1913.
[4] *Outline of Individual Study*, 1910.
[5] *Die cerebrale Sekundärfunktion.*   [6] *Ibidem.*   [7] *Ibidem.*

tional dominance of the " primary " and the " secondary " functions of the nervous system.

> " Each nervous element whose (primary) functional excitement means the occurrence of a presentation in consciousness, persists (secondarily) after the presentation has quitted the span of consciousness. That is to say, it remains for a further long period in a state of after-function. This after-function . . . remains regulative of the further direction of associative activity." [1]

This notion of a primary and a secondary function was soon taken over by Heymans, Wiersma, and their school, with the result of building up the theory that individual differences rest upon three bases : emotionality ; activity ; and the proportion of primary to secondary function. So far as scientific status is concerned, this Dutch work stands upon a very high plane. In it mere casual observations— shown over and over again to be grossly misleading—are replaced by most careful and systematic investigations. One of these in particular was founded on the fact that no person is likely to be better acquainted with the characters of a group of other persons than is a physician in respect of a family tended by him for many years. Accordingly, Heymans and Wiersma induced 450 such physicians to make exhaustive reports upon 2,523 individuals in 458 families. The wealth of detail thus secured would appear to constitute one of the finest contributions that have been made to modern psychology. [2]

Introverted and extroverted attitudes. Ideas substantially the same as those mentioned above re-appeared not long afterwards in the work of Jung. [3] But the arduous scientific research of his predecessors, notably the Dutch school, now gives way to attractive literary embellishment. The anti-

----

[1] *Die cerebrale Sekundärfunktion.*

[2] *Zeit. f. Psychol.* xlii. xliii. xlv. xlvi. li.

[3] *Psychological Types*, trans. by Baynes, 1923.

types put forward have the arresting titles of " introverts " and " extroverts." The introversion

" means a turning inwards of the *libido* (identified by the author with mental energy), whereby a negative relation of subject to object is expressed." [1]

As for the mental make-up of a person of this type :

" Intensity is his aim, not extensity. . . . In thinking out his problems to the utmost of his ability, he also complicates them, and constantly becomes entangled in every possible scruple. The subject perceives the same things as everybody else, only he never stops at the purely objective effect, but concerns himself with the subjective perception released by the objective stimulus. The peculiar nature of introverted intuition, when given the priority, also produces a peculiar type of man, viz. the mystical dreamer and seer on the one hand, or the fantastical crank and artist on the other." [2]

Turning to the opposite trait, that of extroversion, this

" means an outward turning of the *libido*. With this concept I mean a manifest relatedness of subject to object in the sense of a positive movement of subjective interest towards the object.[3] So far as the practical thinking of the merchant, the engineer, or the natural science pioneer is concerned, the objective interest is at once manifest. Feeling in the extroverted attitude is orientated by objective data, *i.e.* the object is the indispensable determinant of the kind of feeling. It agrees with objective values. . . . This kind of feeling is very largely responsible for the fact that so many people flock to the theatre, to concerts, or to church, and what is more, with correctly adjusted positive feelings. His aim is concrete enjoyment, and his morality is similarly orientated. His intuition is employed ' in the service of action and accomplishment ' rather than ' in the service of cognition and inner perception.' " [4]

[1] *Ibidem.*   [2] *Ibidem.*   [3] *Ibidem.*   [4] *Ibidem.*

For all his resemblance to the Dutch school, however, Jung on certain points displays originality. He no longer regards such introversions and extroversions as abilities, or even as innate temperamental characters. Instead, he declares that they are nothing more than a pair of alternative *mechanisms which can be inserted or disconnected at will.* Only by force of their habitual predominance in any person do the corresponding traits of character develop.

Original also is the need which he finds for dividing this mechanism into separate parts. One is allowed by him for each of four faculties : sensation ; thought ; feeling ; and what he calls "intuitive knowledge." This sub-division of the mechanism may perhaps be required by the facts ; but it certainly introduces so much complication as must greatly diminish the value of the whole standpoint. For instead of only two types, there are now actually sixteen (counting as a different type every arrangement of introversion and extroversion among the four faculties).

Miscellaneous other types. In addition to all the preceding types that have from time to time received emphatic support and elaborate development, numerous others have been advocated in a more occasional manner.

An instance is the pair of antitypes called by Meumann " static " and " dynamic " respectively.[1] But seeing that the former is taken to be he who can pursue his purpose persistently, whilst the latter needs being continually spurred anew, one may wonder why these titles were not rather bestowed the other way round.

Another pair brought forward by the same author consists of the " analytic " and the " synthetic " types. He himself appears to have regarded the former tendency as that which is measured by speed of scratching out any given letter on an ordinary printed page.[2] But Stern portrays it more attractively as follows :

> " The former (analytic type) inclines to regard details in isolation from each other, to draw boundaries, and

---

[1] *Die Experim. Pädagogik,* 1911, ii. pp. 393-4. [2] *Ibidem*

to detect faults. The latter (synthetic type) inclines rather to bring what is separate into a single view, to connect the remote, and to arrange the chaotic, whilst often deficient as regards the truth in detail and sharpness in single judgments." [1]

Yet another pair is supplied by Stern's division of persons into the "spontaneous" and the "merely reactive." The former are characterized in that they

" do not wait until their mental work is demanded, but incline to set it going themselves." [2]

An antithesis that has found wider echo among psychologists is that between "theoretical" and "practical" mindedness. This contrast has been stressed by Lipmann [3] and many others, especially McFarlane in her careful experimental work. [4] But, unfortunately, it has been interpreted in very diverse ways. With some authors, "practical" means capacity for dealing with concrete situations as opposed to abstract ideas ; when so taken, Napoleon would be practical as compared with Plato. In other writings, as those of Stern, however, the " practical " man is he who faces some situation quite new to him, and therefore has to adapt himself to it on the spur of the moment. The " theoretical " man, on the other hand, seems to be he who adapts himself to a situation by means of his accumulated past experience. But most often of all, perhaps, the " practical " seems to be understood as synonymous for " motor " ; taken in this sense, the pre-eminently practical man would not be he who faces serious situations of any kind, but rather he who breaks stones on the road.

The last type to be mentioned here—and one that may possibly have a large psychological future—is the " eidetic " kind that has recently been investigated by Jaensch and his school. It comprises those persons whose images are

[1] *Die Intelligenz der Kinder und der Jugendlichen*, 1922, p. 22.
[2] *Ibidem.*   [3] *Zeit. f. ang. Psych.* 1924, xxiv.
[4] *Brit. Journ. Psych. Mon. Suppl.* viii. 1925.

extremely vivid. Among its most interesting features is that such persons are said to fall into two varieties, named T and B respectively. The T-constitution is

" marked by galvanic and mechanical hyper-excitability of the peripheral, especially of the motor, nerves " ; also by a tendency to the " tetanoid " type of psychosis ; the persons are silent and anxious ; the images tend to be uncontrollable and are often negative.

The B-constitution tends towards the Basedow syndrome ; the images are positive, well under control ; the persons sweat easily, have lively skin reflexes, low skin, resistance, widely opened eyes, lively pupil reactions, and bright eyes. Pregnant women incline to be eidetic, which indicates that this character is dependent upon some inner secretion.[1]

ANTICIPATION BY EARLIER PSYCHOLOGISTS

Ancient times. As usual, most of these modern doctrines of types have had forerunners in the past. Already with Plato we encounter—incidentally—hints at the distinction between the " shallow " and the " deep " kinds of men. He writes that commonly,

" such as learn with facility, have a good memory, are sagacious and acute, and endowed with all qualifications thereto allied, are yet not at the same time of so vigorous and lofty an intellect as to live orderly, with calmness and constancy, but are carried hapchance by mere buoyancy of spirits and are deserted by everything like stability." [2]

Aristotle discourses in similar vein, but with a stronger bias towards physiological interpretations.

The Renaissance and afterwards. Here again—as indeed also in the Middle Ages—such a physiological tendency was very pronounced. Throughout history, the differences

[1] *Sitzungsb. d. Ges. z. Beförderung d. ges. Naturwissenschaften.*
[2] *The Republic.*

between man and man—far more than the mental constitution common to all men—has been taken as especially
open to explanation on physiological grounds. And this
tendency may perhaps be not without profound metaphysical
significance.

The following is a characteristic passage from Malebranche :

" It is easy to account for all the different characters
that are encountered in the minds of men ; on the one
hand, by the abundance and poverty, the agitation and
sluggishness, the largeness and smallness of the animal
spirits ; and on the other hand, by the delicacy and
coarseness, the moisture and dryness, the ease and
difficulty of bending the fibres of the brain ; and finally,
by the relation that the animal spirits bear to the
fibres." [1]

In those old times, people spoke with the same naïve confidence about the " animal spirits " as they do nowadays
about the almost as little understood " nerve impulses."

Half a century later, with Wolf, the language became
predominantly psychological again, and the exposition
acquired much more detail. That which Gross was afterwards
to call the power of building up large systems of ideas is by
Wolf attributed to the " conservation of attention." His
chosen example is a mathematician who wrote such lengthy
demonstrations, that no living man could read through
them.[2]

More important still for our present purposes is the work
of that distinguished Herbartian, Beneke.[3] For him, the
whole psychology of individual differences was essentially
based upon three " ground-properties " (*Grundeigenschaften*).

The first of these was entitled " excitability by stimulation " (*Reizempfänglichkeit*), and was said to consist in the
ease, fullness, and fineness with which the mind is able to
" pick up " (*aufnehmen*) the sensory impressions. It corresponds in large degree with what Wolf had called sensory

---

[1] *La Recherche de la Vérité*,   [2] *Psychologia empirica*, para. 244.

[3] *Lehrbuch der Psychologie*, 1845. *Pragmatische Psychologie*, 1850.

"attention." The person favoured in this respect will, it was said, tend to have not only his percepts but also his thoughts turned towards external objects of cognition. These latter, then, by force of their manifoldness, will diminish mental stability, and in this way will be injurious to clearness of abstraction and to coherency of logic. Further, such extroversion of the mind will naturally spread from matters of cognition to those of affection and conation ; there will ensue a greater inclination to seek for happiness in things outside rather than inside one's self. There will also be a greater tendency to adopt one's opinion from other people instead of forming judgment independently. As conspicuous examples of this first ground-property, with all its corollaries, Beneke quotes the feminine sex and the French nation.

The second ground-property was said to be that of the mental " powerfulness " (*Kräftigkeit*) with which the sensory excitations are assimilated (*angeeignet*). The corollaries of this property are assumed to act largely in opposition to those enumerated above. In particular, those persons who are more favoured in respect of the second than of the first property will have their main source of cognition inside rather than outside themselves ; they will perceive, think, and feel less about what happens in the external world and more about what goes on within themselves. Again, such an introversion will tend to impoverish the person in respect of manifoldness of scope, but on the other hand to enrich him in firmness of abstraction and power of logic. And what is of still greater moment, such an inwards turning will, it was said, bring the person's behaviour more under the sway of stable principles, and in this manner carry in its train the virtues of trustworthiness, industry, and even courage. Women were alleged to be superior in the externally directed kind of cognition, but inferior in the internally directed kind. Among nations, the Germans were said to be just the reverse. To the English were credited both excellences.

After thus delineating these two ground-properties, Beneke

rather unexpectedly introduces yet a third, which seems in many respects to hark back to the first. As defined, it is the " liveliness " (*Lebendigkeit*) of mental operation. The person who excels in this respect will not linger at his first impressions—Beneke declared—but pass lightly on to manifold further activities, both reproductive and combinative. Hence he will enjoy such advantageous traits as those of tact, address, and resourcefulness. On the affective and conative sides of his nature, he will tend towards gaiety, sympathy, sociability and leadership. But on the debit side of his account will stand a diminution of independence and even of trustworthiness. To exemplify excess of the third property are quoted (as in the case of the first property) women and the French. Examples of deficiency in it are furnished by the male sex as also by the English and the German nations.

On the whole, it would appear that already Beneke, some seventy years ago, had in many respects gone as far as—and perhaps even farther than—such casual and literary expositions as are current nowadays. But he lacked the treatment of the subconscious, which enriches the writings of Jung. And in particular, he had not at his disposal the scientific methods which impart such invaluable solidity to the work of Müller, Stern, Heymans, and Wiersma.

CRITICISM

Essential sameness of character. Hasty as has been our review of all these types so confidently advanced and vividly delineated by writers both ancient and modern, at least one feature about them will hardly escape the reader's notice; this is the general kinship between them all. And on closer examination, this family likeness shows itself to go surprisingly far.

As most fundamental of all the concepts involved, we may pick out that of " perseveration " due mainly to G. E. Müller and that of " secondary function " introduced by Gross. Evidently these two exactly supplement each other.

For whereas the perseveration indicates that percepts and ideas once vividly aroused have a marked tendency to persist or revive in subsequent consciousness, the secondary function implies that the percepts and ideas remain markedly influential even when they have become unconscious. Joining these two concepts together, we get simply that, with some persons, there is a tendency for mental processes to persist in activity long after the cessation of the conditions to which they were originally due.

When once this firm basis has been established, all the rest of what has been said about the types may possibly be nothing but its natural consequences.   Consider first that type of person who, according to Beneke, perceives, thinks, and feels less about what happens in the external world and more about what goes on within himself ; or who, according to Stern, is " subjective " in the sense that when describing a picture he tends to give above all things himself ; or who, according to Jung, is " introverted " and " never stops at the purely objective effect, but concerns himself with the subjective perception released by the objective stimulus " ; such a state as this seems natural enough with those persons whose present sensory experiences are crowded out of mind by the persisting activity, conscious or unconscious, of experiences in the past.

Take next the type so concordantly depicted by Wolf, Beneke, Müller, Gross, Stern, and Jung, as being intensive rather than extensive ; it is said to manifest " a dissolution of the spiritual personality into single large systems of ideas, which is each in itself closely connected, highly developed, and deeply rooted, but which are defectively associated between each other."   Just such intensity, such deep but comparatively isolated systems of ideas, may plausibly enough be expected in those minds where any impression, once made, thereafter persists to the exclusion of other impressions.

A further type was encountered by us which Plato, Beneke, Müller, and Stern invested with such virtues as constancy and trustworthiness. These again are just such qualities as might with fair show of reason be derived from superior mental persistency and therefore stability.

Yet another prominent feature in the literature on types is the way in which the perseverating, secondarily functioning, subjective, introverted, systematizing and excessively scrupulous person is portrayed as tending furthermore towards being melancholic. This view finds perhaps its sharpest expression in the writings of Gross, Heymans, Wiersma, and Jaensch, these being fundamentally inspired by the contrast between melancholia on the one hand and mania on the other. Even for this additional trait an explanation is easily enough forthcoming, if recourse be allowed to some current (but highly speculative) physiology ; for both the perseveration and the melancholy admit of being attributed to one and the same feature in the bodily metabolism, *i.e.* a predominance of dissimilation over assimilation, of breaking down over building up.

The old difficulty, correlation. So far, the doctrine of types would seem to go as merrily as marriage bells. But there remains one very grave obstacle still to be encountered ; it is no other than that which baffled both the doctrines considered in the earlier chapters. Such a name as lag, perseveration, secondary function, or introversion only serves in the first place to bring together an indefinitely large *class* of mental tendencies. It does not (pending further evidence) indicate that all the tendencies falling within this class will vary proportionately in any individual. Yet such correlation it is that we need, if the whole class of tendencies is to be treated as a single-behaviour unit and measured, or even described, for this individual by a single value or statement.

As an illustration of this difficulty, take the report made by Müller that he himself, after experimenting with syllables, was plagued by their involuntary return to consciousness, whereas his wife—who had done quite similar experiments —had no such trouble. Now, nothing that we are told here would prevent the rôles from being reversed, say after hearing an opera ; in this latter event, the subsequent obsession with fragments of melody might perhaps befall her instead of him.

Or consider how Jung, after setting out with one pair of mechanisms for intro- and extro-version respectively, found himself in later publications constrained to provide a separate pair for each of his four faculties. Presumably, experience had shown him that a person need not necessarily be of the same type for all four ; he who is an introvert for the faculty of perceiving may conceivably be an extrovert for that of thinking, and so on independently for the other two faculties. If this is right, then introversion or extroversion is no longer any single thing, but splits up into four, each demanding a measurement of its own.

But how can we tell that the sub-division may not have to be carried yet further ? Take for example the faculty of thinking. Extroversion in this is declared to injure a person's power to form original judgments. This defect, it is said, will be manifested in a great variety of mental operations ; thus, such a person will complacently adopt the prevailing custom of wearing a greatcoat in the winter, instead of trying to harden himself against the cold ; when he goes to hear a new singer, he will docilely accept the estimate made by other people. But do we really know that such ways of behaviour tend to go together ? Why should a man not *both* wear a greatcoat in the cold *and* think for himself about music ? Possibly, just as Volkmann said that every idea has its own memory and its own imagination, so too it may have its own perseveration.

Here, again, then, we find that any genuine science of individual differences must needs depend upon ascertaining what correlations exist. Nothing else can avail instead. Beneath the flowers of literature that we have quoted there *may* indeed lie mines of scientific gold. But until these have been actually discovered—which can only be done by the light of correlations—the preceding doctrine of types can at most be taken as a hope, not as an achievement.

CHAPTER V

ANARCHIC DOCTRINE: "GENERAL LEVEL," "AVERAGE," OR "SAMPLE"

DOCTRINE OF INDEPENDENCE

Crude view that all abilities are independent. The trend of the preceding chapter was once more towards further analysis. Already in the two previous chapters, we had been compelled to break up the sovereign "intelligence" into several different ruling faculties or types. All these were found to need separate treatment—and especially measurement—since they appeared to be more or less independent of one another. And then this same fate befell the faculties and types themselves; each of these, also, had to be further broken up; for it covered a variety of mental operations which, so far as could be seen, were more or less independent.

To what point, then, must all this sub-division be eventually carried? No stopping place seems to present itself short of the most elementary processes ; every one of these may derive from a separate and independent ability. Such a movement over into the doctrine of all-round independence —or the " anarchic " doctrine, as it may be called—was taken at once by Herbart and his followers. Having demolished all defence for the view that ability is tied up into a few great separate faculties, they naturally enough went on to proclaim that ability is really subdivided into innumerable independent parts. Volkmann, as we saw, roundly declared that every idea possesses its own memory, its own imagination, and so forth.

And a similar view appears to have been advanced even in quite recent times. It may be found, for instance, in some of the earlier writings of no less an authority than Thorndike. He expresses his opinion that

> " the mind is a host of highly particularized and independent faculties." [1]

And indeed, at the moment when he made this statement, it was fully warranted by the most exact research then known. For shortly before (1901) there had been published a momentous investigation by Cattell and Wissler. [2] These authors had devised tests for no less than 22 different mental powers and had tried them upon 325 university students. Furthermore—for the first time in psychology— the degree of dependence between one ability and another had been submitted to definite quantitative measurement, the means employed being the then little known " correlational coefficients." [3] The issue was blankly negative ; the

[1] *Educational Psychology*, 1903, p. 39. [2] *Psych. Mon.* iii.

[3] A correlational co-efficient, as is now generally known, consists in a number that indicates how far the changes in any variable magnitude are accompanied by corresponding changes in another one.
Procedures for showing such correspondence have during the last few years been invented in great number and variety. And so far as theoretical significance goes, it might be hard to demonstrate that any one of them is more valid than the rest. But at any rate in one important respect, that of being amenable to mathematical elaboration, easily foremost is the procedure which was substantially given in a beautiful memoir of Bravais and which is now commonly called that of " product moments." Such

tests displayed no appreciable correlation, either among themselves, or with success in academic work. So manifest was the superiority of this research to anything done previously, that to be incredulous would not have been wise but rather the reverse.

Unfortunately, however, these investigators had fallen victims to their own insight and enterprise. They had rightly grasped the immense value of the new mathematical tool invested by statisticians ; but they had no means of knowing that this tool was still vitiated by a fatal flaw, that of " attenuation " (see appendix, p. i). After this flaw had been detected, such negative results never again made any appearance. On the contrary, sets of tests almost always produced high—and often very high—inter-correlations.

Later view that all abilities are correlated. Not infrequently, certain authors—notably Ziehen and Thorndike—are still cited as championing the aforesaid crude doctrine of independence. But in all such passages as have come under the notice of the present writer, there are to be found some explicit reservations. Ziehen does indeed declare that " the intellectual aptitude falls into numerous aptitudes " ; but he quickly adds the qualifying clause that the latter " stand in complicated connection with one another." [1] So also Thorndike does appear to continue to assert the existence of many different abilities ; but now he carefully proceeds to note that these are more or less inter-correlated.

By the aid of these safeguards, the doctrine may indeed be said to have been rendered absolutely irrefutable. Beyond all reasonable doubt, human ability does admit of being regarded as being made up of very numerous particular abilities that are mutually correlated. But has not

procedures have been further improved by Galton, who invented the device—since adopted everywhere—of representing all grades of interdependence by a single number, the " coefficient," which ranges from unity for perfect correlation down to zero for entire absence of it. These coefficients, varying from 1 down to 0, are generally calculated to two or three decimal places.

[1] *Paedag. Mag.* 683, 1918, p. 32.

this security been purchased at the price of significance ? The collapse of the earlier and crude view, that all different abilities are independent, had come from establishing just this fact of their inter-correlation. Thereafter, the whole problem at issue was to discover some aspect from which the inter-correlation could be rendered intelligible. And towards solving this problem, such statements as we have been considering do not appear to make even a commencement ; the bare proposition that the intellectual aptitudes stand in complex relations to one another says nothing wrong only because it says almost nothing at all. To this fact must be ascribed such reproaches against it as have been brought by T. Moore, that it has been sterile and unprogressive.[1]

Hypothesis of independent elementary factors. Yet a road for progress lay open obviously enough, namely, by pursuing the analysis still further. This in the preceding view comes naïvely to an end at each distinct mental operation. But with far greater likelihood every concrete operation itself— even the simplest—depends upon numerous abstract influences, or " factors " as they have been called in psychology. This is obvious even in the physical world ; not the smallest movement of the smallest particle of matter can occur but that a part is played by many different factors, such as weight, heat, or electricity.

If so, then the correlation displayed between any different concrete operations admits after all of being readily explained. For it may well be due to these operations having one or more of their elementary factors in common. It is these basic factors, then, not the entire concrete operations however simple, to which the doctrine of independence should naturally be applied. And when so applied, all the objections that we have hitherto seen against it become void.

Interestingly enough, this is the very road that has led to the general mathematical theory of all correlation. The

[1] *Psychol. Monogr.* xxvii. 1919.

original work of Bravais himself was fundamentally established upon the basis of assuming that each single observable correlated magnitude is a function of multiple unobservable uncorrelated elements. And his successors have had to content themselves with following in his footsteps. Recently, definite proof has been supplied by Garnett, that such an analysis is always mathematically possible. Any number of total magnitudes however correlated with each other—he shows—can always be expressed as functions of elements that are themselves uncorrelated.[1]

Had but this more finely analytical direction of thought been followed by the advocates of independence, their theory could scarcely have failed to merge eventually into the one that will chiefly occupy us later on (ch. vi.).

DOCTRINE OF A "GENERAL LEVEL" OR "AVERAGE"

Origin of the doctrine. This promising line in which to pursue the doctrine of independence, however, appears to have escaped notice. We arrive now, instead, at that view which among those who are actively engaged in mental testing is probably having the greatest influence. For the belief in a monarchic "intelligence" (ch. ii.) seems not to affect the actual testing so much as the conclusions drawn from its result. The assumption of unitary faculties (ch. iii.) or types (ch. iv.) is most prominent in theoretical discussions ; its supporters usually drop them again on getting down to the actual testing. But the doctrine to which we now turn appears to be pre-eminently that which inspires confidence in the tester when busy at his work. It consists in regarding that which is measured by the tests as the "general level," the "average," or a "sample" of the person's abilities.

Now, there is some reason to suppose that this way of thinking started from a suggestion of the present writer. He—almost alone at that time, it would seem—had been

---

[1] *Brit. J. Psych.* 1920, p. 243.

much impressed by the difficulty of submitting the individual differences to any genuine measurement at all. To every one of the current doctrines there had appeared to exist some insuperable objections (those which we considered in chs. ii.-iv.). In each case, the fatal flaw had lain in assuming the existence of some correlation that was unsupported —or even contradicted—by the available evidence. The remedy seems to be necessarily based upon some deepening of the theory of correlations. An attempt was actually taken in this direction, with the result of finding that there does indeed exist something measurable which might possibly be entitled general intelligence. But the procedure which the theory indicated for obtaining the measurement was of a most curious kind. For up to now the trend that we have been examining has always been towards finer and finer analysis. Seemingly flouting all this, the procedure dictated by this correlational theory was to take almost at random very numerous tests quite different from each other and to throw all the scores for them indiscriminately into one common pool.[1]

A little more than a year afterwards appeared the great work of Binet and Simon.[2] Here, this paradoxical recommendation to make a hotchpot was actually adopted in practice. Nevertheless the elaborate correlational theory which had in point of fact generated the idea, and had supplied the sole evidence for its validity, was now passed over. The said authors employed a popular substitute. " Intelligence," as measured by the pool was depicted as a " general level " of ability. So far as doctrine is concerned, this is the only thing introduced by them that was novel. And most surprisingly Binet, although in actual testing he took account of this " general level " alone, still in all his theoretical psychology continued to rely altogether upon his old formal faculties, notwithstanding that these and the " general level " appear to involve doctrines quite incompatible with each other.

[1] Present writer, *Amer. J. Psych.* xv. 1904, p. 274.   [2] *Année Psych.* 1905.

Interpretation of " general level " as average or sum.
Such a replacement of an elaborate correlational theory by
the simple concept of a " general level " was—if valid—a
remarkable achievement. But before being finally accepted,
it needs at least some critical examination.

To begin with, what is intended to be the meaning of this
term " general level " (or any other term taken to involve
this, such as "mental age" or the " I.Q."[1]) ? Really, a
person's abilities will in the ordinary course of events be
most *un*level ; with everybody, some kinds of ability very
much surpass others. The level, then, must be taken as
some theoretical line or plane, not necessarily coinciding
with any of the actual abilities at issue, but bearing some
general relation to them all. Where is any such thing to be
found ?

One suggestion that has been attempted to meet the case
may at once be put out of court, namely, that of a base-
level, such as the sea furnishes for measuring the heights on
land. No such well-defined datum is known, from which all
the abilities of a person can be measured upwards. The only
exception is the level of zero ; and this, of course, would not
vary from one person to another, as is here required.

We are compelled to interpret the person's general level of
ability as being some theoretical *central* altitude, whilst his
different actual abilities lie, on the whole, as much above
as below it. And the most natural value to take as central
is the *average*.[2]

Accordingly, this does appear to have been the view of
all or almost all writers (including Binet himself) who used
the term " general level," and even of many who employ
" general intelligence " or " general ability." Some are
careful to state as much. Others, instead, write of the " sum "
of abilities, or of the " total efficiency " ; but this comes to the
same thing ; for an average is, of course, only the sum or

---

[1] The I.Q. is the percentage that the " mental " age is of the real age.

[2] This, as is well known, brings the sum of the squared deviations above
and below to its minimum value.

total divided by the number of cases.   Many more make no definite statement as to what they intend such terms to mean, but the interpretation in the sense of an average seem best to accord with their context.

This concept of an " average," then, we will adopt as the basis for the following considerations.   But, as may readily be seen, our arguments would apply just as well to any other kind of central value (as median, mode, geometric mean, harmonic mean, etc.).

Violated postulate of unequivocal domain.   Now, speaking broadly, there can be no doubt but that averages are not only a legitimate statistical device, but one of extremely great value.   Even in ordinary life, their use is frequent and very convenient, as for example, when calculating an average weekly expenditure.   And in science, they are used for almost every value of importance.   As for psychology, in this even more than in physics, the procedure of averaging dominates all quantitative work ; an average is determined of reaction times, of memory spans, of errors committed, of " right and wrong cases," and so forth without limit.

Nevertheless, we must venture to raise the question as to whether this procedure of averaging, so widely and so successfully employed in other cases, may also be employed in the special case here interesting us.   That the average score can be calculated for *all the tests* applied to any person is, of course, obvious.   But can the value so obtained ever be regarded as the average of *all the person's abilities*?

In order to answer this question, let us consider what postulates are indispensable, if any genuine average is to be obtained.   One, evidently, is that the domain should be settled within which the averaging is intended to run.   It would be absurd, for instance, to pretend to give the average rainfall for Burma without having first said whether it referred to Lower Burma (which has about 200 inches) or to Upper Burma (which has only about 40).   But then analogously idle must be any averaging of a person's " intelligence," unless there has first been some settlement as to whether motor ability, sensory perception, memory, imagination, etc., are to be counted in or not.

An illustration may help to show this more pointedly. We will take a test-scale that has been widely used and is unquestionably among the most excellent hitherto produced ; that of Yerkes. The author (here, as elsewhere, exceptionally thorough) has carefully indicated the scope of each of the component tests—or " sub-tests," as they have been called. These sub-tests are 15 in number, and the following table shows an exemplifying set of scores obtained for them respectively by a particular person :

Subtest.	Score.
(1) Motor coordination - - - -	12
(2) Perception (visual) - - - -	11
(3) Discrimination (visual) - - -	9
(4) Discrimination (kinesthetic) - -	14
(5) Association - - - - -	6
(6) Suggestibility - - - - -	3
(7) Memory - - - - - -	8
(8) Memory (auditory) - - - -	9
(9) Memory (visual) - - - -	7
(10) Imagination - - - - -	8
(11) Judgment (aesthetic) - - -	1
(12) Judgment (practical) - - -	4
(13) Judgment (logical) - - - -	1
(14) Analysis and comparison - - -	4
(15) Ideation - - - - - -	1

Now, in this instance, if motor ability, sensory perception, memory, and imagination are all to be included, the average amounts to 6·5. But if they are to be excluded, it goes down to 2·9 or only 37 per cent. of that obtained in the other way !

Violated postulate of comparable cases. Another fundamental requirement in order to obtain any genuine average is that the cases to be averaged should be equivalent to one another, or at any rate in some way comparable. It would be ridiculous to try to take the average expenditure for a number of periods, if some of these happened to be weeks, some months, and others of unknown duration. Yet just such arbitrariness and uncertainty vitiate any attempt to average abilities. In our illustration, Judgment and Memory are taken to comprise 3 abilities each, Imagination and Ideation being allowed only 1 each. Why should not the allowancing have been done reversely ? Or, indeed, in any other proportion whatsoever.[1]

Violated postulate of no repetition. Equally futile must be any averaging where the same items are introduced repeatedly. In the instance of weekly expenditure, no valid result would be expected if, say, Xmas week were brought in several times. Turn, then, to the mental scale. Does, for example, Analysis really occur only in sub-test 14 for which it is marked ? The author himself, at least, does not think so ; he expressly states that it occurs also in 11, 13, and 15. Suppose that, to avoid thus counting analysis four times over, we omit 11, 13, and 15 (so that there now only remain 5, 6, 12, and 14). Thereupon the person's average jumps from the 2·9 to 4·25, or 60 per cent. more than before !

Violated postulate of no omission. This is the converse of the preceding requirement. Its indispensability is no less obvious. What would be the use of a man averaging his expenditure, if those weeks were omitted in which he paid his rent ? Yet no one can seriously believe that any scale of tests is able to escape making grave omissions. In our illustrative scale take as example Imagination. The actual test consists in uttering for three minutes as many sentences as possible that contain three given words. Now, is this feat going to prove corresponding ability for poetic flights, for scientific hypotheses, or for any other imaginative performances of serious value ? If not, then all these have been left out of account.

---

[1] This need of making different abilities comparable with each other as regards the qualitative range to be included in each must not be confused with the need of making them comparable as regards their respective quantitative ranges. Whereas the former problem seems to be insoluble, the latter is at once settled by measuring each ability in terms of its own mean square variation.

On the whole, there appears to be no possibility of satisfying a single one of the postulates which—for any genuine averaging—are indispensable.

Pleas in defence. From all these criticisms that can be brought against the doctrine of measuring a general level in the sense of an average value, let us turn to what can be said in its defence.

As one plea, it might be urged that all these difficulties may be removed simply by virtue of psychologists coming to some agreement. Let only a World Court of them settle upon any definite number of definite traits. Thenceforward, there need be no equivocality of domain, no incomparable cases, no repetitions, and no omissions. But this pleasing prospect quickly shows itself to be delusive. For if the lines of agreement are to be arbitrary, then science becomes none the better for it ; the value obtained can be no more significant than would be that got from any list made of desirable traits of body ; it would at best be comparable with some average mark derived from an individual's height, weight, strength of grip, soundness of heart, capacity of lungs, opsonic index, and so forth *ad lib.* How can any such concoction of heterogeneous traits, bodily or mental, be taken seriously ?

Another possible plea is that our postulates are too rigorous, too subtle, too refined, too pedantic, for ordinary practical purposes. But this suggestion would be quite intolerable. Every one of the said postulates is acknowledged and fulfilled throughout the entire range, not only of physical science, not only of psychological science, but even of every-day domestic economy. Shall the scientific treatment of " intelligence," with its elaborate mathematics of standardizations, calibrations, frequency distributions, mental ages, mental ratios, achievement ratios, correlational coefficients, reliability coefficients, multiple and partial coefficients, measures of skewness, curve fittings, and so forth—with its aims at reforming education, at re-vitalizing industry, at re-shaping the laws of immigration, at dictating the right to have children, at upsetting the very constitution of society—shall all this be founded upon a quantitative basis that would not be good enough to estimate the spendings of the humblest housewife?

Only one other plea seems to have been hitherto forthcoming. It is that the theory of a general level or average has actually led to approximately valid results, since the different test-series—whatever else may be said about them —undeniably do show fairly high correlations with each other. But against even this plea must be answered that no such theory of a level or average ever *led* Binet to his hotchpot procedure; for, in truth, his theoretical views were entirely alien to anything of the sort (still immersed, as he was, in " faculties "). He only took up the general " level " as an afterthought, a " rationalization," to account for a procedure which he really had adopted from elsewhere.

In any case, the fact that the hotchpot test-series have high correlations with one another, or in any other way actually " work," is no proof whatever that they do this by virtue of any impossible " levels " or averages. As is much more natural, every virtue possessed by the hotchpot procedure will find its genuine explanation in the doctrine from which this procedure really emanated.[1]

DOCTRINE OF SAMPLING

Recurrence of the same violations. There remains open a recourse to the allied doctrine of " sampling." The test-scale, it may be conceded, does not in itself supply any general level, average, or sum of a person's abilities, but it does furnish instead a sample of these. And herewith we reach, probably, the position that among the most active testers can boast of the largest number of adherents.

Now, what does the term sample mean? The dictionary tells us, a part or group selected at random as representative of the whole. And the introduction of the word " representative " seems to indicate that the chief relative

[1] See the theorem of indifference of indicator, ch. xi. p. 197.

quantities of the sample and those of the whole must be approximately similar ; any way, such similarity is absolutely essential, if the sample is to fulfil any scientific purpose. But to secure this representativeness, in what sense are we to take the words " at random." This certainly cannot mean that the selecting may be done anyhow at haphazard. All who have studied sampling know full well that *to obtain any part or group fairly representative of the whole is usually a most difficult matter.*

On examination as to where such difficulty lies, it will be found to consist in fulfilling just the same fundamental postulates as before. To begin with, there is the need of settling the precise limits of the domain over which the sampling has to run. For instance, before any one started to sample the weight of Americans, he would have to decide whether he meant by this the population of the United States. Then, he would have to settle whether to include all immigrants, or only persons who had resided in the country for some particular period, or only such as had been born there, or perhaps only those whose parents had been born there. Similarly, he would have to settle whether negroes were to be included ; whether both sexes, or only one. Again, he would have to fix the age limits for the persons to be taken into account. And so on, for a large number of vital points.

Turning back to mental ability and asking analogous questions, we once more come up against the equivocalities in the concept of " intelligence." Shall or shall not our sample be made to include memory, imagination, motor activity, and so forth ? In our illustrative test-scale, more than half of the sub-tests are involved in this fatal dilemma.

After the need of marking out the domain from which to draw the sample, comes that of letting every case, or sort of case, have its proper chance of being drawn. For example, any sampling of the consumption of beer by Germans would be illusory if most of the persons included in the sample were taken from the specially beer-drinking region of Bavaria, or from the specially schnapps-drinking East Prussia, or from the specially wine-drinking Rhine districts. Instead, each region should contribute its due quota. But here we come up against the second great postulate that is not possibly fulfilled by any selection of the mental abilities to be tested. For, as we have seen, there exists no rational way of deciding what quota of these should be taken respectively from judgment, imagination, and so forth.

The preceding requirement, that each sort of case should be given its proper chance of being drawn in the sample, involves also the third and the fourth of our postulates. Obviously, we should not be sampling a regiment fairly if we took one quota from those who were officers and another from those who were catholics. For in this way, two chances would be given to the catholic officers, one each to the protestant officers and to the catholic rank-and-file, and no chance at all to the protestant rank-and-file. But in respect of mental abilities, both repetitions and omissions are, as we saw, present to a degree that touches the outrageous.

New difficulties superadded. Not only do all the obstacles to averaging thus re-appear in sampling, but the latter procedure adds on new difficulties of its own. For no sample will in general be representative, unless it contains cases in such large numbers as to smooth away accidental irregularities. Now, is this really achieved in respect of abilities. Take the scale of Binet himself. Only a small portion of it is applied to any particular child, the easier components being taken as unquestionably within his power and the harder components as unquestionably not within it. Central in the portion actually used are the components that belong to the year of his " mental age." Let us, then, consider as typical this main year (what will be said applies equally to the others also). Now, for the age of three years the component tests are five in number, and two of them deal with " memory." For the age of seven years, there are four tests, of which memory gets none at all. For the eleventh year, there are five tests, and again memory is left out altogether. But for the twelfth year, memory once more get two out of five. To advance such a meagre and vacillating sample as scientific and representative seems a strange claim.

Shall, then, the claim of effective sampling be renounced for this Binet series, but still maintained for other series where the components are more numerous? Surely this would be a logical fallacy. The Binet series succeeds just as well as those others, in spite of its making no approach towards genuine sampling. And the same may be said even more forcibly of other series, as that of Wyatt, which has been conspicuously successful despite having only three components altogether. Such success as is at present obtained, therefore, can by no means be accredited to any bare virtue of sampling.

Suggestion of an " S.Q." If anything more need be said, let us compare a person's mental measurement (his " intelligence quotient " or " I.Q.") as based on averaging or sampling with his record in any other sphere of activity, say that of sports. Suppose some lad to be champion of his school in the 100 yards race, the $\frac{1}{4}$ mile, and the $\frac{1}{2}$ mile, as also in the high and broad jumps. Could all this be taken as a representative sample of his sporting ability in general? So far as here indicated, he might perform very badly indeed in countless other branches of sport, such as cricket, lawn tennis, shooting, baseball, rowing, putting the weight, riding, mountaineering, or flying. And even if he were to be measured in every one of these also, how could the results be reasonably pooled into any sort of average? Shall all sports mainly dependent on the " eye," as cricket, tennis, billiards, etc., be reckoned as one ability? Or as a myriad? A similar question arises where the dominant influence happens to be strength, or speed, or heart, or lungs, and so forth indefinitely. In a rough way, no doubt, a person can sometimes be said to have had much success at such sports as he has attempted. But there appears no serious prospect of calculating his " S.Q." to several places of decimals, and then piling upon this result a mass of higher mathematics.

Inconsistency with actual practice. The worst about this theory of sampling, however, has yet to be mentioned. It is that, in actual practice, the procuring of a genuine sample has not really even been attempted.

One of the many indications of this is the prevalent procedure, in the construction of a series of tests, of trying out a large number and then selecting those which exhibit the highest correlations with all the rest. Such a procedure seems to have been more or less influential, directly or indirectly, in the framing of all generally accredited series at the present day. It has been formally designated as the " principle of coherence."

But who, when attempting to get a fair sample of Americans, and finding in his preliminary selection the majority to be Easterners, would thereupon proceed to eliminate even such Westerners as he had already obtained ? Or who, on gathering together what was meant to be a representative sample of some mixed wheat for sale and on noticing that the larger part happened to be of his best quality, would proceed to weed out even such representatives of the inferior quality as were present—on the ground of making his sample " coherent " ? Not improbably, such a procedure would bring him within reach of the law. In order to obtain a genuine sample, one carefully retains, and even adds to, the sorts which were at first little represented, and which therefore tend to be *least* correlated with, the remainder.

CONCLUSION

To summarize this chapter, every version of the " anarchic " doctrine has failed to make good. To maintain that the abilities for different operations are independent of each other is now, by universal admission, untrue. To say that they stand in complicated inter-relations is true but sterile.

As for the prevalent procedure of throwing a miscellaneous collection of tests indiscriminately into a single pool this— whether or not justifiable by the theory which gave birth to it—certainly cannot be justified simply by claiming that the results give a " general level," an " average," or even a " sample." No genuine averaging, or sampling, of anybody's abilities is made, can be made, or even *has really been attempted*. When Binet borrowed the idea of such promiscuous pooling, he carried it into execution with a brilliancy that perhaps no other living man could have matched. But on the theoretical side, he tried to get away too cheaply. And this is the main cause of all the present trouble.

CHAPTER VI

ECLECTIC DOCTRINE : TWO FACTORS

DISCOVERY OF THE "TWO FACTORS"

History. Next to examine will be that doctrine from which the notion of pooling together a miscellaneous lot of different tests really emanated. This doctrine was based upon what we have all along been finding of such paramount importance, namely, the correlations between abilities. Unfortunately, the current accounts of this doctrine—its origin, development, and essential nature—are extraordinarily incorrect. To clear up the matter, a historical exposition would be most effective. This, however, might possess but little interest for those readers who have not been personally concerned in its early development or in the controversies to which it has upon occasion given rise. Consequently, the historical aspect of the doctrine will here be reserved for the appendix (i-xiv). In the present chapter it must suffice to remark that whilst Binet, followed by psychologists in all civilized countries, was busily culling the first practical fruit of the doctrine—that is to say, the procedure of miscellaneous pooling—the originators of the doctrine chose the part of developing the tree from which that fruit had grown. There remained still plenty to do ; in the twenty years that have lapsed, more than double that number of laborious researches have been carried through, each bringing the whole work a step further forwards. And very recently there has at last been achieved what may be regarded as the keystone to it all. With respect to the empirical results of these multitudinous investigations, an account of them will be kept for Part II. of the present volume. Here, we will confine ourselves to the main points in the theoretical foundation.

Criterion of " tetrad differences." The start of the whole inquiry was a curious observation made in the correlations calculated between the measurements of different abilities (scores for tests, marks for school subjects, or estimates made on general impression.) [1] These correlations were noticed to tend towards a peculiar arrangement, which could be expressed in a definite mathematical formula. And the formula thus originally reached has ever since been maintained without any essential change. Only from time to time, for convenience, it has been converted from one form to some other that is mathematically equivalent.

The form recently preferred is given below. In it, as usual, the letter r stands for any correlation, whilst its two subscripts indicate the two abilities (tests, school marks, etc.) that are correlated.

$$r_{ap} \times r_{bq} - r_{aq} \times r_{bp} = 0.$$

This formula has been termed the *tetrad equation* and the value constituting the left side of it is the *tetrad difference*.

An illustration may be afforded by the following imaginary

---

[1] It will be remembered that the correlation between any two things is measured by a number or " coefficient," which ranges in value from 1 down to 0, according as the correlation varies from perfect dependence down to perfect independence. For inverse correlations, the coefficients take similar but minus values. See note to p. 56.

correlations between mental tests (actually observed correlations will be given in abundance later on) :

	Oppo-sites.	Completion.	Memory.	Discrimination.	Cancellation.
Opposites - 1		·80	·60	·30	·30
Completion - 2	·80		·48	·24	·24
Memory - - 3	·60	·48		·18	·18
Discrimination 4	·30	·24	·18		·09
Cancellation - 5	·30	·24	·18	·09	

For instance, let us try the effect of making :

a denote Opposites.

b ,,   Discrimination.

p ,,   Completion.

q ,,   Cancellation.

From the table of correlations above, we see that r_{ap} will mean the correlation between Opposites and Completion, which is ·80. Obtaining in a similar fashion the other three correlations needed, the whole tetrad equation becomes—

$$·80 \times ·09 - ·30 \times ·24 = 0$$

which is obviously correct. And so will be found any other application whatever of the tetrad equation to this table.

The Two Factors. So far, the business is confined to matters of observation; we simply try out the tetrad equation on any table of actually observed correlations and examine whether it fits. The next step, however, is not observational, but purely mathematical; we have to ask how, if at all, this equation between the correlations bears upon the individual measurements of the correlated abilities. The answer is that there has been shown to exist a very remarkable bearing indeed. It is to the effect that, whenever the tetrad equation holds throughout any table of correlations, and *only* when it does so, then every individual measurement of every ability (or of any other variable that enters into the table) can be divided into two independent parts which possess the following momentous properties.   The one part has been called the " general factor " and denoted by the letter g ; it is so named because, although varying freely from individual to individual, it remains the same for any one individual in respect of all the correlated abilities.   The second part has been called the " specific factor " and denoted by the letter s. It not only varies from individual to individual, but even for any one individual from each ability to another.   The proof of this all-important mathematical theorem has gradually evolved through successive stages of completeness, and may now be regarded as complete.[1]

Although, however, both of these factors occur in every ability need not be equally influential in all.   On the contrary, the very earliest application of this mathematical theorem to psychological correlations showed that there the g has a much greater relative influence or " weight " in some of the abilities tested than in others.   Means were even found of measuring this relative weight.   At one extreme lay the talent for classics, where the ratio of the influence of g to that of s was rated to be as much as 15 to 1. At the other extreme was the talent for music, where the ratio was only 1 to 4.[2]

Here at once we have before us the essence of the whole doctrine, the seedling from which all else has sprung.   But notice must be taken that this general factor g, like all measurements anywhere, is primarily not any concrete thing but only a value or magnitude.   Further, that which this magnitude measures has not been defined by declaring what it is like, but only by pointing out where it can be found.

[1] The theorem is quite general : its application is not in the least restricted to psychology.   Its proof is given in the appendix, pp. ii-vi.   The precise mathematical expression of the divisibility into two parts is afforded by the following equation :

$$m_{ax} = r_{ag} \cdot g_x + r_{as} \cdot s_{ax}.$$

Here, m_{ax} is the measurement or other value obtained for any individual x in the variable a ; g_x is the individual's amount of g, the factor common to all the variables ; and s_{ax} is the individual's amount of s_a, the factor specific to the variable a.   See appendix, p. xiv.

[2] Present writer, *Amer. J. Psych.* 1904, xv. p. 202.   For explanation of this inequality, see ch. xii.

It consists in just that constituent—whatever it may be—which is common to all the abilities inter-connected by the tetrad equation. This way of indicating what g means is just as definite as when one indicates a card by staking on the back of it without looking at its face.

Such a defining of g by site rather than by nature is just what was meant originally when its determination was said to be only "objective."[1] Eventually, we may or may not find reason to conclude that g measures something that can appropriately be called "intelligence." Such a conclusion, however, would still never be the definition of g, but only a "statement about" it (see ch. ii. pp. 17, 18).

Suggested universality of g. The vital problem, in respect of empirical observation, is as to how far and how regularly our tetrad equation actually holds good. In the original work, an extremely wide generalization was adventured. The suggestion was made that

> "all branches of intellectual activity have in common one fundamental function (or group of functions), whereas the remaining or specific elements seem in every case to be wholly different from that in all the others."[2]

Here, then, lies the justification for attributing so much importance to g, despite its purely formal character. The view is put forward that this g, far from being confined to some small set of abilities whose inter-correlations have actually been measured and drawn up in some particular table, may enter into all abilities whatsoever.

Such a universal law could only be advanced very tentatively. The express caution was added that

> "it must acquire a much vaster corroborative basis before we can accept it even as a general principle and apart from its inevitable corrections and limitations."

This caution was the more imperative, seeing that the law not only had such a tremendous scope, but moreover

---

[1] Present writer, *Amer. J Psych.* 1904, xv. p. 202.   [2] *Ibidem.*

came into sharp conflict with the most authoritative psychology then prevailing, the latter being at that time wedded to the doctrine of independence.[1]

Utility of the doctrine in practical testing. The preceding doctrine—as we shall see later—admits of usage throughout almost every kind and description of problem within the whole domain of individual differences of ability. For the present, however, we will only allude to two of the most obvious of these applications.

The one consists in the power conferred of measuring any individual in a genuine manner (instead of giving a pseudo-average or level, see ch. v.). We can determine the magnitude of his g, which will tell us nearly everything about some of his abilities and something about nearly all of them (see p. 75). And then we can do the same as regards any of his s's, one for each distinct kind of performance : this supplements and completes the information supplied by his g. For the details of calculating g and s, see the appendix, pp. xvii-xviii.

The other immediate application of the doctrine is in the construction of mental tests. We are enabled to ascertain just the degree of accuracy with which any given test, or series of them, will measure either a person's g or any of his s's. Further, we learn how this degree of accuracy may be raised to its maximum. Procedures for both purposes are given and explained in the appendix, pp. xviii-xix.

We can already see, too, that some crude approach towards measuring g can be obtained by the seemingly unscientific course of throwing very miscellaneous tests into a common hotchpot. So doing does not indeed supply an average, or even a representative sample, of the person's abilities ; anything of the sort seems to be for ever precluded by the impossibility of fulfilling the necessary postulates (see ch. v. pp. 62-64). What the pooling does effect is to make the influences of the many specific factors more or

[1] Partridge, for instance, wrote about that time as follows : " If now Spearman's method be valid, there is decided correlation among mental abilities, and the conclusions of many, especially among American investigators, are wrong." *Outline of Individual Study*, 1909, p. 34.

less neutralise each other, so that the eventual result will tend to become an approximate measure of g alone.[1]

DISCREPANCIES BETWEEN THEORY AND OBSERVATION

Effect of sampling errors. Although we have above suggested that the range of g as indicated by the tetrad equation is really universal, this must not be taken to mean that the said equation is under all conditions well satisfied. To expect this would be as absurd as to infer from the law of conservation of energy that the distance a man can walk is always proportional to the amount of food he eats.   The manifestations of all such laws, whether mental or physical, are bound to be more or less intermingled with, and modified by, further influences.   For such influences, then, all due allowance must be made.   In order to verify the law of Two Factors, actual experiment should *not* satisfy the equation exactly, but instead should present exactly the right departure from it.   If a marksman wishes to hit the bullseye he does not aim plump at it but more or less to one side, according to the direction and strength of the wind.

Now, all such inevitable complications of the theorem will be treated in detail later on (ch. x.). But about two of them—to obviate gross misapprehensions—a few words may be said forthwith. One such complication derives from the " errors of sampling." In any actual investigation only a limited number of individuals—ranging generally from 50 to 1,000—can actually be measured ; these have to be accepted as a representative sample of the entire class of persons under consideration. But between the correlation found for any such mere sample and that truly holding for the entire class, there must naturally be expected some random discrepancy. The general size of this for any single correlation has long been ascertained ; about half of the discrepancies will be greater and about half less than a calculable value called the " probable error " of the correla-

---

[1] Present writer, *Amer. J. Psych.* 1904, xv. p. 274. See also app. pp. xviii-xix.

tion. Every table or correlation must, then, be looked upon as consisting of the true values peppered over with, and more or less disguised by, random positive or negative additions; the general size of these, however, will bear a predictable relation to that of the said " probable error."

Such disturbances of the correlations cannot but exercise some effect upon our " tetrad differences," since the latter are constructed out of the former. Consequently, if the true value of the tetrad differences is always zero as shown in the tetrad equation (p. 73), then the actually manifested values ought *not* to be always zero, but instead should present some deviations from this. We need to ascertain how large these deviations should tend to be.

To discover this—or more broadly speaking, to make allowances for the disturbance of the correlations by their errors of sampling—has been the greatest trouble in the whole development of the doctrine. In the earlier investigations, the degree of allowance was left for anybody to estimate as high or as low as he pleased. Such a procedure, of course, is unscientific and misleading. Later on, the artifice was devised of replacing the tetrad equation by another criterion, which would at any rate be approximately correct and which did admit of calculating the allowance to be made for the errors of sampling. This substitute criterion was called that of " inter-columnar correlation "; an explanation of it will be found in the appendix, pp. viii-x. Quite recently, however, this long-standing grave defect in the doctrine has at last been overcome. Means have been discovered for evaluating the effect of the disturbance in the case of the true criterion, the tetrad equation itself. Knowing (as we always do) the probable errors of the four correlations that enter into the tetrad difference (see p. 73) we can now deduce from these the probable error of the tetrad difference as a whole. The formula for this purpose is given in the appendix (pp. x-xi).

Overlap between specific factors. As mentioned, there is another conspicuous limitation to the doctrine we are con-

sidering. Obviously, the specific factors for any two performances can only be independent of each other when these
performances are quite different. When, on the contrary,
two performances are much alike, their respective specific
factors will necessarily cease to be mutually independent.

For example, take as one test the cancellation of all the a's
in a printed page, and as another test the cancellation of all
the e's. These two performances, being so extremely alike,
may naturally be expected not only to have the g factor in
common, but also to present a large overlap in respect of
the s factor. The case may be symbolized in the following
figure, where the vertical shading (top left and the bottom
circles) stand for the s and the g in cancelling a's, whilst the
horizontal shading (top right and the bottom circles) stand
for the s and g in cancelling e's.

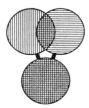

Whenever such cases are introduced, then our tetrad equation must in general *cease* to be valid.

But where, it may be asked, shall the line be drawn
between those performances which are and those which are
not " quite different." The answer must be that this is
not a point to settle intuitively, but to ascertain by experiment. Performances should be regarded as quite different
—in the present signification of this phrase—so long as the
tetrad equation is satisfied and no longer. To give some
notion, however, of how this rule pans out in actual practice,
it may at once be said that the most striking instance of such
an overlap was afforded by just these two tests that both
consist of cancelling letters and only differ as to which letter
should be cancelled. Another instance of likeness found
to produce marked overlap was that between counting

dots one at a time and doing so three at a time.[1] A somewhat different instance was found in school subjects ; the
correlation between marks for Latin Grammar and those
for Latin Translation proved far too large to fit into our
tetrad equation.

Evidently, such overlaps are akin to the " common
elements " which have been taken by Thorndike, Judd,
Sleight, and others to account for any " formal training "
that may exist (see ch. iii. p. 36). But our overlaps might
also derive, it was found, from various more or less accidental
circumstances. Thus, some of the children had been learning Latin for a longer period than the others, and therefore
naturally enough tended to excel at both the Grammar and
the Translation. By this fact, of course, the correlation
between the two abilities must have been increased beyond
the amount due to g alone.

In general, the early investigations indicated that the
cases of appreciable overlap are surprisingly scarce : that is
to say, it appeared only to link together abilities that were
allied very obviously. But already at this early period an
exception was announced. It consisted in the overlap
found between the memorizing of syllables and that of
numbers. This observation was said

> " to indicate the possibility of a rather extensive group
> of performances being so nearly related, that they might
> be gathered together as a more or less unitary ability
> under the concept of ' memorization ' ".[2]

And the point was again emphasized in 1912.[3] Herewith,
then, was actually encountered something at least akin to
the formal faculties (ch. iii.) or the types (ch. iv.).

After this discovery, such broad factors capable of em-
bracing very extensive ranges of ability were placed in
the forefront of enquiry. There has been a steady stream
of investigations in our laboratory devoted to ascertaining

[1] Krueger and Spearman, *Zeit. f. Psychol.* 1906, p. 102.
[2] Krueger and Spearman, *Zeit. f. Psychol.* 1906, p. 103.
[3] Hart and Spearman, *Brit. J. Psych.* 1912, p. 75.

whether various notable characters of ability do or do not act as specific factors of broad extent (the results will be given in Part II.).

Overlapping specific factors have since often been spoken of as " group factors." They may be defined as those which occur in more than one but less than all of any given set of abilities. Thus, they indicate no particular characters in any of the abilities themselves, but only some kinship between those which happen to be taken together in a set. Any element whatever in the specific factor of an ability will be turned into a group factor, if this ability is included in the same set with some other ability which also contains this element. The most that can be said is that some elements have a broader range than others, and therefore are more *likely* to play the part of group factors.

COMPARISON WITH RIVAL DOCTRINES

Controversy. The welcome so far accorded to such portions of the preceding doctrine as have been hitherto published show certain divergencies of opinion. Most writers appear to have been favourable. For instance, no less pre-eminent an authority than W. Stern has said that the general factor

" is one of the most certain results of investigation hitherto."[1]

[1] *Die Intelligenz d. Kinder u. d. Jugendlichen*, 1922, p. 9.

A claim can now be made even for the important support of William Brown, despite his earlier more conservative attitude. For the latest publication of his views treats the matter as follows :

" He (Brown) was inclined to favour the view that there was such a thing as general ability with sub-factors. . . . Prof. Thomson said that the hierarchy was due to chance, but witness was not convinced that this view was right."

(*Report of Evidence laid before a Committee of the British Board of Education*, 1924).

Indeed, even McCall, who has sometimes been quoted as an opponent, would seem really to be the reverse. He writes :

" There is an objectively and practically measurable something, which constitutes the core of most aptitudes. It is overlaid with various incidental abilities, and furthered or retarded by emotional or physical characteristics of the individual."

(*How to Measure in Education*, 1922.) Call this " something " " g," and you have the kernel of the doctrine put forward in the present chapter.

A few psychologists, however, have raised some opposition. But they have done so upon contradictory grounds ! The one party has devoted itself to demonstrating that such a "hierarchical" arrangement as is shown on p. 74 does not actually occur. Whereas the other party urges that it must necessarily occur by mere "chance," and therefore has no scientific significance.

But both these parties, unfortunately, seem to have misunderstood the doctrine against which they were contending. And indeed it has been published in such a fragmentary manner as made it peculiarly liable to erroneous interpretation. Still, we must here emphatically state that it has never from the very beginning undergone any substantial change whatever : only a continual development of more detail ; in particular, an unceasing increase of exactitude and cogency.[1]

For the present, the only controversial remarks that appear needed are the following. As regards the reported cases of the "hierarchical" arrangement *not* occurring, these cases will be considered in chapter x., and will be found really quite harmonious with all the other evidence. And as regards the opposite view which holds that the hierarchy must needs occur by mere "chance," this—even if it were to be accepted—could by no possibility enter into conflict with the doctrine given above. The foregoing equations would not be altered by a hair's breadth ; nor even would any of the accompanying comments require so much as a change of emphasis. The utmost that could ensue would be to indicate that the g may somehow be the product of numerous elements distributed in a "chance" manner. This, no doubt, is a view as to the nature of g which deserves due consideration. And such it will receive later on (pp. 94-97 ; append. pp. xiii-xiv).

Eclectic nature of view advocated here. The experimental facts quoted in the present chapter have aimed rather at illustration than at cogent evidence (which is reserved for

[1] See app. pp. i-xiii.

Part II.). But if we provisionally accept these experiments as conclusive, the inference follows that a certain amount of truth is to be found in *each* of the three great rival doctrines set forth in the earlier chapters.

Thus, the " monarchic " view is justified by *g* if we admit this ruler to be constitutional, not despotic ; it forms a mighty factor in the state, but not the sole one. And a further truth—qualifying and restricting the other—is contained in the " anarchic " view. For besides the factor *g* which rules throughout all mental processes, there is also the factor *s* which is in every process independent ; under the monarchic reign there is still some freedom for the individual citizens. And as much may be said, finally, for the third or " oligarchic " view, seeing that something of the nature of faculties or types—quite distinct from the universal factor and fairly distinct from the ordinary narrow factors—has revealed itself in what we have been calling the broad factors.

Implicit recognition in current procedure of testing. Besides this eclectic relation of our doctrine to all the prevalent theoretical doctrines, there should be noticed its curious connection with the prevalent practice in actual testing. Our *g* is, in fact, really obtained by this practice, with rough—much too rough—approximation. And it will be obtained the more exactly, as the procedure is freed from undeniable defects by means of the methods given in the appendix, pp. xviii-xix.

The explanation may be ventured that psychologists have been assimilating this doctrine of Two Factors more than they knew. The first and greatest move was made when they tacitly adopted (in flat contradiction to their then professed doctrines of faculties) the procedure of throwing many miscellaneous tests into a single pool. There followed their momentous step, whereby (in flat contradiction to their now professed principle of averaging or sampling) each of these component tests was selected by reason of its correlation with the rest of them. Recently has been added a more and more open usage of the very terms " general ability " and " special abilities " as together constituting a person's mental make-up, terms which were originated by and are essentially characteristic of the doctrine of g and s. Such " peaceful penetration " of the doctrine is still progressing. Even the writers professedly most antagonistic have nevertheless all the time been unconsciously drifting towards it.

Need of Explicit Recognition. But let a plea be entered here, that this conversion should be frankly admitted. For the procedure of testing will surely admit of very great improvement when once the basis upon which it really rests is taken openly into consideration. As already mentioned, the power will be obtained of constructing more efficient tests and that of applying these in a more effective manner (see p. 77.) A solution, also, will be supplied to the urgent practical problem as to what tests are of legitimate kind. Ought memory to be admitted ? Or imagination ? Or motor ability ? In every case the reply now is simply—Yes, if and in so far as any of these show a sufficiently high correlation with g.

More important still, however, is the need of frankness for theoretical purposes. So long as mental testers appropriate only the procedure and the terms, not the doctrine upon which these were founded, then the tests possess, in truth, no foundation at all. With only too much justice have they been subjected to the scathing criticisms quoted in chapter ii. There was small exaggeration in calling them a " bunch of stunts " or " jazz examinations," which " may test intelligence and may not ; nobody knows." Particularly damaging has been the reproach that the measurements obtained from such artificialities have unwarrantably been taken to hold good for the ability displayed in ordinary life. Now, on taking cognizance of the present doctrine, all this criticism of undue generalization loses its relevance. An instrument has been furnished for ascertaining just how far the range of g actually does extend. And no demand need be made for the smallest generalization beyond.

But of such prospective advantages we have said enough. The list of them could be extended without end. They may be summed up by claiming that the frank adoption of Two Factors would seem to supply an adequate basis—the only one possible—for a unified science of all human ability. The definite establishment of this claim will be attempted in Part II.

CHAPTER VII

PROPOSED EXPLANATIONS OF *G*

PSYCHOLOGICAL BASIS

Aim of present chapter. The chapter preceding set forth the conditions under which every ability is divisible into two factors, the one universal and the other specific. The suggestion was made—although no rigorous proof was attempted —that these conditions are actually fulfilled. But even the most complete demonstration that this is really so, and that therefore *g* and *s* certainly exist, would not of itself afford the smallest indication as to the nature of what these two factors represent. To reveal this nature is quite a different business, and one that leaves room for widely divergent views. The chief of these views—or " sub-theories " of *g*, as they may be called—will now be summarily outlined. But for the most part no endeavour will as yet be made to decide which if any of them is correct. Such a decision can only develop in a gradual manner, as the relevant actual observations are accumulated ; and these observations are reserved to be the subject-matter of Part II.

Interpretation as " intelligence." We lead off with the fact shown in the last chapter, that g is measured (roughly) by the current tests of " general intelligence." This bare title, indeed, carries us no great way, seeing that the word intelligence has no definite meaning (ch. ii.). But some of the particular interpretations given to the word, although inadequate to define it, may still afford valuable " statements about " it. In this way we may perhaps with profit come back eventually to such properties as " conscious adaptibility to new situations," or " capacity to learn," or the power of " combination." Phrases of this sort are especially promising when tightened up by means of restrictive clauses. For example, we shall meet some interesting experimental work, which aims at deciding whether g measures " immediate " or else " progressive " adaptability, taking the former to signify success in the first attempt at a new task, whilst the latter is the eventual success after prolonged practice (see pp. 284-5).

Another and still more promising version of intelligence would seem to be that which would identify it with the power to abstract. On this also we shall find that much information has been obtained by experimental methods.

Even the best of these renderings of intelligence, however, always presents one serious general difficulty. This is that such terms as adaptation, abstraction, and so forth denote entire mental operations ; whereas our g, as we have seen, measures only a *factor* in any operation, not the whole of it.

Recourse to attention or will. After " intelligence," the most widely supported interpretation of g seems to be as the power of " attention." This has been advocated by the two British authorities who, each from his standpoint, are admittedly pre-eminent : Burt, from the psychological side ; [1] and Garnett, from that of mathematics.[2] In Germany, too, such a solution would appear to find especial favour, no less

---

[1] *Brit. J. Psych.* 1909, iii.   [2] *Ibidem,* 1919, ix.

a man than Wundt having led the way.[1] In the United States, a similar conclusion has been reached by that brilliant investigator, Woodrow.[2]

The main 'trouble about bringing " attention " into the field lies once more in its ambiguity. It may be taken to mean—as by Stout, for instance—some conation or effort of will; and in point of fact, this is perhaps the meaning intended by Garnett. But instead, its meaning may be taken as akin to that of mental energy (to be discussed later) ; and this seems to be more what has been advocated by Woodrow.

Even when *g* is explicitly derived from the will, at least two different explanations remain to be distinguished. The one is by what may be called the intensity of conation ; the view is in fact equivalent to simply saying that those persons succeed best at the tests who try hardest. The other explanation (perhaps that of Garnett) is more subtle ; it is approximately equivalent to volitional control ; the most successful testee is he who can most effectively dispel all distraction caused by other matters.

Something again different would seem to be contained in the characterization of intelligence by Stern, as the power of a person " consciously to adjust his thoughts to new demands." For this seems to include all intentional but exclude all unintentional adjustment.

Upon each of these possible interpretations of *g*, as derived from attention or from will, we shall be able to find plenty of experimental evidence.

Hypothesis of " mental energy." The next explanation of *g* to be mentioned here takes the adventurous step of deserting all actually observable phenomena of the mind, and proceeding instead to invent an underlying something which—by analogy with physics—has been called mental energy. To this view the present writer attaches such great importance, that it will be reserved for exposition in two chapters specially devoted to it (viii. and ix.).

[1] *Physiol. Psych.* 6th ed. 1911, iii. p. 598.   [2] *Journ. Exper. Psych.* i. 1916.

Depreciatory views. There have been several further attempts at psychological explanation which—although less prominent in current literature than those just mentioned—still cannot be allowed to pass here quite without notice. For the most part, their tendency is to interpret g in such a manner as to diminish its scientific significance.

The most extreme among these disparaging versions is that which declares the scope of g to begin and end with the tests themselves—or with, at most, the addition of ability for puzzles and other stunt-like performances. But this certainly goes too far. Among the many opposing reasons is the correlation which the tests are well known to have with success at school work.

Not so easily warded off, however, is the more moderate charge, that success at the tests depends upon mere verbal ability. Harsher critics have even said, verbal " agility." This is a view that later on will need careful examination (see chs. xi. and xii.).

More important still is the interpretation of g as being a product, not of innate aptitude, but only of education. That person does the tests best, it is said, who has been best taught.

Also worthy of mention, though hardly of prolonged examination, is the taking of g to have reference only to children, being in fact no more than a measurement of their maturity. One child does better at the tests than another of the same age, it is said, only because of being more precocious. For measuring the ability of adults, then, the tests would obviously be useless. Such a view has in its day been much favoured by critics of the tests; but now it would seem to have become almost extinct.

PHYSIOLOGICAL BASIS

Energy. The next group of things that claim to constitute that which is measured by g derive from the field of physiology. One of them is the above mentioned mental energy, but translated into terms of the brain. It will be kept for discussion later on together with the mental version of the energy.

Plasticity. Another attempt, ventured long ago by the present writer in collaboration with Professor Krueger, was to regard *g* as measuring the " plastic function " of the nervous system.

> " A nervous system of superior plastic function would not be distinguished in that its conducting paths could enter more quickly into any desired combinations ; this is what would seem to be needful for mere speed in forming any chance associations, as for example in the memorizing of senseless syllables. What it would be able to perform would be to shape out with time in all psycho-physiological territories finer and more stable complexes of conductors. In this way, it would function with more precision and constancy (in the sense of systematic regularity) ; the eventual advantage would be a greater speed and also exactness of the normal much practised abilities. A nervous system whose development had been favoured by a superior plastic function would in its performances surpass other nervous systems in much the same way as a machine made of steel would surpass one similar but made of iron." [1]

As for the question why the brain that is plastic for one kind of configuration should be expected to be so for other kinds, the following answer was suggested :

> " It is on very analogous grounds that the hair on one region of a person's scalp usually resembles that on other regions." [2]

The blood. Next, we may naturally think of the influence which must necessarily be exerted by the state of the blood.

---

[1] *Zeit. f. Psychol.* xliv. 1906, p. 108. Not unlike would appear to be the view recently advanced by Freeman in a valuable work on *Mental Tests*, which has reached the present writer too late for discussion here.

[2] Hart and Spearman, *Journ. Abnormal Psychology*, 1914.

This, too, was long ago taken into account. Over and above any energy, it was said :

" We immediately come across a general factor beyond all dispute, namely, the common blood supply ; quantitative and qualitative alterations of this necessarily produce effects upon all the cortical functions." [1]

Various. There would seem to be cogent evidence for a third universal and physiological factor, namely, the state of the endocrine glands, as is strikingly illustrated by cretinism. Yet a fourth arises from the respiratory apparatus, as is evidenced in the way that mental efficiency can be disturbed by adenoids. In fact, from this physiological standpoint, the universal factors would seem to be multipliable almost without limit.

POSSIBILITY OF COMPLEX BASIS

Early regard paid to sub-factors. The foregoing physiological considerations forcibly bring up the question as to whether the universal factor g can or cannot, consistently with the tetrad equation (p. 73), be composed of *two or more* sub-factors (universal or otherwise). This question was already put forward—and even, with certain restrictions, answered affirmatively—in the original publication of 1904 (p. 284) ; g might, it was said, represent a whole group of functions or sub-factors.

Impossibility in general. This matter is peculiarly important for those numerous renderings of " intelligence " which involve several different constituents of the nature of " faculties." A well-known instance is Binet's division of it into comprehension, invention, direction, and censorship. Another is Freeman's analysis into " sensory capacity," " capacity for perceptual recognition," " quickness and range and flexibility of attention," " facility in imagination," " span and steadiness of attention," and so forth.

[1] Hart and Spearman, *Brit. J. Psych.* 1912, v. p. 71.

Now any resolution of g into such factors as these—and they represent the great majority of those which come into serious consideration—would seem to be altogether impossible ; for the tetrad equation could not ever be satisfied. This can be deduced from what has been said in ch. vi. And a direct special proof is given in the appendix (p. vii). Such factors may or may not occur *additionally* to g ; but they certainly cannot form any part of this.

Possibility in certain cases. There are, however, certain special cases where the g does admit of resolution into a plurality of sub-factors.

One such case is where these are fixedly inter-linked, as occurs when one of them acts through the medium of the other. Thus, g could quite well involve both the sub-factor of blood and also that of the endocrine glands, since the latter only exerts its influence by way of the former.

Somewhat more subtle is the case of sub-factors that are fixedly *inter-changeable*. As an illustration from ordinary life, suppose a man to derive part of his income from England and part from France. So long as the rate of exchange between pounds and francs is everywhere the same, he can always pay in either money equally well, and its derivation from two separate sources makes no difference to him. But this would cease to be true if the pound stood at a higher rate in some places and the franc in others ; the two would no longer be inter-changeable in any fixed manner.

Now just the same holds of any psychic influences, say, for example, ability and zeal. If in all the tests the respective influences of these two always remained in any constant ratio, then both could quite well enter into g together ; for the tetrad equation would still be able to hold. But if, instead, some tests depended more on ability and others more on zeal, then g can no longer possibly contain both at once ; for the tetrad equation must necessarily break down.[1]

[1] All such exceptions can be brought under a single heading from the mathematical standpoint, that variations of quantity may have different " dimensions of freedom." Imagine a man's total income to come from the single bank X. If we know how much he receives from

DOCTRINE OF " CHANCE "

The lawless and the law-abiding kind. There remains one more proposed explanation of g, or rather of the tetrad equation which conditions it. This is by crediting the fulfilment of the equation to pure " chance."

But here arises a troublesome ambiguity. The term chance has two almost opposite meanings. In the one, it implies the wildest irregularities, such as the shiftings of a weathercock in a storm. In the other meaning, it becomes regular and accordingly follows laws. These ordain, for instance, that red cards shall in the long run tend to be cut as often as black ; or that the throwing of a die shall tend to be either a four or a five in one third of all trials. In such cases the theoretical foundation is twofold ; first a set of basal events are assumed to remain uniformly probable throughout the range at issue ; and then the further assumption is made that on an average of very numerous trials all influences additional to these basal probabilities will tend to neutralise each other. Thus, in the case of the cards it is assumed that the theoretical probabilities of cutting red

this, obviously we can settle offhand the amount of his total income. The latter, since it can be fixed by one single fact, is said to have only one dimension of freedom. But next imagine him to get his money from two banks, X and Y. In order to settle his total income this time, we are obliged to know the receipts from both banks ; the freedom of variations is now said to have two dimensions. If there are n banks at issue, the number of dimensions will also be n.

It may occur, however, that the freedom given with one hand is taken back again with the other. Thus, suppose that in the case of the two banks we introduce the condition that the receipts from X are always three times as large as those from Y. Hereupon, the knowing of *either* of these receipts will suffice to settle the total income.

All this may be generalized by saying that, if any variable total magnitude depends upon n part-variables, the total variable can always be reduced back to one dimension of freedom by imposing upon the part-variables n-1 independent conditions between each other. On such reduction, and then only, the total variable can satisfy the tetrad equation and therefore produce g and s (with the s's mutually independent).

We need hardly add that whenever g involves n sub-factors, its total value must be some mathematical function of the values of these respectively. In the simplest case, but one of especial importance, it is merely their *average*. Still even here, just as in any other case, they must be inter-connected by n-1 independent conditions.

and black are equal, and that therefore with a large number of trials (whether successive or simultaneous) the actual proportions of the two colours will approximately be equal also. Similarly, as regards the six sides of the dice throughout a large number of throws, or the two faces of coins throughout many tossings. After these two assumptions, all the rest of the argument is only a matter of counting the different ways in which such uniformly probable events can combine favourably or unfavoutably for some occurrence at issue. This part of the business is wholly determined by inexorable mathematics ; and the calculations involved may be as elaborate as in any other mathematical branch.

Now, it is only in this second sense of law-abidingness that " chance " can possibly explain the tetrad equation (or anything else !). But in the course of ordinary life—as distinguished from the artificialities of card-cutting, dice-throwing, etc.—any such uniform probabilities together with additional influences that neutralize each other in the long run would appear to be surprisingly rare. For instance, the chance of a marriage or of a suicide might to a superficial observer seem to remain the same year after year ; whereas actual records reveal that in truth the probability undergoes continual changes, often of great complexity. The same may be said of every field in economics, politics, and even physical events. And if there is any sphere in which the assumption of uniform probabilities together with additional influences that tend to exactly cancel each other is *least* plausible, surely it is that of mental operations. To be deprecated in psychology, then, is any description of such assumptions as representing " the natural course of events." Nevertheless, the possibility that mental events should actually take such a course must not be ignored.

Statement of the doctrine. The way in which the said assumption of uniform probabilities has been applied to the doctrine of mental powers consists in the view that mental ability depends on a set of very numerous ultimate elements, and that all individuals have a uniformly equal probability of being well or ill endowed in respect of each element.

This view in its simplest form may be illustrated by the following arrangement. Put into a bag a large number of counters, each representing one element of ability. Then, let every individual have one fair throw of dice for each element ; the higher the throw the greater is taken to be his endowment.

A Conclusive Objection. The first to suggest the possibility of some such arrangement of " chance " seems to have been the present writer, who deduced mathematically its chief consequences for a table of correlations.[1] Subsequently, this point of view was interestingly advocated by Thomson (who does not appear to have noticed the previous work) ; this time, there was no mathematical deduction of its consequences, but instead three or four actual trials with dice and cards.[2] Then followed Garnett, who once again—and in a much more exhaustive manner—determined the consequences by rigorous mathematics.[3]

Between these three investigators there ensued a good deal of discussion. But all this, it would seem, may immediately be short-circuited by the following consideration. The very core of this doctrine of " chance," throughout all its possible varieties in detail, is that every individual should have a uniformly fair throw of the dice for each of very numerous ability-elements. Now, if this really happened, then every individual would in any pool of many different operations tend to equality with every other individual. Anything more opposed to the known facts could hardly be imagined. Beyond all question, the dice are very heavily loaded in favour of some individuals as compared with others. And as Dr. Ballard has luminously expressed the matter,

[1] His first mention of it was in *Psych. Rev.* 1914, xxi. p. 109.

[2] For references to his works, see appendix II. 2 and 3, where the matter is discussed in greater detail.

[3] *Brit. J. Psych.* 1919, ix.

it is just this loading of the dice that gives value (other than zero) to g.[1] With this suggestion of " chance," then, there seems no need for us to trouble ourselves further ; one very simple consideration has sufficed to condemn it conclusively and finally.

[1] See the appendix, pp. xiii-xiv.

CHAPTER VIII

UNIVERSAL MENTAL COMPETITION

DESCRIPTION OF THE PHENOMENON

Occurrence with cognitive operations. We now turn to that interpretation of g which—in the present state of psychology—appears to have the greatest importance of all; it is that which regards this g as measuring a person's " mental energy."

But this necessitates some digression. Before dealing with the theory itself, an exposition seems needful of the phenomenon which has at bottom inspired it. To indicate the general nature of this phenomenon may be quoted the dramatic words of Pascal:

" The spirit of this sovereign judge of the world, man, is not so independent but that it is liable to be troubled by the first disturbance about him. The noise of a cannon is not needed to break the train of his thought, it need only be the creaking of a weather-cock or a pulley. Do not be astonished if at this moment he argues incoherently, a fly is buzzing about his ears, and that is enough to render him incapable of sound judgment. . . . Here is a droll kind of a God! O most ridiculous hero ! " [1]

The human weakness thus derided by Pascal is familiar enough to us all. A man's stream of lived experience runs in such a tiny bed, that anything entering into this must needs displace some previous occupant. Of all the competitions for existence, of all the wars for " a place under the sun," surely none is more relentless than that which is continually waging between the various contents of our own mind.

So far, the most exact information about this phenomenon has been obtained in the sphere of sensory perception. The first definite measurement is usually ascribed to the forerunner of modern experimental psychologists, Charles Bonnet, who remarked that the number of objects clearly visible at the same time is about six.[2] But much earlier a similar observation had been made by Nemesius, who arrived at a somewhat smaller estimate.[3] Many subsequent psychologists have repeated the observation with growing scientific acumen. Hamilton writes :

" If you throw a handful of marbles on the floor, you will find it difficult to view at once more than six, or seven at most, without confusion ; but if you group them into twos, or threes, or fives, you can comprehend as many groups as you can units ; because the mind considers these groups only as units—it views them as wholes, and throws their parts out of consideration." [4]

Particularly curious is the similar but much more elaborate trial made by Jevons with beans ; for he concludes that it is

" one of the few points in psychology which can, as far as we yet see, be submitted to experiment." [5]

---

[1] *Les Pensées*, trans. by Kegan Paul.

[2] *Essai de Psychologie*, ch. 37, p. 132.

[3] Numerum autem eorum, quae cernuntur, si plus tribus est aut quatuor, qui uno aspectu non cernitur, motus etiam et figuras multorum angulorum numquam (visio) sola, sed cum memoria et cogitatione sentit. *De Natura Hominis*, 1566, ch. 7, ed. Malthaei, p. 164.

[4] *Lectures on Metaphysics*, 1865, Lect. XIV. p. 254.

[5] *Nature*, 1871, p. 281.

This was in 1871 ; less than eight years afterwards, Wundt had founded a laboratory for the purpose of submitting the whole range of psychology to experimental treatment !

In this same original laboratory—more perhaps than in any of its innumerable followers and rivals—interest for the present problem has been faithfully conserved. The steady flow of investigation which started with the clever pioneer work of Cattell,[1] has culminated with the masterly volume of Wirth.[2]

Thanks to all these labours, the primitive experimental results have been confirmed, corrected, and extended. We have now learnt that the narrow limitation originally noticed in visual perception applies no less to the other senses. The impossibility has been ascertained of perceiving simultaneously and clearly more than half a dozen auditory tones ; the same has been found about the number of tactile impressions, or of impressions combined from different senses. Researches by Flugel have manifested the similarly confined range that exists when the discrete visual objects are replaced by a continuous design, and also when the duration of the impression instead of being momentary is indefinitely prolonged.[3]

Even more impressive is the competition that has been revealed to exist on passing from the sphere of percepts to that of ideas, from the present experience to reproduction of the past. The wealth of such reproducible ideas is so vast as to have excited enthusiasm in all ages. Hear the passionate utterance of Augustine :

> " I come to the field and spacious palaces of my memory, where are the treasures of innumerable images, brought into it from things of all sorts perceived by the senses. . . . All these doth that great harbour of the memory receive in her numberless and inexpressible windings, to be forthcoming and brought out at

[1] *Philos. Studien*, iii. 1886.

[2] *Die Experimentelle Analyse der Bewusstseinsphenomene*, 1908.

[3] *Brit. Journ. Psych.* v. 1913, p. 357.

need. . . . Yea, I discern the breath of lilies from violets, though smelling nothing ; and I prefer honey to sweet wine, smooth before rugged, at the time neither tasting nor handling, but remembering only. These things do I, in that vast court of my memory. For these are present with me, heaven, earth, sea, and whatever I can think of therein, besides that I have forgotten. . . . Great is this force of memory, excessive great, O my God ; the large and boundless chamber!—Whoever sounded the bottom thereof ? " [1]

Hegel likewise speaks of the " limitless pit " for the storage of our ideas.[2]

Yet of all this potential immensity, what a beggarly pittance is available at any one moment ! A man may have spent a lifetime in memorizing the whole Bible, and still remain unable to recall to mind any half a dozen iines quite simultaneously. As Fortlage said :

" Our soul is like a full treasury vault, in which a wretched lamp is burning, whose glimmer can only reach to illuminate a scanty number of objects at a time." [3]

So, too, Herbart :

" Reproduction by memory and imagination betrays indeed, that no idea once created is ever quite lost. . . . But when we compare the multitude of all that the mind of an adult man has collected with that of which he is conscious in any single moment—we must be astounded at the disproportion between the former's wealth and the latter's poverty." [4]

And if the intensity of the competition is astonishing, no less so is its universality. Not reproduction alone, but perhaps in even higher degree all insightful and creative operations (p. 28) are also governed by it. In all alike,

---

[1] *Confessions*, bk. x.   [2] *Encyl. d. Philos. Wiss.* para. 403.
[3] *Acht Psychol. Vorträge*, ii. " Ueber das Gedächtnis," 1872, p. 65.
[4] *Lehrbuch der Psychologie*, 1816, p. 69.

the actual amount of simultaneous mental activity is infinitesimally small as compared with the potential amount. As was said by Publius Syrus two thousand years ago : " To do two things at once is to do neither."

The competition appears not even to be restricted to those mental events which are manifestly conscious, but to extend in some degree to those underground regions of cognition—constituting by far its larger part—which fail to be introspectible.   For instance, a research of the present writer has shown that, under certain conditions, the harder a person tries to feel the position of an unseen point pressing against his skin, the worse he succeeds.   In an experimental series with one subject [1] the effort to localize with extreme exactness produced a mean error of no less than 154 mm., which was immediately reduced to less than half as soon as the localizing was done with natural negligence.   Similar results were obtained with twenty other subjects.[2]

Now, this paradox of the localization becoming worse the more the subject tries to make it better was eventually traced to the fact that the apparently simple act of locating the prick is really based on many not manifestly conscious, but yet indispensable, contributory mental processes.   These latter suffered by the competition which ensued when any intense notice was directed to the prick sensation itself.[3]

Occurrence with states of feeling. So far, we have examined only the competition that prevails between all simultaneous processes of a cognitive nature. But the question then arises as to whether anything of the sort befalls also our affective states.

Rarely, it seems, has the question even been raised. Such indications as can be gathered from casual observation, however, suggest that these affective states are ruled by just the same universal competition.   Any person addressed in an offensive manner may at first from sheer astonishment

---

[1] Professor Krueger was kind enough to serve here.

[2] Among them was Professor Wirth.

[3] Normaltäuschungen, *Psychol. Stud.* 1906, i. p. 387.

not break into anger ; so, too, on unexpectedly entering into a great inheritance, he may for a while be too perturbed for much happiness.   An interesting case of one state ousting another is recorded of Scott.   The latter, whilst dictating his novels, was often impeded by great bodily pain.

"But when dialogue of peculiar animation was in progress, spirit seemed to triumph altogether over matter, he arose from his couch, and walked up and down the room, raising and lowering his voice and, as it were, acting the parts." [1]

Such exclusion of one feeling by another would seem capable of even more drastic effects ; martyrs are said to have been burned alive without suffering—all agony having been expelled by absorbing ecstasy.

Not only does cognition thus compete with cognition, and affection with affection, but so too does the one kind of process with the other.   It is a common observation that anger tends to make us "blind."   Joy, if sufficient in quantity, is able to "daze" us.   Proverbially, a man may be "scared out of his seven senses."

More impressive still is the witness borne by pathology. Excessive emotion is said by high authority to be the main cause of the modern scourge, neurasthenia :

It makes "those who are its sport lose their faculties of judgment and intellectual control."   "A man is neurasthenic from the moment that in him emotion gains a permanent supremacy over reason." [2]

Still more vividly is depicted a similar origin of hysteria :

"The emotion may exercise a blighting action on the mentality of the subject undergoing it.   He who is under the influence of the emotion becomes incapable of cognition, incapable of judgment ; he is insane.   This is particulaily the characteristic of intense emotional

[1] Lockhart's Life of Scott, ch. xliv.

[2] Déjérine and Gaukler, *Les Manifestations Fonctionelles des Psychonévroses*, 1911, pp. 323, 369.

shocks which, so to speak, make abrupt and total invasion of the individual conscience. Deprived of perceptions, even the most elementary, not feeling any more, not seeing any more, not understanding any more, transformed into a simple automatism, the subject is, so to speak, in a state of psychological swoon." [1]

Support of less startling but even more cogent sort is afforded by the introspections of our best psychologists. Carveth Read recently communicated a record of a series of minor but painful surgical operations upon himself. One of the main hindrances to obtaining the record was found by him to consist in the fact that " when the pain is very intense, it occupies the whole mind." [2]

Up to the present, these affective states have only to a very limited extent been submitted to experimental investigation. But so far as this has gone, at any rate, the results are concordant with the preceding indications. Thus, Ach notices that the feelings disturb the course of consciousness. Hamlin finds them the most effective of all sorts of distraction. More sensational were the " shock-stimuli " of Alexander-Schäfer. Whilst his experimental subjects were diligently memorizing a series of colours, he from behind and without warning fired off a small pistol. The ensuing emotion of the subjects was found to produce a large and measurable loss of memory. He repeated the experiment several times on the same subject, so that—although the auditory experience remained unchanged—the emotional effect wore off ; thereupon there was also a decrease in the disturbance of memory. [3]

An investigation of Yerkes and Dodson showed that a similar effacement of cognition by affection holds good of the lower animals. Dancing mice were put into a chamber with two outlets of only just distinguishable appearance ; but whereas the one conducted to food, the other led across some wires that gave an electric shock. It was found that

[1] *Ibidem*, pp. 319-320.   [2] Paper read to the Brit. Psyc. Soc., 1912.
[3] *Zeit. f. Psychol.* xxxix. 1905.

the rate at which the animals learnt to select the right outlet depended on the intensity of the shock ; a mild one helped, but a severe one hindered. The most reasonable interpretation is that, though all pain from the shock increases the volition to select the other outlet, yet an excess of the pain neutralizes this advantage by diminishing the cognition of the different appearances.[1]

This accords with a vivid reminiscence of the present writer's early school days. His teacher had adopted the maxim that Latin Grammar could best be driven into the minds of small boys by dint of severe blows of the fist in the middle of the back. The actual result of this stimulus, however, was that, instead of further cognition arising as to whether the past participle of a verb ended in -tum or in -sum, the whole posse of rules and exceptions incontinently vanished into oblivion.

The preceding considerations seem to demonstrate clearly enough, that affection interferes with cognition. But does also the reverse occur ? Once more the indications appear to be in the affirmative. Certainly, at any rate, popular experience is on this side. Not many days ago, a protest was made in Parliament that " learning is apt to produce a swollen head at the expense of weak bowels." In pleasanter fashion, a similar belief was voiced by Tennyson's Lucilia, when she " found her master cold " with " his mind half buried in some weightier argument." In a similar sense, too, we may take the line, " whistling to keep himself from being afraid."

Corroborative evidence is given by pathology. Carpenter relates that, before the introduction of chloroform, patients sometimes went through severe operations without giving any sign of pain, and afterwards declared that " they felt none," having concentrated their thoughts on something else.[2] Even to this day, surgical operators and dentists are

[1] *Journ. Compar. Neurology and Psychology*, 1908, pp. 459, 482. Similar experiments have been made by Cole, *Journ. Animal Behaviour*, 1911, pp. 111-124.

[2] *Mental Physiology*, 1874, p. 138.

said to make frequent use of such distractions. And any one who is experienced with young children knows how readily their griefs, whether due to physical injury or otherwise, may be banished simply by bringing something else to their notice. Miss Shinn, for instance, writes that her niece, when discomforted by teething, would demand constant diversion.[1]

The more precise and reliable evidence of scientific psychology brings again support. Read, in his above mentioned communication, expressly stated that his pain was diminished by studying it. W. Stern found that a too intense observation of a picture interfered with the aesthetic enjoyment of it.[2] Dürr wrote that the disturbance of feeling by reflection is demonstrated in all kinds of experience.[3]

From the foregoing observations, it is hard to resist concluding that the competition is not confined to the cognitive processes, but extends in just the same way to the emotions also, as anger, fear, surprise, and joy.

Occurrence with acts of will. There remains still to be considered the third great class of mental process, namely, that of conation or will. Do these, too, enter into the same competition ? This time, the answer is more difficult. Often, indeed, the remark has been made that different desires have a mutually weakening effect. As the French say, one nail drives out another. But proof is not easy that this mutual hindering really derives from the universal competition, and not merely from some particular interference.

If, for example, the attraction of a woman's beautiful features is decreased by a repugnance at her vapid expression, this may be sufficiently explained by the intrinsic incompatibility between attraction and repugnance to one and the same object. Or if miserliness excludes generosity, this may be simply because the impulse to retain and that to

[1] *Notes on the Development of a Child*, i. 1895, p. 241.

[2] *Differentielle Psychologie*, 1911, p. 38.

[3] *Die Lehre von der Aufmerksamkeit*, 1907, pp. 116-117.

relinquish are contradictory.   Perhaps we can account in a similar manner for many of the Freudian " conflicts."

And even should there be no direct incompatibility between the desires themselves, there may still be one between their respective means of realization, which will eventually react upon the desires also.   There is no intrinsic contradiction in wishing to be both a saint and a millionaire ; but the active pursuit of either of these ideals is likely enough to impair success with the other.   Such interference will probably arise, if for no other reason, at any rate through the limits of any person's time, or endurance, or financial resources.   He who devotes himself to science is apt to slacken in his quest after fashionable clothes.   A man with an insane craving to fight has been cured by putting him into a smithy where he could deal his blows to metal plates.   All these mutual weakening of desires on *specific* grounds must not be confounded with any weakening that might be traceable to the perfectly general competition here at issue.

But although evidence is so hard to obtain with respect to one conation competing with another, it appears to be got readily enough as regards competition between, on the one hand conation, and on the other hand either affection or cognition.   For the reply, alike of casual experience and of trained psychologists, is emphatically affirmative.   Hamlet says :

> " The violence of either grief or joy,
>   Their own enactures with themselves destroy."

And any one would agree that a person may be so overwhelmed with grief at his misfortunes, as to be incapable of a vigorous effort to repair them.   With regard to joy, also, Shand writes decisively :

> " In proportion to the degree in which the impulse of joy is prominent in consciousness is the emotion of joy destroyed." [1]

He finds a similar opposition between intensity of surprise and efficiency of action.[2]   James points out that the man

[1] *Foundations of Character*, 1914, p. 283.   [2] *Ibidem*, p. 431.

"who spends his life in a weltering sea of sensibility
and emotion . . . never does a manly concrete deed."[1]

So, too, Bain :

"The active man manifests power, but the passive man
may be he that luxuriates in the sentiment itself.   It is
the essence of the pure energetic temperament, still to
energize, and not to enjoy even the fruits of energy."[2]

More general is the declaration of Lehmann :

"There is a real opposition between the manifestations
of emotion and impulse ;   their respective energies during a mental movement (Gemütsbewegung) are, other
things equal, inversely proportional."[3]

So, once more, in the small but masterly work of Elliot
Smith and Pear :

"His intelligence seemed (to himself) to have become
numbed by his experiences of dread, and he became
conscious of the unreliability of his memory and of his
inability to understand not only complex orders, but,
as he put it, ' even the newspapers.' "[4]

Further confirmation has been afforded by experiment.
In the investigations of Ach, feelings of pleasure and un-
pleasure occurred frequently and they often reached considerable intensity.   It was found, however, that such feelings were in every one of the subjects completely absent *at
the moment of strong willing.*[5]   This has quite recently received full confirmation from the very important series of
researches that have been made in the laboratory and under
the direction of Aveling.

Analogous appears to be the relation between the conative
and the cognitive processes.   Koffka describes how excessive

---

[1] *Principles of Psychology*, i. p. 125.

[2] *The Study of Character*, 1916, p. 202.

[3] *Die physischen Äquivalente der Bewusstseinserscheinungen*, p. 193.
Elemente der Psychodynamik 1905, p. 362.

[4] *Shellshock*, 1917, p. 21.

[5] *Ueber den Willensakt u. d. Temperament*, 1910, p. 245.

strain to comprehend a foreign word only increases the difficulty of doing so.[1] Meumann relates a similar observation.[2] Still more emphatically Book warns against the danger of the learner's energy going " into the trying instead of into the work-activity."[3] Titchener states in quite general terms that, the greater the effort to make any mental representation clear, the less the ensuing clearness.[4]

Extraordinary neglect by psychologists. In view of its paramount importance, this law of universal competition might well be expected to have everywhere and always constituted a dominant feature in psychological discussion, investigation, and speculation. And indeed, our quotations indicate that some thinkers have been impressed by it most profoundly. Strange to say, however, these appear not to have been the rule, but only rare exceptions. In earlier times, the larger half of eminent psychologists seem not so much as to have mentioned the phenomenon ; this includes such widely divergent writers as Hartley and Tetens, Destutt de Tracy, and Cardinal Mercier, Hume and Spinoza, La Mettrie, Maine de Biran, and Adamson. Still more numerous are the authors who seem only to run into it by accident, as it were ; this is all that can be said of Hobbes, Bossuet, Reid, Condillac, and James Mill—to name only a few. Even Descartes, whose whole doctrine, epistemological, metaphysical, and ethical, is fundamentally based on clearness of cognition, does not pause to consider that this clearness is so curiously restricted in extent.

Nor can any great improvement be chronicled for the majority of the most modern writers. The bare facts, no doubt, do nowadays usually receive a more adequate treatment than formerly. But there still remains the same dearth of effort to treat them scientifically ; the same limitation to comparatively few among all these facts ; the same

[1] *Zur Analyse der Vorstellungen u. ihrer Gesetze*, 1912, p. 45.

[2] *Vorl. z. Einführung in d. Experim. Pädag.* i. 1911, p. 203.

[3] *Journ. Educ. Psych.*, i. 1910, p. 194.

[4] *Textbook of Psychology*, 1911, pp. 295, 276.

consideration of cognate events disconnectedly from one another ; and the same slackness in seeking for even so much explanation as will serve for practical purposes.

But perhaps the most curious attitude is to regard the phenomenon as offering no point to be explained. Thus Thomas Brown, who seems to have enjoyed a greater popularity than any other psychologist in modern times, could write as follows :

> " Let us imagine a castle, which commands, from its elevation, an extensive view of a domain, rich with all beauties of nature and art. . . . Instantly, or almost instantly . . . the landscape becomes to our view altogether different. Certain parts only, those parts which we wished to know particularly, are seen by us ; the remaining parts seem almost to have vanished. . . . When one becomes more vivid, the others become fainter. . . . If one can discover any reason why this should have become more vivid, the comparative in-- distinctiveness of the other parts of the scene may be considered as following *of course*." [1]

And at the present day, even such an exceptionally thoughtful author as Calkins would dispose of the whole matter in a similar way—with offhand curtness to boot. " Attention to part of one's total object of consciousness *of course* implies inattention to the rest." [2] Why in the name of all that is psychological these " of course's " ?

Surely, the phenomenon is mysterious enough even from the merely physiological aspect. For what reason does the eye not perceive more than six objects clearly at a time, possessing, as it does, three to six million cones for receiving the visual impressions on the retina, and half to one million fibres for conducting them on to the brain ? So, too, some half a million fibres exist to accommodate stimulations of pressure ; [3]

---

[1] *Philosophy of the Human Mind,* 21st ed. 1870, p. 200. Here, as in the next quotation, the italics are introduced by the present writer.

[2] *A First Book in Psychology,* 1910, p. 98.

[3] v. Frey, *Würzburger Ber.* 1899, *Ueber den Ortsinn der Haut,* p. 4.

while even the less richly endowed ear spreads at any rate a quarter of million basilar fibres to catch the different tones.[1] And wherefore has the mind but a minuscule of thought at a time, seeing that the cerebral cortex contains some 92,000,000,000 nervous cells devoted to this service ? [2] This question is not to be eluded simply by saying that the brain, like every other apparatus, must needs have some or other constant maximal limit to its output. Such a reply misses the essential point, which is that the maximal output for *each kind of activity* is *not* constant, but becomes changed and lowered by any simultaneous occurrence of *other* activities. What a contrast to such internecine rivalry in the mental functions of the brain is presented by the non-mental functions of the rest of the body, as circulation, respiration, secretion, digestion, nutrition, or the production of heat. Here, the narrow limitation vanishes. The digestive activity of the salivary glands proceeds without arresting the digestion in the stomach ; secretion is effected by the liver without hindering that which goes on in the kidneys ; the heart steadily beats without thereby causing any abatement in the expansions and contractions of the lungs. The whole bodily performance is no longer a succession of jealous soloists ; instead, it assembles, unites and combines all parts into a harmonious chorus.

UNSUCCESSFUL EXPLANATIONS

Mere verbiage. The more closely and fully the preceding facts are envisaged, the more evidently they constitute one of the fundamental quantitative laws of the mind—indeed the first in rank among such laws. How, then, shall it be explained ?

We may begin by summarily dismissing certain views that

[1] Tetzius, *Das Gehörorgan d. Wirbeltiere*, 1884, ii. p. 346. Hensen, *Zeit. f. wiss. Zoologie*, xiii. 1863. Hermann's *Handbuch d. Physiologie*, iii. (2), 1880.

[2] Helen Thompson, *Journ. Comp. Neurol.*, June, 1899.

cannot properly be called any solution at all, but rather an anodyne to allay the craving for this. These views are generally embodied in popular phrases—not disdained in emergency even by the professed psychologist—which possesses no reasonable meaning whatever.

For example, the explanation why Archimedes did not notice the Roman soldiers approaching to kill him is commonly said to be because he was " giving his whole mind " to his thought about circles. But what is the " whole mind " and what is meant by " giving " it ? Most moderns seem to deny that the mind is anything more than a series of processes, such as sensations, thoughts, feelings, desires, and so on. It is not evident how any one of these can be bestowed upon any other one. How, for example, shall a boy's thought of a cricket match be given to his remembrance of football, or to his desire for pastry ? Other psychologists, it is true, maintain that all the processes are manifestations of an underlying durable substance or soul. But how even this could be given or lent is not too obvious. And, in any case, why should it not be lent to twelve marbles or tones or ideas just as well as to six ?

A similar usage is often made of the word " attention." As usually employed, this word "means not, but only blunders about a meaning." On looking it up in the dictionary, we merely learn that it is " the act of attending " : and on turning over to " attend " we find that this is to regard with attention. On having recourse to psychologists for an interpretation, we get indeed very many ; but if there is any point in which these tend to agree, it is that all bearing upon the phenomenon of mental competition illusively vanishes. Suppose, for instance, we adopt the view that a concentration of attention on any part of the mental field simply means a becoming-clearer of this part. We are still left asking, as before, why the clearness of one part should preclude that of the remainder. Or if, instead, we agree that attention consists in " conation so far as it requires for its satisfaction fuller cognisance of its objects "

—then why should this satisfaction always be restricted to half a dozen beans and never be allowed a full dozen ?

Unity of the soul. Turning to the more serious assaults upon the problem, it is to Aristotle that we are indebted for the first great explanation offered, one which has perhaps been more widely accepted than any other, and which has preserved its vitality down to the present day. He suggested that the restriction of our consciousness is due to our being able to perceive *only one object at a time ;* and this, in its turn, he attributes to the fact of the perceiving psyche being itself an indivisible unity.[1]

But this doctrine, despite all its illustrious sponsors, must here be rejected. For if really the unity of the mind were that which prevents a person from perceiving a dozen objects at the same time, surely it ought also to prevent perception of six, or even of two. And should the defender of this view go on to say that the six can be perceived because they are linked in the unity of mutual relation, then why should not also twelve be linked in such unity ?

Specific antagonisms. The next great attempt to explain our phenomenon is by attributing it to what may be called specific antagonisms.

Now, the fact of these latter really existing is beyond all doubt. In the domain of physiology, they have been studied with great success, notably by Sherrington, under the name of the " reciprocal inhibition " of reflexes.[2] For instance, the hind limb has one system of nerves and muscles to flex and another to extend it ; but when the flexor muscles are excited reflexly by a suitable stimulus, there ensues a corresponding relaxation of the extensors ; conversely, any reflex innervation of the extensor muscles inhibits the flexors.

This purely physiological interference possesses, without doubt, a remarkable counterpart among the operations of

[1] *De Sensu,* ch. vii.

[2] *Integrative Action of the Nervous System,* 1906, and many subsequent writings.

the mind, as has been shown by many recent investigators, especially Sherrington and McDougall. For example, the figure given below can equally well elicit the appearance of a chamber or of a boss. But the appearing of the one

inevitably prevents that of the other. So, too, when different objects are presented to the two eyes (by using a stereoscope, squinting, or other device), the complete vision of the one object infallibly precludes that of the other.

Nevertheless, all such cases would appear to be sharply and widely separated from the general mental competition which we have been considering. In calling these antagonisms " specific," it is meant that each occurs between two particular kinds of mental process, which are, as it were, in permanent hostility to each other. The said reflex innervation of the flexor muscles will (whatever the strength of the stimulation) tend to prevent innervation of the extensors ; the one perspective will invariably oppose the other one. But in the experiments with beans, etc., nothing of the kind occurs. When the group of them is exhibited, *any* two may both be seen clearly—so long as not too many others are seen clearly also.[1]

Degree of reinforcement. In the next attempt to explain the phenomenon, the failure of a percept or idea to reach consciousness is attributed, not to active repression by competitors, but to its own weakness through lack of reinforcement.

This view has found no less a proponent than James, for

[1] Similarly, one can easily follow any two instruments in a numerous orchestra. Most impossible of all, perhaps, to ascribe to any specific antagonism is the competition which Flugel has shown to exist even between adjoining parts of the same line seen without change of ocular fixation (*Brit. J. Psych.* 1913, v.).

whom the reinforcing consists in what has been variously
known as " pre-perception," " pre-imagination," or " idea-
tional preparation." This, he says, may be so effective as
even to produce illusion.

> " When watching for the distant clock to strike, our
> mind is so filled with its image that at every moment
> we think we hear the longed-for or dreaded sound."

A similar view seems to have been taken of the reinforcement that may be derived from the " constellation "
(Ziehen), or from concomitant movements (Ribot).

Now the facts here cited are no doubt perfectly true.
But they do not seem adequate to explain our present
problem, even partially. At most they cause the problem
to shift its ground. They ascribe the narrow span of simultaneous perception or thought to narrow span of reinforcement ; but the latter stands in just the same need of explanation as the former does.

General mental brake. Many of the objections that are
fatal to the theories hitherto mentioned have been cleverly
overcome by the following hypothesis, which we owe to
Wundt. He suggests that the small amount of ideas possible
at any one moment may be due to the existence of some
general mental brake or " inhibitory centre." A rough
analogy can be afforded by the action of the piano ; here,
only a very few of the wires, namely, those directly struck
at the same time, are set into appreciable vibration ; this is
because all the other wires struck previously are restrained
from still vibrating by a " damping " apparatus. Wundt
is able even to propose a possible locality in the brain for
such a psycho-physical damper, to wit, the frontal convolutions. For damage to this region, he says, is almost
always followed by a loss of inhibition—as if some sort of
brake had been impaired.

But even this ingenious hypothesis can scarcely be
accepted. If these frontal convolutions (or any other neural
apparatus) really acted as such a brake, then destruction of

the apparatus should increase the mental span. Put the piano damper out of action (as by pressing the loud pedal) and the simultaneous range of sound will increase indefinitely. But no such result is known to the pathology of the mind. In the case of damage to the frontal convolutions, there ensues, indeed, a particular increase of function ; but this is only in the violence of impulses (at the expense of force of control), not in the span of perception or of cognition ; the brake impaired is not cognitive, but solely moral.

Up to the present point, then, every one of the attempts to render intelligible our phenomenon of universal mental competition—the leading quantitative law of the mind— would appear to have hopelessly broken down.

CHAPTER IX

HYPOTHESIS OF MENTAL ENERGY

NATURE AND HISTORY OF THE HYPOTHESIS

Sponsorship by Aristotle. We turn now to yet another attempt, and the final one, at rendering intelligible this first quantitative law of all mental process—that of mental span. The proposed view is at the same time yet another and the final interpretation to explain our g. The sole solution that is plausible for the one great problem is able at the same time to satisfy the other problem hardly less great. To fulfil this double office, recourse is had to the concept of mental " power," " force," or, in particular, " energy."

The originator of the last term ($\dot{\epsilon}\nu\dot{\epsilon}\rho\gamma\epsilon\iota a$) was, as is well-known, Aristotle. But its meaning for him was far from equivalent to that which is current nowadays. This " energy " he took to signify any *actual manifestation* of change, whereas the power ($\delta\dot{\upsilon}\nu a\mu\iota s$) was but the latent potentiality for this. An instance given by him is that during the waking state an act of knowing occurs actually or " in energy " (ἐνέργειᾳ), whereas during sleep there exists only the " power " to know.[1]

Changes introduced by physical science. This manner of thinking—common perhaps to all men, put into definite expression by Aristotle, and heartily adopted by the psychologists of the middle ages—became from the Renaissance onwards the corner stone of the science of physics. Here, however, were brought in three very important modifications.

The first was that this concept of energy, as above described, became restricted to material phenomena. It claimed reference to *physical movements*, but no longer concerned itself with such events as those of knowing.

The second modification, if viewed superficially, might seem to have been merely one of words. What Aristotle had called energy, the physicists now termed " kinetic energy " ; and what for him had been potentiality became for them " potential energy " ; that is to say, the word energy now denotes a *persistent entity* always identically the same—at one time latent, and at another manifest.

The third change—and that which is of the greatest importance for us at present—consisted in assuming this persistent energy to be *transferable from one thing to another*. The physical cosmos is taken to possess a permanent stock of it, which is therefore always constant in total amount. Any alteration can only be in the manner that it is distributed ; we reach here the law of conservation of energy.

Conservation asserted of the mind. This concept of physical energy had an unparalleled success. By its aid, the once despised science of physics climbed up to, and securely seated itself on, its present pinnacle. And success, as usual, bred imitation. The psychologists did not long remain content to see the concept of energy—originated, as it was, by themselves—carried off and exclusively exploited by the physicists. Soon the various modifications introduced by

[1] *Metaph.* bk. iv. ch. 12 ; also bk. viii.

the latter began to distil—more or less apart from each other —over to psychology also.

Among the earliest to claim constancy of total mental power was Malebranche ; [1] he declared this total power to remain always—in spite of some seeming exceptions— absolutely unalterable. And just this fact, he said, is one of the most dangerous pitfalls in the pursuit of truth ; for the capacity of the mind is so readily occupied by " pleasures, sorrows, and in general all intense sensations, likely imaginations, and great passions," that but small room is left for calm reason.[2]

As for the still stronger view—that of one and the same persisting entity—this arrived at clearest possible expression with Immanuel Fichte, according to whom the master-key to the comprehension of the mind with all its processes and changes consists in

" the great principle of the so-called conservation of energy, amid change in mode of manifestation."

This, he declares, explains also

" those numerous facts which are commonly interpreted as the dependence of the mind on the body. . . . These facts indicate nothing but the changing distribution of the mind's primary quantity of force among its conscious and unconscious functions."

A corollary drawn by him from this indestructibility of the energy is that the mind (or " soul ") possessing it must necessarily be immortal.[3]

" **Open** " **systems of energy.** Such indestructibility and therefore conservation, however, really appertain only to what has been called a " closed " system of energy, namely,

---

[1] *Recherche de la Vérité*, 1674, bk. vi. pt. i. ch. 2. Of his forerunners may be specially mentioned Gilles de Lessines, as early as the thireeenth century. The French word generally taken as equivalent to δύναμις was capacité, see the quoted work of Malebranche, pt. viii. ch. 5.

[2] *Ibidem*, bk. vi. pt. i. ch. 2.

[3] *Psychologie*, 1864, pt. i. p. 67 ; pt. ii. p. 7. Of his forerunners, especially notable was Schmid in his *Versuch einer Metaphysik der inneren Natur*, 1834.

one where no energy passes in and none passes out. The sole perfect physical example of this is the cosmos taken as a whole.

Engines as they are ordinarily constructed have the other sort of system, that which is called " open." Far from permitting neither entrance nor exit of energy, their essential business is to facilitate both ; they take in fuel, electricity, and so forth ; and they render back a quantum of work. There is no persistence of the same entity, but a continuous succession of different entities. Nevertheless, as regards constancy of amount, their energy may—for a time—rival even that of the closed systems. In general, however, this constancy remains of a more precarious nature ; it is at the mercy of any fluctuations in the supply from without, as also of any imperfection in the mechanism itself.

Now, this fundamentally different " open " system of energy it is that we find to have been attributed to the mind by Beneke. His doctrine was developed with the utmost precision of language, completeness of elaboration, and range of application. The mind was no longer regarded as a machine perpetually conserving its energy, but as one continually consuming it and receiving a further supply. The consumption was said to take place chiefly during the hours of wakefulness, whereas most of the replenishment was believed to occur during sleep. The constancy of power was regarded as approximate only, just as with ordinary machines. Nevertheless here, too, the concept of energy was used as an argument in favour of the mind being immortal.[1]

Physiological interpretation. The next great step in the theory of mental energy consisted in investing it with a physiological substrate. Far from taking any such step himself, Beneke had declared that psychic and physical events are absolutely incommensurable. He had written :

" The history of psychology has shown that it has been found impossible for the smallest part of the de-

[1] *Lehrbuch der Psychologie*, 1845, ch. i. sect. ii.

velopment of the mind to be explained or constructed out of that of matter." [1]

With his immediate successors, however, the anti-physiological attitude was no longer present. Although his ideas reappear with little or no change otherwise in the works of Fechner,[2] Bain,[3] J. S. Mill,[4] and Herbert Spencer (whom they seem to have reached between the first and the second editions of his *Principles of Psychology* [5]), yet now everywhere the energy invoked to explain the mental phenomena is not itself mental but neural.

LINES OF ADVOCACY AT THE PRESENT DAY

Psychical version of energy. All the preceding earlier views of the energy underlying mental process have since thriven. Some psychologists have enthusiastically followed Beneke and Fichte in treating the energy as being purely mental (though they have not been so explicit as to whether a closed or an open system is intended).

Thus Th. Lipps—who stands unsurpassed among authors ancient or modern for an exhaustively systematic exposition of the mind as a " force "—nevertheless declares (with Fries and Beneke) that the investigation of human nature must necessarily be undertaken from the two sides, mental and material, quite independently. Between these two, he says, there is a wall of such a kind that from no point of view can the proceedings of both be seen simultaneously.[6]

Supporting him have been almost all sections of the

[1] *Ibidem*, p. 19 ff. Before him, Fries had written : " Let no one fancy that anything bodily either is explained by, or can explain, anything mental." *Handbuch der psychischen Anthropologie.*

[2] *Elemente der Psychophysik*, 1859, i. pp. 39-42.

[3] *The Senses and the Intellect*, 1868, 3rd ed. pp. 51, 353.

[4] His notes to *Analysis of the Phenomena of the Human Mind* by James Mill, 1869, i. p. 118.

[5] The second edition was published in 1870.

[6] *Grundtatsachen des Seelenlebens*, 1883, p. 7.

school of Brentano.   Thus, Meinong,[1] Jodl,[2] and Witasek [3] unanimously treat the energy as psychical.   Höfler [4] not only takes the same side, but pushes it to extremes that rival those of Imm. Fichte.

Another very important school inclining in the same direction is that of the Neo-Scholastics.   Maher, for example, uses the notion of mental energy a great deal.[5] Geyser develops it with remarkable thoroughness and acuteness.[6] Like Fichte, he sees in it a conclusive proof of immortality :

" The mind does not in principle lose its active form through separation from matter, and must consequently be capable by nature of separate existence."

Much in common, but with a shift from theological to biological and metaphysical interest, is to be found in the view developed by Bergson, Wildon Carr, and others of this school.[7]   Of conspicuous value have also been the contributions of the following authors :   Höffding,[8] who keenly attacks the standpoint of Fichte ; della Valle,[9] who gives a luminous general account of the topic, especially from the educational aspect ; and Wirth,[10] to whom we owe a precious advance by the more exact way of experiment.

To all these must be added a large number of widely reputed psychiatrists.   One group of these, among whom may be specially named Breuer, Freud,[11] and Jung,[12] have obtained from the concept of mental energy or force much assistance for their doctrines of sexual perversion.   Another

[1] "Beiträge zur Theorie d. psychischen Analyse," *Zeit. f. Psychol.* vi. p. 379.

[2] *Lehrbuch d. Psychologie*, 1908, i. pp. 145-6.

[3] *Grundlinien d. Psychologie*, 1908, p. 85.

[4] *Psychische Arbeit, Zeit. f. Psych.* viii. 1895, pp. 223, 565, 594.

[5] *Psychology*, 1911.   [6] *Lehrbuch d. allg. Psychologie*, 1908.

[7] *Mind Energy*, by Bergson, trans. by Wildon Carr, 1920.

[8] *Psychologie in Umrissen*, 1893, pp. 87, 130, 148, 320, 457.

[9] *Le Leggi del Lavoro Mentale*, 1910, ch. vii.

[10] *Die Experim. Analyse der Bewusstseinsphenomene*, 1908.

[11] *Traumdeutung*, 1911 ; *Das Ich und das Es*, 1920 ; *Jenseits des Lustprinzips*, 1920.

[12] *Collected Papers on Analytical Psychology*, 1917.

group has found in the concept a foundation for the theory of other mental abnormalities. Prominent names are those of Janet,[1] Déjérine and Gaukler,[2] Deschamps,[3] Régis,[4] Hesnard,[5] and Lévy.[6]

For example, Régis and Hesnard, in considering the derangement known as " mental confusion," ascribe the simultaneous effacement of widely different mental activities to the fact of these being " manifestations of the same energy." Lévy accounts on the same lines for the curious exaltation of intellectual power that may occur in a state of hypnosis, somnambulism, or even ordinary sleep. Imagination is then so vivid that it becomes indistinguishable from actual experience ; memory may be able to function so vigorously that we recall events long forgotten in normal waking life. Such facts are easily explained, he says, by noticing what a man does when going to sleep. He seeks darkness and silence, in order to escape visual and auditory impressions ; he lies down so as to relax every muscle ; he covers himself moderately, that he may avoid impressions either of warmth or of cold ; finally, he tries to banish all ideas which begin to occupy his mind ; in short, he does everything possible to reduce the extent of his consciousness. But thereby he saves and accumulates mental energy. If this, after all, does find some vent or other in consciousness, small wonder, he says, that such consciousness should be abnormally intense.

Physiological version. But more numerous still appear to have been those authors who—following Fechner—have explicitly followed physiological lines. W. McDougall, for example, writes as follows :

" The constituent neurones of the nervous system with all their branches are regarded as a vast system of channels in all parts of which potential chemical energy

[1] *Les Médications Psychologiques*, 1919.   [2] *Les Psycho-névroses*, 1911.
[3] *Les Maladies de l'Energie*, 1909.
[4] *Traité International de Psychologie Pathologique*, 1911, p. 827.
[5] *Ibidem.*   [6] *L'Education Rationelle de la Volonté*, p. 62.

is constantly being transformed, in virtue of the normal vital activity of the neurones, into a particular form of active energy. This energy, which in the present state of our ignorance can be most profitably regarded as a fluid, tends always to flow, like heat, electricity or water, from places of higher to places of lower potential, following the paths of least resistance, and for convenience of description it may be called ' neurin.' " This fluid, he says, " constitutes a reservoir of energy upon which the various forms (of the nervous system) draw in turn as they become active." [1]

Further may be mentioned Maudsley,[2] Ribot,[3] Lasswitz,[4] Ladd,[5] Spiller,[6] James,[7] Claparède,[8] Ioteyko,[9] Woodworth,[10] Lehmann,[11] Woodrow,[12] Pyle,[13] Goddard,[14] and Thurstone.[15]

The view has met with the approval of several among the leading physiologists themselves. Mott expressed his belief that

" the total nervous energy is at the disposal of the whole nervous system." [16]

[1] " Physiological Factors of the Attention-process," *Mind*, ii. N.S. 1902 ; iii. 1903. " Inhibitory Processes within the Nervous System," *Brain*, 1903, p. 170. *Physiological Psychology*, 1905, p. 161. " The Sources and Direction of Psychophysical Energy," *Amer. J. Insanity*, 1913, p. 861. *Outlines of Psychology*, 1923.

[2] *Physiology of the Mind*, 1876, p. 305.

[3] *Psychologie de l'Attention*, 1898, p. 33.

[4] " V. d. psychophysischen Energie u. ihren Faktoren," *Archiv f. System. Philosophie*, i. 1893, pp. 46-64.

[5] *Psychology Descriptive and Explanatory*, 1894, pp. 61, 85.

[6] *Mind*, x. N.S. 1901, pp. 506, 602.   [7] *The Energies of Man*, 1906.

[8] *Psychologie de l'Enfant*, 1909, ch. v. para. 6.

[9] " La Conception Idéoenergétique de la Psychoméchanique," *Journ. de Neurol.*, 1908.

[10] Ladd and Woodworth, *Elements of Physiological Psychology*, 1911, p. 648.

[11] *Grundzüge der Psychophysiologie*, 1912, bk. 8, ch. 19.

[12] *Psych. Rev.* 1915, xxii.   [13] *Psychology of Learning*, 1921, p. 171.

[14] *Human Efficiency and Levels of Intelligence*.

[15] *The Nature of Intelligence*, 1924, p. 27.

[16] " Importance of Stimulus in Repair and Decay of the Nervous System," *Journ. Mental Science*, Oct. 1902, pp. 668-9.

And on this remark Sherrington put his endorsement that

> " One of the most helpful of the assumptions we can use in dealing with the problems of the nervous system is that which regards the nervous system as more or less a reservoir of energy to be discharged." [1]

Psycho-physiological equivalence. In comparatively recent times a further modification of view has been suggested. Intermediate between the advocates of the mental and those of the physiological energy there stands a third school, which holds that these two energies are interchangeable, or at least in some way mutually equivalent.

At once the earliest and the boldest exposition of this doctrine seems to have come from the Russian philosopher, v. Grot. On death, according to him, the energy of the mind will not be completely resolved into the physio-chemical energy of putrefaction. Just as a current of electricity can be transported from one point to another in space, so too the mind—conceived as a current of ethereal energy diffused in the cerebrospinal system—will pass through the ether, either into another body, or else into other spaces.[2]

These wings of speculation were soon clipped down to the modest dimensions of empirical science by Ostwald, who, in his well known lectures, arrives at the conclusion that

> " the facts, on the whole, make another conjecture probable ; namely, that mental processes derive from the creation and transformation of a special kind of energy, which we will provisionally call ' mental energy.' " [3]

Among the later interesting developments of this view may be mentioned that of Lieder.[4]

Most recent of all is an original theory elaborated by Heymans.[5] This is based upon the philosophical doctrine

---

[1] End of Mott's Paper.

[2] " Die Begriffe d. Seele u. d. psych. Energie," *Arch. f. system. Philos.* iv. 1898, pp. 281 ff.

[3] *Vorles. u. Naturphilos* 1902.   [4] *Die psychische Energie,* 1910.

[5] *Ueber die Anwendbarkeit des Energiebegriffes in der Psychologie,* 1921.

of psychical monism, according to which all that appears to be going on in the material world is in truth but the outward aspect of what inwardly is mental (conscious or unconscious). Thence he argues that the laws of physical energy—both that of conservation and that of entropy—must needs have a counterpart in the domain of mind. Indeed, he takes these laws of mental energy to be already so well established that—being, as they are, the inner side of reality—they may some day render superfluous any further reference to the energy of physics, which does but concern the outer show.

OBJECTIONS TO THE HYPOTHESIS

General hostile reception. In remarkable contrast to this array of names—including many of the greatest authorities both past and present—in favour of the energy as a hypothesis to explain the mental phenomena, stand the great majority of psychologists who, for their part, are not only adverse but very decidedly so.

Most often, the whole concept is passed over in chilling silence. For instance, both the voluminous philosophical dictionaries, the American (Baldwin) and the German (Eisler), although professedly depicting all theories and concepts that—right or wrong—have any serious psychological interest, leave this energy as good as unmentioned. Some writers vouchsafe to it only a remark of curt dismissal; Dürr, for example, contents himself with saying that it

" may well be rejected without discussion." [1]

During the last year or two, however, an inclination has grown up to treat it with somewhat greater respect ; at least a discussion of it is taken to be worth while. It was chosen as the topic of a symposium at the International Congress for Psychology in 1923, and attracted such eminent speakers as Adrian, Head, and Myers. To the results thus gleaned, moreover, there has been added a welcome after-

[1] *Die Lehre von der Aufmerksamkeit*, 1907, p. 169.

math, as exemplified by the papers of Gillespie,[1] Morris,[2] and Wrinch.[3]

Alleged superfluity of all hypothesis.   Passing over various criticisms of no serious importance,[4] one prominent objection that has been raised against bringing on the stage any " energy " is that this can at best be only hypothetical ; whereas, these authors say, psychology ought to renounce all hypothesis. It should do this, they urge, in order to supply a pure record of experience, and so secure a flawless

[1] *Brit. Journ. Psych.* 1925, xv. p. 266.

[2] *Proc. Aristotelian Soc., Suppl.* vol. v. 1925.   [3] *Ibidem.*

[4] One such is the charge against the energy of being an ancient relic of some long past " metaphysical " stage of psychology, now happily replaced by the more scientific " positive " stage.   This, as a matter of history, seems to be the truth inverted.   The concept of mental energy happens to be of much later origin than most of the views attributed to the stage of positivism, these being really of very ancient date.

Again, when Maxwell Clark says that any such mental energy would possess the miraculous power of remaining undiminished in spite of doing work, this, on making the distinction between open and closed systems, becomes obviously inapplicable to either of them.

Similarly irrelevant is the objection frequently made—and excellently refuted by Busse (*Geist und Körper*, 1903)—that the concept of mental energy would involve untenable views as to the relation between mind and body.   For such energy is, in truth, equally compatible with any view whatever as to this relation.

Nor is the energy to be disposed of by the plea of Wundt, Varisco, and others, that in the mind—unlike matter—the whole is greater than the sum of its parts.   This dictum of " sums " and " parts " does indeed rest upon a very important fact, but brings the said fact to a most misleading form of expression.   Moreover, it is, in truth, just as applicable to matter as to mind.

And as little notice, finally, need be taken of the protest that all such terms as " energy," " force," or " work," are relevant only to matter, not to mind.   The latter, it is said, involves solely conscious processes, in which no such exercise of causation can possibly be discovered.

Against this, the counter-argument has been brought that, far from such terms being meaningful in physics and meaningless in psychology, more nearly the opposite holds good.   For as regards physics, when a weight is raised by a machine, no " work " (nor even " mass ") can really ever be seen, heard, felt, or in any other manner directly cognized ; all that we actually perceive is the movement.   The appropriateness of the term " work " derives solely from the associated idea of some person or animal pulling with conscious effort.

In any case, however, the whole objection misses the mark.   For the kind of energy here at issue by no means consists in any conscious effort. It is no conscious phenomenon at all, but something that is taken to *underlie* not only effort, but all other conscious phenomena.

foundation for the philosophy of knowledge—and even for that of existence. But why should psychology thus make itself a mere tool for philosophy ? It is a science in its own right, and can no more fulfil this mission without hypotheses than a man can run properly with his legs tied in a sack. What would physics do without its electrons, its ether, or its heat, none of which are, or perhaps ever can be, directly perceived ?

Indeed, there is no necessity for believing that such entities really exist at all. They with their " concealed masses " and their movements are by many authorities taken to be nothing more than devices for portraying the course of events in a compact and vivid manner ; devices, even, that sometimes admittedly break down (as appears to occur, for instance, in the case of " dissipation " of energy). The root-idea of physical energy is neither mass nor movement, but (as we have seen) transfer ; one and the same causative entity is taken to have the property of assuming different forms, which may be those of movement, heat, magnetism, electricity, or chemical activity.

Even this transfer itself is speculative. If the physicists were to confine themselves to what they really knew, there would remain nothing to state beyond quantitative *equivalencies* ; for example, the raising of a cubic foot of water by one degree of temperature is equivalent to the lifting of it by a height of 430 metres. The physical energy would, as Nunn has said, reduce itself to

> " merely a means of expression, useful from the technical point of view, of our conviction that the events of the world run in lines of sequence such that the present phase in the development of any line represents, and so may be regarded as equivalent to, the vanished phases which preceded it." [1]

But if, then, physics is to be allowed this useful shorthand

[1] See his short but admirable account of the evolution of the concept of energy in physics, *Proc. Arist. Soc.* 1912, pp. 25-64. For a more technical account, see *Die Energetik* by Helm, 1898.

way of expressing measured equivalencies, surely the same privilege should be accorded to psychology also.

Alleged impossibility of mental equivalents. Here, however, we do encounter an objection of indubitable gravity. Beyond question, the bulk of the advocates of a mental energy have never measured any of the required mental equivalents ; they have not possessed the experimental and statistical resources needful for so doing. They have never even realized the necessity. And doubts have been widely and loudly proclaimed as to whether such measurements can ever possibly be effected. Thus Külpe, himself a master-experimentalist, nevertheless wrote :

> " All physical processes can be reduced to a unit of work or energy, which can be exactly defined, and through which the physical phenomena can be expressed in terms of a uniform and common measure. To set up any such unit of energy or work for the totality of psychic events must—in view of the impossibility of reducing its manifoldness to one and the same performance—be regarded as a hopeless undertaking." [1]

Still, history is full of warning against taking such negative predictions too much to heart. Once Kant declared that the future of chemistry as a science was hopeless, on account of its insusceptibility to mathematical treatment ! So, too, Comte asserted that among the unknowables must for ever remain the constitution of the stars, because they can never be visited. And yet only a short time afterwards, men learnt their constitution with great exactitude. Again, the great physiologist, Joh. Müller, announced that never possibly could there be any measurement of the velocity of nerve impulse ; yet only six years later on, Helmholtz actually measured it.

And as for the measuring of equivalents in the case of the mental energy, this would seem to have already begun. As an instance may be cited the research of Lehmann into the

---

[1] *Einleitung in die Philosophie*, 1903, sect. 19, para. 8 ; sect. 22, para. 6,

interaction between arithmetical and motor activity. The diagram following shows how the strength of a pull (using the familiar ergograph) was diminished by a simultaneous task of reckoning.

Here, the height of each vertical line represents the strength of a single pull. Arrow No. 1 shows when the first reckoning began, and No. 2 when it finished. Nos. 3 and 4 do the same for the second reckoning.

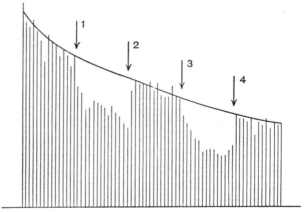

The result of many such measurements under varying conditions led him to the following law :

$$\frac{S - V}{S} = \text{constant},$$

where V denotes the amount of muscular work performed when distracted by the reckoning, and S is the amount that was to be expected if the distraction had not occurred. Now, this law was found by Lehmann to be exactly that which governs the relative amounts of water flowing out of different pipes from the same reservoir ; again, the same law was found to regulate the intensities of different electric currents all derived from a common electric source.

An example is given below of each of these two cases, that of the water-flow and that of the mental activity. In the case of the water, two experiments produced the following values respectively :

		S	V	$S - V$	$(S - V)/S$
Experiment I.	- -	91	68	23	·25
Experiment II.	- -	76	58	18	·24

As will be seen, the two values in the last column are nearly the same. In the case of the mental activity, the two experiments resulted as follows :

		S	V	$S - V$	$(S - V)/S$
Experiment I.	- -	53·9	42·4	11·7	·22
Experiment II.	- -	34·5	27·5	7·0	·20

Evidently, the mental case seems to match the physical case, not only in principle but even in precision. From such results he concludes that the diminution of muscular work caused by the simultaneous mental work

> " indicated exactly that fraction of the free energy of the brain which was consumed by the said mental work." [1]

Now, this physiological inference certainly admits of being contested. But no such doubt would seem to impair the validity of the mental results in themselves.

As another notable example, we may quote a research by the eminent psycho-physicist Wirth. This consisted in dividing the visual field into a large number of areas. The subject of the experiment kept his eyes turned towards the centre of the whole field, but shifted his " attention " from one part to another ; also, that attention was sometimes concentrated on a comparatively small area, and sometimes distributed over a larger one. Under all these varying conditions, Wirth measured the subject's power of perceiving minimal changes of brightness in the different areas. The

---

[1] *Körperliche Äusserungen psychischer Zustände*, ii. 1901, p. 199. *Ibidem*, iii. 1905, p. 362.

striking general law was deduced that, whatever the direction or concentration of the attention, the sum of the perceptual power remained always exactly the same. Wirth's conclusion—judiciously avoiding contentious physiology—is to the effect that :

> " All the results indicate one constant limited sum total of mental energy."

Moreover, for the purposes of the present argument, all this appeal to such outstanding experimental achievement is rather a luxury than a necessity. In principle, a measurement of equivalence was already attained in the work of Hamilton, Jevons, Bonnet, and indeed Nemesius. For to state that only five marbles or beans can be seen clearly at the same time is, at bottom, only another way of saying that the different marbles, etc., are mutually equivalent. Still more obvious does the fact of equivalence become on discovering that the number of items remains approximately the same even when some of these are visual and some auditory.

Recent dissent by physiologists. A few words may be added on the rather adverse opinion that has recently been expressed by some of our leading physiologists, as typified in the already quoted paper of Adrian.

On the psychological side, he appears to have misunderstood what was really meant by " energy," and to have taken this as being that which a person has when said to be " energetic." In truth, this popular phase has little to do with what is under discussion here (see pp. 117-119 of this chapter).

As for the physiological side—which is naturally his main theme—the discussion of this will be reserved for ch. xxiii.

USEFULNESS FOR PSYCHOLOGY

Law of constant output. What, then, is the upshot of our discussion in the preceding and the present chapter up to this point ? Overwhelming evidence would seem to have been found for the phenomenon described here as the

universal mental competition.   This means that in ordinary
waking life the commencement of any mental activity (using
this term in its broadest sense) causes other activity to
cease, whilst conversely the cessation of any activity causes
other activity to commence.   Such mutual influence proceeds in a regular manner so that—after making due allowance for all specific interaction, facilitating or inhibiting—
there are quantitative equivalencies between the activities
that come and those that go.

Accordingly, we here in the sphere of consciousness—with
as much right as in that of physics—are brought to the
conclusion of Nunn that events

> " run on lines of sequence such that the present phase
> of development may be regarded as equivalent to the
> vanished phases which preceded it."

Otherwise expressed, the constancy of total output shows that
all the mental activity, just like the physical, consists in
ever varying manifestations of one and the same underlying
thing, to which may be given the name of energy.

No such energy, however, can possibly work in a vacuum,
but only in some or other " engine."   We conclude, then,
that in the case of the five clearly seen marbles, each of
these percepts must be credited with an engine of its own ;
similarly, as regards the reckoning or the ergographic
work, etc.

Now comes the question as to how this general energy
and these specific engines may best be conceived physio-
logically.   With respect to the engines a suggestion is supplied at once ; for the different kinds of mental output
would naturally be subserved (mainly, at any rate) by
different neural systems (see pp. 400-403).   These latter,
then, are suggested as being the engines.   With respect to
the energy, the available information is less definite.   But
for psychological purposes, this lack seems to be of minor
importance.   We may venture to employ the following
diagram.   If the representation be not allowed to pass as a

working hypothesis in physiology, it will nevertheless retain its usefulness as an illustrative diagram in psychology.

The whole area represents the cerebral cortex, whilst the shaded patch is some special group of neurons (for convenience of the figure, taken as collected in one neighbourhood). The arrow heads indicate the lines of force coming from the whole cortex.

Law of fatigue. But this constancy of mental output has not been the sole reason that has moved so many eminent psychologists to adopt the concept of mental energy. A further and hardly less powerful reason has been found in the phenomena that fall under the heading of fatigue.

Here, naturally enough, the widest and fullest recognition has come from the psychiatrists. Foremost has been Janet,[1] who attributes a large share of neurotic disorder to insufficient reserves of mental energy.

Substantially in accord is the classical work of James, entitled *The Energies of Man* (1906). A typical instance of the facts quoted here is the achievement of Colonel Baird-Smith, who maintained unimpaired vigour throughout the siege of Delhi, in spite of suffering from scurvy, a gangrened foot, a sprained arm, and constant diarrhoea. From such facts James draws the conclusion that :

> " Our organism has stored reserves of energy that are ordinarily not called upon, but that may be called upon : deeper and deeper strata of combustible or explosible material, discontinuously arranged, but ready for use by anyone who probes so deep."

[1] *Les Médications Psychologiques*, 1919.

The matter was taken up on physiological lines by W. McDougall in one of the most brilliant papers produced even by him. He enunciates his hypothesis as follows :

> " The energy liberated by chemical change, by katabolic process, in one part of the nervous system may be conducted through the nervous channels and may operate in other parts of the nervous system. This may be called *the hypothesis of the vicarious usage of nervous energy.*" [1]

In support he cites Descartes, Hale White, Horsley, and Sharkey. A few months later, an elaborately and carefully reasoned defence of the theory of energy in connection with the phenomena of fatigue was published by Claparède.[2]

Besides the preceding laws of constant output and of fatigue, there are three others (retentivity, conative control, and primordial potencies).[3] All five will be considered at length in Part II. In every case, the hypothesis of mental energy and engines would seem to fit the facts as a glove does the hand. Should, however, any one pedantically still reject the energy on the ground of its being hypothetical, he can salve his conscience by only saying that the mental phenomena behave " as if " such an energy existed.

To sum up the indications of the last two chapters, the facts of general psychology—quite apart from those of individual differences—strongly support the suggestion of mental energy and engines. Moreover, such an energy would seem to be just what is wanted to explain g, whilst the engines might go far towards explaining the s's. Here, accordingly, we have a hypothesis that deserves at any rate careful confrontation with all the actual facts which we are about to communicate and consider.

[1] " Inhibitory Processes within the Nervous System," *Brain*, 1903.
[2] *Psychologie de l'Enfant*, 1909, ch. v.
[3] See chs. xvi, xviii, xx, xxi, xxii.

PART II

THE FUNDAMENTAL FACTS

CHAPTER X

PROOF THAT *G* AND *S* EXIST

EARLIER RESULTS BY IMPERFECT METHODS

Scope of present chapter. In the preceding Part I, we began by setting forth the general doctrines that have been, and still are, most widely held concerning individual differences of ability. All these doctrines showed themselves open to grave criticism, partly because of such intrinsic faults as equivocality, and partly because of contradicting undeniable facts.

What we then brought forward was primarily not so much

a doctrine of ability as rather a method by which any of the doctrines can now at last be submitted to exact trial. In particular, this method laid down the criterion needed in order to decide whether or not every ability in any given set can be divided into two factors, *g* and *s* (*g* remaining throughout the same, whilst every *s* varies independently both of *g* and of the other *s*'s). Further, the suggestion was made, but no rigorous demonstration as yet attempted, that this criterion is in point of fact well satisfied by actual experiment.

Next, we considered the chief different ways in which the *g* and the *s* admit of interpretation. We found that the whole of psychology would be illuminated if they could be taken, *g* as the amount of a general mental energy, and the *s*'s as the efficiency of specific mental engines.

But all this, clearly, leaves still untouched the chief requirement of all, namely, to prove definitely whether these two factors, *g* and *s*, do or do not actually exist. To achieve this effect experimental work must be brought forward of unimpeachable quality and overwhelming quantity. To this task, then, we will now address ourselves.

Fallacious reliance on general impressions. To begin with, a note of warning must be sounded against all attempts to replace the rigorously demonstrated criterion by anything else. Many writers have tried to invent a new one for themselves ; others have declared that so many are in the field as to produce a difficulty in choosing between them. Against this, we must formally declare that no other rigorous criterion than that demonstrated here (including mere equivalent conversions of it) has ever been proved or *ever can be*.[1] Hence, any attempted different criterion can only be valid to the extent that it has the support of the correct one.

---

[1] If two rigorous criteria existed that were in the least degree independent of each other, then they might lead simultaneously to contradictory conclusions, which would be absurd. Of course, two criteria may lie on such different lines as to seem independent to a superficial view ; but they must always turn out to be completely dependent on each other when examined more profoundly.

There is one pseudo-criterion that has been employed particularly often, but in point of fact is especially treacherous. This consists in simply inspecting the table of correlations concerned and straightway forming a *general impression* as to whether their values fall into a "hierarchical" order (see p. 74).

In the earlier investigations this impressionistic method often led to confident denials of agreement between the doctrine of two factors and the actually observed facts, whereas the subsequent use of the correct method indicated, on the contrary, the agreement to be little short of perfection. Undeterred by this lesson, however, later writers have persisted in relying upon such general impressions—with, of course, similarly illusive results.

Previous evidence from substitute criterion. On the whole, there appears to be only one substitute for the genuine criterion that needs being taken into serious account; it is the already mentioned one which involves the "intercolumnar correlation" (see p. 79 and the appendix, pp. viii-x). When this correlation approaches towards perfection or unity, then, in general, every measurement of ability admits of the division into g and s without an overlap. When it falls much short of unity, then, in general, such a division becomes impossible.

Already at the first announcement of this substitute criterion, its application was made to all the tables of correlations that had been published previously. This included work from various periods, up to thirty years back. It came impartially from strong supporters of each doctrine then prevalent on the matter, as well as from other investigators who had not yet heard of the point at issue. Among these tables was an especially notable one by Bonser, which emanated from the laboratory and supervision of Thorndike ; there was also one published by the latter under his own name. Altogether, there was presented in this way the work of 14 experimenters on 1463 men and women, boys and girls, sane and insane.

The general result was to show that out of the several hundreds of different pairs of abilities thus arrayed, only three failed to conform with the substituted criterion. Apart from this very small exception (which will be considered later on) the average value of the inter-columnar correlations proved to be no less than ·96, or almost perfect.

Two years later, further additions could be made, so that now the total result was given in the following list : [1]

Year.	Investigator.	Subjects.	Mean Inter-columnar correlation.
1889	Oehrn - - - -	10 students - -	> + ·93
1902	Thorndike - - -	160 boys and girls -	+ 1·04
1904	Spearman - - -	37 boys and girls -	+ 1·16
1904	Spearman - - -	24 boys and girls -	+ 1·01
1906	Krueger and Spearman -	11 students - -	> + ·96
1908	Peterson - - -	96 students - -	> + ·94
1909	Foerster and Gregor -	11 insane patients	+ 1·12
1909	Burt - - - -	30 boys - -	+ 1·06
1909	Burt - - - -	13 boys - -	+ 1·06
1910	Brown - - - -	56 boys - -	+ ·86
1910	Brown - - - -	39 girls - -	+ 1·02
1910	Brown - - - -	40 boys - -	+ ·97
1910	Brown - - - -	23 students - -	+ ·93
1910	Brown - - - -	56 women - ··	+ ·89
1910	Bonser - - -	385 boys - -	> + ·97
1910	Bonser - - -	372 girls - -	> + ·96
1912	Simpson - - -	37 adults - -	+ ·96
1913	Wyatt - - - -	75 children - -	+ ·97
1914	Abelson - - -	78 children - -	+ 1·02
1914	Webb - - - -	200 students - -	+ 1·02
		Average - -	+ ·99

Since that date there appears to have been published only four more applications of this inter-columnar criterion. The first was by McCall, and the other three by Thorndike. For these cases, the said criterion of inter-columnar correlation

[1] *Eugenics Review*, Oct. 1914, p. 8. For the reason that some values exceed 1·00, see appendix, p. i.

was reported to have definitely failed.   But in none of them, unfortunately, had the criterion been applied in the proper manner.   In one case at least, however—that of McCall—it really would not have been satisfied even by the proper procedure.   The reason for these particular experiments being discrepant from the whole great array just brought forward will be explained subsequently (p. 151).

The general trend, at any rate, of all this evidence lies beyond reasonable doubt : it is that in the great majority of cases the criterion of inter-columnar correlation shows itself to be excellently satisfied.   On the other hand, we must remember that this criterion itself leaves much to be desired (ch. vi. p. 79) ; its evidential virtue is only borrowed, not intrinsic ; it is valid to the extent only that it can show itself to agree with the genuine criterion, namely, the tetrad equation (p. 73).   It has been, in short, a mere provisional make-shift.   And now that the genuine criterion has become available, to this alone we must look for evidence that may be regarded as really conclusive.

FAILURE OF GENUINE CRITERION WITH NON-MENTAL TRAITS

Employment of the " probable error."   Let us turn accordingly to this genuine criterion itself.   It consists, as we have seen (p. 73), in the " tetrad difference," which must be zero throughout a table of correlations, if the g and s are to exist without overlap in the s's.   But this condition holds only of the " true " correlations (see p. 79) ; and these in actual practice are always replaced by the correlations which derive from mere samples, and which therefore suffer from the sampling errors.   In practice, then, the tetrad differences should *not* tend towards zero, but instead should tend to have just such values as would result from the sampling errors alone (see the appendix, pp. x-xii).

The most perfect comparison between the two, the observed tetrad differences and those to be expected from sampling errors alone, is obtained by making a complete frequency distribution of each of these two sets of values. A more summary comparison is got by seeing whether or not about half of the observed tetrad differences are greater and half less than their "probable error." Much the same thing is to see whether the median observed tetrad difference and the probable error are about equal. Most summary of all is to see whether or not the largest observed tetrad difference exceeds about five times the magnitude of their probable error.

A case of bodily dimensions. Before proceeding to our main work—the application of this criterion to the correlations observed between mental abilities—let us first make trial of it upon some individual traits *other than* mental abilities. By this we shall obtain a useful basis for comparison, which will have especial importance in view of the statement sometimes made, that the criteria of *g* and *s* are satisfied for any sort or kind of correlations merely by virtue of the laws of "chance." (ch. vii., pp. 94-97.)

As first example may be presented a case closely parallel to that of correlations between mental abilities, except that now these latter are replaced by bodily dimensions. Seven such were measured by McDonnell for 3,000 male adults, and gave the following table of correlations, every one of them positive.[1]

	1	2	3	4	5	6	7
1. Head length -	—	·402	·394	·301	·305	·339	·340
2. Head breadth -	·402	—	·618	·150	·135	·206	·183
3. Face breadth -	·394	·618	—	·321	·289	·353	·345
4. Left mid-finger -	·301	·150	·321	—	·846	·759	·661
5. Left cubit -	·305	·135	·289	·846	—	·797	·800
6. Left foot -	·339	·206	·363	·759	·797	—	·736
7. Height -	·340	·183	·345	·661	·800	·736	—

From such a table there can be derived tetrad differences to the number of 105. These have to be arranged in a frequency distribution, which shows the relative frequency with which different magnitudes occur. For comparison

[1] *Biometrika*, 1901, i.

with this, we have to calculate the frequency distribution that would be produced merely by the errors of sampling. The two distributions are given below.

DISTRIBUTION OF TETRAD DIFFERENCES FOR THE CORRELATIONS OF McDONNELL.

The theoretical distribution (required for the divisibility into g and s) is given in the curve ; half fall between a and b ; none beyond c or d. The distribution actually observed is given in the rectangular columns. In either case, horizontal position indicates the magnitude of the tetrad difference, whilst height indicates its relative frequency.

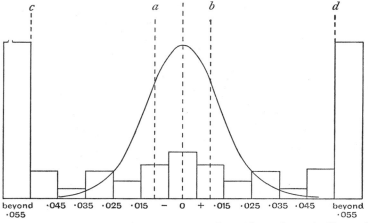

| beyond | ·045 | ·035 | ·025 | ·015 | − | 0 | + | ·015 | ·025 | ·035 | ·045 | beyond |
| ·055 | | | | | | | | | | | | ·055 |

Clearly, more discrepant distributions than those indicated by the curve and by the columns respectively could hardly be conceived.

A case of traits of maturity. Even more instructive in some ways is a table of correlations recently published between various physical traits which were taken to indicate degree of maturity. For the author, A. Gates, expressly says that this table exhibits the close resemblance between the two kinds of correlations, those of mental abilities and those of merely physical traits :

" Apparently, in appraising physical traits we have a very close, perhaps a perfect, counterpart of the situation in measuring mental abilities. In both fields different single measures correlate positively, but far from perfectly with each other ; in neither field does it seem likely that any one trait will satisfactorily represent general abilities." [1]

These correlations, derived from 115 subjects, were again all positive, as he says, and had the following values :

	1	2	3	4	5	6	7	8
1. Area of ossification -	—	·88	·60	·62	·43	·31	·25	·26
2. Ratio of ossification -	·88	—	·52	·58	·41	·21	·24	·29
3. Height - - -	·60	·52	—	·69	·44	·51	·45	·11
4. Weight - - -	·62	·58	·69	—	·65	·39	·40	·83
5. Chest girth - -	·43	·41	·44	·65	—	·59	·36	·69
6. Lung capacity -	·31	·21	·51	·39	·59	—	·46	·26
7. Strength of grip -	·25	·24	·45	·40	·36	·46	—	·14
8. Nutrition - -	·26	·29	·11	·83	·69	·14	—	—

Applying, now, the criterion of tetrad differences, the ensuing frequency distributions of observed and theoretical values respectively are given below.

DISTRIBUTION OF TETRAD DIFFERENCES FOR THE
CORRELATIONS OF GATES.

The two distributions are shown in the same way as in the preceding case :

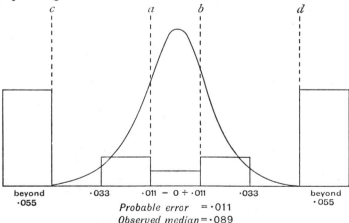

| beyond ·055 | ·033 | ·011 − 0 + ·011 | ·033 | beyond ·055 |

Probable error = ·011
Observed median = ·089

[1] *Journ. Educ. Research*, 1924, p. 341.

Between the two distributions, those shown by the curve and by the columns respectively, there is again no resemblance whatever.

A case of anthropological measurements. The only other set of correlations so far published that admit of the comparison with those found between abilities appears to be the following, obtained by Doll with 477 boys and girls, once more positive throughout.

		1	2	3	4	5	6
1. Right hand grip -	-	—	·885	·525	·579	·455	·620
2. Left hand grip -	-	·885	—	·570	·595	·570	·620
3. Standing height -	-	·525	·570	—	·805	·630	·430
4. Sitting height -	-	·580	·595	·805	—	·680	·475
5. Weight - -	-	·455	·570	·630	·680	—	·390
6. Vital capacity -	-	·620	·620	·430	·475	·390	—

On turning to the tetrad differences, the result is the same as before. For brevity, we may this time content ourselves with comparing the median value of the observed tetrad differences with their probable error. To satisfy the theory, these two values should not greatly disagree. In point of fact, the said probable error is ·010, whereas the median observed tetrad differences comes to the far greater magnitude of ·103. These correlations of Doll, then, are as far as the others from satisfying the conditions of divisibility into g and s without overlap.

Concordance with the older method. In all these three cases the new and correct criterion shows that the divisibility into the two factors does *not* occur. What would be the result of trying these same cases by the older method that was formerly used instead, the inter-columnar correlation ? The conclusions reached by the two methods prove to be quite concordant. The older one—which a few pages back showed us the very high average inter-columnar correlations of +·96 and therefore indicated the divisibility—now in these present three cases shows instead the extremely low inter-columnar correlations of + ·01 + ·17, and − ·02 and therefore this time indicates the *non*-divisibility.

SUCCESS OF CRITERION WITH NEARLY ALL ABILITIES

The correlations already considered. After these three cases, which do not deal with mental abilities, let us turn to the cases that do so. And we may conveniently begin with those that have already been evaluated by the older method, as shown in the list on page 139.

First of all, we will take the investigation which has been most prominent in the literature on the topic, that of Simpson.[1] Here, 14 tests were applied to 37 persons, and resulted in the following correlations, all positive :

	1	2	3	4	5	6	7	8	9	10	11	12	13	14
1. Completion - -	—	·98	·94	·79	·62	·91	·71	·54	·78	·88	·55	·42	·33	·25
2. Hard opposites -	·98	—	·84	·80	·64	·81	·79	·70	·73	·74	·52	·43	·26	·25
3. Memory words -	·94	·84	—	·62	·55	·82	·49	·56	·73	·71	·53	·40	·28	·21
4. Easy opposites -	·79	·80	·62	—	·57	·52	·68	·53	·42	·56	·45	·29	·38	·48
5. " A " test - -	·62	·64	·55	·57	—	·55	·54	·73	·39	·51	·39	·59	·25	·22
6. Memory pass -	·91	·81	·82	·52	·55	—	·53	·57	·59	·66	·54	·31	·28	·19
7. Adding - - -	·71	·79	·49	·68	·54	·53	—	·45	·39	·47	·51	·57	·17	·25
8. Geometry forms -	·54	·70	·56	·53	·73	·57	·45	—	·35	·49	·34	·56	·25	·25
9. Learning pairs -	·78	·73	·73	·42	·39	·59	·39	·35	—	·69	·36	·29	·26	·09
10. Recognised forms -	·88	·74	·71	·56	·51	·66	·47	·49	·69	—	·44	·37	·34	·28
11. Scroll - - -	·55	·52	·53	·45	·39	·54	·51	·34	·36	·44	—	·31	·19	·27
12. Completed words -	·42	·43	·40	·29	·59	·31	·57	·56	·29	·37	·31	—	·21	·07
13. Estimated lengths -	·33	·26	·28	·38	·25	·28	·17	·25	·26	·34	·19	·21	—	·24
14. Drawing length -	·25	·25	·21	·48	·22	·19	·25	·25	·09	·28	·27	·07	·24	—

For this table the older criterion, inter-columnar correlation, amounted to + ·96 (see p. 139), and therefore decisively indicated divisibility.

Let us now treat this same table with the new and correct criterion, that of tetrad differences. Much labour has been entailed, seeing that these differences are no less in number than 3,003. But the work seemed worth while, and the ensuing frequency distributions are shown below.[2]

[1] See present writer, *Psych. Rev.* 1914, pp. 101 ff.

[2] The observed tetrad differences were calculated quite independently of the present writer by Mr. Raper, to whom cordial thanks are here tendered.

DISTRIBUTION OF TETRAD DIFFERENCES FOR THE
CORRELATIONS OF SIMPSON.

The two distributions, theoretical and observed, are shown in
the same way as in the previous cases.

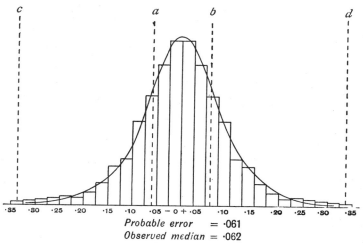

Probable error = ·061
Observed median = ·062

This time, the two distributions, curve and rectangles, far
from being totally discrepant as before, display instead one
of the most striking agreements between theory and observation ever recorded in psychology. Indeed, it would not
easily be matched in any other science. The divisibility,
then, is indicated more decisively than ever.[1]

The other most important case of similar kind is that of
the investigations made by Brown (William). Here again,
the original verdict based on general impression was adverse
to the theory of two factors, whereas the subsequent verdict
based on the inter-columnar correlation was no less decisive
in its favour. Of these investigations we have now selected
the one with largest number of subjects (66) for trial by the

[1] Note, however, that the conformity is not *quite* perfect. At the extreme wings of the frequency distribution are some very few cases as large
as ·35, which is more than five times the probable error, and therefore
cannot well be attributed merely to sampling errors. For the explanation
of these exceptional instances see p. 151.

new and correct criterion. The observed correlations were as follows : [1]

	1	2	3	4	5	6	7	8
1. Combination - -	—	·52	·52	·39	·46	·13	·00	·15
2. Memory, poetry -	·52	—	·49	·39	·27	·12	·05	·13
3. Memory, mechanical	·52	·49	—	·29	·34	·14	·12	·10
4. Addition - - -	·39	·39	·29	—	·41	·12	·03	·20
5. Letters - - -	·46	·27	·34	·41	—	·37	·10	·00
6. Motor ability - -	·13	·12	·14	·12	·37	—	·04	·00
7. Illusion - - -	·00	·05	·12	·03	·10	·04	—	·16
8. Bisection - -	·15	·13	·10	·20	·00	·00	·16	—

For this table, the probable error of the tetrad differences comes to ·028, whilst the actually observed median of these differences is ·027. Once more, then, the observations—in extraordinary contrast to all those obtained from bodily measurements—agree perfectly with the correct criterion (thereby, incidentally, again corroborating the older and provisional method).

Yet another work of exceptional importance for our purposes is that which we owe to Bonser ; this, like that of Simpson, was done in the laboratory and under the supervision of Thorndike. Moreover, the two researches illuminatingly supplement each other ; for whereas Simpson used a small number of subjects (37) but a large number of tests (14), Bonser did just the reverse (757 subjects and 5 tests). The resulting correlations were as follows : [2]

	1	2	3	4	5
1. Mathematical judgment -	—	·485	·400	·397	·295
2. Controlled association - -	·485	—	·397	·397	·247
3. Literary interpretation - -	·400	·397	—	·335	·275
4. Selective judgment - -	·397	·397	·335	—	·195
5. Spelling - - - -	·295	·247	·275	·195	—

When previously treated by the provisional criterion of inter-columnar correlation, the agreement with theory had

[1] *Brit. J. Psych.* 1910, p. 309.   [2] *Ibidem*, 1912, p. 62.

here again shown itself to be excellent (the value obtained being again +·96, see p. 139). And on now applying the correct criterion, the result is just as before. For the tetrad differences have a probable error of ·011 and an observed median of ·013 or almost exactly the same.[1]

This is as far as the new criterion has up to the present time been applied to the great mass of earlier results arrayed on page 139. In every case, the new and correct criterion has fully corroborated the earlier and provisional method; wherever the one is satisfied, so is the other; conversely, when the one fails, the other does so also. The suggestion is, then, that the old method was after all a reliable guide when applied properly. If that be so, the whole array given on that page may be taken to involve abilities which are in general really and truly divisible into g and s with s independent throughout.

Correlations of later date. But to make assurance doubly sure, we may proceed to consider the correlations that have been obtained more recently. One such has been supplied by Holzinger, where the Otis tests—which closely resemble the American Army Alpha (this latter having been largely borrowed from them)—were employed with 50 children. The correlations proved to be as follows :

Test.	a	b	c	d	e	f	g	h	i
a -	—	·50	·54	·34	·47	·40	·50	·33	·24
b -	·50	—	·39	·56	·51	·43	·36	·32	·15
c -	·54	·39	—	·49	·52	·27	·27	·26	·27
d -	·34	·56	·49	—	·30	·27	·52	·13	·35
e -	·47	·51	·52	·30	—	·35	·14	·33	·18
f -	·40	·43	·27	·27	·35	—	·38	·40	·19
g -	·50	·36	·27	·52	·14	·38	—	·19	·38
h -	·33	·32	·26	·13	·33	·40	·19	—	·29
i -	·24	·15	·27	·35	·18	·19	·38	·29	—

[1] See Appendix ii. 3.

DISTRIBUTION OF TETRAD DIFFERENCES FOR THE
CORRELATIONS OF HOLZINGER.

The two distributions, theoretical and observed, are shown in
the same way as on p. 5.

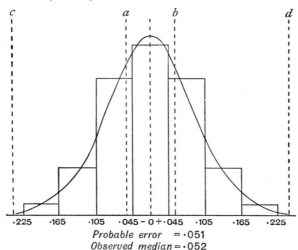

Probable error   = ·051
Observed median = ·052

Evidently the agreement could hardly be bettered.

Another instance is the investigation, done with 149
subjects, which has just been published by Magson.[1] The
following is the table of correlations :

	1	2	3	4	5	6	7
1. Analogies - - -	—	·50	·49	·55	·49	·45	·45
2. Completion - - -	·50	—	·54	·47	·50	·38	·34
3. Understanding paras. -	·49	·54	—	·49	·39	·44	·35
4. Opposites - - -	·55	·47	·49	—	·41	·32	·35
5. Instructions - - -	·49	·28	·39	·41	—	·32	·40
6. Resemblances - - -	·45	·38	·44	·32	·32	—	·35
7. Inferences - - -	·48	·34	·35	·35	·40	·35	—

Here, the tetrad differences gave a probable error of ·03
and an observed median of ·04, so that again the agreement
leaves nothing to be desired.

[1] *Brit. J. Psych. Mon. Suppl.* 9, 1926.

Still further corroboration, should it be required, is available to almost limitless amount. Indeed, the remainder of this volume will provide it in great abundance incidentally.

Herewith, then, the first and greatest portion of our present task would seem to have been accomplished. An answer has been obtained to the question, whether the divisibility of abilities into g and s (with s throughout independent) really occurs anywhere to any large extent. To this question our evidence appears to have answered convincingly in the affirmative. Such two independent factors have been demonstrated for at any rate a great number of the sets of tests commonly used for " general intelligence." [1]

FAILURE WITH ABILITIES THAT "OVERLAP"

Operations obviously similar. Our next business is to examine the cases where the criterion of tetrad differences, on being applied to abilities, *fails* to be satisfied.

The most arresting feature about these cases is their comparative rarity. Out of the many hundreds of pairs of abilities that have been submitted to one or other of the

---

[1] The preceding agreement of observed with theoretical errors of sampling in the case of the tetrad differences may be interestingly compared with the agreement that has been found in the case of ordinary correlational coefficients. Here we can obtain light from a valuable statistical investigation of Thorndike (Empirical Studies in the Theory of Measurement, *Archives of Psych.* 1907, No. 3). He arranged several series each of 1,000 values in such a manner as to depart in various typical ways from the " normal " distribution. The correlations found between these original different series were regarded as " true " amounts. Then from each series were drawn random samples of about 50, 100, or 200 corresponding values, and the correlations were now calculated for each sample. Naturally, the amounts obtained from these samples diverged more or less from the original or true ones. Such actually occurring divergencies were compared with the probable errors (calculated in the usual way). The results proved to be as follows :

Theoretical probable errors - ·035 ·049 ·070 ·044 ·062 ·088 ·023 ·032 ·045
Observed median error 9 trials - ·033 ·054 ·084 ·054 ·088 ·128 ·037 ·027 ·100

On the whole, the agreement is certainly no better in this case of simple correlations than that which we have been finding in the case of the tetrad differences.

two criteria (old and new) not a dozen have failed to conform.

As to the nature of these exceptional cases, a large proportion of them are characterized by the two operations being closely similar. Three such pairs have been met by us already; one consisted of Latin grammar and Latin translation; another was the counting of dots one at a time and three at a time; the third was the memorizing of syllables and that of numbers (p. 81).

There seems to have been only five other pairs of this kind hitherto noticed. And all five, curiously enough, have had just the same origin; all came from using together in the same set of tests two varieties of the well known Cancellation test (see Whipple's *Manual of Physical and Menial Tests*). Two of these pairs occurred in the work of W. Brown.[1] For two more Simpson was responsible. The fifth case was provided by McCall, who went so far as to employ four such varieties together.[2] Just such a series might well have been devised, if the intention had been to construct one where, according to the doctrine of two factors, the criterion ought *not* to be satisfied.

Different measurements based on common data. From the preceding kind of case may be distinguished that where measurements, which were put forward as being derived from independent data, have really been to a greater or less extent derived from the same data. In such cases, naturally, the criterion will often fail; the specific factors will not be mutually independent.

This appears to have happened to Thorndike in collaboration with Lay and Dean. Measurements were obtained by these authors for 25 children in the following respects: (1) discrimination of weight; (2) discrimination of length (visual); (3) intelligence as estimated by teachers and fellow-pupils; and (4) record of school success. The

---

[1] See Hart and Spearman, *Brit. J. Psych.* 1912, p. 73.

[2] Teachers' College, Columbia Univ., *Contr. to Educ.* No. 79.

ensuing correlations were found not to satisfy the criterion then used. But, doubtless, both the teachers and the fellow-pupils were acquainted with the school success, and in large measure based their estimates upon this; for this reason the (3) and the (4) did not supply independently obtained data.[1]

Some special cases. Rather an exceptional case, but still of considerable interest, is afforded by the following correlations which Baldwin found between six successive applications of the Binet test-series at intervals of six months.

	1	2	3	4	5	6
1 -	—	·85	·73	·77	·81	·81
2 -	·85	—	·84	·80	·81	·75
3 -	·73	·84	—	·91	·83	·79
4 -	·77	·80	·91	—	·91	·86
5 -	·81	·81	·83	·91	—	·94
6 -	·81	·75	·79	·86	·94	—

Here, a rash reasoner might jump to the conclusion that he had before him the very model case of the two factors, one always constant (" intelligence "), and the other varying each time independently (the errors of the successive measurements). In point of fact, however, the median of the observed tetrad differences comes to ·072, which is far greater than their probable error, ·016, and therefore cannot be ascribed merely to sampling.[2] Any surprise at such a result is dissipated by recalling that the Binet tests continually change in nature as the age of the testee increases (see ch. v. pp. 68-69). Consequently, the tests for any two neighbouring ages will have much in common that does not extend to ages farther apart.[3]

[1] *Am. J. Psych.* 1909, xx.

[2] It should be noted that the only probable error so far determined is for any *single* tetrad difference. The probable error for the median (or average) must certainly be much smaller, but we do not yet know *how much* smaller.

[3] For a very elaborate and exact investigation of this matter, see The Constancy of " G " by Slocombe, *Brit. J. Psych.* 1926.

Our next and last illustration of overlap due to similarity presents some remarkable features. Four years ago the writer was invited to test the " general intelligence " of nearly 30,000 members of the British Civil Service. And advantage was taken of this occasion to promote not only the practical but also some theoretical ends. For the latter purpose, three of the tests were given in two varieties that may be called " selective " and " inventive." The former variety was characterized by the subject having only to select an answer out of three or four offered to his choice ; whereas in the other variety he had to originate an answer for himself. The ensuing correlations were calculated for 2,599 cases, and proved to be as follows :

	1	2	3	4	5	6	7
1. Completion, selective	—	·516	·606	·416	·429	·479	·433
2. Analogies, inventive	·516	—	·468	·480	·457	·436	·398
3. Completion, inventive	·606	·468	—	·394	·421	·430	·409
4. Analogies, selective -	·416	·480	·394	—	·331	·347	·334
5. Instructions - -	·429	·457	·421	·337	—	·363	·355
6. Passages, inventive -	·479	·436	·430	·347	·363	—	·390
7. Passages, selective -	·433	·398	·409	·334	·355	·390	—

For this table, the tetrad differences were divided into two groups. One consisted of those which involve any correlations between two varieties of the same test ; such correlations are r_{13}, r_{24}, and r_{67}. In these, of course, overlap is only to be expected. And accordingly, as is evident in the figure below, the theoretical and the observed frequency distributions do not in the least conform with each other.

The two distributions, theoretical and observed, are shown in
the same way as on p. 142.

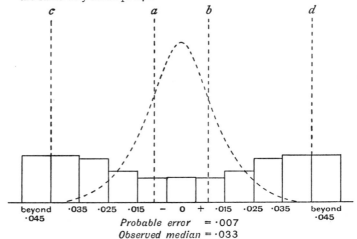

| beyond ·045 | ·035 | ·025 | ·015 | − | 0 | + | ·015 | ·025 | ·035 | beyond ·045 |

Probable error = ·007
Observed median = ·033

But turn to the remaining tetrad differences which did *not*
involve two varieties of the same test, that is to say, did
not include r_{13}, r_{24}, or r_{67}. Here, the obvious reason for
overlap is removed. And accordingly, the agreement of
observation with theory at once becomes admirable.

DISTRIBUTION OF TETRAD DIFFERENCES FOR THE TETRADS
THAT DO *NOT* INVOLVE TWO VARIETIES OF THE SAME TEST.

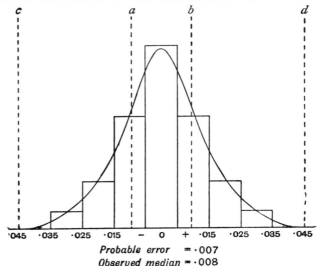

| ·045 | ·035 | ·025 | ·015 | − | 0 | + | ·015 | ·025 | ·035 | ·045 |

Probable error = ·007
Observed median = ·008

DISTURBANCE BY SPURIOUS CORRELATION

Partial measurements of efficiency. We have now considered two general cases. The first is where no significant tetrad difference exists, so that the abilities can be split up into g's and s's, the latter being independent both of g and of each other : there is no overlap. The other case is where significant tetrad differences do occur, so that the s's cannot be independent of each other ; instead, they must have an overlap attributable to some special resemblance between the mental operations concerned.

But unfortunately these two cases are not the sole ones where a significant tetrad difference can occur. For this may happen even when the mental operations at issue have no such special resemblance between each other ; but, then, in general, it will be found to be " spurious."

Illustrations of such spurious correlation are not infrequently afforded when any mental operations are measured only for speed, regardless of quality. For if this be done, some of the subjects may have a general inclination to strive for speed even at the risk of the quality thereby suffering. Such conduct will necessarily produce an increase of correlation between all the speed measurements ; this increase, however, will not derive from ability for speed, but only from preference for it.

Diversity of age, training, or sex. Still more dangerous is the admission of such influences as diversity of age, training, or sex, when these—as usually happens—are irrelevant to the purpose in hand.

Only in such a manner, it would seem, can any adequate explanation be afforded for the occasional occurrence of appreciable *negative* correlations. Probably, this accounts for the negative correlation obtained by McCall between the usual tests of " intelligence " and that of Cancellation. For efficiency in such cancelling would largely depend on age, and just the oldest children in a class are as a rule the most stupid.

Plurality of experimenters. Another instance, but on larger scale, has been supplied by the testing of the American Army. For about a thousand of the men were picked out as a " special experimental group " to represent the American Army in general ; and the results obtained from this group were submitted to extraordinarily elaborate statistical treatment. In particular, a calculation was made of the correlations between all the eight sub-tests of which the whole series (the " Alpha," as it is called) was composed. These correlations were as follows :

	1	2	3	4	5	6	7	8
1. Directions -	—	·730	·590	·710	·686	·680	·670	·658
2. Arithmetic	·730	—	·745	·791	·763	·773	·736	·742
3. Prac. judg.	·590	·745	—	·805	·754	·613	·671	·775
4. Sun.-antin.	·710	·791	·805	—	·834	·681	·730	·861
5. Diss. sent. -	·686	·763	·754	·834	—	·674	·778	·823
6. Num. ser. -	·680	·773	·613	·681	·674	—	·704	·693
7. Analogies -	·670	·736	·671	·730	·778	·704	—	·672
8. Inform'tion	·658	·742	·775	·861	·823	·693	·672	—

Now, the result of applying our criterion here is strangely unlike that obtained on other occasions even when using very similar tests (*e.g.* in the work of Holzinger, see p. 149). The median observed tetrad difference, instead of being near to the probable error, is now over four times greater, the respective values being ·043 and ·009.

Can this time any explanation be found in the degrees that the different tests resemble one another ? The author of the official report made a brave attempt to find out. Between every pair of sub-tests he calculated—at very great labour—the " partial coefficients of sixth order," assuming himself to obtain thereby " the amounts of actual resemblance between tests." [1]

But the upshot was, as the author himself concedes, that the resemblance indicated by these partial coefficients

[1] Off. account, p. 652.   For method of calculation see Yule's *Introduction to the Theory of Statistics*, ch. xii.

showed no tendency whatever to agree with those indicated by psychological analysis. This curious result seems only explicable by considering how the correlations were actually obtained. In the endeavour to procure fairly representative samples of the Army, the plan had been conceived of sending round to twelve different camps, asking each that the tests should be given to " approximately 100 relatively unselected men." Nine of the camps responded, their contributions of men ranging from under 20 to over 200. But by such a procedure the subjects, and still more so the testing, must have become heterogeneous to the last degree. For instance, when in any camp the testing or marking happened to be more generous than in others with respect to any of these tests, then the men here would tend to shine in these particular tests ; the result must be to generate additional correlation between these tests quite independently of any resemblance or psychological connection between them. And the cumulative result of such influences could scarcely fail to produce the highly irregular character that we actually find.

Miscalculation. To the preceding causes of spurious correlation must be added another not usually suspected. The experience of the present writer has convinced him that there is only too much truth in the recent statement by a prominent psychologist, that few of the published correlations are safe from the danger of downright errors of calculation. Time and again, grave mistakes have been detected, and this even in the correlations published by authors who stand in high repute both as mathematicians and as careful workers.

Above, it must be added, we have only had in view errors of large magnitude. But as soon as the subjects become very numerous, the whole calculation becomes a most delicate business. Serious disturbance begins to arise even from those inaccuracies which are commonly passed over as being negligibly small.[1]

---

[1] Among these must be counted the deviations of the frequency distributions from the " normal " type, the effect of coarse grading, the non-use

SUMMARY

Summary. In Chapter VI. a mathematical theory had been built up ; in the present chapter a home has been found for it. The attempt was favoured over those made previously in several decisive respects. First and above all, the correct criterion had become available for use, instead of the formerly employed provisional substitute. Then, assistance was derived from comparison and contrast with some tables of correlations that had been obtained in fields other than those of mental ability. Finally, the number of subjects included in a single experiment had been greatly increased ; in one instance it rose to no less than 2,599.

The general result has been to demonstrate that the said criterion usually holds for the sets of mental performances now commonly employed for testing " general intelligence." In a very large number of cases, such tests have yielded correlations closely agreeing with the new and correct criterion, as also with the older provisional one. In this way, incidentally, the older method has after all shown itself to be remarkably effective when properly applied.

Of the cases—surprisingly few—where either criterion has failed to be satisfied, the majority are at once explicable by the fact of the abilities possessing some conspicuous resemblance to each other, so that " overlap " is indicated.

There have remained some rare cases where, although the criterion failed to be satisfied, yet no special resemblance was evident. But in every such instance, there has been

of Sheppard's correction, any uncorrected approximation when taking an arbitrary origin of measurement, the source of deviation explained in the appendix, p. xv, not to mention innumerable other sources of slight irregularity.

As an illustration, suppose that for any series of abilities and class of persons the *true* tetrad difference was :

$$\cdot 84 \times \cdot 60 - \cdot 80 \times \cdot 63 = 0.$$

Suppose further that for a *sample* of 625 persons the actually observed values led to the following tetrad differences :

$$\cdot 87 \times \cdot 63 - \cdot 77 \times \cdot 60 = \cdot 0741.$$

Here, not one of the observed correlations deviates from the true one by more than $\cdot 03$. And yet this calculated tetrad difference of $\cdot 0741$ is nearly seven times larger than the probable error (this being only $\cdot 0108$).

correlation of some " spurious " sort. Usually, either the way of sampling, or the administration of the tests, or the procedure of marking, has been vitiated by illegitimate influences. Sometimes, there have even been gross errors of calculation. And as for heterogeneity in age, sex, etc., this influence has been allowed to run riot.

It may here be remarked that nearly all these pitfalls in investigating the doctrine of two factors were pointed out in its very earliest exposition.[1] This already foresaw the " inevitable eventual corrections and limitations to the doctrine." The evidence for or against it was said to be attainable " on sole condition of adequate methodics." Long consideration was given to the topic of " overlap " or " group factors." And the greatest stress was laid upon the danger of heterogeneity of subjects ; especially harmful were said to be inequalities of age, training, or sex. Another publication two years later asserted the same needs with even greater emphasis : this side of the work was said to engender the most formidable of the difficulties to be encountered.[2]

But all this scrupulous care, so strongly urged by those who were developing the doctrine, would seem to have been regrettably overlooked by writers criticizing it : these, apparently, looked to find a " hierarchical " order in any correlations got by anybody, anywhere, anyhow. Such fool-proof doctrines, we must urge, do not enter into science at all, psychological or material. Think of the thousand and one precautions that have been found needful to demonstrate any great law in physics. Not otherwise could possibly be the fundamental laws of the mind.

Indeed, even now after all the preceding evidence, there remains still need for further warning. Science knows no finality. Research can only push forward and bring down the errors to smaller and smaller dimensions. Wholly eliminated they can never be. Assuredly, there will in

---

[1] Present writer, *Am. J. Psych.* 1904, xx.

[2] Krueger and Spearman, *Zeit. f. Psychol.* 1906, xliv.

time be revealed many yet further complications that have not hitherto been taken into account. As originally, so now once more, the plea must be urged that all conclusions drawn in the present work are subject to "inevitable eventual corrections and limitations."

Even with the degree of exactness attained already, however, the agreement of the observed values with those required by theory must be admitted by any unbiased person to have been surprisingly close. In general, it seems quite as good as, if not better than, that usually reached in determining the mechanical equivalent of heat and thus establishing the law of conservation of physical energy.

CHAPTER XI

UNIVERSALITY OF *G*

REQUIRED GENERAL SURVEY OF COGNITION

Use of fundamental laws. The preceding chapter has supplied us with a foothold from which to make further advances. We have found a sphere—the usual sets of mental tests—where in general all the' correlation (other than spurious) indicates the existence of our two factors. Wherever the abilities involved are sufficiently distinct—and that is in the great majority of cases—our tetrad equation (ch. vi. p. 73) is satisfied with surprising exactitude, so that here each ability must be divisible into *g* and *s*. The letter *g* becomes, in this manner, a name for the factor—whatever it may be—that is common to mental tests of such a description. This is the very definition of *g*. All else about it—including the question as to whether it has the least right to be regarded as a genuine measure of " intelligence "—lies still before us to ascertain.

For this purpose, the first step is to find out how far the range of such tests obeying the tetrad equation really extends.

This involves nothing less than a general survey of the entire range of possible operations of knowing. To execute this gigantic task, there appears to be only one effective means. It consists in an appeal to the complete system of ultimate laws that govern all cognition. Nothing of such a nature, indeed, would appear to be provided by the psychologies now current, which James could portray as

"a string of raw facts ; a little gossip and wrangle about opinions ; a little classification and generalization on the mere descriptive level ; . . . but not a single law in the sense in which physics shows us laws, not a single proposition from which any consequence can be causally deduced."

But recently an attempt to supply this indispensable foundation has actually been undertaken. A new doctrine has been advanced, one which does not necessarily conflict with any of those now prevalent, but which carries the analysis to a further stage, and which does seem to have succeeded in reducing all observed cognitive phenomena to a complete system of *ultimate laws*, and also—what is at least equally important—to a concatenation (often immensely complex) of *ultimate processes*.[1]

After the exposition of the said laws and processes—it can fairly be claimed—not one of them has been, in substance, even challenged. All writings opposed to them appear to have been, either mere misunderstandings, or else only just these laws and processes over again but viewed from a slightly different angle. Nor, it would seem, has any case falling outside the scope of these laws and processes been hitherto demonstrated—or even seriously urged.

But it is not enough that the laws should be valid, or even that they should be exhaustive. We must also require of them scientific significance. They should be able to array all the known facts into a unitary whole, which by reason of its orderliness renders these facts intelligible ; which, by

[1] *The Nature of " Intelligence " and the Principles of Cognition*, 1923, by present writer. For reasons given in that work (p. 61), the said doctrine has been called that of "noegenesis."

bringing all of them into mutual relation, affords an all-round check upon their accuracy ; and which, by virtue of relevance to the problems really at issue, do allow of " consequences being causally deduced." Above all, such a doctrine should possess the virtue of inspiring further and fruitful investigation. Here, also, the newly proposed laws would seem already in this short time to have fulfilled their promise. As instances may be quoted the fine research of Gopalaswami into learning by trial and error,[1] that of Hamid into economical memorizing,[2] that of Strasheim into the mental development of children,[3] that of McCrae into mental hygiene,[4] that of Bradley into the psychology of error,[5] and that of Wild into the influence of conation upon cognition.[6] Further instances, outside of our own laboratory, have been the novel analysis and diagnosis gained by Sherlock for the study of dementia ; [7] the fresh light that Sullivan has thrown upon the disorder of schizophrenia ; [8] the new direction given by Ballard to the most vital of all educational problems, that of " formal training ; " [9] the fine study of " Judgment " by Stevanović ; [10] the very practical treatise of Aveling on *The Directing of Mental Energy*,[11] as also his profound works on *External Perception* [12] and on *The Psychology of Conation and Volition*.[13]

But the crucial ordeal of these laws will be found in the remainder of the present volume itself. To the inspiration furnished by them it is that the great majority of the researches to be chronicled here have really owed their origin. And to these same laws all the results of the researches must eventually turn for their scientific illumination.

[1] *Brit. J. Psych.* 1924, xiv. ; *ibidem*, 1925, xv.   [2] *Ibidem*, 1926.
[3] *Educational Psychology Monographs*, 1926.
[4] *Thesis* in Library of University of London.
[5] Not yet published.   [6] Not yet published.
[7] Metropolitan Asylums Board *Annual Report* for 1924.
[8] *Amer. Journ. Psychiatry*, 1925.   [9] *The Changing School*, 1925, p. 142 ff.
[10] *Brit. J. Psych.* Mon. Suppl. 1927.   [11] University of London Press, 1927.
[12] In *The Mind*, by Various Authors, 1927.   [13] *Brit. J. Psych.* 1926, xvi.

The apprehension of one's own experience. The task of mapping out the entire domain of cognition, so as to show just what area in it is occupied by any particular mental operation or test, commences with the three ultimate *qualitative* laws (and their corresponding processes) ; for these prescribe how all new cognition (*i.e.*, all cognition that is not merely reproductive) is ever possible. Of these laws, the first may be formulated by saying that a person has more or less power to observe what goes on in his own mind. He not only feels, but also knows what he feels ; he not only strives, but knows that he strives ; he not only knows, but knows that he knows.

To demonstrate the validity of this law would seem to be superfluous. To it we are indebted for the greater part of ordinary conversation ; as when a man remarks " I was angry at this," or " I tried to do that," or " I saw something red," or " I thought of the future." Its manifestations become most copious in autobiographies, and most exact in experimental introspection.

Although on closer scrutiny this law gives rise to many problems that are extremely difficult, still these do not appear to touch the matters with which we are concerned at present. The only stumbling-block which seems to demand attention here is the opinion of many authorities, that to have a mental experience and to become aware of doing so are as indissoluble as the convexity and the concavity of one and the same curve. If such a view were to be accepted, no scope would be left for individual differences in this respect ; this first law would be irrelevant to our topic. But other psychologists—as it seems, with better reason—hold contrariwise that a person may know his own experience with varying degrees of clearness ; at the limit, the clearness may even sink to zero, so that the knowledge —but not the experience—vanishes. Upon this second and more reasonable view, clear introspection may well lie within the power of one person more than another ; scope does remain for individual differences of ability.

On proceeding to inquire, then, how far this power has been brought within the range of mental tests, the answer would seem to be blankly negative. Nothing of the sort appears to have ever yet been measured, save only a person's knowledge of his own sensations ; and even the knowing of these has been inextricably mingled with the knowing of likeness and difference between them, a feat which comes within the purview of the second rather than of the first law. Still less, of course, have any measurements been obtained as to how far this introspective power is correlated with any other abilities. Here at once, then, we detect an immense gap in the range of the mental tests, and consequently in the information to be derived from them as to the range of *g*.

The eduction of relations. Turning to the second law, this states that when a person has in mind any two or more ideas (using this word to embrace any items of mental content, whether perceived or thought of), he has more or less power to bring to mind any relations that essentially hold between them.[1]

This law, also, seems to be indisputable enough. It is instanced whenever a person becomes aware, say, that beer tastes something like weak quinine, that the number seven is larger than five, or that the proposition " All A is B " proves the proposition " Some A is B." For the attributes involved here—resemblance, comparative size, and logical evidence—are undeniably of the kind called relations.[2]

The process may be symbolized in the following figure, where *r* stands for the relation, whilst f_1 and f_2 denote the " fundaments " as they are termed, between which the relation is known. The continuous lines represent what is given originally ; the dotted line, what is educed by the process. If hitherto the cognition of relations has been so extraordinarily neglected by almost all psychologists, this

---

[1] By " essential " relations are meant those which derive from the very nature of the fundaments.

[2] *The Nature of Intelligence*, etc., pp. 65-67.

can only be explained by their not seeing the forest for trees !

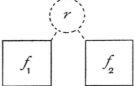

Our need here is a survey of the entire mental territory which such processes constitute. And means for this purpose are at once to hand. For all possible relations have been systematically classified, so that we can proceed to examine each class in turn. As regards the different kinds of fundaments, these will be considered in a more incidental manner. For the present, it must suffice to remark that they are inexorably limited to the mental content supplied by the first law, together with what can be evolved out of this content by the action of the second and third laws.

The eduction of correlates. Proceeding to the third and last of these laws, this enounces that when a person has in mind any idea together with a relation, he has more or less power to bring up into mind the correlative idea.

For example, let anyone hear a musical note and try to imagine the note a fifth higher. If he understands the relation of " fifth " and moreover possesses an ear for music, he will more or less accurately accomplish the task. Or let him notice the relation of horizontal to vertical length in Fig. 1 below, and then try to draw in Fig. 2 straightway (that is, without reflection or correction) a horizontal length in the same relation to the vertical one as before. Again the feat proves to be possible.

Fig. 1.　　　　　　　Fig. 2.

Such educing of correlates may be symbolized as follows, where the continuous and the dotted lines have the same meaning as before.

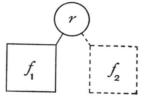

This third form of process, although just as abundant in ordinary life as the preceding one, seems hitherto to have in strange degree escaped psychological notice. But this time there is perhaps more excuse ; for here the analysis often does encounter very great difficulty. Nevertheless, several highly important theorems have now been established about it ; overtopping all else is the discovery that this process supplements the two preceding ones, so that together the three make up absolutely all the cognition (other than purely reproductive) of which the human mind is ever in any circumstances capable.

With regard to mapping out the region supplied by this third law, the same may be said as above in respect of the second. We have only to go through the several classes of relations and the possible kinds of fundaments.

DETECTION OF *G* WITH ALL TEN RELATIONS

Procedure. Our next course, then, is to examine each class of relation to see whether the eductive processes characterized by it do or do not involve the general factor *g*. To prove that they do involve it, we have to show that they are among the abilities where—on duly eliminating manifest overlap—every tetrad of correlations satisfies the tetrad equation to just the extent that should be expected from the errors of sampling.[1]

---

[1] A further resource is conveniently at our disposal. When the presence of *g* in any ability cannot be proved by showing this ability to satisfy the tetrad equation, it may sometimes still be provable by the indirect method of showing the ability to correlate with some further one that does satisfy this criterion. For the preceding chapter has indicated that all correlation (other than spurious) either derives from *g* or else is due to overlap. Consequently, then, whenever overlap cannot be suspected, any correlation that makes its appearance must be taken as due to the presence of *g*.

The complete list of relations is as follows :

"*Ideal.*"	"*Real.*"
Evidence.	Space.
Likeness.	Time.
Conjunction.	Psychological.
	Identity.
	Attribution.
	Causation.
	Constitution.

As for the distinction here made between the " ideal " and the " real " classes, this descends from an ancient controversy as to which relations possess real existence over and above that of their fundaments. In general, such a prerogative has been asserted of those which are called real, but denied of those called ideal. This point, however, is a metaphysical nicety with which we fortunately need not here concern ourselves.

Relation of evidence. The report to be now made of experimental results may perhaps most illuminatingly commence with that mental power which in all ages has been regarded as belonging essentially and indisputably to the " intellect," namely, the power to cognize relations of evidence.[1] A case of this kind already encountered by us is Magson's test of Inferences, of which the following is an example :

> " All Russians travelled with Danes, some Danes travelled with Dutch, all Dutch travelled with Spaniards. What can you conclude as to whether Russians travelled with Dutch ? "[2]

Here, clearly, the subject is asked in the second of the two

---

[1] A careful distinction must be made between cognizing the relation *of* evidence and cognizing relations *by* evidence. Only the former performance constitutes specially the class which we are considering. The cognizing *by* evidence applies to all ten classes (see *Nature of Intelligence*, etc., p. 72).

[2] See ch. x. p. 149. The example is an elaborate case of educing a correlate. The given fundament consists in the stated situation of the Russians, Danes, Dutch, and Spaniards. The given relation consists in evidencing. The required correlative fundament consists in what is evidenced by the stated situation.

sentences to state what is evidenced by the first of them. This test entered into 54 different tetrad differences ; the observed median value of these showed itself to be ·03, which was almost exactly the same as the probable error of those differences (also ·03). Such an observed median value of the tetrad differences, then, can be wholly accounted for by the mere errors of sampling ; no portion of the value remains over to be attributed to any " overlap " or " group factor " (see pp. 150-151). Accordingly, the power to make such inferences can be wholly analysed into *g* and *s*, where every *s* is independent both of *g* and also of all other *s*'s in the set of tests.

For our present purposes, an even better instance is afforded by the work of H. A. Peterson as early as 1908.[1] Here, 63 students were submitted to 5 tests entitled respectively Reasoning, Generalization, Abstract Thought, Memory, and Accuracy. These took from 30 to 70 minutes each (which is as long as testers nowadays usually allot to their whole series of 8-10 different single tests). The following are examples of each kind :

(1) Reasoning.

" State whether the following conclusions are *necessarily* true or not. If not, where is the error ? Point it out. If the reasoning is sound, but the premises false, point out what is false in the premises.

" Giving advice is useless. For either you advise a man what he means to do, in which case the advice is useless ; or you advise him what he does not mean to do, and the advice is ineffectual."

Here again, obviously, the main point at issue is as to whether the stated premises afford evidence for the suggested conclusion.

(2) Generalization.

" What general statement or statements can you make which will be true of all the following instances of the way in which Colonial schoolmasters were paid ?

[1] *Psych. Rev.* xv.

" In Watertown, Mass., in 1680, the schoolmaster got 25 pounds and the benefit of the Latin scholars. In Newbury, Mass., 1696, the schoolmaster was offered 30 pounds in country pay by the selectmen provided he demand but 4 pence per week from Latin scholars, and teach the town's children to read, write, and cipher without pay. In Lynn, Mass., in 1702, a schoolmaster was allowed 40 pounds by the selectmen, and Latin pupils were charged 6 pence per week. In this case, assuming an average of 6 Latin scholars attended the whole year, we see his total wages would be about 237 dollars. In Hartford, in 1643, the town agreed that the schoolmaster should receive 16 pounds, that this should be raised by tuition fees of 20 shillings a year per pupil as far as possible, but the town was to make good any deficit. The indigent were free. Salem, Mass., had a subscription for its school, but the town provided for the poor by a rate."

This time the substance of the task consists in discovering what general fact is evidenced by the given particular facts.

(3) Abstract Thought.

" Study the selection numbered 1 and tell the meaning of it in your own language. No notice will be taken of papers which quote the selection, even in altered words. Express *all* the ideas that you get from it.

" 1. No one will doubt that men are more possessed by the instinct to fight, to be the winner in serious games and contests, than are women ; nor that women are more possessed than men by the instinct to nurse, to care for and fuss over others, to relieve, comfort and console. . . . The fighting instinct is, in fact, the cause of a very large amount of the world's intellectual endeavour. The financier does not think for money, nor the scientist for truth, nor the theologian to save souls. Their intellectual efforts are aimed in great measure to outdo the other man, to subdue nature, to conquer assent. The maternal instinct in its turn is the chief source of woman's superiorities in the moral world. The virtues in which she excels are not so much due to either any general moral superiority or any set of special moral talents as to her original impulse to relieve, comfort, and console."

Here, as in the following two tests, little or no cognizing of the relation of evidence appears to be involved in the " critical " (see p. 4) part of the mental operation required.

(4) Memory.

About a page was read to the subjects, and they were warned that they would be tested immediately afterwards. A week later, without any warning, they were again asked to write out as much as possible. They were told that only substance, not actual words, were wanted. Marks for both first and second recall were pooled.

(5) Accuracy.

The subjects copied a bibliography from the blackboard, without knowing that it was a test. Enough time was given for the slowest to finish. Mere errors of punctuation or capitalization were not counted, but only serious errors.

The general result of all these five tests was the table of correlations given below :

	1	2	3	4	5
1. Reasoning - - -	—	·95	·83	·40	·45
2. Generalizing - - -	·95	—	·86	·40	·28
3. Abstract Thought - -	·83	·86	—	·64	·48
4. Memory - - -	·40	·40	·64	—	·31
5. Accuracy - - -	·45	·28	·48	·31	—

Now, we can apply to these correlations the method of tetrad differences, in order to ascertain whether any factor is shared by all five tests. And the answer proves to be in the affirmative ; the scores made in each of these tests do involve one and the same *g*.   In particular, the essentially evidential tests 1 and 2 involve just the same *g* as the other three which are *not* essentially evidential.   Incidentally, it may be noticed that not only test 1, but also 2 and 3, are among the " highest " of which the mind is capable.   *G* is, then, forthwith established upon a basis of best repute.[1]

Among later tests, only one series would seem to have touched anything like the same high level, and this was the brilliant *Development of Reasoning* by Burt (*loc. cit.* p. 201). Here, however, no correlations with any three other tests appear to have been as yet published.   We can, then, no longer emplqy the direct method of proof, as in the two preceding cases ; but there remains the indirect method (p. 167, footnote).   Burt's *Reasoning* was shown by him to correlate highly with teachers' estimates of " intelligence," and these latter have already been found by us to contain *g*.   Hence—seeing that the *Reasoning* and the estimates appear to have no mutual overlap—the *Reasoning* also must involve *g*.

Relation of likeness.   Next may be considered the " ideal "

[1] The method of proof has two steps.   In the first of these we show that the analysis into *g* and *s* holds good of tests 1, 3, 4, and 5.   For this purpose, we may extract the following tetrad from the preceding table :

					Abstract Thought.	Memory.
Reasoning	-	-	-	-	·83	·40
Accuracy	-	-	-	-	·48	·31

Here, the tetrad difference $= ·83 \times ·31 - ·40 \times ·48 = ·065$.   This is just about the size that should be expected from mere sampling, since the probable error is ·055.   From any four things correlated, as may easily be seen, there always arise three different tetrad differences ; and the other two in the present case have an average value of ·059.   Thus, the observed values all hover close to the probable error.   Consequently (within the limits of the error of the experiment) all these four abilities have the same common factor, which may be called *g*, but have nothing else in common between any of them.

In the second step, we select for consideration the tests 2, 3, 4, and 5. These four again supply three tetrad differences, whose average value comes to ·044 and therefore once more approximates to the value of the probable error.

But by the first step we see that whatever is common to 3, 4, and 5 is also shared by 1.   And by the second step we see that the element common to 3, 4, and 5 is furthermore shared by 2.   Thus, one and the same common element exists in all five.   But notice that—for all that has been shown so far—1 and 2 may or may not have some *further* element in common.

relation called that of likeness or resemblance (including its varying degrees as also its opposite). In ordinary life, this appears to be the most universal of all cognitive tools. To cope with the immense variety of mental content, one has to sort this into classes, putting together the like and keeping apart the unlike. In testing, also, these relations of likeness and unlikeness have had an extremely wide range of usage. One conspicuous instance of educing such relations has been given in the Synonyms-Antonyms used by Otis and then by the American Army. The instructions were :

" If the two words of a pair mean the same or nearly the same, draw a line under *same*. If they mean the opposite or nearly the opposite, draw a line under *opposite*."

Then, below, a number of pairs of words were given, each pair being followed by the words " same " and " opposite," between which the subject had to choose. Thus :

Command—Obey. Same Opposite.

Since all the subjects would naturally have been well acquainted with the meaning of each of these paired words by itself, the critical process must (in so far as not merely reproductive) have consisted in educing their relation of oppositeness.

Now, this test of Synonyms has, according to the correlations reported by Otis and others, showed itself to conform with the criterion of *g* very exactly.[1] The sphere of *g*, then, must be extended to the cognising of the relation of likeness.

Peculiarly interesting from a theoretical standpoint are the results that have been obtained from this relation when applied to *sensory discrimination*. For here we might seem

[1] The following is a typical tetrad from the work of Otis (*Journ. Ed. Psych.* 1918, ix.) :

		Synonyms.	Narrative Completion.
Following directions	- -	·781	·815
Memory for digits	- -	·322	·341

The tetrad difference $= ·781 \times ·341 - ·815 \times ·322 = ·004$, or less than the probable error, which is ·020.

to reach the very antithesis to intellect or intelligence, as these words have in all ages been usually employed. Although the relation is the same as in the preceding case, the fundaments stand at the opposite pole. Is or is not our g present here also ? Once more, the answer given by experiment would appear to be decidedly in the affirmative.[1]

Similar results have been obtained for sensory discrimination of many other kinds. Already in the research just quoted the range of g was extended to the discrimination of light and of weight, although in these cases—especially the last—the correlations were very small.[2] Two years later, corroboration was got for discrimination of pitch. Next came the work of Burt.[3] This corroborated the foregoing as regards pitch ; and it furnished a similar result, though with still lower correlations, for visual discrimination of length ; but for discrimination of weight the correlations were this time so low as scarcely to be significant at all (in one school it averaged only $+ \cdot 07$ and in the other $+ \cdot 08$). Not long afterwards came the work of William Brown, which brought confirmation as regards visual discrimination of length ; the correlations were just about large enough to be taken as significant. Later, the very extensive work of Carey issued in similar results for both auditory and visual discrimination. But for four tests of tactile discrimination (thickness of wire, size of balls, and weight of cartridges) the correlation with other tests only averaged $+ \cdot 01$, and was therefore insignificant.[4] Another investigator, Abelson, tried the visual discrimination of length, and found an average correlation with the other tests amounting to $\cdot 29$ (131 cases).[5]

Everywhere, then, the proof is striking in the case of sound. It is less so in that of vision, but still usually un-

---

[1] Here is a typical tetrad, taken from the table given by the present writer in *Amer. J. Psych.* 1904, xv. p. 275.

	Classics.	English.
Discrimination of pitch - - - -	·63	·51
Mathematics - - - - - -	·70	·64

The tetrad difference $= \cdot 63 \times \cdot 64 - \cdot 70 \times \cdot 51 = \cdot 047$, whilst the probable error comes to $\cdot 055$.

[2] *Ibidem.*

[3] *Brit. J. Psych.* 1909, iii.

[4] *Ibidem,* 1915, viii. p. 88.

[5] *Ibidem,* 1911, iv.

deniable. In that of the tactile sense it often seems to fail; but sometimes, at any rate, the *g* seems to be present in appreciable degree, nor can one easily suppose that this last sense differs quite radically from the other two. On the whole, the conclusion seems irresistible, that *g* is more or less involved in educing relations of likeness, even when the fundaments are of a sensory nature.

Relations of conjunction, space, and time. The next class of ideal relation has a much more restricted scope. This is that ultra-simple kind which is called conjunction and is indicated by the word " and." Its chief sphere lies in arithmetic. It has often been introduced into mental tests, and the power to cognize it has always revealed the presence of *g*. An instance has already been supplied in the tetrad given on the preceding page; for what is there entitled mathematics consisted really of arithmetic and little else.

Turning next to the " real " relations, the most convenient to take first are those of space and time. These furnish the primary qualities of matter (including, of course, the body) as conceived by modern physical science. In this class of relations, then, we are examining the very basis of a person's stimulation by and reaction to his material environment.

In order to treat this kind of relation completely, we should have to start from the aboriginal apprehension of the spatial characters in experience. This might lead us back to the stage imagined by J. Müller, where the nerves are " capable of sensing their own extension." But such a power is still very controversial; and at any rate, it has never yet been rendered amenable to measurement.

The most primitive ability hitherto measured would appear to be that of distinguishing two tactual points from one. And in this respect the first results *failed* to indicate any presence of *g*; the average correlation with various other tests known to contain *g* amounted only to the negligible value of +·03.[1] But other experimenters have sometimes obtained appreciable values, as was done by Lipska and

[1] Krueger and Spearman, 1906, *Zeit. f. Psychol.* xliv. p. 75.

Librach working under the direction of Ioteyko. 420 children were divided into three groups according to their estimated intelligence. They were then examined in the power of distinguishing two points. At all three ages tried, 9-10, 10-11, and 11-12, the more intelligent children did markedly better than the less intelligent.[1]

Passing to the probably less primitive process of perceiving spatial relations visually, measurements have here been procured in abundance. We have already encountered the comparison of length of lines (page 174). And several of the tests used by Burt come more or less under this heading. One consisted in putting out a set of cardboard letters in random order and then making the subject arrange them as fast as possible in their natural sequence. Another brought into use the well known " dotting apparatus " of W. McDougall ; here dots irregularly placed along a band of paper pass rapidly in and out of the view and reach of the subject ; each dot has to be marked with a pencil as it passes by. Yet another was the test where the subject had to trace over a pattern seen only in a mirror. All these showed correlations with all the very varied further tests, and the ensuing tetrad differences were just such as to be attributable solely to the errors of sampling.

Another kind of simple spatial perception often tested, as by Brown, Simpson, and Wyatt, was the cancellation of some given letter or letters in a printed passage. This, too, has shown the same conformity with the criterion of g.[2]

More complicated eduction of spatial relations is afforded by the test of " geometrical figures." [3] For example, the

---

[1] *La Revue Psychol.* vi. 1913.

[2] Here is an example from Wyatt (*Brit. J. Psych.* 1913, vi.) :

	Analogies.	Part-Whole Association.
Cancelling a n o s - -	·57	·75
Interpreting fables - -	·34	·57

The tetrad difference = ·57 × ·57 − ·75 × ·34 = ·06, whilst the probable error is also ·06.

[3] First used by Hart and Spearman, *Journ. Abnormal Psychology*, Oct.-Nov. 1914 ; afterwards by Abelson, *Brit. J. Psych.* 1911, iv. and in the American Army tests.

subject was shown the following figure and told to point out a spot " inside the triangle but outside the circle and outside the square."

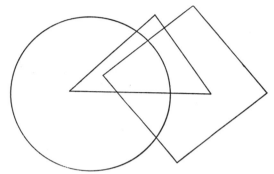

Among other well-known cases have been the ' Form-boards ' of Goddard,[1] of Dearborn,[2] and of Doll,[3] the Mazes of Porteus,[4] and the elegant ' Engineer Tests ' of Rupp.[5] Evidence of *g* can be found throughout.

The preceding tests introduce chiefly the eduction of relations, but there have been others which bring into play rather that of correlates ; here, some relation already observed between any two spatial ideas is applied to a third, whereby is generated a fourth idea, the correlate. An example from ordinary life is when anybody has seen one thing fall and thereafter can imagine another thing doing so ; or when he has observed one piece of paper being unfolded can imagine another piece being treated in a similar manner. But such in essence is the well-known test of Binet, where the experimenter cuts a notch out of a piece of doubly folded paper and the subject has to say how the paper will look when unfolded.

A more elaborate example may be taken from the series

---

[1] *Training School Bull.* 1915, xi.   [2] *Journ. Educ. Psych.* 1916, vii.

[3] *Journ. Psycho-Asthen.* 1916, xx.

[4] *Journ. Exper. Pedag.* 1915, iii.   *Journ. Educ. Psych.* 1918, ix.

[5] *Psychotechnische Zeitschrift*, 1925.

constructed by Cox.[1] Here the subject was given the following instructions and diagram :

> AB and CD are two rods fixed at their centres to upright supports by pivots so as to turn like a pair of

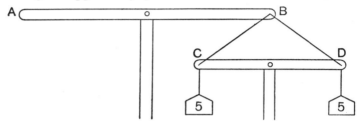

> scales. C and D are then fastened to B by strings exactly as shown. 5-pound weights are hung at C and D. What would you expect to happen
>
> (*a*) if 15 pounds were hung at A ;
> (*b*) if 2 pounds were hung at A ;
> (*c*) if 15 pounds were hung at A and BD were cut ;
> (*d*) if 2 pounds were hung at A and BD were cut ?
>
> And
>
> (*e*) if 15 pounds were hung at A, both weights removed from C and D, what weights would you hang and where so as to make AB balance horizontally ?

All such tests showed correlation with all others that were known to contain *g*.

Not different at bottom from such cases of imagining changes of position is that of voluntary movements. For the first phase in executing one of these would seem to consist always in imagining it (consciously or sub-consciously) But with this we arrive at all bodily action or behaviour—in particular, at all feats of skill, all practical adaptation to the material environment.

So far, we have examined the relation of space as cognized separately, and also as cognized in movements where it combines with that of time. There must further be taken into account the cognizing of the relation of time separately.

[1] Not yet published.

Of this relation the simplest forms are simultaneousness and successiveness. Tests in such respect have been carried out by Carey ; the subjects had to compare different rates of a metronome.[1] There ensued a correlation of ·32 with the teachers' estimate of intelligence, and again the criterion of tetrad differences was satisfied.

There remains one more kind of spatial and temporal relation to be considered. It is of a highly abstract kind, not so much quantitative as qualitative. For instance, the subjects might be required to complete the following analogy :

" Here is to There as Now is to . . . ? "

To answer correctly, the subjects must first educe the relation of Here to There, and then they must apply this relation to Now, so as to educe the correlate Then. Such tests as these always show correlations with all operations known to involve *g* ; they therefore involve it themselves.

On the whole, then, the conclusion from the evidence must be that the cognizing of either spatial or temporal relations—whether these be perceptual or abstract, whether in isolation or combined as movement, and whether taken quantitatively or qualitatively—never fails to involve *g*.

The " Psychological " relation. From the two preceding relations which supply the woof and warp of physical matter, we may turn to that which is peculiarly and exclusively psychical. This arises from the dual constitution of mental processes in that these imply, on the one hand a " subject " that knows, strives, or feels, and on the other an " object " that is known, is striven for, or evokes feeling. The relation between these two may, for want of a better word, be called " objective " (perhaps " objectivating " would be an improvement). It probably characterizes more than half of the concepts ordinarily current. Of course, it enters into all that are of cognitive nature, as intellect, thought, attention, inquiry, comparison, discrimination, evidence, demonstration, discovery, belief, truth, expectation, supposition, communication, interpretation, concealment, news, report,

[1] *Brit. J. Psych.* 1915, viii.

painting, language, poetry, and so forth. Equally, of course, it occurs in all conation, as will, impulse, behaviour, obstinacy, pursuit, business, importance, haste, advice, attack, submission, authority, prison, offer, wealth, etc. And almost always it at least co-operates intimately even with the affective processes as in the cases of temperament, passion, endurance, excitement, gladness, irritation, relief, amusement, interest, hope, fear, wonder, pride, love, resentment, pity, and penitence.

Originally, it would seem, this " psychological " relation together with all that depends on it is apprehended by a person within his own experience ; such apprehension comes under the heading of the first of the noegenetic laws, and has therefore been treated by us already (pp. 164-165).

But by analogy with his own inner experience a person proceeds to generate thoughts—and even percepts—of other persons round about him. The form of such mental generation is laid bare in the mental test of Analogies, as exemplified a few lines above. First a pair of ideas is given, between which a relation has to be cognized ; and then this relation has to be applied to a third idea, so as to generate a fourth one called the correlate. Accordingly, for a person to pass from his own inner experience to any thought or even percept of other persons, the essential process is one of educing correlates, where the relation chiefly involved is of the psychological or objectivating kind.

Now, in what manner, if at all, has this perceiving and thinking of fellow persons by analogy to ourselves been so far submitted to measurement. In its most primitive stage, naturally enough, it still eludes scientific treatment. But at a somewhat more advanced stage, it has been effectively handled by means of various pictorial tests ; for example, Binet's *Interpretation*,[1] Decroly's *Sequence*,[2] and the *Picture Completion* of Healy[3], Fernald, Pintner[4] and Anderson. All of these essentially depend upon constructing ideas

[1] *Année Psych.* 1905, xi.   [2] *Année Psych.* 1914, xx.

[3] Healy and Fernald, *Psych. Mon.* xiii, 2, 1911.

[4] Pintner and Anderson, *Picture Completion Test*, 1917.

To face page 181

of other persons as knowing, striving, and feeling analogously to ourselves. And it is certain enough that such tests—if properly made and used—have correlations with all that are known to contain *g*.

From such perception of what people are doing, there is an easy and continuous passage to the imagination of what they have done before and what they will do next. Much of this, too, enters even into the ordinary pictorial tests. Facing is one of the pictures employed for this purpose in the laboratory of the present writer. Underneath is what one talented student " saw " in it :

" Incident in small lower middle-class Quaker family of early twentieth century. Father is out at work, probably giving a drawing lesson or otherwise trying to add a little money to the family store. The young mother, scrupulously clean and neat in her habits, has come in from the kitchen to receive two unexpected visitors, viz., the old minister and his daughter. They have asked to see the drawings of the elder child, a gifted boy of ten or eleven, who has been sitting at the table painting. When his mother brought in the visitors he got up, pushed his chair back, and at their request fetched the portfolio in which his work was kept. They are surprised and pleased at the talent shown by the boy, who blushes and fidgets with the brush he has picked up. The younger child, a girl of four or five, usually a noisy, boyish little thing, has stopped her chatter for a moment and watches the young lady, by whom she is very much impressed." [1]

Passing on to the cases where the imaginative construction becomes much more complex and extensive, here the development of tests has been regrettably scarce. But at any rate there has been the admirable work of Webb.[2] The following is one of his tests called Problematic Situations. He reported it to have a high correlation with *g*.

" Imagine the following situation : You and a young lady friend have taken a return day trip by steamer

[1] Every item in this description, due to Miss Benham, is really justified by the picture.   [2] *Brit. J. Psych., Mon. Suppl.* 1915, No. III.

from a small coast town A to another small coast town B, on a fine summer day. You spend the day pleasantly at B, but lose the only return boat which starts back at 6.30 p.m. The only train connection from B to A is by a long loop line *via* C thus :

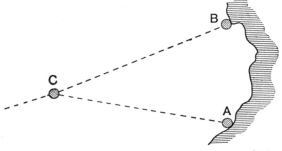

and if you took the train from B to C you would be too late to catch the last train from C to A. You are expected back at A by the young lady's mother, whom you are anxious to propitiate. She is nervous and has a rather strict sense of propriety. The distance by road is about 15 miles. You do not know anybody in B. You are not very well-to-do, but have about £2 in your pocket.

"You are required to state *concisely* (1) what are the alternative plans of procedure which you could adopt under these circumstances, (2) which of these plans you would actually choose, and (3) the reasons for your choice."

Finally, like the spatial and the temporal classes of relation, so too the psychological class admits of being taken in a highly abstract and purely qualitative aspect, as is exemplified in the following Analogy test :

"Virtue is to Reward as Sin is to . . . ?"

All such tests as this certainly have correlation with all in which g plays a part.

Relations of identity, attribution, causality, and constitution. The remaining four classes of relation are to some extent of more ontological than psychological interest. They concern the basic structure of the universe, both mental and material.

The relation of identity—to begin with this—has perhaps originally come to awareness through cognition of the *ego* as persisting identically the same despite all changes in its state of activity. Such a relation could subsequently be applied by analogy to percepts of material bodies, imparting to these also (by way of correlate eduction) a seeming identical persistence.

The attributive relation could originally have come to awareness in the cognition of the *ego* as existing in some state or activity.

The causal relation may perhaps have been first cognized in the *ego's* awareness of its own conation, and then have been transferred by analogy to the percepts of matter.[1]

The constitutive relation is that which any fundaments and relations (of whatever class) bear to the whole which they jointly constitute. Its simplest instance is afforded by the conjunctive class ; for example, when a person understands that two and two " constitute " four. Another example is when three lines are seen to constitute a triangle ; another is when successive words are comprehended as constituting a coherent sentence.[2]

[1] This whole question has been recently illuminated by the admirable exposition of Aveling (the Psychology of Conation and Volition, *Brit. J. Psych.* 1926, xvi. part 4). The following are some relevant passages :

" This notion of conating, striving, tending, inclining, we apply not only to living organisms, but even, by analogy, to inanimate beings as well. . . . I lay it down as an evident principle that all concepts (as, *e.g.* of the ether, force, or God) are in some way derived from immediate experience. . . .

" There remains as the basic fact from which the teleological concept can be derived the immediate experience of one thing conating, or tending towards or away from, another thing, or end, or event. This alone fulfils the requirements. But we, admittedly, have no such experience with regard to animals, or plants, or minerals. The only possible experience of this sort must be—and here, for the moment, I argue hypothetically—an experience of the self as one term in conative relation to another. Theoretically, I submit, such an experience is *necessary* if we are to be able to account for the notion of conation at all, or to apply it in the teleological view of the world. It is also *sufficient*; as can be shown by the application of the principle of correlative-eduction."

[2] *The Nature of Intelligence*, etc., ch. viii.

In mental tests, these four relations are most conspicuously manifested in the very abstract qualitative manner mentioned before (p. 179). The following exemplifies this in the case of the attributive relation :

　　" Stove is to Heat as Knife is to (Sharpness)." [1]

In the test of interpreting pictures the causal relation becomes much more concrete.

Now, on appealing to the work of Hamid,[2] ability to cognize any of these four relations always shows itself—as in the case of the other six—to have undeniable correlation with all ability that is known to involve g ; they must, then, involve it themselves.

G AND THE CURRENT FACULTIES

Sensory Perception. In ascertaining the range of g, we have so far been moving along the lines indicated by the doctrine of " noegenesis " (p. 162). Let us now briefly examine the range of g from the standpoint of the ancient and crude, but still prevalent, doctrine of faculties (ch. iii.). Confining ourselves to those which have been most conspicuous in theory and in controversy, we may take first the faculty of sensory perception.

This is the power which in all ages has been most widely and emphatically regarded as the very antithesis to " intelligence." Nevertheless, our recent analysis has shown it to possess just the same forms of process as are to be found in all the non-perceptual abilities to which the title of intelligence is commonly credited ; notably, it involves the same two eductive processes which we considered on pp. 165-167.[3]

Concordantly with this analytic result, the correlations which we have been meeting in this chapter would seem to demonstrate that sensory perception even of the simplest kind—such as the bare discrimination of tones—does beyond all doubt involve g. And this is all that for the present

---

[1] For many instances, see Hamid, *Brit. J. Psych.* 1925, xvi.
[2] *Loc. cit.* p. 204.　　[3] *The Nature of Intelligence*, etc., ch. xv.

we need to know. As to whether anybody chooses to admit—or still to deny—that sensory perception involves "intelligence," this seems to have become a mere matter of words.

Memory. Another faculty whose unsettled inclusion in the domain of intelligence has caused much trouble is that of remembrance. A special source of confusion about this is the common error of taking it to depend altogether on bare retentivity. Instead, it involves two very active further operations ; the first is that of originally weaving an awareness of one's own experience as something passing in time ; [1] the other is that of subsequently filling up the gaps which have been made in this awareness by the ravages of forgetfulness ; the one operation is constructive, the other reconstructive.

Now, in the original and constructive operation, indeed, the relations and correlates involved are chiefly restricted to those of simple simultaneousness and succession ; and these are so easily grasped that in general they do not give rise to any marked individual differences. But in the reconstruction, on the other hand, the relations and correlates present any degree of variety and difficulty. The first effect of trying to recall an experience is apt to be fragmentary enough ; all the missing portions have to be filled in afterwards in much the same way as occurs with the test of Completion.

From this analysis then, taken together with the results given earlier in the chapter, we can easily predict that *g* will at any rate be found in the so-called " logical " memory of prose and poetry ; since here, not only the original understanding, but also the eventual re-construction, will usually involve relations and correlates in abundance.

And this inference of the presence of *g* is thoroughly corroborated by actual observation. As one example may serve some (unpublished) experiments made by the present writer on 114 children in collaboration with Miss Bones,

[1] *The Nature of Intelligence*, ch. xix.

Miss Buysman, Mr. Fenning, and especially Mr. Dockerill.[1] Among other researches from which similar results can be gathered are those of Simpson,[2] and W. Brown.[3]

A more open question is whether g will also enter into the kind of memory where the influence both of the original understanding and the subsequent re-construction is comparatively slight ; instances would be the memorizing of digits or of letters. In point of fact, the first attempt in this direction seemed to indicate that g was *not* present ; for the correlations with the tests that contained g averaged only $+ \cdot 03$.[4] But somewhat more appreciable correlations were got later on by Burt,[5] W. Brown,[6] Simpson,[7] and Wyatt.[8]

Imagination. We will pass on to the faculty of " imagination." This term can be interpreted in two widely different ways, of which the one consists in the ability to form more or less clear and vivid " images." The importance of these comes chiefly from the view held by many psychologists, that they constitute the essence even of thinking itself. For any such view, however, but little support is afforded here ; the forming of images seems to be just the one ability the correlations of which with those involving g never in any circumstances rises appreciably above zero ! A great deal of evidence for this has been published, including one in 1910 by Rusk ; but the most elaborate and instructive investigation would seem to have been that of Carey.[9]

Turning to imagination in the very different sense of inventiveness or creativeness, this offers a curious contrast to sensory perception ; for whereas the latter has been

---

[1] Here is a typical result:

	Opposites.	Inferences.
Memory - -	$\cdot 44$	$\cdot 30$
Questions - -	$\cdot 49$	$\cdot 33$

The tedrad difference $= \cdot 44 \times \cdot 33 - \cdot 30 \times \cdot 49 = - \cdot 003$, which is insignificant. For a description of these tests, see pp. 201-202.

[2] *Loc. cit.* p. 145.　　　　[3] *Loc. cit.* p. 147.

[4] Krueger and Spearman, *Zeit. f. Psych.* 1906, xliv.

[5] *Brit. J. Psych.* 1909, iii.　　　[6] *Loc. cit.* p. 147.

[7] *Psych. Rev.* 1914, xxi, p. 102.　　[8] *J. Exper. Pedag.* 1914, ii.

[9] *Brit. J. Psych.* 1915, vii.

denied participation in " intelligence " on account of being something quite inferior, this creative power has been denied it on account of being altogether superior (see p. 33).

Analysis, however, would appear to demonstrate that *no such special creative power exists.* All three " noegenetic " processes described at the beginning of this chapter are generative of new mental content and of new knowledge ; and no other cognitive generation can possibly be attained in any other way whatsoever, not though a Shakespeare, a Napoleon, and a Darwin were rolled into one. That which is usually attributed to such a special imaginative or inventive operation can be simply resolved into a correlate eduction combined with a mere reproduction.[1]

From this analytic standpoint, then, we must predict that all creative power—whether or not it be dubbed " imagination "—will at any rate involve *g*. And such an *a priori* conclusion seems to be corroborated by all the experimental evidence. Some results can be quoted here from an investigation devoted to this matter by Hargreaves.[2] Among the tests (applied to 151 children) were the following :

(1) Inkblots. The subjects were shown four of these for a minute each, and had to write down all the objects seen in them.

(2) Free Completion Test. This was the ordinary test of filling up gaps left in passages of prose ; but the special feature was introduced that the gaps could be filled in a large variety of ways at the choice of the subject.

(3) Unfinished Pictures. Four pictures were drawn, in each of which only one or two objects were represented. The subjects were told that " an artist had just begun a picture and had left it unfinished ; you are to write down all the things you would put into the picture if you were going to finish it."

(4) Unfinished Stories. The opening sentence of a story was given, as for example : " A small girl, after

[1] *The Nature of Intelligence,* etc. ch. **xx.**
[2] *Brit. J. Psych. Mon. Suppl.* 1927.

her first visit to the Zoo, had a very strange dream. She dreamt that . . ." Then the subjects were allowed 20 minutes to write their stories.

In all cases there ensued quite an appreciable amount of correlation with all the other tests where g had already been established.

As regards still higher flights of imagination, especially on the esthetic side, the exact verdict of experiment has yet to be awaited. But what we do know on the topic affords no warrant for expecting the nature of such higher flights to be totally unlike that of the lower ones.

Intellect and " intelligence." There remains among the most commonly advocated faculties the pre-eminent one of " intellect." That this—and in its most characteristic form —involves g has already been shown. In fact, this intellect was purposely taken by us as the ability from which the delimitation of the scope of g should begin (pp. 168 ff).

Not impossibly, however, the very fact of this evidence having been obtained experimentally will for some critics seriously lessen its value. There are still writers who believe that the working of the mind inside a psychological laboratory is somehow radically different from what it is outside. Such writers are especially inclined to quote, as rebutting evidence, the fact that the current tests sometimes show only moderate correlations with the children's intelligence as estimated by the teachers on the basis of practical experience. The most striking case of this kind has been the recent admirable work of Wilson, who tried several well known series of tests [1] on 340 children, and found that their correlations with the estimates of teachers came only to values between ·30 and ·40.

Now, without doubt, all such poor correlation between, on the one hand g as measured by the tests, and on the other hand estimates as formed in practical experience, has at any rate need of thorough investigation.

[1] These were the Terman Group, the Otis Group, the National, the Northumberland (Thomson) and the Simplex. See *Brit. J. Psych.* 1924, pp. 44 ff.

To begin with, these respective kinds of ratings—by tests and by estimates—may be compared in respect of " reliability " ; this means the amount of correlation between two or more ratings of the *same* kind. Now, as regards the tests, two independent sets of these produce ratings that are generally found to correlate with one another to an amount in the neighbourhood of ·70 – ·80 (see work just quoted of Wilson). And the present writer does not hesitate to add that, by the means given in the present Appendix, (iv, 6), this amount can and should be raised to at least ·99.

Turning to the estimates, the most important of the older investigations devoted to this point would seem to have been that of Waite.[1] He found that the judgments made about the same schoolboys by different masters resulted in a correlation of only ·47 for a group of 1,405 pairs of judgments, and ·50 for a second group of 2,018 pairs. Even when children were estimated by the very same teacher, but after an interval of nine months, the correlation only rose to ·66. And this surprising unreliability of the estimates was all the more remarkable in view of the fact that the investigator himself had evidently set out with a strong bias in their favour. It was the story of Balaam, but reversed.

Quite recently, a far more elaborate research on the matter has come from Magson.[2] He divided estimates of intelligence into two classes, those based on prolonged acquaintance (a year or more) and those formed at a single interview as is customary in engaging employees. The subjects of the investigation were 149 students at a training college and 727 children at schools. The judges, 35 in number, were chosen from a variety of types, inclining especially towards such as had had much practice at judging in ordinary life. They were of both sexes and included headmasters, headmistresses, training college lecturers, school attendance officers, and several business managers.

[1] *Biometrika*, 1912, viii.

[2] *Brit. J. Psych. Mon. Suppl.* 1926, ix. " How we judge Intelligence."

In the case of impressions formed at a single interview the average correlation between different judges came only to ·52. Even in the case of judgments formed after prolonged acquaintance, it came to no more than ·53. And as for that between, on the one hand judges whose acquaintance had been prolonged, and on the other hand those who had had a single interview, the average correlation came down to ·18 ! Altogether, there seems to be little doubt but that, in respect of reliability at any rate, the tests are far superior to the estimates.

There is, however, yet another and more instructive way of comparing the two different kinds of ratings. It consists in picking out all the individuals respecting whom the tests and the estimates show very large discrepancies, and then submitting these individual cases to an intensive examination. This method has been pursued by the present writer and his students for many years. It has been applied by them to a great number of schools of all classes ; also to such outstanding institutions as the British Civil Service, the College for Military Cadets, and the Naval Staff College. Of similar nature, too, has been a careful study during the last four years of all cases where students at University College of the University of London have displayed a marked discrepancy between their performance at tests given on entrance into the University and their subsequent academic success there.

Throughout, the results have been to indicate that the tests and the estimates aim essentially at one and the same mental power ; but whereas the tests tend to measure this power in a comparatively pure and simple manner, the estimates are profoundly modified by a multitude of other circumstances.

To some extent, these disturbing circumstances are of a more or less accidental character. Usually, for instance, the estimators appear incapable of making due allowance for differences of age ; whereas standardized tests have here no difficulty whatever. Another instance is that teachers are very apt to over-estimate children who have been long at their school and have thoroughly adapted themselves to its particular ways. Turning from the estimates to tests, even the latter indeed are far from blameless in respect of accidental errors. Still, disturbances of this kind are capable of being diminished to any extent by the use of more perfect procedure in testing (see app. iv. 6). Whereas little if any diminution appears possible for most of the accidents that befall the estimates.

Far more serious, however, than all such accidental errors in the procedure of estimating or testing a person's ability are the various influences that may *prevent his ability from being exerted in full degree*. And these influences appear to have an incomparably greater effect on the estimates than on the tests. All normal children, and the great majority even of adults, can easily be induced to try at the tests quite as hard as is likely to improve their performances. But not nearly all children, and still less all adults, will consistently try their utmost in their ordinary work (whether scholastic or industrial) upon which the estimates are mainly based.

For example, one child was found by Abelson to be third out of a class of eleven by the tests, whereas she was only tenth by the teacher's estimate. Closer examination of the case revealed that the child was

> " cunning and underhand, scatterbrained and unstable and incapable of sustained attention. She is frivolous minded and will never take anything seriously. Reprimanding has no effect on her." [1]

This child showed every sign of doing her utmost at the tests, but she certainly could not be expected to do so in the daily routine of the school.

The amount of effort put forth by children at school work is not only influenced by such more or less permanent traits of character, but also by temporary relations to their environment. Thus, a child well known to the present writer

[1] *Thesis*, to be seen in the Library of the University of London.

performed excellently at the tests, but nevertheless earned a distinctly bad report from her teacher. On being transferred to another school, however, she gained the largest number of " firsts " that was on record there. The simple cause of the change appears to have been that the girl got on very badly with her first teacher, and very well with her second.

The influence of effort upon success, and therefore upon estimated intelligence, is by no means confined to schools. It was found to be very strong, for instance, in a comparison made by Dr. White and the present writer between the test scores and the academic success of about a thousand students recently tested at University College of the University of London. Here, cases of students doing very badly at the tests and yet very well academically were so rare as to be practically negligible. But the reverse case, where the students did very well at the tests and yet very badly at their university work, were only too common. Now, the largest portion of these were found to consist in persons whose interest in their academic work was subordinate to their fondness for games or for social gatherings. Another portion of fair size did, indeed, give themselves wholeheartedly to their academic work, but in so doing kept mainly to such study as seemed to them most helpful towards their general culture, rather than that which was most likely to aid them in examinations.

Not always sharply distinguishable from the children or students who do not try hard enough at their scholastic work are those who suffer from inferior health, especially mental. In general, this has little or no appreciable effect on their ability as manifested in tests, but a great effect on their daily work—and, through this, on the estimates formed about them.

The following is a thoroughly typical case taken from the British Naval Cadets. On the present writer sending a representation that one cadet had done much better at the tests than accorded with the estimates received about him, his tutor was kind enough to reply as follows :

" I am not at all surprised to find he was higher than his ordinary place. He is developing fast and I think he has started to go up. . . . Has a very clever brother —one of the most brilliant scholars recently turned out by Rugby."

Here is another instance where a similar representation had been sent to the headmaster of a school of highest standing. The following was the reply:

" Clearly, I think, a temperamental case. X is a bundle of nerves ; twitchy at times, almost jumpy. One day his nerves are in good, or fairly good, condition ; and he gives his teacher satisfaction ; the next day his nerves play tricks with him, and he hates himself and earns disfavour. To do himself justice in study-work, he would need to have entirely sympathetic teachers. A (one of the masters) says that he is one of the most intelligent boys he has under him this term. B (another master) who is suffering from a bad sore throat, says that he is slow-brained and exceptionally stupid. When he first came here X was condemned by C (another master) as wholly unsuitable. C is the sort of personality who would set all X's nerves on edge ! "

As another case may be cited a boy of ten years well known to the present writer who—contrary to the evidence of tests—got quite a bad report from his school. But the following term he rose from the bottom quarter of his class to the top of all, having made 1,600 marks as compared with 1,200 by the second boy. Nothing had changed in the conditions, except that during the vacation he had been cured of " worms ! " These had disturbed his sleep and injured his general nervous state.

Many other cases have been encountered by the present writer that probably are akin to some of the foregoing. For example, a clerk in the Civil Service was found by the tests to be second out of the twelve in his office, but by estimate he was bottom of all. On a second estimate being formed next year he went up from twelfth to fourth.

S.A.M. N

Yet another case may be mentioned, not that it is of frequent occurrence, but only to show to what extremes the errors in estimates can upon occasion go. A lad at one of the best—if not *the* best—of the scholastic institutions in England came out far better by the tests than by the estimates. On a note to this effect being sent to the headmaster, the latter forwarded the following report from one of the masters who had been deputed to examine the case—

"In the matter of Y, there is almost complete unanimity among the masters who are teaching him this term and those who tried to do so last term (including myself). I cannot do better than quote his mathematical master, who sums up concisely in the words : ' Y, intelligent in manner, but not in performance.' This is precisely my own impression. At the first blush he seems very wide-awake in class and prepared to snap out answers at once, but they are almost invariably inaccurate and quite often totally irrelevant. His written work is always of poor quality. His English master—and I am inclined to attach very great importance to work in this subject—describes his performance as being ' the limit.' . . . The general impression among us is, then, that he certainly lacks intelligence, two men go even further."

A week later, however, the headmaster wrote again ; this time as follows :

"Interesting light has been thrown on the case of Y., who came out better in your tests than with us. It has just been discovered that he is deaf and relies largely on lip-reading ! "

GENERAL REVIEW

Universality of *g*. We have been examining the whole range of cognition, in order to see how far the scope of *g* extends. For this purpose, the three noegenetic laws have supplied an adequate map of the mind.

The result has been to indicate that the current tests of ability have had some very large deficiencies. One of these amounts to almost the whole field of self-awareness. Another great domain which proves to have been very inadequately handled is that of psychological ability ; by this is meant the understanding of the thoughts, feelings, and strivings of other people, as also the devising of effective behaviour towards them.

Still, throughout nearly all the immense area into which these tests do appear to have penetrated, the presence of *g* has been decidedly affirmed. Moreover, this *g* given by the tests has shown itself to measure that which the usual estimates of " intelligence " are *trying* to measure— but with indifferent success, owing to a variety of difficulties.

Comparison with other views. Does this result, it may be asked, admit of reduction to the simple formula, that *g* measures the power to grasp relations ? The answer must be in the negative. In the first place, such a formula would suggest only the educing of relations, and would therefore leave out of account the power—at least equally important —of educing correlates. In the second place, it would overlook the possibility, indeed probability, that *g* also enters into the power indicated by the first noegenetic law, that of knowing one's own experience. Yet again, it would unjustifiably imply that *g* constitutes the *whole* of any such power, whereas the evidence indicates that *g* is never more than a *factor* in it.

A far greater clash with our results, however, is presented by the not infrequent assertion that *ordinary life* involves ability of quite a different kind from that which has been submitted to test. Those who enounce this view are for the most part regrettably backward in explaining what different kind of ability they really mean. When they do give some explanation, often nothing more seems to have been intended than that under the conditions of testing some persons may get nervous or " rushed." How far anything of the sort occurs is, naturally, a matter that needs careful investigation. This point will be considered in detail later on (ch. xx.).

Of very different status, however, is an interesting suggestion which we owe to J. Green. The current tests, he says, are those which deal with a " universe common to all " ; whereas 10 per cent. or so of humanity are fortunate enough to be carried :

> " into universes of activity as varied as they are attractive, and their minds grow up with the parts they play. They are constantly coming up against new situations which call for new integrations which mean, not so much new knowledge, as new selves, and new power. . . The difficulty of intelligence tests after fourteen (years of age) comes from the diversity of universes, to the calls of which intelligence is applied." [1]

But such a suggestion, however plausible it might have been formerly, would seem to have now been dissipated by means of the ultimate analysis which has been at our disposal in the present chapter. From this analysis it would seem that *no man ever enters into a new universe.* Both the original material of cognition (experience), as also the forms in which alone it can be elaborated (eduction of relations and of correlates), appear to remain eternally fixed. The most that can happen, then, with this " exceptional 10 per cent. of humanity " is that they may pursue the elaboration to a higher degree of fineness and complexity. And this affects *g* in respect only of amount ; not of existence, or even of nature.

Moreover, the fact of *g* penetrating to the " big " walks of life is beginning to be supported by empirical evidence also. In not one of the cases where eminent men have been said to break down at the tests, does any good evidence appear to have been brought to show that they were tested properly. So far as the experience of the present writer goes, the most eminent man measured by him did, in point of fact, easily surpass everyone else that was tried. Moreover, an important indication has been furnished by Terman, that the children who do the tests extraordinarily well have had an extraordinarily high proportion of " big " fathers and grandfathers ; these are reported to have filled " positions of honour, trust, and responsibility," such as those of senators, mayors, bank presidents, bishops, managers of large factories, and so forth.[1]

Obviously, however, *g alone* would never make a big man of any sort. For it measures only the cognitive aspect of mental activity, and therefore abstracts from the dominant influence of the affective and above all the conative aspects (see ch. xx.).

Theorem of indifference of indicator. A corollary—more practical than theoretical—to be derived from the universality of *g* is what may be called the theorem of the indifference of the indicator. This means that, for the purpose of indicating the amount of *g* possessed by a person, any test will do just as well as any other, provided only that its correlation with *g* is equally high. With this proviso, the most ridiculous " stunts " will measure the self-same *g* as will the highest exploits of logic or flights of imagination.

Another consequence of the indifference of the indicator consists in the significance that should be attached to personal estimates of " intelligence " made by teachers and others. However unlike may be the kinds of observation from which these estimates may have been derived, still in so far as they have a sufficiently broad basis to make the influence of *g* dominate over that of the *s*'s, they will tend to measure precisely the same thing.

And here, it should be noticed, we come at last upon the secret why all the current tests of " general intelligence " show high correlation with one another, as also with *g* itself. The reason lies, not in the theories inspiring these tests (which theories have been most confused), nor in any

[1] *Genetic Studies of Genius*, 1925, ch. i.

uniformity of construction (for this has often been wildly heterogeneous), but wholly and solely in the above shown "indifference of the indicator."   Indeed, were it worth while, tests could be constructed which had the most grotesque appearance, and yet after all would correlate quite well with all the others.

CHAPTER XII

AMOUNT OF *G* IN DIFFERENT KINDS OF EDUCTION

INFLUENCES OF DIFFERENCES IN RELATIONS AND FUNDAMENTS

Present problem. Having ascertained which abilities involve *g*, our next step is to find out the *degree* that they involve it or are " weighted " with it (p. 75). At times, this problem takes two somewhat divergent directions, the theoretical and the practical. The former aims at throwing light on the intrinsic nature of the two factors. The latter has the less ambitious purpose of constructing tests or estimates more effectively. That there is still room for such practical improvement is found, for example, by Jaederholm, who concludes a recent admirable publication by saying that :

" Several kinds of tests very much used in intelligence testing . . . do not show any correlations of the same magnitude (as the others) . . . and should preferably not be used in the measurement of intelligence." [1]

The best means for measuring the amount of g in any ability, say a, consists simply in the correlation between the two, or, as it may be symbolized, r_{ga} (see app. pp. xvi-xvii). Even less than this will suffice when we are not seeking the absolute amount of g in any ability, but only want to compare this amount with that present in some other ability. Such a merely relative valuation can be obtained by comparing together the respective correlations which the two have with *any further* ability, provided only that this latter has no " overlap " (pp. 150 ff.) with either of the others.

In a preliminary rough way, our present problem can evidently be solved by information very similar to that which served in the previous chapter. But eventually, the present problem needs a much more intensive study. In the values observed, there will have to be a careful separation of what is due to the intrinsic nature of the abilities from what must be regarded as of extrinsic and adventitious origin.

Relations of likeness, of evidence, and of mixed kinds. We will begin by accepting provisionally the experimental results at their face values. And first we will look in this way at the influences that appear to be exerted by differences in the class of relations concerned.

The class of these which at present dominates mental testing is, unquestionably, that of *likeness*. As representative of this class may be taken the test of Opposites, or the closely allied Synonyms (p. 173). These seem not only to have been employed most often, but also to have in general yielded the highest correlations.

Much less frequent has been the usage of the relation of *evidence*. But H. A. Peterson showed that this also can give excellent results ; for his Reasoning has a correlation with g of nearly ·80. So, too, the Reasoning of Burt in its original oral form and as administered by its author himself

---

[1] *Scandinavian Scientific Review*, 1923, ii. p. 81.

proved to be correlated with teachers' estimates to the large amount of ·70 (easily surpassing the Binet-Simon series, which was tried at the same time).[1] More recently, Burt has joined it together with four others, the well-known Opposites, the Analogies (invented by himself),[2] Mixed Sentences,[3] and Completion (p. 185) into a series called the National Institute Group Test. On this series being tried out by Dobson, the Reasoning seemed to be the weakest of the five ; but subsequently with McCrae it appeared to be the best, its correlation with *g* rising this time to ·86.[4]

The preceding investigations, however, had not aimed at the same problem as occupies us now ; and the results—for various reasons which we shall see later on—are not very conclusive for our special purpose. This lack induced the present writer, in collaboration with Mr. Dockerill and others,[5] to carry out some experiments with the express intention of comparing different relations with one another. To 114 children, about 12-13 years of age, were applied eleven tests of the following description. Three were directed to bring into play the relation of likeness. Two did the same for that of evidence. Five others had a mixed character, but especially avoided the relations of conjunction, of space, and of time. The remaining test was one of memory. The correlations with *g* are given on the following page. Examples of each kind are added in a footnote.

From this list, the main impression one gets is that the differences of kind of relation have a surprisingly small effect on the amount of correlation with *g*.

Relations of conjunction, space, and time. Turning to the three classes of relation that had been specially omitted from the preceding investigation, these are distinguished by their prominence in mathematics. That of conjunction, as mentioned before, supplies the basis of arithmetic. Usually it

---

[1] *Mental and Scholastic Tests*, 1921. [2] *Journ. Exper. Pedag.* 1911.

[3] The words of a sentence are mixed randomly, and the subject has to re-arrange them in proper order. [4] *Loc. cit.* p. 163.

[5] Especially Miss Buysman, Miss Bones, Mr. Fennings, and Mrs. Spittle.

appears to have yielded somewhat smaller correlations than have the other relations which we have been considering. Still when the test is suitably constructed, especially in the form of a problem rather than as dependent on memorized formulas, its inferiority has not been excessive. In the results quoted previously from Otis, for instance, Arithmetical Problems came indeed only sixth out of the ten tests, but still the difference, even from the best test, was remarkably small (the correlation of the former with g being ·84, that of the latter ·88).

Nature of Test.	Correlations with g (corrected for "attenuation," see App. I.)
1. Relation of Likeness :	
(a) Opposites - - - - -	·89
(b) Synonyms [1] - - - - -	·85
(c) Classification [2] - - - -	·77
2. Relation of Evidence :	
(a) Inferences [3] - - - - -	·74
(b) Likelihood [4] - - - - -	·92
3. Mixed relations :	
(a) Analogies - - - - -	·79
(b) Completion of sentences - - -	·86
(c) Completion of paras. (written) [5] -	·78
(d) Questions [6] - - - - -	·80
(e) Comprehension of paras. (written) -	·94
4. Memory [7] - - - - - -	·79

[1] The following is an example : " ' Artful ' means most nearly the same as what ?   Wise ?   Skilful ?   Cunning ?   Clever ? "

[2] The subject had to say which of four given words had a meaning most unlike the rest, as for instance, " Fast.   Hurried.   Galloping.   Large."

[3] An example : " If I can run faster than Tom, and the same as Harry, but slower than Dick, who will win the race, Tom, Harry, or I ? "

[4] The subjects had to decide whether some given statements were quite certain, only likely, very unlikely, or downright absurd.

[5] Except the two tests here marked as " written," all were given orally.

[6] Substantially similar to 3 (b), but arranged in the form of answering questions instead of completing passages.

[7] A short story was read to the subjects, who immediately afterwards had to recall its substance.

From the same work of Otis may also be instanced the relation of space, for it is presented by the Geometric test (see p. 177 of last chapter). This lags still further behind, but again only by an insignificant amount (the correlation with g being ·79). When this test was used originally by Hart with the present writer, it took the third place out of fourteen, having a correlation of ·69 with g. When afterwards used by Abelson, it occupied in general a moderately high position.

As regards the relation of time, the only instance available seems to be that supplied by Carey, where the correlation with g came to no more than ·32 [1] ; whereas Opposites here showed one of ·71. Here at last, then, we do encounter a large difference.

The psychological relations. There is another class of relations about which something must be said, both because of its very inadequate representation in the " mixed " relations quoted above, as also on account of its pre-eminent importance for daily life ; this is what we have called the "psychological" class (ch. xi. pp. 179-192). How far does the power of dealing with this class depend on the universal factor ; or, conversely, how far does it involve a specific one ?

To answer this great question the evidence is deplorably meagre. In fact, it appears to be almost confined to a single investigation, the very notable one of Webb (*loc. cit.* p, 181). For his five tests, he found the following correlations with g :

Reasoning - - - - - - -	·94
Comparison - - - - - -	·85
Problematic situations (psychological) - -	·67
Definitions - - - - - - -	·42
Opposites - - - - - - -	·37

That is to say, the psychological relations present no exceptional feature, but instead take up a medium position. On the whole, from this rough survey, the factor g would not appear to characterize any relation in particular. It enters about equally into mental processes involving relations of

[1] The test consisted in discriminating slightly different rates of a metronome.

any kind. The only seeming exception has been the low degree in which it entered into the perceiving of the relation of time.

Need of considering each process separately. All the researches quoted so far, however, suffer from a weakness for our purpose ; they all throw together as a single test what really comprises several different operations. For instance, what is called the test of Opposites consists not in finding any single opposite, but a whole series of them. A useful corrective supplement to all the preceding work, then, may be had from that of another sort which has recently been executed by Hamid.[1] This, too, was based upon mental tests, but each operation that involved a separate response was treated separately.

Such separate operations—to the number of 757—were studied in the responses of 373 adults and children specially selected as being " bright " " medium," or " dull." The total number of responses thus available for the research came to 48,842.[2] The classifying of the subjects into " bright," etc., was based, either upon estimates formed by the teachers, or upon positions at school, or else upon total scores in the entire test-series employed. These three bases of classification would seem, in view of what has been proved above, to be equally permissible for our present purpose ; and in point of fact, all three led throughout to similar results.

The general procedure was to compare the average score of the " bright " with that of the " dull " for each of the operations, and then to pick out for closer scrutiny a certain number (126) where the difference between the bright and the dull was greatest, as also a similar number where the difference was least. The former operations were regarded as " good " tests, the latter as " bad " ones.

In the present investigation regard was paid, not only to the influence arising out of different relations, but also to

[1] *Brit. J. Psych.* 1925, xvi.

[2] As regards arriving at this number, it must be remembered that to some extent the different subjects did different tests.

that from different fundaments entering into relation ; note
was taken, too, of the difference shown between the educing
of relations and that of correlates (see pp. 165-167).

Of the two last named processes—to consider this point
first—neither was found to be markedly superior to the
other. But the educing of correlates occurred much more
frequently than that of relations, and therefore would seem
to be, for testing purposes at any rate, the more important.
The actual frequencies were as follows :

	1st Group of Subjects.		2nd Group of Subjects.	
	Good Tests.	Bad Tests.	Good Tests.	Bad Tests.
Eduction of relations -	4	8	8	10
Eduction of correlates -	21	29	32	19

In respect of the different fundaments, here no general
effect was noticeable. The author writes as follows :

" The nature of the fundaments themselves, apart
from their complexity, abstractness, and novelty does
not seem to make any marked difference in the diag-
nostic value of intelligence tests."

In respect of the different relations, there was found—in
seeming conflict with the results on p. 202—a distinct advantage for those of likeness. The following were the
frequencies :

	1st Group.		2nd Group.	
	Good	Bad	Good	Bad
Similarity and opposition - -	24	8	20	6
Quantity and space - - -	5	8	2	1
Psychological - - - -	9	7	5	9
Attributive - - - -	26	22	7	7
Causal - - - - -	16	13	2	4
Constitutive - - - -	14	9	4	5
Miscellaneous - - - -	18	20	0	8

Upon these figures Hamid makes the following comments :

" From the above results it appears that among the different classes of relations, those of Similarity and Opposition are the most effective for purposes of testing ability or intelligence."

Such a discrepancy from the results on page 202 recalls the need already mentioned, that such results cannot be naïvely accepted at their face values, but should be carefully studied. In particular, search should be made for any disturbances of what we have called an extrinsic character. To these we now will turn.

INFLUENCES OF EXTRINSIC KIND

Disturbance from method of sampling. A portion of these extrinsic influences derives from the selection of persons for investigation ; the " subjects."

In this, there are a number of influences that may be very harmful for some purposes, but nevertheless do not seriously affect the particular point that we are considering at present. One such influence is the error of sampling which caused us so much trouble in earlier chapters. Another is the heterogeneity introduced by neglecting differences of age, sex, etc. These, although they may introduce grave disturbances when the tetrad equation is at issue, do not often mislead about the comparative amounts of g in different operations.

Disturbance from accidents of procedure. Much graver for our present purposes would seem to be the disturbance caused by accidents in the procedure of measuring. In one mental operation, for example, a subject may be helped by having to deal with a difficult term recently studied by him at some cross-word competition ; in another operation, he may be distracted by breaking the point of his pencil. Again, out of two possible ways for solving a problem, sheer luck may decide whether he lights upon the easier one. Yet again, he may either puzzle himself for a long time over a difficulty, or else he may draw his bow at a venture ; the relative advantages of these two behaviours will depend upon whether the experimenter happens to put a heavy penalty upon errors.

A specially important case falling into this category occurs when a test is either too hard for the testees or too easy. If the former, then any right answers will tend to be mere flukes ; if the latter, any wrong answers that occur will only consist of mere accidental slips.[1] In neither event is the test *critical*.

Now, in the results obtained by the present writer with Mr. Dockerill and others, the effect of such random accidents was—by a statistical device [2]—eliminated. Whereas the results given by Hamid did not admit of any such elimination. Hence, the superiority shown in his case by the relation of likeness might quite possibly have been due to tests of this relation being less affected, on the whole, by some of these accidental disturbances.[3]

Variations in the " breadth " of an ability. More serious still would seem to be the following trouble. In speaking of an ability or a test, we usually mean to comprise a whole class of more or less similar performances. But we can make each class as broad or as narrow as we please. For instance, we can throw together as a single class every kind of judgment, logical, practical, and esthetic (see ch. v. p. 64). Or instead, we can confine one class to " logical," another to " practical," and so on. But the broader we make a class (other things equal), the larger, in general, become its correlations.[4]

In comparing one relation with another, then, due account

[1] A very valuable investigation of such irregularities has been supplied by Courtis, *Why Children Succeed*, 1925, ch. vii.

[2] The correction for " attenuation," see appendix, p. i.

[3] The validity of this suspicion can at once be verified. We can see how large the correlations given on page 202 were *before* being corrected for attenuation. Hereupon, those involving the relation of likeness do actually become much superior to the others. The seeming discrepancy is in this way explained.

[4] See " Correlations of Sums and Differences," present writer, *Brit. J. Psych.* 1913, v.

must be taken of any inequality of breadth involved. The estimation of such inequality seems, indeed, only feasible in an extremely general manner. But even so, it appears to be effective in smoothing out the experimental results we have been examining.

For instance, this standpoint would at once explain the success of the relation of evidence in the work of Peterson and that of Burt; for both introduced variety, and therefore breadth, into their tests. Again, it would make intelligible the somewhat lower position of the spatial and the conjunctive relations; for the tests of these have certainly tended to be somewhat uniform. And still more striking would be the explanation of the much lower correlation with g exhibited by the relation of time; for nothing could be much more monotonous than simply comparing different rates of a metronome.

Conclusions to be drawn. Taking everything into consideration, the several kinds of relation are certainly not very disparate in respect of the degree that they make calls upon g. There is, indeed, nothing to indicate that—when properly compared—they are even unequal at all. The same may be said to some extent even as regards the fundaments (see p. 165).

This conclusion has particular importance in view of the still prevalent tendency to regard " intelligence " as peculiarly, or even solely, appertaining to those operations which involve the relation of evidence (in particular, " reasoning "). Such a doctrine is expressed, for instance, in a recent valuable paper by A. Wolf.[1] Now, possibly there may be found adequate grounds for restricting the title of "intelligence" to this comparatively small domain; but at any rate there would seem to be no justification whatever for thus restricting the scope of g.

Another current tendency here brought into question is the advocating of some special compartment or level of ability for mental operations dealing with *mechanics*. For

[1] *Proc. Aristot. Soc.* 1925, suppl. vol. v.

these essentially involve the relations of space ; and any claim that the latter constitute such a separate compartment finds no warrant in the facts elicited here. The probable origin of such a doctrine will appear in the following chapter.

ABSTRACTION, LANGUAGE, AND DEGREE OF DIFFICULTY

Current procedure of investigation. Having thus failed to discover that the saturation with *g* is markedly affected by any differences in the fields of cognition, let us see whether it is more influenced by the manner in which any such fields may be developed. And here we come across a view which is being advocated with continually increasing emphasis ; it is that the intelligence measured by the customary tests is essentially characterized, not by the nature of the content cognized, but rather by the fact that this content—whatever it may be—is cognized *abstractly*. In such fashion, the whirligig of time completes its cycle. The modern mental tester—little though he may sometimes be aware of it—is in fact joining hands with the medieval schoolman.

Most conspicuous here has been the fine work of Stockton. In general, he holds that intelligence

" is a method of active solution of problems through focus upon the possibilities of the situation, pause, selection of significant elements, and the recognition of relationships between the selected elements. But what are the elements between which relationships are found ? They may be perceived between *material things, images* of things, or *symbols* of things." [1]

In this way, he divides the process of relation-finding into three classes, according as the basis consists of material things, images, or symbols (*i.e.* words). These classes, he goes on to suggest, constitute a rising series of levels. In particular, the two lower classes, thrown together by him as " perceptual," are contrasted with the class which he calls

[1] *Psych. Mon.* 1921, xxx. whole No. 137.

symbolic, verbal, or abstract ; the three latter terms are taken by him as almost synonymous.

Now, in order to investigate this contrast, he devised an experimental procedure of the following kind. Children, to the number of 222 and from grades iv. to viii, were submitted to the Binet-Stanford test series, which served as a standard of reference ; they were then given nine perceptual tests and eleven symbolic or verbal ones. The correlations with the standard proved to be as follows :

PERCEPTUAL TESTS.			ABSTRACT TESTS.		
Picture completion	-	·42	Arithmetic reasoning	-	·63
Series completion	-	·46	Written directions	-	·58
Comparison	-	·40	Information	-	·68
Symbol digit	-	·45	Synonym-Antonym	-	·65
Form combination	-	·34	Practical judgment	-	·65
Copying design	-	·30	Analogies -	-	·68
Pictorial sequence	-	·43	Arithmetic (elements) -		·59
Pictorial identities	-	·46	Vocabulary -	-	·75
Recognitive memory	-	·29	Sentence completion	-	·68
			Mixed-up sentences	-	·53
			Logical selection -	-	·60
Pooled perceptual -	-	·60	*Pooled abstract*	-	·60

Another similar experiment was made, but with children of younger age (135 of them, grades ii. and iii.). To these were given, besides the standard series, five perceptual and three abstract tests. There ensued the following correlations with the standard :

PERCEPTUAL TESTS.			ABSTRACT TESTS.		
Symbol digit	-	·39	Practical judgment	-	·62
Picture completion	-	·46	Opposites -	-	·56
Maze -	-	·39	Vocabulary -	-	·72
Pictorial sequence	-	·47			
Pictorial identities	-	·39			
Pooled perceptual -	-	·58	*Pooled abstract*	-	·72

Once more, then, the abstract tests manifest a striking superiority.

In the same year was also published another work of kindred tendency ; it was by Herring.[1] But this time

---

[1] *Journ. Educ. Psych.* 1921, xii.

the abstract and the symbolic (verbal) manners of thinking, instead of being identified, were distinguished from one another. The experimental procedure included, as before, the establishment of a standard of reference ; this was now formed of various tests, including both the Binet-Stanford series and some of the group kind. Then many further tests were arranged in two scales ; the one was according to whether each test was deemed abstract or concrete ; the other was according to whether it was verbal or non-verbal. In this way, the Army Beta Maze test was estimated to be very concrete and very non-verbal. The Beta Cube-counting test was distinctly abstract, although very non-verbal. Arithmetic problems were very abstract The Stanford-Binet series was, on the whole, rather abstract than concrete, and verbal than non-verbal. The extreme of verbality was attained by the Thorndike Reading Alpha 2. That of abstractness, by the Analogies of the National Intelligence tests. As for the standard, this lay just about half-way between either extreme.

The subjects, 118 in number, came from grades iv. to vii. To avoid heterogeneity of age, the results for 10, 11 and 12 years were calculated separately, and then averaged together. The results were grouped on two scales, that of abstractness and that of verbality.

Scale of Abstractness.	Correlations.	Scale of Verbality.	Correlations.
Concrete - -	·47	Non-verbal - -	·49
Medium - -	·58	Medium - -	·58
Abstract - -	·84	Verbal - -	·88

From all this the author concludes that the leading part in intelligence is played by the ability to handle, not merely abstract ideas, but above all symbols.

" Total human nature and the mutual demands of human beings have become such that intelligence . . . comprises largely the ability to deal effectively with

> situations involving the use of language and of mathematical symbols, both subjective and conventional. It is the hod-carriers who typically deal with concrete situations. The master architect . . . reaches by way of many and abstract processes involving complex symbolisms."

On proceeding to examine this experimental procedure more closely, however, there appears little to indicate any regard for what we have above been calling the extrinsic influences upon the correlation. In particular, no attempt seems to have been made to arrange that the two sets of tests, perceptual on the one hand and abstract or verbal on the other, should be in all other respects fairly matched. Indeed, the only information that we do get points rather in the opposite direction. For the perceptual tests are said to have been easier than the others. May they not have been *too* easy ? Consider in this reference what has been found on page 207.

Procedure by matching. Let us then turn to another investigation where such influences did receive very careful regard. This was due to Davey.[1] Here 243 children were given four well known abstract and verbal tests, namely, Analogies, Completion, Classification, and Questions. But with each of these was matched another test having in every possible way the same form, but this time being pictorial instead of abstract and verbal.

In order to compare the relative amounts of g in these abstract and pictorial tests, *two* standards were supplied ; of these themselves the one was abstract and the other pictorial. The abstract standard consisted of a pair of further tests called Inferences and Likelihood (for their description see p. 202 of this chapter). For the pictorial standard, there was a pair of tests called Sequence and Enumeration (for a description of these four tests, reference must be made to the original paper).

[1] *Brit. J. Psychol.* 1926, xvii.

The remarkable result of these experiments was to show that the respective correlations of the abstract and the pictorial tests were *just about equal,* and this regardless of which standard was used. The following are the actual correlations :

	Abstract Standard.	Pictorial Standard.
Abstract tests (av.) -	·34	·34
Pictorial tests (av.) -	·32	·31

Thus, on the tests abstract and pictorial being scientifically matched, so as to eliminate all disturbing influences (even differences in breadth of ability), the great advantage which the current procedure seemed to demonstrate for the abstract over the pictorial tests now wholly disappears.

Effect of degree of difficulty. Much in the preceding considerations has suggested the need for taking more notice of variations in degree and kind of difficulty. And this was, in fact, done in the already quoted investigation of Hamid. Here, four kinds of difficulty were selected for study ; the frequencies were noted of good and bad tests for great, medium, and smaller degrees of difficulty of each kind. The results are shown on the following page.

Evidently, the rule for all four kinds of difficulty—including abstractness—is that the degree should not be extreme either way, but medium (see p. 207). This, however, is no essential property in a test, but only the accident of appropriateness to the subjects tested. With less capable subjects, the advantage would perhaps shift round from the medium to the smaller degrees of difficulty ; with more capable subjects, conversely, the advantage would go over to the greater degrees.

In this way, the results of Stockton and Herring would appear to be explained, but at the same time to be shown not to touch the point really at issue. If they had gone on to still higher degrees of abstractness, the correlations would probably not have still further increased, but instead would have decreased.

Kind of Difficulty.	Degree in which it is present.	Frequencies.	
		Good Tests.	Bad Tests.
Fineness of distinction.	Great [1]	31	83
	Medium	52	8
	Small	13	15
Novelty of process.	Great [2]	4	20
	Medium	55	19
	Small	18	17
Complexity of process.	Great [3]	10	27
	Medium	60	30
	Small	9	20
Abstractness.	Great [4]	14	50
	Medium	56	20
	Small	21	21

Abstraction as climax of eduction. From all these results it would appear that the prevalent theories as to the part which abstraction and language play in ability and in mental testing have at least some need of revision. Let us return for a moment to the age-long problem as to how abstraction is originated.

Some new light on the matter seems to have been shed by the recent research of Strasheim.[5] His subjects were

[1] Example of great fineness : "Loss is to Sorrow as Gain is to Profit ? Advantage ? Mirth ? *Enjoyment ?*"

[2] Example of great novelty : "What must a deaf man have in order to understand people at all ? Arms ? Patience ? *Sight ?*"

[3] Example of great complexity : "Some people seem to find . . . even in achieving small things, others . . . in great ones."

[4] Example of great abstractness : "Underline the correct word out of the three given in each bracket. 'We are not, strictly speaking, responsible for the future, but (greatly, partially, *only*) for the use we make of the (*present*, occasion, past).'"

[5] *Educational Psychol. Monogr.*, 1926.

children of about equal standing at school, but half of them were comparatively young and therefore " bright," whilst the other half contrariwise were old and " dull." Of his experiments, the larger portion consisted of putting these subjects into some situation, letting them learn to solve it, and then seeing how well they could " adapt " themselves to another one somewhat different. Among the kinds of situation thus examined by him, we will select that of having to thread a maze ; for this operation is of peculiar interest to us, having above been singled out as the extreme case of concreteness and non-verbality.

In the first of Strasheim's situations, a large number of mazes had to be threaded which, although very unlike in general appearance, nevertheless all followed the same simple principle. First of all, there was one path going straight ahead, and several others turning to the right ; the correct route was to follow the straight path to its end. When this situation could be solved by the subject readily, he went on to the second ; this again employed numerous mazes, but now some paths to the left were introduced ; the correct route was, first to the left, and then straight on to the end. In the third situation, the first of the previously introduced paths to the left was furnished with some further paths turning out of it to the right ; the whole correct route was, first to the left, then first to the right, and then on to the end. In the fourth situation, the correct route became, first left, first right, first left, and then straight on. None of the later situations, it will be noticed, ever contradict the earlier ones, but only bring in some additional complication.

As result of these experiments, it was found that all the situations could be solved *either with or without* the power of formulating the rule verbally and therefore developing it from the perceptual to the abstract stage. Still, the abstracting of the rule, when achieved, was discovered to possess important characteristics. It rendered the operation far less hesitating and liable to error. It greatly facilitated transfer of ability from the simpler situations to the more complicated ones. It was much more often accomplished by the young-bright subjects than by the old-dull. It was found increasingly difficult as the number of relations involved became more numerous. It was only possible when the relations were cognized *very clearly*.

The explanation of the whole matter, then, seems to be that all cognitive growth—whether by eduction of relations or by that of correlates—consists in a progressive clarification ; the mental content emerges out of a state of utter indistinguishability and ascends into ever increasing distinguishability. So soon as any item of mental content has become sufficiently clear and distinguishable, then and then only it admits of being abstracted ; that is to say, it can be " intended " apart from its context. And when this happens, it can be thought of separately and given a name. This clarification may be likened to the ripening of a fruit ; abstraction, to its consequent eventual falling from the stalk. Now, tests of *g* should not be limited to ascertaining whether the fruit has already fallen ; they should measure instead the degree of ripeness at whatever stage is most appropriate to the ability of the persons tested.

VARIOUS OTHER INFLUENCES

Sensory and motor apparatus. Akin to the preceding problem of perception—so much so as often to be confused with it—is that of bare sensation. How far does *g* enter into such low-level abilities as that of merely discriminating between one sensation and another ?

At any rate, a new influence comes into play, that of the sensory apparatus (including the receptors, neural tracts, and cerebral areas). These were also required to function, no doubt, in the preceding perceptual operations ; but not usually in a way that made any difference between different individuals. If a person's sight was altogether defective, he was unquestionably handicapped or even crippled. But so long as it was nearly normal, he needed no more ; supernormal acuity would have afforded him little or no advantage.

Turning, then, to the experimental results for this sensory discrimination, the chief seem to be : (*a*) that even here *g* does play some part ; but (*b*) that this part is comparatively small. Such smallness may perhaps be partly explicable by the narrow breadth of the operations involved (see p. 207). The deciding many times in succession which of two tones is the higher, or which of two lines is the longer, can for monotony rival any test whatever.

But a further explanation can be found in that these operations bring largely into use the peripheral parts of the nervous system, and even non-neural structures. These, by universal consent, do not subserve mental processes directly, but only influence them indirectly.

In this manner can be explained another striking experimental result, the exceptionally low correlations shown by all the motor abilities. For here again, the dominant part is played by peripheral engines. The comparatively small demands made upon the general energy may be inferred from the fact that many skilful motor actions can be performed simultaneously. A rider, for example, can quite well employ skilfully all four limbs—indeed, the trunk and head too—at one and the same time, although he could never carry on four lines of thought (even though related to the same topic).

Class of person under consideration. Another important influence upon the saturation of an ability with *g* appears to be the class of person at issue.

The most drastic example of this is supplied by a comparison between normal children and those who are mentally defective. Evidence is supplied by the work of Abelson, as here the same tests were applied by the same experimenter to both classes. The correlations obtained for the two respectively were as follows : [1]

[1] *Loc. cit.* pp. 174 and 191.

78 NORMAL CHILDREN (Corrected for Attenuation).

	1	2	3	4	5	6	7	8	9	10	11	12
1. Opposites - -	—	75	78	71	62	64	72	78	57	40	46	33
2. Observation - -	75	—	72	58	60	58	67	56	58	56	52	29
3. Absurdities - -	78	72	—	53	41	44	79	68	41	46	34	29
4. Memory sentences -	71	58	53	—	54	61	54	37	54	55	19	43
5. Crossing o's - -	62	60	41	54	—	73	48	54	38	36	52	35
6. Geometrical figs. -	64	58	44	61	73	—	45	48	30	42	48	35
7. Discrim. length -	72	67	79	54	48	45	—	56	49	30	31	06
8. Crossing patterns -	78	56	68	37	54	48	56	—	30	21	27	18
9. Memory form - -	57	58	41	54	38	30	49	30	—	24	31	29
10. Tapping - - -	40	56	46	55	36	42	30	21	24	—	29	18
11. Strength of grip -	46	52	34	19	52	48	31	27	31	29	—	28
12. Interpret. pictures -	33	29	29	43	35	35	06	18	29	18	28	—

Mean = 0·466.

22 DEFECTIVE CHILDREN (Corrected for Attenuation).

	1	2	3	4	5	6	7	8	9	10	11	12
1. Absurdities - -	—	1·0	1·0	98	97	1·0	1·0	1·0	98	94	94	79
2. Opposites - -	1·0	—	97	95	87	91	85	76	85	87	70	72
3. Crossing patterns -	1·0	97	—	91	80	88	68	92	74	78	76	67
4. Crossing o's - -	98	95	91	—	85	77	84	67	76	81	73	55
5. Memory sentences -	97	87	80	85	—	73	90	68	88	65	78	68
6. Observation - -	1·0	91	88	77	73	—	76	83	71	86	59	65
7. Memory form - -	1·0	85	68	84	90	76	—	65	67	70	77	75
8. Interpret. pictures -	1·0	76	92	67	68	83	65	—	74	80	80	59
9. Geometrical figs. -	98	85	74	76	88	71	67	74	—	65	60	62
10. Discrim. length -	94	87	78	81	65	86	70	80	65	—	51	45
11. Tapping - - -	94	70	76	73	78	59	77	80	60	51	—	61
12. Strength of grip -	79	72	67	55	68	65	75	59	62	45	61	—

Mean = 0·782.

All round, obviously, the correlations are much smaller in the case of the normal children. This indicates that with these the influence of the energy has gone down and that of the engines has correspondingly gone up.

Compare, next, young children with older ones. Here may be quoted once more the work of Burt. Applying his test of reasoning to numerous children of different ages, he obtained the following correlations with the estimates of the teachers; in general, the older children show smaller amounts:

Ages - -	10-11	11-12	12-13	13-14
Correlations -	78	81	64	59

No less marked is this tendency on comparing children with adults. As exemplifying this may be taken the correlations obtained by Otis[1] and Carothers[2] respectively for what appear to have been similar tests in each case :

Tests.	Correlations with *g*.	
	Otis, Grades IV-VIII.	Carothers, Students.
Analogies - -	·84	·71
Completion - -	·88	·53
Directions - -	·86	·45
Digits, memory -	·41	·22

Similarly, Stead has found that even motor abilities have considerable correlations with tests of *g* up to about 11-12 years of age, but not later.[3]

Now, all the changes we have been considering follow a general rule. The correlations always become smaller— showing the influence of *g* on any ability to grow less—in just the classes of person which, on the whole, possess this *g* more abundantly. The rule is, then, that the more " energy " a person has available already, the less advantage accrues to his ability from further increments of it. But this is analogous to a well known property of engines in general. Suppose that a ship at moderate expenditure of coal goes 15 knots an hour. By additional coal the rate can readily be increased another five knots. But by doubling the addition of coal, the additional knots will certainly not be anything like doubled also. This relation may be observed not only in engines, but also widely elsewhere. In the science of economics, for example, it is expressed in the familiar law of diminishing returns. A moderate amount of capital spent on a given piece of land will produce a certain return ; but on adding further doses of capital, the return will not increase proportionately.

[1] *J. Educ. Psych.* 1918, ix.   [2] *Archives of Psychol.* 1921, No. 46.
[3] *Brit. J. Psych.* 1926, xvi.

In our psychological case of different classes of persons, there enter no doubt various complications which render the interpretation more dubious. For one thing, there are reasons (to be seen later) to expect that increasing age tends to differentiate individuals more and more in respect of s. Again, there is the fact that the classes better endowed with g have usually undergone more or less selection. For example, the university students of Carothers had, of course, been cleared of the weaklings who could not matriculate. This in itself would tend to lower all correlations due to g. It must remain questionable, however, whether such facts can account for the phenomenon wholly. Possibly, there exists further a genuine law of diminishing returns for mental as for material processes.

Any way, this large influence exercised here upon the amount of g by the nature of the subjects is in striking contrast with the very small influence previously shown to be exercised by the nature of the eductive process.

Corollary about genius. The next and final point to be raised here is a corollary of what has been said. Since a great many abilities depend almost entirely upon the efficiency of the engines involved and this efficiency varies independently from individual to another, we may conclude that these abilities themselves vary almost independently from individual to individual.

Let us try, then, to get a notion as to how such abilities of any single person must be distributed in respect of excellence. By all experience—and also by statistical theory, in which we cannot enter here—the great bulk of his abilities will tend to be mediocre ; that is to say, they will be near the general average of the class of individuals under consideration. A fair number will be distinctly above this average, and a fair number below. A small number will be much above ; and so also, below. The whole frequency distribution will, in fact, have a bell-like shape more or less similar to that which was shown by the curves of the tetrad-differences to be expected from sampling errors (see, for instance, page 146). At the extreme ends of the distribution will lie a very small number for which the person is, on one side a genius, and on the other an idiot. Every normal man, woman, and child is, then, a genius at something, as well as an idiot at something.

It remains to discover *what*—at any rate in respect of the genius. This must be a most difficult matter, owing to the very fact that it occurs in only a minute proportion out of all possible abilities. It certainly cannot be detected by any of the testing procedures at present in current usage ; but these procedures seem to be susceptible of vast improvement.

The preceding considerations are apt to arise on looking at a procession of the unemployed, and hearing the common remark that they are mostly the unemployable. That they are so actually, one can hardly help concurring. But need they be so necessarily ? Remember that every one of these, too, is a genius at something—if only we could discover what. No illusion, indeed, can be cherished that among them may be marching some " mute inglorious Milton, some Cromwell guiltless of his country's blood." For these are walks in life that appear to involve a large amount of *g*. But perhaps every one of these persons could at any rate do something that would make him a treasure in some great industrial concern ; and there seems no reason why a few should not have even become famous—in such occupations, for instance, as those of dancer, jockey, or player of a popular game.

CHAPTER XIII

"SPECIAL ABILITIES" AND "GROUP FACTORS"

THE PROBLEM

Urgent need of solution. We have now arrived at the " group factors " which have played such a baffling part in controversial writings. They make their appearance here, there, everywhere, nowhere ; the very Puck of psychology. On all sides contentiously advocated, hardly one of them has received so much as a description, far less any serious investigation.

And yet they are of immense importance, not only theoretically, but also practically. By dint of nothing else can all those who claim to measure " special abilities "—holding out magnificent promises for industry—be saved from the charge of living in the fool's paradise of " faculties." [1] For a test

---

[1] Strictly speaking, there are no such things as " special abilities " ; for all abilities involve more or less *g* and therefore are not altogether special. What really exist are special—or better," specific "—*factors*. But these are in some abilities so preponderant that, for most purposes, the *g* factor can be neglected.

only measures any ability other than g by having correlation with it other than that due to g.   Such super-added correlation will, of course, be caused by any overlap of the specific factors ; or, in other words, by any " group factor " (see p. 82). It may conveniently be termed " specific correlation." For the method of calculating it, see appendix, pp. xxi-xxiii.

Procedure to be adopted. The main cause of trouble, probably, is that the current mental testing has never been built up on any genuine theoretical foundation (see ch. vi.). In consequence, no means have been available for ascertaining how much of any observed correlation does derive from g and how much remains over to be attributed to anything else, such as overlap.

The sole valid means of solving this problem is just the same as that which we have been employing hitherto.   It still is furnished by the tetrad differences.   Before, the absence of these in any significant amount supplied the proof that specific correlation was absent ; now, conversely, nothing but the presence of significant tetrad differences can prove that any specific correlation is present. Hence, whereas before we were searching for all cases where the tetrad equation (p. 73) is satisfied, we now want to discover all cases where it fails to be so.   Whenever this happens, there must necessarily exist some " specific correlation " ; and often this can actually be measured.   Therewith is also established and measured the group factor.[1]

[1] To find out whether any two abilities are linked together by overlap, specific correlation, or a group factor, there must be obtained two further abilities—*reference abilities* they may be called—so as to make up the tetrad.   For this purpose, any two of the ordinary tests of g will serve ; they need not even be highly saturated with g (as they would have to be for measuring this g *effectively*) ; but they must, of course, be distinct from each other, as also from the pair under comparison (see p. 80).

Some complication is introduced when the available reference abilities are more than two in number ; for not more than two can be used at the same time.   The simplest course is to pick out any two at will ; but this would bring in the danger of arbitrariness.   A more thorough way is to try out every possible pair in turn ; but this line of demonstration, besides being tedious, would lack in lucidity.   Best on the whole appears to be the plan of dividing the reference abilities into two sets, pooling together all those that enter into the same set ; and this is what we are going to do

THE DIFFERENT CLASSES OF RELATIONS

Evidence. Passing on to the experimental results as yet obtained, we may once again rapidly survey the whole field of cognition by running through the different classes of relations which it can involve.

Beginning, as before, with the relation of evidence, we have already in the previous chapter been obliged to reject the view that this class is more characteristic of g than are the other classes. But there remains to see whether it may not, over and above its connection with g, involve throughout its domain some additional factor. Such a factor would give rise to a special ability of pre-eminent importance.

Now, facts bearing on this question are afforded by the work quoted in the previous chapter on page 203 ; for there the relation of evidence was represented by two tests specially constructed for this purpose ; they were those of Inference and Likelihood. In addition, there are available two " reference values " (see previous page) ; for these can be made by throwing the nine other tests of g into two pools.[1] We get in this way the following tetrad of correlations [2] :

			Inferences.	g pool$_a$
Likelihood	-	-	·172	·321
g pool$_b$ -	-	-	·343	·749

The presence of a group factor or not will be decided by there being or not a tetrad difference of significant size ; and this tetrad difference is simply $·172 \times 749 - ·321 \times 343$. This amounts to only ·018, which is *not* significant, seeing that the probable error comes to ·039. The result, accordingly,

here. But as a precaution against possible arbitrariness in the manner of division, this ought to be done in some way applicable to all cases quite uniformly. Such a procedure is given in the appendix.

[1] The nine consisted of Opposites, Synonyms, Classification, Completion, Questions, Analogies, Paragraphs, Meanings, and Memory. As to the manner of pooling, see appendix.

[2] Throughout this chapter (except where otherwise indicated) the correlations given are not corrected for attenuation (see ch. vi. p. 72). In the case of the reference values, such correction is superfluous. Even in the case of the abilities under comparison, it is not needed unless the attenuation happens to be excessive.

is to show that the two evidential tests do not have any appreciable overlap, group factor, or " specific correlation." The fact of both involving characteristically the relation of evidence has been insufficient to produce any such common element additional to g.

The same two evidential tests were subsequently employed by Davey, the subjects being this time 243 in number. Even more decisively than before, the results indicate that there does not exist any special ability broad enough to include both [1]; *a fortiori*, then, there is none broad enough to include the whole class of evidential relations.

With this result may be contrasted that obtained with the two evidential tests used by H. Peterson, those of Reasoning and Generalization (described on p. 169). Proceeding in the same manner as before, the tetrad difference proves to be very large indeed (about seven times as large as its probable error). The specific correlation has the extraordinarily high value of ·93.[2] This is all the more remarkable in view of our previous finding, that neither the Reasoning nor the Generalization has any specific correlation with Abstract Thought, a test that might easily be taken as nearly akin (see its description on p. 170).

Combining this result with the previous one, we must conclude that, although no factor additional to g extends through the entire domain of the relation of evidence (as would be indispensable in order to characterize the relation of evidence as such), nevertheless there does exist a very

---

[1] Here, the reference values are supplied by Synonyms, Classification, Questions, Completion, and Analogies. The resulting tetrad is as follows :

					Reasoning.	g_a
Likelihood -	-	-	-	-	·260	·452
g_b	-	-	-	-	·445	·709

This time the tetrad difference = ·017 with a p.e. of ·024.

[2] Reference values are supplied by Abstract Thought, Memory, and Accuracy.

				Reasoning.	g_a.
Generalization	-	-	-	·950	·348
g_b	-	-	-	·380	·579

The tetrad difference comes to no less than ·417 (p.e. = ·059).

large additional factor common to the tests of Reasoning and of Generalization.

The explanation seems to be that these two call into play very similar concatenations of elementary logical processes ; the same methods of thinking are dominant in both cases. Here, then, we appear to have discovered a " special ability " or group factor, broad enough to include a sphere of mental operation that is very valuable for many purposes in ordinary life. Quite possibly, indeed, this special logical ability may not be innate, but acquired by training or habit. Even so, its importance would not lose in degree, but would only shift from the region of aptitude to that of education.

Likeness. Turning next to the relation of likeness, this too has often been assumed to furnish a unitary power ; different individuals, it has been assumed, are unequally endowed with special ability for detecting resemblances and differences.

No such thing, however, appears to be indicated by exact research. Compare, for example, the test of Synonyms with that of Classification. In the former, the subject has to decide whether two given words are very like or very unlike ; in the latter, he is given four words and has to pick out the one whose meaning is most unlike those of the remainder. In both cases, then, nothing is required of the subject save to distinguish simple likeness from simple unlikeness in respect of the meanings of single words. From the standpoint of *a priori* assumption, the two tests might plausibly enough be taken to possess a very large group factor in common over and above g. But the results of actual experiment indicate no such thing. The tetrad difference is insignificant.[1] This is the concordant verdict,

---

[1] Reference values are supplied by Completion, Questions, Analogies, Paragraphs, Meanings, Memory, Inferences, and Likelihood. The result is as follows :

					Synonyms.	g_a.
Classification	-	-	-	-	·566	·615
g_b	-	-	-	-	·615	·725

The tetrad difference $= ·032$ with a p.e. of ·029.

both of Dockerill's research mentioned on p. 186, as also of that made by Davey.[1]

In the case of the relation of likeness, then—despite all *a priori* assumptions to the contrary—the specific factor s has shown itself to be extremely narrow ; no " special ability " is manifested broad enough to have any general importance.

Time and space. Passing on to the relation of time, about this—except as conjoined with space into "movement" —there is nothing to say. For nobody so far seems ever to have supplied the correlations needful for proving anything. Not even any interest in the matter has been manifested.

Very different is the scene which presents itself when we turn to the relation of space ; about this, the literature is abundant. As to the abilities involving it, these have been taken by some authors to be radically unlike all non-spatial kinds. But other authors, again, have raised the protest that the power of co-ordinating movements cannot differ fundamentally from that of co-ordinating ideas (the German *Kombinationsgabe*). Yet another doctrine which has excited much interest is that of the existence of a " geometrical intelligence " as something quite different from and supplementary to the intelligence of the " intuitive " sort.[2] To a large extent, however, such views seem to have been disposed of already, being incompatible with our finding (especially in the previous chapter) that the spatial cognition coincides with all the other classes to the extent that it involves the same g. Still, as happened in the case of the evidential relations, there remains to be discussed the pos-

---

[1] Reference values are supplied by Questions, Inferences, Completion, Analogies, and Likelihood, with the following result :

					Synonyms.	g_a.
Classification	-	-	-	·600	·673
g	-	-	-	-	·538	·632

The tetrad difference = ·018 with a p.e. of ·021.

[2] If " intuitive " be taken to mean knowledge that is self-evident and unmediated, then the term applies to all three noegenetic processes and to no others whatever.

sibility that either all, or else a large part, of the spatial cognition possesses over and above its *g* some overlap or group factor.

Now, the more extreme of these last two views, namely, that *all* spatial cognition possesses a common group factor, has been submitted to trial by the spatial tests of McCrae. One of these was the Maze (Porteus). Another was Cube Construction, where the subject is supplied with blocks painted on some sides but not on others ; out of these he is required to construct larger blocks that also are painted on certain sides but not on others. A further test was the Goddard Formboard, which involves fitting a number of blocks as fast as possible each into an aperture made of corresponding dimensions. Yet another was the Dearborn Formboard, which differs from the foregoing in that two or more blocks must be fitted together into the same aperture, so that here skilful arrangement is needed in order to discover some place for every block. There were three other tests, the Triangle, the Diagonal, and the Healy A ; these were very similar to the Formboards and extremely similar to one another ; each consisted in a most elementary sort of jigsaw puzzle ; four or five triangles or rectangles had to be fitted together into one or two apertures.

The result of all this work, on applying the same criterion as before, is that no overlap or group factor becomes appreciable until we arrive at comparing together the three jigsaws which appear to be almost identical with each other. As for the remaining tests, not even the two Formboards manifest any such mutual overlap.[1]

---

[1] Reference values are supplied by the known tests of Picture Completion, Cube Imitation, and Substitution, none of which seems to involve essentially any relations of space. The spatial pools have been arranged so as not to include the correlations of the three jigsaws with one another ; but as a matter of fact, even the inclusion of these values makes little difference in the result.

	Space$_a$.	g_a.
Space$_b$ - - - -	·311	·306
g_b - - - -	·306	·262

The tetrad difference comes to = ·012 with a p.e. of ·051.

Markedly contrasting with this, however, is the result obtained from another field of spatial cognition, one which comprises much of what is often called constructive mechanical ability. Here, on analysis, the characteristic process proves to be an eduction of correlates ; given are a spatial situation together with a relation (or system of these) ; to be educed is the correlative situation. This kind of performance has been very carefully investigated by Cox ; an example of his tests has been given already (ch. xi., p. 178). On applying the criterion to these tests in the same manner as to the others, a significant tetrad difference does occur, and specific correlation makes its appearance to the considerable amount of ·366.[1]

The relevant results of other investigators are probably to be interpreted in a similar way. But they did not have at their disposal the present (and sole valid) criterion ; nor do they even seem to have obtained all the data requisite in order to reach any definite conclusion. This appears to apply to the otherwise excellent work of Stenquist,[2] and of Blumenfeld.[3] One recent research, however, does supply the needed data ; it is due to McFarlane.[4] On submitting them to the criterion, there ensues a result of peculiar interest; *quite a large overlap and high specific correlation is manifested for boys, but none for girls.*[5] This striking sexual difference raises the query as to whether such a group factor in the

[1] Using ordinary tests of g for the reference values, the tetrad is as follows :

					Space$_a$.	g_a.
Space$_b$ -	-	-	-	-	·535	·360
g_b	-	-	-	-	·302	·410

The tetrad difference $= ·110$ with a p.e. of ·023.

[2] *Columbia Univ. Contr. Educ.*, Teachers' College Series, 1918, No. 89.

[3] *Zeit. f. Psychol.* 1922, xci.   [4] *Brit. J. Psych.* 1925, Mon. Suppl. xiv.

[5] The following are the respective tetrads :

Boys (172 subjects).				Girls (184 subjects).		
	Space$_a$.	g_a.			Space$_a$.	g_a.
Space$_b$ -	- ·571	·217	Space$_b$	-	·552	·662
g_b	- ·004	·700	g_b	-	·548	·745

For the boys, the tetrad difference has the high value of ·399 with a p.e. of ·039 ; whereas for the girls it is only ·051 with a p.e. of ·024.

case of the boys may not derive from acquired rather than innate ability. Daily observation shows that many boys, unlike almost all girls, tend already in their second year of life to play with mechanical instruments in a very thorough way, which can scarcely fail to help them subsequently in all performances of a kindred nature.

Conjunction. After the relation of space may conveniently be taken that of conjunction ; for these two are linked by the fact that they respectively underlie the two great branches of mathematics, the geometrical and the arithmetical.

Now, arithmetic shows specific correlation throughout. Take, for instance, the work of Rogers.[1] In this there were five arithmetical tests, named Algebraic Computation, Matching Equations and Problems, Matching n^{th} Terms and Series, Interpolation, and Missing Steps in Series. When these are divided into two pools in just the same manner as we have been doing, there ensues the large tetrad difference of ·254 with a p.e. of only ·023 or less than a tenth.[2]

A similar conclusion emerges from a remarkably thorough and valuable investigation of arithmetical ability by Collar.[3] About 200 boys were for six weeks given carefully planned tests in :

(1) Computation (addition, subtraction, multiplication, and division).

(2) Higher arithmetical operations, viz. Problems, Rules, and Mental Arithmetic.

(3) Two of the usual tests for g.

---

[1] *Columbia Univ. Contr. Educ.*, Teachers' College Series, 1923, No. 130.

[2] For reference values there are here available Analogies, Opposites, Completion, and Thorndike's Reading Test. The following tetrad ensues.

	Arithmetic$_a$.	g_a.
Arithmetic$_b$ - - - - -	·684	·348
g_b - - - - -	·348	·561

The tetrad difference amounts to ·254 with a p.e. of ·023.

[3] *Brit. J. Psych.*

From his results may be extracted the following typical table (for a single class) :

	1	2	3	4	5	6
1. Computation - -	-—	·325	·495	·397	·125	·180
2. Problems - - -	·325	—	·760	·792	·587	·417
3. Mental arithmetic -	·495	·760	—	·742	·397	·255
4. Rules - - - -	·397	·792	·742	—	·517	·202
5. g_a - - - -	·125	·587	·397	·255	—	·577
6. g_b - - - -	·180	·417	·255	·202	·577	—

We can now, in just the same way as previously, throw the four arithmetical results into two pools and then see whether any significant tetrad difference is manifested. The answer is in the affirmative ; and the specific correlation amounts to no less than ·658. Thus, these four arithmetical abilities have much in common over and above such g as enters into them respectively.[1]

Collar raises the interesting question as to whether arithmetical ability may not fall into two main subdivisions, a lower one for mere computation, and a higher one which is involved in the Problems, Rules, and Mental Arithmetic. On applying the criterion, this suggestion seems at first sight to be verified ; the inter-correlations between the arithmetical abilities lead to tetrad differences of quite large magnitude. But then the author wisely proceeds to eliminate from these correlations the disturbing influence of g (see pp. 201-203). Thereupon the said tetrad difference sinks to insignificance. That is to say, on such elimination, the inter-correlations of the arithmetical abilities are traceable to a single factor over and above g ; the suggestion that there is one specific factor for the lower operations and

---

[1] Proceeding as usual, there ensues the following tetrad :

	Arithmetic$_a$.	g_a.
Arithmetic$_b$ - - - -	·739	·390
g_b - - - - -	·390	·577

The tetrad difference comes to ·273 with a p.e. of ·055.
This seems to agree with the results of W. Brown (*Biometrika*, 1910, vii.).

another for the higher proves not to be tenable ; the higher are only different in that they involve more g.[1]

There is another question of much interest. We have found one group factor which seems to extend throughout geometry, and another throughout arithmetic. Do these two to any extent coincide, and thus constitute a special ability for mathematics in general ? The common belief, not only of the " plain man," but also of the mathematical teacher, is that such a special ability for mathematics in general does exist. To obtain some definite evidence on the point, let us return to the work of Rogers. This investigator introduced three tests of an almost purely geometrical character, called Superposition, Symmetry, and Matching Solids and Surfaces. These we can throw together into one pool ; the five distinctly arithmetical tests we can put into another ; and for the " reference abilities " (see p. 223) there are the two independent pools of tests for g, which we have already used in footnote 2 on page 230. From all this we get the following tetrad of correlations :

		Arithmetic.	g_a.
Geometry	- -	·249	·367
g_b -	- - -	·424	·561

The tetrad difference $= ·249 \times ·561 - ·367 \times ·424 = - ·015$ (p.e. $= ·035$). There appears, then, no real basis for the common opinion which would take arithmetic and geometry to furnish one single special ability. Their union as " mathematics " seems, rather, to be merely one of practical convenience.

Psychological class of relations. Of the remaining five classes of relation, we must pass over four, those of identity,

---

[1] *Before eliminating g*

				Computation$_a$.	Higher Arithmetic$_a$.
Computation$_b$	-	-	-	·85	·50
Higher Arithmetic$_b$	-	-	·50	·84

Here, the tetrad difference $= ·454$.
After eliminating g

				Computation$_a$.	Higher Arithmetic$_a$.
Computation$_b$	-	-	-	·74	·68
Higher Arithmetic$_b$	-	-	·68	·70

Here, the tetrad difference is only ·058.

attribution, causality, and constitution (see ch. xi. pp. 182-184). For as to whether each or any of these involves a factor extending throughout its domain but not further, there is at present no means of deciding. Researches supplying the needful correlations have yet to be made.

There is only, then, still to be considered the class of relations that we have been calling psychological. Do these form the basis for any special ability ? Or, what comes to the same thing, are they all inter-correlated by specific correlation over and above what is due to g ?

For want of other pertinent investigations, we must again return to the work of Webb. His subjects had to state the most advisable social behaviour in two widely different situations. Our question, then, is as to whether the two tasks showed any correlation additional to that which was due to g. The answer is Yes. Between these two there proves to be a specific correlation of ·495.[1] Here, accordingly, would appear to lie another special ability at any rate broad enough to merit being tested.

In the foregoing case, both the relations and the fundaments involved were of psychological nature. With it may be contrasted another case where only the fundaments, not the relations, were psychological. This happened in the previously mentioned research by Dockerill and others (p. 281). Here, three tests involved the relation of likeness (Opposites, Classification, and Meanings). And the ideas between which the likeness had to be cognized were sorted by the authors into four classes, viz. :

(1) Concrete objects, as grapes, fur, bedroom.

(2) Abstract ideas, as heavy, equal, absent.

(3) Moral concepts, as spite, praise.

(4) Psychological concepts other than moral, as wish, pleasure, attention.

[1] The following is the tetrad :

					Situation$_a$.	g_a.
Situation$_b$	-	-	-	-	·710	·485
g_b	-	-	-	-	·485	·576

The tetrad difference = ·164 with a p.e. of ·024. *Loc. cit.* p. 181.

Do some subjects tend to excel when the likeness has to be cognized between such terms as wish, pleasure, or attention ; other subjects, with such terms as spite, or praise ; others again, with such as heavy, equal, or absent ; and yet others, with such as grapes, fur, or bedroom ?   The reply is in all four cases negative ; in no case is any specific correlation manifested.[1]

This contrast between the tests of situations and those of likeness admits of being explained in various ways. But their discussion would occupy more space than can here be afforded.

THE " FACULTIES "

Sensory and motor ability. After the preceding consideration of special abilities from the standpoint of analysis into the ultimate relations and fundaments involved, we may briefly examine the same topic from the cruder standpoint of the supposed unitarily functioning " faculties." Together with these are included, of course, all their synonyms, such as capacities, powers, levels, and even abilities, so long as these names are taken to denote so many mental forms or tools, each capable of being applied to any sort of material.

Beginning with the faculty or level of sensory discrimination, we have to enquire whether the endowment of an individual for one kind of sensation tends to go with that for other kinds to any amount exceeding what is already explained by their respective shares in g.

The first answer to this question came from the work of the present writer, and was negative.   In fact, such a denial furnished the original hint which eventually led up to the whole theory of Two Factors (appendix, p. i).   Soon afterwards, corroborative results were obtained by Burt for the

---

[1] The following tetrad is typical :

	Psychological$_a$.	Concrete$_a$.
Psychological$_b$ - - -	·622	·343
Concrete$_b$ - - - -	·343	·229

The tetrad difference $= ·025$ with a p.e. of ·025.

visual, auditory, and kinesthetic senses.[1] Conflicting seemed to be the later result got by Thorndike, Lay, and Dean ; but this has been explained away already (ch. x. p. 151). Still later came a further investigation under more satisfactory conditions than any of the foregoing ; among other things, the number of subjects, which had previously been extremely small, was now raised to 150 (children). It was the work of Carey, who tested both visual and auditory discrimination, and found that they manifested no specific correlation whatever.[2]

But still more striking evidence was to come from the laboratory of Thorndike, namely, in the results of Simpson. For here two kinds of discrimination were compared which did not come from different kinds of sensation, or even from different sensory aspects. Instead, both alike consisted of discrimination of visual length. The sole difference lay in the technical method of testing. This, as is well known, has the choice between three main lines (those of " reproduction," of " right and wrong cases," and of " minimal changes "). Simpson tested in two of these ways (" reproduction " and " right and wrong cases "). But even with this extremely close resemblance, the correlation between the two tests only came to ·24, and none of the ensuing tetrad differences was large enough to be significant (see ch. x. p. 146).

A cognate question arises about motor ability. That no group factor runs *throughout* this is obvious already. For since the entire correlation between any two different motor operations has shown itself to be for the most part negligibly

---

[1] Here is the resulting tetrad :

			Discrimination$_a$.	g_a.
Discrimination$_b$	-	-	-	·167	·386
g_b	-	-	-	-	·386	·813

The tetrad difference $= ·013$ with a p.e. of ·07.

[2]

			Visual Discr.	g_a.
Audit. discr.$_b$	-	-	-	·260	·383
g_b	-	-	-	-	·374	·381

The tetrad difference $= ·037$ with a p.e. of ·032.

small,[1] *a fortiori* any part of this correlation not attributable to g must be very small indeed.

On the other hand, there may quite well exist high intercorrelations that cover fields large enough to have much importance. One such is at any rate supplied by those motor performances which depend upon the so-called " reaction-time." The existence of high correlations between these were revealed in some (unpublished) experiments conducted in the laboratory of the present writer by Rao. More recently, they have been demonstrated in an interesting work of Reymert.[2]

Intellect, abstraction, and language. From Sense we may pass to its antithesis, Intellect. And the latter may most pregnantly be taken to mean the power to operate with abstract ideas expressed in words. Does this constitute any single faculty or ability ? Can it be treated as a tool usable in diversified operations, and therefore as supplying these with a common group factor ?

At the present time this view appears to have been adopted with equal emphasis by two opposing schools— those who desire to extol such a power as the crown of creation, and those who scoff at it as remote from what they call practical.

Turning to the actual evidence, a certain amount of information has been supplied on page 233, which indicated that there does not exist any special ability for handling the abstract ideas " heavy," " equal," " absent," etc., as com-

---

[1] Carey's results show rather high correlations between writing, painting, and needlework. But for non-scholastic experimentally tested dexterities, both this investigator and others in our laboratory have found extremely low correlations.

[2] Reymert's research was communicated in the *Scandinavian Scientific Review*, 1923, ii. The following is one of his tetrads for reaction-time to sound :

	Simple reaction with lips.	Simple reaction with thumb.
Simple reaction with teeth - -	·78	·55
Choice reaction with finger - -	·43	·76

The tetrad difference is thus $·78 \times ·76 - ·54 \times ·43 = ·355$, which can scarcely be due to chance, even with the very small number of subjects here employed (20).

pared with the more concrete " grapes," " fur," " bedroom," and so forth.

Much more decisive, however, has been the already quoted work of Davey (ch. xii. p. 213). For there the abstract-verbal operations were compared with those that were frankly perceptual, the two kinds being equalized in every other possible respect. On submitting the correlations that ensued to the same criterion as before, the result is to show that the so widely assumed special ability for verbal-abstract operations has here at any rate no appreciable magnitude.[1] Much the same result ensues, moreover, when the verbal-abstract operations are compared with what have been called " performance " tests and were described earlier in this chapter (p. 228) as investigated by McCrae.

On the whole, then, the conclusion seems enforced upon us, that not even abstractness combined with verbality—much less, abstractness alone—introduce any group factor or special ability of important magnitude. In order that such a factor should arise, there must be some further condition in play. Still the work of Davey and of Stephenson (*Journ. Ed. Psych.*, 1931) have shown that such further conditions *usually occur*. Above all, the operation involved is in most cases not merely verbal in general, but dependent upon some particular linguistic talent or attainment ; a dominant case, probably, is the dependence upon linguistic memory. In this way may be explained the fact proved by Davey and Stephenson, that most of the ordinary tests of the so-called " general intelligence " do involve verbal factors in large degree.

Memory and imagination. Most conspicuous among the remaining assumed faculties are those of Memory and Imagination. The former will be reserved for next chapter. The imagination falls into two widely different powers, that

---

[1]

				Visual Discr.	g_a.
Auditory discr.	-	-	-	·260	·383
g_b	-	-	-	·374	·381

The tetrad difference $= ·037$ with a p.e. of ·032.

of forming sensation-like images and that of inventing new ideas (or systems of these).

For a brief illuminative comparison of these two, it would be hard to match the chapter recently devoted to them by Ballard.[1] Nothing more need be said here.

As for the images, this came within the scope of Carey's investigation. The outcome contrasts strongly with the other cases which we have been considering. Between the abilities to form visual and auditory images respectively, there does exist a specific correlation, and to the large amount of ·60.[2]

As regards imagination in the other meaning, that of inventive power, the results have been very different. Most definite by far seems to be the evidence supplied by Hargreaves (see ch. xi. pp. 187-188). The result is to indicate the occurrence of only very small specific correlation, from causes that are still rather obscure and are being further investigated.

Interesting in this connection may be a comparison between the two classes of tests that have been called "inventive" and "selective" respectively. The former comprises those which leave the testee at liberty to devise his answers out of his own head ; with the other class, three or four answers are supplied to him, from which he has only to select. And much has been written against this latter sort of test, reproaching it with not touching the subject's power of invention, of initiative, of spontaneity, and so forth. But all such criticism implies that the inventive power functions in a unitary way, that is, involves a group factor. In order to verify the correctness of this assumption, the tests employed by the present writer with some 30,000 candidates for the British Civil Service were made to contain three tests, each of which was given in both the inventive

---

[1] *The Changing School*, 1925, ch. xii.

[2]

			Visual Imagery.	g_a.
Auditory imagery	-	-	·600	·046
g_b - - -	-	-	·087	·686

The tetrad difference $= ·404$ with a p.e. of ·02.

and the selective form (see ch. x. p. 154). The result, on applying the usual criterion, was to prove that specific correlation does not occur and the faculty of invention, initiative, or spontaneity—in the way that has been assumed —does not really exist.[1]

INFLUENCE OF FORM OF PRESENTATION

Oral and written forms. This chapter may be brought to its close by briefly noticing a constituent of s which has hitherto been little investigated, although it is of a very obvious kind and seems not unlikely to possess great importance. It consists, not in the essence of the task to be performed, but rather in the manner that the task is presented to the subjects.

Thus, the presentation may be either by word of mouth or else by writing. Will the one manner tend all round to be favourable to some testees, the other to others ? As much is often stated, or at least implied ; but for any definite evidence either way, one may look in vain. Now, bearing on the point is the previously mentioned work of Dockerill and others (pp. 201 ff.). For this included ten oral and two written tests. On applying the criterion, the result is rather indecisive.[2] But a subsequent investigation (not yet published) by Hanlin, would seem to settle the question negatively ; no specific correlation was manifested. The choice between oral and written tests, then, would seem to introduce no group factor of appreciable magnitude. According to this, both kinds of tests, oral and written respectively, ought (if adequate in other respects) to produce

---

[1] The following is a typical tetrad :

	Completion, Inventive.	Completion, Selective.
Passages, inventive - -	·430	·479
Passages, selective - -	·409	·433

The tetrad difference = ·010 with a p.e. of ·007.

[2]

	$Oral_a$.	$Written_a$.
$Oral_b$ - - - - -	·751	·476
$Written_b$ - - -	·521	·451

The tetrad difference comes to ·090, which is only three times its p.e. (·030) and therefore is not conclusive (see p. 141).

just the same measurements. But such a theorem, of course, can only be expected to apply to normal conditions such as occur here. It would certainly fail for various exceptional conditions, such as with children beginning to learn to write, or with tests which largely depend upon speed of writing.

Individual and collective testing. Another influence also investigated by Hanlin is that of administering tests to numerous persons simultaneously as compared with taking each individual by himself. The choice between these two modes of procedure has frequently been regarded as affecting different persons in a different manner; sometimes, the individual treatment has been extolled as doing better justice to those subjects whose thoughts lie deeper; sometimes, instead, it has been blamed for incapacitating those who incline to be nervous. But obviously, such an effect either way would, if large, generate a group factor; and the present investigation shows no group factor to occur. The two modes of testing, then, would seem to be practically equivalent for the great majority of persons; but there may well be some exceptional persons for whom this is no longer true.

Alternative manners of expressing a task. We now arrive at the last topic to be considered in this chapter, and it raises some curiously suggestive issues. In constructing two of the tests for Dockerill's investigation mentioned above (p. 201), a peculiar procedure was adopted; numerous tasks were systematically devised, and then were divided as evenly as possible into two sets. The one set was brought to expression in the form of the Completion test; the other, in that of Questions. Thus these two tests were perfectly similar in the substance or essential nature of the tasks to be executed, and only differed in the form that these tasks were expressed to the subjects. Very unexpected was the result; the fact of these two tests having been made perfectly similar in substance, and only different in form of expression, introduced no group factor common to the two;

it has no apparent effect whatever.[1]   The difference, then, between tests of any such kind does not lie at all in their substance, but solely in their form of expression.

The interesting further question arises as to how the form of expression becomes so effective.   Possibly, it is by means of inducing the subject to employ some particular mental procedure, which may be based on the haphazard of old habits and present suggestion.

Should this result be eventually corroborated, it would appear to have importance for both theory and practice. For instance, if only a test could be so fashioned as to eliminate all possible difference in the subjects' manner of procedure, then this single test might by itself conceivably afford a perfect measure of g.

SUMMARY

The main upshot of this chapter is negative. Cases of specific correlations or group factors have been astonishingly rare.   Over and over again, they have proved to be absent even in circumstances when they would most confidently have been anticipated by the nowadays prevalent *a priori* " job analysis." Of " special abilities " sufficiently broad to admit of measurement after the fashion that is becoming more and more frequent and pretentious in applied psychology, there have been but the scantiest indications. The modern version of the doctrine of " faculties " has shown itself none the happier for discarding the old name whilst retaining the old fallacy.   The criticisms of Herbart and Thorndike have found abundant justification.

Among the exceptional cases where, on the contrary, specific correlations and group factors do become of appreciable magnitude, the four most important have been in respect of what may be called the logical, the mechanical,

[1]
					Questions.	g_a.
Completion	-	-	-	-	·412	·619
g_b	-	-	-	-	·571	·751

The tetrad difference $= -·040$ with a p.e. of ·031.

the psychological, and the arithmetical abilities.   In each of these a group factor has been discovered of sufficient breadth and degree to possess serious practical consequences, educational, industrial, and vocational.

The same might be said of yet another important special ability which was reluctantly omitted from our preceding account for want of space; this is the ability to appreciate music.   For elaborate investigations of this, reference may be made to the admirable work of Seashore,[1] Pear,[2] Revesz,[3] and Rupp.[4]

A third result that may prove to have significance, especially theoretically, is that in the few cases where the broad group factors and special abilities did make some appearance, there was commonly a suggestion of their being due to past experience rather than to native aptitude. This was notably the case with the mechanical and the psychological abilities.   The special ability found for arithmetic seems less easy to explain in this way; perhaps it is merely due to the extremely narrow basis (simple addition and subtraction) upon which all purely arithmetical operations are ultimately founded.   And at any rate narrowness of basis appears to be the only explanation for such functional unitariness as is presented by musical ability.

Lastly, some indications have been given that the specific factor in ability, as compared with the universal factor, may depend to a large extent upon influences of a very *fortuitous* kind.

[1] Out of Seashore's very numerous publications, one that contains a great amount of information for the present purpose is that in which he collaborated with Mount (*Psych. Mon.* xxv. Whole No. 108, 1918).

[2] *Brit. J. Psych.* 1911, iv.; also subsequently.

[3] *Zeit. f. Psych.* 1920, lxxxv.   [4] *Zeit. für angewandte Psychologie*, ix.

CHAPTER XIV

GOODNESS AND SPEED OF RESPONSE

COGNITIVE QUANTITY

The universal quantitative law. At this point we pass over, as it were, to another psychological hemisphere ; from that of quality to that of quantity.

Looking back upon all the ground traversed in the last few chapters, it has everywhere been dominated by the three ultimate laws of cognition, as set forth in ch. xi. (pp. 164-167)—the mind becomes aware of its own experience ; it educes relations ; and it educes correlates. To the first of these three, indeed, we were obliged to pay but scant notice ; for of this there has been so far little or no scientific investigation ; it remains an unknown continent for future explorers. But the second and the third qualitative laws, those of eduction, have throughout been our twin guiding stars. By means of them we have been able to delimit the entire scope of cognition, to divide up the whole into its main divisions, to ascertain the occurrence of g as also of s

243

in each, to determine everywhere the relative influences of these two, and finally to discover where and to what extent the group factors and special abilities that are so much talked of really exist.

Notwithstanding their ultimateness and universality, however, these three qualitative laws (like those of all science) are in truth mere abstractions for convenience of thought. Every mental process necessarily possesses— additionally to, interfused with, and no less ultimate than, its aspect of quality—the further aspect of quantity. No mental process can occur at all, but that it occurs in some or other degree.

Complementary, then, to the system of qualitative laws, there must, in our doctrine of "noegenesis" (p. 162), be another system of those which deal with quantity. These laws of quantity fall into two categories; the universal kind which characterise all cognition whatever; and the special kind which have a more restricted application. The universal kind it is which supplies the topic of the present chapter. It may be summed up into the single proposition, that *all knowing develops by way of increase in clearness and speed; that is to say, every item in the cognitive field, every constituent in whatever object (mental) is perceived or thought of, comes into being by a continuous emergence out of utter obscurity up to some degree of clearness; and as this description implies, the emerging occupies some duration of time.*[1] The other and more restricted quantitative laws will be treated in the five following chapters; for the present, they may be summarily indicated as those of span, retentivity, fatigue, conation, and primordial potency.

All these quantitative laws (of both kinds), as also such processes as may specially derive from them, will naturally raise the same three basal problems as have met us already. Which, if any, of the processes fall within the sphere of g ?

[1] For more profound treatment of this " clearness," it has to be analyzed into two components, called " cognitive intensity " and " determinateness " (see *Nature of Intelligence*, p. 159). The latter it is, not the former, which concerns our present purposes.

In so far as they do so fall, what are their respective saturations with g ? And to what extent do the laws tend to function as group factors and thus produce broad overlap, specific correlation, and " special abilities " ? Within the scope of these three problems will be found to lie many of the perplexities by which current literature is already beginning to become interested—but unsystematically and therefore ineffectively.

Postulates for measuring ability. Now, if we desire any genuine measurement of cognitive ability, it is to these universal quantitative properties of clearness and speed that we are obliged to turn.

In order to render the measuring feasible, there are needed —physics is no better off in this respect—some auxiliary assumptions ; and a word or two about them may be welcome to those who desire to understand the nature of the foundations upon which all else is really built. As regards the measuring of speed, there is no great difficulty ; for (with suitable arrangements) not much risk is run in inferring the duration of a person's mental processes from the amount of time he takes to respond to the stimulus. As regards the clearness, this can legitimately enough (again supposing suitable arrangements) be inferred from what may be called the " goodness " of the person's responses ; by this is meant their freedom from errors and omissions. Suppose, for example, that a man is being tested for discrimination of pitch. On two different tones being sounded, there will tend to arise in his mind—by virtue of the second law—an awareness of one being higher than the other. When his responses rarely go astray, we assume that his awareness has been very clear. Whereas when the proportion of wrong answers becomes nearly as great as that of right ones, we assume the awareness to have been very obscure. And in the limiting case where he fails to respond at all, we must assume that the clearness has risen little if at all above zero.

The chief difficulty derives, not so much from the inward

natures of these several indications of cognitive quantity, as rather from the very fact of there being several of them. For much trouble has arisen in trying to decide which of the two, speed or goodness of response, is in any given operation really responsible for a person's success or failure. Mental tests, in particular, have been emphatically reproached with depending upon speed ; the man, it is said, who can scramble through the largest number of unaccustomed tasks in the brief hour or so allotted to this purpose is by no means necessarily he who can attain to the highest achievement in the course of days, weeks, and years. An instance in the experience of the present writer is that of a high government official who thought to bring damning evidence against all such tests in the following quotation from Landor :

> " Quickness is among the least of the mind's properties and belongs to her lowest estate. The mad often retain it ; the liar has it ; the cheat has it ; we find it on the race-course and at the card table. Education does not give it and reflection takes away from it."

Indeed, many of the testers themselves have made much concession to this view, seeing that they have abandoned the title of " intelligence " for what they claim to measure, substituting the more diffident name of " alertness."

Similar trouble arises from the fact of the goodness itself being indicated in two different ways, either by freedom from error, or by freedom from omission. Any rendering of these two deficiencies comparable with each other has been found, if not altogether arbitrary, at least extremely difficult. Moreover, error itself may arise from different causes ; it may indicate an inability that is permanent for the individual despite the most favourable conditions ; or one that merely comes from such temporary disturbances as fatigue, emotion, carelessness, etc.[1] To meet this last

[1] For a consideration of these influences, see later on, especially chs. xix. and xx.

trouble, there has been a tendency in recent times to introduce the concept of " power," in the sense of ability to perform an operation correctly when all the conditions are most favourable.

DEPENDENCE ON G

Power of response. We will begin with the easiest of our problems. Does our g—measured as it is by mental tests—involve " power," in the sense of goodness of response under most favourable conditions ? Or, as some writers are asserting, does it only involve speed ?

To answer this question in respect of any kind of ability, the first natural step is to obtain a measure of it under such conditions that the influence of speed is somehow eliminated. For this purpose, we cannot simply take the number of right responses given by the testee ; for here speed is obviously influential. But there is less objection to taking, instead, the proportion of the right responses to the total number. An instance of this sort was already supplied in the Accuracy of Adding investigated by Krueger and the present writer (*loc. cit.* p. 81). For such accuracy of adding is obviously free from " overlap " with fineness of discrimination for pitch, and yet the two had a correlation of ·66. This high value, then, must be wholly credited to g.

Still more satisfactory, however, is the evidence supplied by the goodness of response under conditions whereby the influence of speed has been eliminated experimentally ; that is to say, the persons tested have been allowed as much time as they could utilize. As an instance of this may be quoted a test-series constructed by the present author ; this consisted of oral questions, each of which was answered by writing a single word, with an ample time allowance of ten seconds. This series has always shown high correlations with all measures of g. For example, McCrae[1] found it to have a correlation of ·76 with a series of Burt.

Best of all, however, would seem to have been some

[1] *Loc. cit.* p. 163.

evidence derived from the American Army tests. At two of the camps 510 men were given this test in the ordinary way ; but then (using a differently coloured pencil) they were made to work further at it for as much time again. In the shorter period, very few of the component sub-tests were completed ; but on the time being prolonged, a great many of them were so, and the average score increased by about 30 per cent. Despite all this additional work, the two testings—short and long, respectively—had an inter-correlation of no less than ·967. Moreover, on calculating the correlations of both these testings with the officers' estimates of the " intelligence " of the men tested, that for the longer period proved to be the higher of the two. This experiment was repeated at the University of Iowa by Ruch and Koerth, with an important addition. The whole proceeding arose out of a complaint made by some of the students, after having undergone the test of Thorndike, that they had not been allowed enough time to do them-selves justice. In reply to this complaint, the 72 lowest and the 52 highest in the Thorndike test were now tried with that of the American Army (the Alpha). First, this was done in the ordinary way ; next, just as described above, a further equal period of time was allowed ; but then, finally, they were told to go over the test *as long as they liked*, completing anything which was imperfect. So effectively were they urged to persevere, that actually the slowest subject took $4\frac{1}{2}$ times the original and regular period of time. As result of the first extension of time, the score went up 17 per cent ; with the second extension, it rose another 4 per cent. Yet the correlation of the first with the second score was ·966, whilst that of the second with the third was ·945.

On the whole, then, the evidence indicates convincingly that—in contradiction to the assertions mentioned—the power of cognitive response, quite apart from its speed, does display dependence upon the very same g that we have all along had under consideration. As to whether the same applies to higher achievements in much longer stretches of time—weeks and even years—this question must be reserved for ch. xv.

Speed of response.   Indeed, far from the evidence indicating that the tests of g measure speed rather than power, the difficulty is to demonstrate that they really measure speed at all and not power alone.   For although tests can be found in abundance which depend altogether on power, yet of the converse kind which depend exclusively on speed it is hard to discover a single actual instance.

Still, we can hardly doubt but that several of the tests could be arranged so as to meet this requirement.   Thus, in the work of Hart and the present writer, every normal testee, if only allowed time enough, would beyond doubt have been able to perform quite correctly the Addition, the Ticking Rings, and the Cancellation; perhaps even the Geometrical Figures.   And it seems at least probable that those who worked quickest within the time limits of the experiments would, in general, have continued to show the best record for quickness even had each been given just time enough to work without error.

A more rigorous demonstration, however, that g enters into speed can be built upon the already established fact of its entering into accuracy.   For speed in one kind of operations has proved to be correlated, not only with speed in other kinds, but even with accuracy—and therefore power—in other kinds.   It must then, like power itself, be correlated with g.   For instance, the above quoted work of Hart and the present writer showed speed of addition to have the following correlations :

Sentences, Accuracy.	Figures, Accuracy.	Perception, Accuracy.	Ticking Rings, Accuracy.	Cancellation. Accuracy.
+ ·40	+ ·42	+ ·10	+ ·09	+ ·14

Further corroboration has been reached in an analytical manner.   Strasheim, when investigating the eductive processes involved in finding one's way out of a maze, was led by cogent evidence to infer that many of the mistakes made by the " stupid " children were really due to their eductions occurring *too slowly*,[1]

Most convincing of all, however, appears to be a fact which is familiar even in ordinary experience, but has received its most definite demonstration from Courtis (see ch. xx.). This is that—within certain medium ranges— any increase in speed at a mental operation tends towards a decrease in its goodness, whilst inversely a greater goodness can always be attained by some sacrifice of speed.[2] Apart from more or less accidental further influences, then, high accuracy and low speed have a perfect (though inverse) correlation. In consequence, they cannot possibly be based upon any different variable factors ; if power depends upon *g*, so must speed, and *vice versa*.

SATURATION OF POWER AND OF SPEED WITH *G*

Measurement of power and speed separately. Because both power and speed involve *g*, however, it by no means follows that they should do this to an equal amount. Granting that the two are perfectly inter-correlated and therefore equally saturated with *g* so long as they are regarded apart from accidental influences, still these latter actually occur and may quite well affect the two in unequal degree.

Upon this question, also, the experiments we have been quoting appear to throw some light. The following are the correlations with *g* shown respectively by the goodness and speed of the same operation :

	Goodness.	Speed.	Ratio.
Sentences - -	·86	·64	1·34
Figures - -	·81	·64	1·26
Addition - -	·69	·50	1·38
Cancellation -	·24	·35	·66
Ticking rings -	·23	·55	·42

[1] *Loc. cit.* p. 214.

[2] The fact that a person can improve his speed of response at the cost of its goodness has, of course, nothing to do with his degree of total efficiency taking both into account.

From these figures, the surmise was made that with the top three tests the goodness was obtained under very different conditions from those holding with the bottom two. As regards the top three, " it is achieved in the face of some intellectual difficulty " ; but with the bottom two " the mistakes are of the nature of carelessness, being easily avoidable by the worst patients if not obliged to hurry." For the tests of " intellectual difficulty," it was concluded, accuracy surpasses speed in respect of weighting or saturation with g; for the other kind, the reverse happens.

This result, however, stands in need of being reconciled with the extraordinarily different one which has been reported by Whipple ; when here the class-standing of 50 boys was compared with their performance in the Cancellation test, the correlation with accuracy in the test was zero, and with speed it was − ·40 ! [1] The primary explanation for this negative value would appear to be as already given for the results of McCall (ch. x. p. 155). That is to say, the children lowest in a class are generally among the oldest, and therefore tend to cancel at greater speed (if for no other reason, by sheer virtue of greater muscular development) ; in such case, the correlation of class-standing with speed in test will naturally enough be negative. A further and contributory explanation may perhaps be found in the fact mentioned above, that either accuracy or speed may be preferred by the subject at will. Now Whipple tested his children collectively, whereby arbitrariness of preference was allowed unrestricted play ; but Hart and the present writer did their testing individually, whereby such arbitrariness could be, and actually was, kept within very narrow limits ; the over careful testees were incited to go faster, whilst the over impetuous were warned to be more careful.

Measurement by varying relative influence. The preceding difficulty derives from the ambitious attempt to measure the amounts of g in goodness and in speed separately. It

---

[1] *Manual of Mental and Physical Tests*, i. p. 319.

may be avoided by only varying the *relative* influence of these two characters, and examining the effect of this upon the amount of *g* in a measure of total efficiency (wherein goodness and speed are pooled together).

For such purpose, tests may be constructed of the two kinds already encountered in this chapter ; those in which ample time is allowed, so that speed has little or no scope ; and those in which the time allowed is too brief for any but the fastest subjects to reach the end, so that here speed becomes of vital importance. This procedure was adopted in some very notable experiments of Bernstein :

"Tèn sets of tests were devised embodying this principle. Each set consisted of 20 separate tests, this number being made up of four each of the following five kinds : Sentence Completion, Directions, Concomitants, Analogies, and Moral Classifications. The four tests in each case varied in length—two being short ('leisure' tests) and the other two long ('haste' tests). Thus each of the five kinds of tests were worked by the subjects at four different speeds." [1]

For each of these four speeds the correlations were calculated between the total scores (with deductions for errors) and the teachers' estimates of "intelligence." The following was the result :

Degree of Speed.	Very leisurely.	Rather leisurely.	Rather fast.	Very fast.
Correlation - -	·504	·520	·520	·491

The author concluded that :

"No clear advantage can therefore be claimed by either the 'leisure' tests or the 'haste' tests." If anything, "an intermediate length of test seems to be the most desirable."

The general conclusion to be drawn from the preceding researches would seem to be that in principle at least the characters of goodness and speed stand upon similar footing

[1] *Brit. J. Psych.* 1924, *Mon. Suppl.* vii.

in respect of saturation with g. In actual practice, large differences may be manifested ; but these depend upon the nature and amount of the irrelevant influences introduced ; moreover, such influences may sometimes tend to injure more the measurements of goodness and sometimes more those of speed.

THE FACULTY OF QUICKNESS

Trend of general opinion. There remains one further fundamental question about power and speed. Suppose that any person performs excellently in some test of speed, and that he is then going to be tried in further different performances of which some will test speed but others power. Is he more likely to excel in those for speed than in those for power ? Evidently, we are back again at the old problem of specific correlation and group factors. If the person does have more chance of excelling in the further tests of speed, then this is equivalent to saying that speed is a group factor producing overlap and therefore specific correlation. Analogously, of course, as regards power.

Now, the trend of general opinion seems strongly set towards answering in the affirmative. Throughout all ages and from every conceivable standpoint—psychological, philosophical, pedagogical, industrial, social, and otherwise —the distinction has been emphatically drawn between those who can think quickly and those who can do so well.

Nor is this universal opinion incompatible with any result so far quoted in the present chapter. We have, indeed, seen that some inter-correlation between two different measures of speed must be attributed to their common participation in g ; but this does not preclude their having *additional* correlation on account of both being specially measures of speed.

Evidence of experiment. To settle this new question, we must needs revert to the same criterion as hitherto. But we may apply it to either of two different kinds of material (the same two that served the former question).

The one kind consists in the scores for accuracy and those for speed, each of these characters being treated separately. This is the more ambitious of the two kinds of basis of procedure, but also the more precarious.

For brevity we will call the correlation " paired " when it is between goodness in any performance and goodness in another, or between speed in any performance and speed in another ; conversely, it will be called " unpaired " when between goodness in one performance and speed in another. The question is, then, does the product of the two paired correlations tend to be any larger than that of the unpaired ?

An answer is supplied by the work of Hart with the present writer. The paired correlations show no advantage, or in other words there is no significant tetrad difference ; there is therefore no specific correlation or group factor.[1]

The other and more reliable kind of material consists in the total scores (goodness and speed pooled) for the " leisure " and the " haste " tests respectively, as constructed by Bernstein. If accuracy acts as a group factor, it will produce specific correlation between any two of the tests done at leisure ; if speed is one, it will have a similar effect on those done in haste. One or both these " paired " correlations will have an advantage in magnitude over the " unpaired " ones. In the experimental result, nothing of

---

[1] The following tetrad is typical :

	Figures, Goodness.	Figures, Speed.
Adding, goodness	·61	·52
Adding, speed	·42	·26

The tetrad difference comes to ·61 × ·26 − ·52 × ·42 = ·06 with a p.e. of ·04.

To examine the results of this work more exhaustively, we may with sufficient approximation replace all such single correlations by average values. Thus, in place of the correlation between the goodness for Figures and that for Adding, we can put the average correlation between the respective goodnesses for all different tests. Similarly, with reference to correlation between speed and speed, as also between goodness and goodness, for different tests. The ensuing tetrad is as shown. The tetrad difference is only ·006.

	Goodness$_a$.	Speed$_a$.
Goodness$_b$	·21	·23
Speed$_b$	·23	·28

the sort occurs. The product of the paired correlation is just about equal to that of the unpaired, so that the tetrad difference is close upon zero, and the existence of any group factor is disproved.[1]

Delusiveness of ordinary observation. In view, however, of the universally held opposite opinion—based on ordinary observation—that quickness of thought does constitute a special ability in which some persons surpass others, this ordinary observation itself was brought within the scope of Bernstein's research :

> " Two estimates of this quality (slowness) were obtained—one estimate was supplied by the class teachers and the other by the manual instructor. . . . The subjects were kept under observation for some time previous to the estimate being made, their " slowness *irrespective of their grade of intelligence* being constantly noted."

These two subjectively formed estimates of slowness (and therefore of quickness also) were then pooled together and the result was compared with the actual quickness displayed in the experiments. A measure of this latter for any person was readily furnished by the average of all his scores in the haste tests minus the average for all in the leisure ones. Now, between these subjective estimates and the objective measurements the correlation proved to be close on zero ($\cdot075$) ; that is to say, the estimates found no corroboration in the actual facts. This result, the author not unnaturally concludes,

> " is altogether inconsistent with the existence of a general speed factor." [2]

And the same conclusion may be reached in another way.

[1] Dividing the two kinds of tests into two pools as before (see pp. 223) there ensues the following tetrad :

					Leisures$_a$.	Haste$_a$.
Leisure$_b$	-	-	-	-	$\cdot854$	$\cdot856$
Haste$_b$	-	-	-	-	$\cdot856$	$\cdot840$

The tetrad difference $= -\cdot013$ with a p.e. of $\cdot017$. *Loc. cit.* p. 252.

[2] *Loc. cit.* p. 50.

If the subjective estimates of quickness had really been—as they purported to be—" irrespective of intelligence," then their correlation with the leisure tests of intelligence ought to have been about zero ; in particular, they ought to have been much lower than their correlation with the speed tests. Nothing of the sort happened. The actual correlations of the estimates of quickness with the leisure tests was + ·450, and with the haste tests + ·368. This appears to demonstrate that what the observers had taken to be pure quickness and slowness was after all, in spite of their supposing otherwise, mainly a greater or less degree of " intelligence."

Turn where we may, then, no support whatever is found for the common view, that mental speed constitutes a functional unity or group factor ; and the same may be said of goodness. A person may, of course, have more aptitude for speed than goodness (or *vice versa*) in any *special* sort of operation, but he has no such bias *all round*.

Explanation of the fallacy. How shall all this negative experimental evidence be reconciled with the equally unanimous but contrary verdict of daily observation ?   The latter must needs have, if not an adequate reason, at least some cause. Bernstein himself had originally been led to just the same verdict by his own " common sense " observations ; he had started upon his experimental work with an expectation that its results would be the very opposite to what they proved to be.

The key to the paradox seems to lie in the fact that the experimental procedure can succeed in isolating and measuring pure aptitude, or at any rate pure ability, whereas the ordinary observation suffers this to be confused with many other influences. As to the nature of these, Bernstein's conclusion is as follows :

> " The most obvious speed differences observed were those following the lines of cleavage in the interests of the boys. One boy, for instance, invariably outdistanced the others in the group in answering questions in geography ; his written work showed no such

marked superiority. . . . Yet he was most ' alive ' in this subject, ready to pounce upon a question the moment it was delivered.

Conative differences were noted as being responsible for speed differences with several boys. On the one hand were the ' triers ' in whom the effort to answer questions was always evident. On the other hand, were those in whom conation was defective ; effort to answer questions was either absent or required too much time to be effective.

A semblance of ' slowness ' was given by (a) physical defects, or by (b) temperamental peculiarities. One boy in the first group stammered so badly that he abandoned any effort to participate in the oral work. To a stranger he might easily appear slow. . . . In another case belonging to the same group, sheer inanition was responsible for what appeared to be extreme slowness.

Observation revealed a class of thinkers of a deliberate type who preferred to sacrifice speed to accuracy. These boys would not venture to answer until they had satisfied themselves that they had given the question sufficient consideration. . . . With them not only was the start slow, but the whole of the work was done slowly." [1]

These observations indicate that broad group factors, even when not involved in ability itself, may readily be introduced by adventitious influences. In particular, the persons who *try* to be accurate rather than quick at one test are very likely to do so at others also. Conversely, some persons will tend throughout to work in a slap-dash manner. Such tendencies can actually be detected by the tetrads. Here is an example from the investigation of Carothers [2] :

			Cancellation.	Completion.
Word naming	-	-	-	·40	·22
Mixed reactions	-	-	-	·03	·48

[1] *Loc. cit.* pp. 19-21.   [2] *Archives of Psychology*, 1921, No. 46.

S.A.M.   R

The tetrad difference $= \cdot183$ which, since the p.e. is only $\cdot036$, is decidedly significant. This can at once be explained by the fact that both the Cancellation and the Word-naming were measured in respect of speed and not quality, so that in both alike those subjects who were trying specially to go fast would have an advantage over those who were caring more to be accurate.

To call such influences theoretically " adventitious," however, by no means implies that they ought to be neglected in practice. On the contrary, they in all likelihood are often sources of grave misjudgment. Another word of warning may not be out of place. Some readers may be objecting to the term " goodness " of cognitive response, on the ground that it may be of widely different kinds, such as " depth," " originality," and so forth. This question has not been left out of account, but reserved for chapter xx.

CONCLUSION

On the whole, then, g has shown itself to measure a factor both in goodness and in speed of cognitive process. Such " goodness " is here taken as at bottom indicating clearness.

The connection between the goodness and the speed is that of being inter-changeable. If the conditions of the case are such as to eliminate the influence of speed, then g measures goodness, and *vice versa*. When—as is most usual —both influences are in play, then g measures the efficiency compounded of both.

In agreement with this complete inter-changeability between goodness and speed of response, neither of them constitutes a group factor or produces specific correlation. The almost unanimous view that some persons are on the whole unable to think quickly and yet are quite able to think clearly would seem to be a most grave error.[1]

---

[1] The trend of this chapter appears to be in excellent agreement with the recent admirable work of Boring, see *J. Exper. Psych.* 1926, ix. Also much illumination is both imparted to and received from the work of Hargreaves (*loc. cit.* p. 187).

CHAPTER XV

MENTAL SPAN. DISTRIBUTION OF " ATTENTION "

OUTLINE OF TOPIC

Formulation of the law. Our consideration of the ultimate
quantitative laws will now turn from the universal to the
partial ; from that which expresses the very nature of cognitive growth to that which only governs certain fundamental phases of this ; from the twin characters of Clearness
and Speed to the five influences of Span, Retentivity,
Fatigue, Conation, and Primordial Potency.

Beginning in the present chapter with Span, this has been
characterized in the following law : *Every mind tends to keep
its total simultaneous output constant in quantity, however
varying in quality.*[1] Here the " quantity " of the " output "
indicates nothing else than just the clearness and the speed
which we have been discussing. The " constancy " as explained in chapter ix., is analogous to that of physical
energy ; that is to say, it is taken to hold of a hypothetical
entity ; its basis in actual observation consists only of
equivalencies (see pp. 128-129).

---

[1] *The Nature of Intelligence,* pp. 131-2.

259

Problems arising. The points which this law raises are numerous, and in part extremely contentious. We are in danger of plunging into that ocean of controversy which since the most ancient days has been tossed sky-high by windy metaphysics. Save for walking warily, we may be drawn into such discussions as whether the feat of perceiving more than one marble at the same time is compatible with the unity of the human soul ! Or else, tired of buffeting with things and ideas, we may let ourselves be enticed into the harbourage of empty words, such as " attention."

But if, instead, we hold on to our course of plain scientific research into individual differences of ability, the questions to be encountered become straightforward enough. Does the total cognitive output vary in amount from one person to another ? Do any such variations depend upon g ? Are they and those of g simply identical ? If not, why not ? Further problems are originated, and those preceding much complicated, by the fact that the magnitude of the output —like that of physical energy—has two dimensions, intensive and extensive ; the clearness and speed of an operation may either attain to a high grade, or else cover a wide field ; the " attention " may be either concentrated or else diffused.

In this way there cannot fail to arise once more the question of group factors and specific correlation. Which, if any, of the preceding characters generates any such thing ? In particular, is a group factor produced either by the intensity of cognition, or by the extensity, or by both ? Here again we meet a topic that bulks large in literature, but this time not often in a controversial fashion ; the answer seems rather to have been tacitly assumed—and in the affirmative. Indeed, upon such an assumption have been founded many of the most ambitious applications of psychological science to education and to industry. Binet and Henri, for instance, urge that individuals present large differences in their general ability to execute several acts simultaneously.[1] Jastrow inquires how we shall cultivate and develop this "power of carrying on two mental processes at the same time."[2] Cohen and Dieffenbacher propose to measure "the power of executing two operations at the same time," and remark that "this power to dilate the attention is a very variable individual property."[3] Lasurski reckons such dilatability of attention as among the fundamental characteristics of an individual.[4] Meumann declares that the abilities to concentrate and to diffuse attention produce

"two quite different types of intelligence. According as the capacity of a man tends towards the one or other side of attention, he is disposed towards learned observation and scientific thinking or towards the practical vocations of life. The concentrative kind ought to be possessed by the man of science; the diffusive kind, by such men as teachers, officers, conductors of orchestras, and hotel proprietors."[5]

Above all, the measurement of such "concentrative attention" would appear to have been actually made to serve as the basis for selecting the entire personnel of a gigantic railway system (see ch. iii. p. 27).

RELATION OF SPAN TO G

Evidence of tachistoscopic experiments. The trouble about all these wide reaching statements and implications is their lack, as it seems, of any tangible, supporting evidence. The present inquiry will be along experimental lines, which have the advantage that such evidence as may be obtained lies open to inspection and verification.

First, we will take the question as to how far the total simultaneous cognitive output of a person correlates with

[1] "La Psychologie Individuelle," *Année Psychol.* ii. 1895-6.
[2] *Amer. J. Psychol.* iv. 1891.
[3] *Beihefte z. Zeit. f. ang. Psychol.* ii. 1911.
[4] *Pädag. Monogr.* hrsg. v. Meumann, xiv. 1912.
[5] *Vorl. z. Einf. in d. exper. Pädagogik*, 1907.

his amount of g. And since this output has the two dimensions of intensity and extensity, the question divides up into one about each of these.

As regards the intensity, evidence that this depends on g would seem to be forthwith supplied by the common test of Opposites. For no single test, on the whole, displays higher correlations with g than this does ; and yet in none does the mental content essentially involved appear to have a more restricted field, so that the preponderant source of the correlation must be the intensity rather than the extensity of the process.

As regards examining the latter dimension, one naturally thinks at once of what have been called tachistoscopic exposures. Some object or collection of objects is displayed for a fraction of a second ; in this moment of time, the subject has to perceive as many of the objects or other items as he possibly can. For the most part, the objects have consisted of printed texts, isolated words, nonsense syllables, single letters, geometrical forms, dots, lines, colours, and such like.

But, unfortunately, the results of these experiments cannot be accepted as conclusive. When printed texts have been used, the correlations with estimates of " intelligence " have, indeed, sometimes been quite high. This, however, admits of explanation by the fact of the more intelligent children having learnt to read better than the others. When non-verbal objects have been used, the correlations have tended to be considerably lower, although still positive. This lowness, however, seems to be sufficiently explained by the large influence that in such cases devolves upon the sensory organs (see ch. xii. p. 217).

Evidence of simultaneous operations. Frequent also have been experiments where a person has to perform two distinct operations at the same time. Among these have been reading and writing, reading and reciting, reading and cancellation, dotting and mental arithmetic, and unlike motor performances with the two hands.

Of such experiments, however, only one appears to have

been planned and executed in a sufficiently systematic manner to throw light upon our present problem; it was the work of McQueen.[1] His subjects were 40 boys, of ages 11-13, in Grade VI. A of a school. These boys were made to do five tests, each having two forms; in one the " attention " had to be concentrated upon a single operation at a time; in the other, it had to be diffused over two at a time. These tests may be summarily described as follows:

CONCENTRATIVE TEST.	DIFFUSIVE TEST.
1. Tapping and Adding, separately.	Tapping and Adding at the same time.
2. Card Sorting and Counting separately.[2]	Card Sorting and Counting Aloud, at the same time.
3. Threading discs on a needle unseen and Crossing Out every third of a row of *o*'s, each performance separately.	Threading the discs with one hand, whilst Crossing Out the *o*'s with the other.
4. Discriminating the sizes of two circles exposed to view for a fraction of a second.	Discriminating the sizes of four circles so exposed to view.
5. McDougall's dotting test.	The same test, but arranged for both hands simultaneously.

The correlations found between these different tests are given in the following table; the values in brackets are those of each concentrative test with the corresponding diffusive one; *c* indicates concentrative, and *d* diffusive.

	1*c*	2*c*	3*c*	4*c*	5*c*	1*d*	2*d*	3*d*	4*d*	5*d*
1*c*	—	·47	·47	·30	·38	(·61)	·51	·55	·18	·37
2*c*	·47	—	·10	·10	·08	·28	(·62)	·07	·19	·02
3*c*	·47	·10	—	·36	·47	·39	·29	(·84)	·11	·44
4*c*	·30	·18	·36	—	·34	·38	·48	·36	(·42)	·37
5*c*	·38	·08	·47	·34	—	·29	·00	·57	·06	(·89)
1*d*	·61	·28	·39	·38	·29	—	·34	·38	·39	·31
2*d*	·51	(·62)	·29	·48	·00	·34	—	·25	·30	·08
3*d*	·55	·07	(·84)	·36	·57	·38	·25	—	·09	·58
4*d*	·18	·19	·11	(·42)	·06	·39	·30	·09	—	·00
5*d*	·37	·02	·44	·37	(·89)	·31	·06	·58	·00	—

[1] *Brit. J. Psych. Monogr. Suppl.* v. 1917.

[2] The counting was done by 3's, starting from a number given by the experimenter.

We may now collect the scores of each subject into two pools, one for all the concentrative tests and one for all the diffusive. The former pool turns out to have a correlation with g amounting to ·45 ; the latter pool, one of ·42. That is to say, the two kinds of ability, involving intensive and extensive cognition respectively, correlate with g to just about the same amount.

If these experiments can be accepted at their face value, then we have here a corroboration of the law of span, according to which intensity and extensity are but alternative manifestations of one and the same general energy.

A closer view, however, reveals several possible objections. The most serious, perhaps, consists in a doubt as to whether in the operation taken to be diffusive the two operations do really occur quite at the same time. Numerous writers have emphatically denied that any such feat can ever be accomplished ; they have declared that all seeming instances must be nothing more than rapid alternation. Thus Stewart deduces from " the astonishing rapidity of thought " that those activities which have a semblance of occurring simultaneously may really be

> " different successive acts in an interval of time so short as to produce the same sensible effect as if they had been exerted at one and the same moment." [1]

Accordingly, McQueen took especial pains to investigate this matter by means of careful and systematic introspection.[2] His chief results were as follows :

(1) Sometimes, though very rarely, there did occur a simultaneous " attention " to the two tasks as separate. But in some even of these cases, the person's effort seemed to be monopolized by one task, while the other was treated in " distinctly a waiting attitude."

(2) Far more frequently, there occurred a successiveness

---

[1] *Philosophy of the Human Mind*, 1843.

[2] These introspections were not done with the boys, but with special subjects highly trained in introspection.

of attention from the one activity to the other ; this happened for every subject and for every test.

(3) In such cases of successiveness, however, the activity not in the focus of attention was very often still simultaneously in consciousness, only not focalized. At times one, or even both, of the activities seemed to become altogether unconscious.

(4) Very often, the two activities appeared to be in some way unified. Such reports were made by the subjects as the following :

> " I never felt there were two tasks."   " No feeling of two tasks at all ; it seemed as much one act as if I were dotting with one hand."   " When the two things are done together, there is a tendency, I think, to regard them as one task."   " At times, I feel the whole process to be a kind of rhythm, and this seems to unify the two."

These results may be summed up as indicating that a simultaneous extensive cognition is by no means impossible, but that it occurs much more naturally when its constituents are cognized in relation to each other.[1]

Evidence of simultaneous items in a single operation. The preceding work suggests that the most effective study of cognitive extension will not be found in two disconnected operations, but rather in a single operation which has many constituent items intimately inter-related.

Now, a test into which such a multiplicity of items can be introduced with exceptional ease and convenience is the familiar Cancellation. One way of effecting this purpose is by the ordinary procedure of increasing the number of letters to be cancelled. But another way is to make the cancelling done, not to any prescribed letters, but to such letters as may happen to follow each other in a prescribed relation.

Both these ways have been applied by Strasheim,[2] and to

---

[1] The manner in which a single pulse of conation covers an extensive system of mental activity corroborates the research done by Topçiu, under the direction of Wirth (*Psych. Studien*, x. 1917).

[2] *Loc. cit.* p. 214.

two groups of subjects. The one group consisted of 12 children, who had an average age of $8\frac{1}{2}$ years and were selected by their teachers as especially "bright." The other group comprised 24 children of about the same scholastic standing, but nearly three years older, so that they were rated as "dull." The instructions for the test remained in sight of the subjects throughout, in order to reduce the influence of memory. In scoring, the speed and the accuracy were compounded into a single index of efficiency. The actual scores were as follows :

	With prescribed letters. No. of letters.				With prescribed relation.
	2	4	6	8	
Young-bright : -	28	21	15	13	21
Old-dull : - -	38	25	17	12	14

As is apparent, the Old-dull excel at the simpler tasks, whereas the Young-bright do so at those which are more complex, and especially when the complexity derives from the added relation.

On the whole, then, a dependence upon g is shown by the extensity no less than by the intensity of a person's cognitive output at any given moment. These two quantitative dimensions would seem to constitute alternative manifestations of the self-same mental energy, just as they do in the case of physical energy.

Extrinsicalness of specific factors. At this point, the reader may not improbably be tempted to criticize as follows : Take, for example, he will say, McQueen's Adding and Tapping, which were in one case done successively and in the other case simultaneously. In each case the activities involved in the test can be analyzed into two parts. First, there is the essential quality of the processes, namely, those of adding and tapping ; this part contributes the specific factor of s, which is therefore the same in both cases. And then there is the distribution of the general energy of g, which distribution is in the one case intensive and in the other extensive.   Thus, the two tests are identical as regards the first constituent part and functionally equivalent as regards the second.   If this be so, then the two tests should be perfectly inter-correlated.   But this conclusion is at once contradicted by the actual facts ; the correlation of Adding and Tapping successively with Adding and Tapping simultaneously is not $+1\cdot00$, but only $+\cdot61$.[1]

Now, the preceding paradox did not escape the notice of McQueen.   From the fact of the diffusive test not correlating perfectly with the concentrative one, he inferred that the s is *not* wholly the same in both cases.   And he went a considerable way towards showing how such a difference arises. He picked out, for instance, such influences as that of immediate memory, which may enter quite differently into the diffusive test as compared with the concentrative.   So, too, may various emotional influences.

All this recalls a very important fact which we have already encountered more than once.   It is that the elements entering into the specific factor or s of any operation are not restricted to what we have called the intrinsic character of this operation ; they largely include other elements of a more extrinsic or adventitious character.[2]

QUESTION OF GROUP FACTORS

A further problem.   There remains the second great question arising out of the topic of the mental span.   This problem, even if theoretically less momentous than that which we have just been considering, is for practical purposes more important still.   Do or do not the intensity and the extensity of cognition—in popular terms, the concentration and the diffusion of attention—constitute group factors ?   Otherwise expressed, does the person who is better able to concentrate than to diffuse his attention for

[1] The correction for attenuation is so small as to be negligible.
[2] See ch. xii, p. 207 ; also xiii, pp. 239-241.

one kind of performance tend to be so also for other kinds ? In current literature, as we have seen, the answer is unanimously taken for granted as being affirmative. What verdict is reached by the more laborious way of experiment ?

On this point, the experimental results so far quoted have brought nothing decisive. To the extent that the concentration depends upon g, of course, it cannot possibly be a group factor ; and the same applies to the diffusion. But we have just seen that each of these two depends further upon an s of its own ; and this latter might or might not—for all we have found hitherto—constitute a group factor ; that is to say, the different concentrative operations might or might not overlap in respect of the s ; similarly, the diffusive operations.

Experimental evidence. An answer to this problem, however, has been supplied by McQueen in another way ; indeed, the settlement of this point was the chief aim of his whole research. He submitted his data to a great variety of statistical methods, and by each of them concordantly he arrived at the verdict, that there is no evidence whatever for the existence of an ability to concentrate attention, or inversely to diffuse it.

There may still perhaps be room to cavil at the statistical methods at his disposal. But now we can treat the same data by the conclusive criterion of tetrad differences. In this manner, using the same procedure as hitherto, we get from the table on page 263 the following tetrad of correlations :

	Concentration$_a$.	Diffusion$_a$.
Concentration$_b$ - - -	·516	·502
Diffusion$_b$ - - -	·502	·470

The tetrad difference is -- ·018 (p.e. = ·027). By this low value the conclusion of McQueen is fully corroborated.

For completeness of proof, the possibility must be reckoned with, that a group factor might make its appearance on turning from the artificial diffusion involved in two disconnected performances to the more natural diffusion of a

single performance having manifold inter-related constituents. For examining this point, use may be made of the
collaborative work mentioned on p. 201, where Completion
and Inferences were markedly complex, whilst for contrast
Synonyms and Classification were markedly simple. The
tetrad is as follows :

	Synonyms.	Completion.
Classification	·57	·45
Inferences	·21	·18

The tetrad difference is only ·007. Once more, then, there
is no sign whatever of any group factor.

CONCLUSION

To sum up the present chapter, the chief theoretical result
has been that both the intensity and the extensity of cognitive operations depend on g. In so far as they do so, the
two constitute alternative dimensions of the same constant
cognitive output characterizing each individual.

In this way the evidence derived from objectively measured
individual differences comes into perfect agreement with
that obtained from direct introspection. For, as Wirth
remarks :

" One of the most certain introspective results is that
the competition of ideas consists just in the mutual
restriction of degree of consciousness." [1]

Hereby, strong support is afforded to the hypothesis of a
general mental energy.

On the practical side, the most important result has been
that neither the intensity nor the extensity generates any
kind or degree of group factor. Although faculties for each
of these—otherwise expressed, for concentrated and diffused
attention—have been implied or stated very widely ; and
although upon them have been based projects and even
actions of grave moment for education and industry ; still,
according to our present experimental evidence, neither
faculty has any real existence.

[1] "Zur Theorie des Bewusstseinsumfanges," *Phil. Stud.* xx. 1902.

CHAPTER XVI

LAW OF RETENTIVITY OF DISPOSITIONS

OUTLINE OF TOPIC

Formulation of the law. Next after the quantitative principle of Span or Constant Output comes that of Retentivity. Here we arrive at a topic whose treatment in current literature has been incomparably more abundant and more scientific. Still, even in this case, the psychological analysis has left much to be desired. Among all the copious discussion and even experimentation about " memory," " reproduction," and " association," there has been unexpectedly small success at penetrating down to and grasping distinctly the ultimate principle of pure retentivity in its simplest and most fundamental significance ; that in which it pervades all material solid substances, organic or inorganic, and especially colloidal.

Perhaps, indeed, this principle scarcely admitted of being adequately grasped before the development of the other concept which has so much occupied us, that of eduction. To understand the respective natures of eduction and re-production—in their trenchant contrast, in their ubiquitous co-operation, and in their genetic inter-linkage—to do this would appear to be for the psychology of individual abilities, and even for that of cognition in general, the very beginning of wisdom.

The retentivity may be formulated in a single law as follows : The occurrence of any cognitive event produces a tendency for it to occur afterwards.[1] Such a tendency, however, manifests itself in two ways so widely unlike that perhaps we should more properly talk of two laws instead of one. The first of these—which alone supplies the topic of the present chapter—is that *cognitive events by occurring establish dispositions which facilitate their recurrence.* This includes as a special case of peculiar importance the law of *association,* which is here taken to mean that cognitive events by accompanying each other establish dispositions to do so thereafter.

Such associative connections are taken by most writers as fully explaining the process of *reproduction.* But they would seem inadequate for this purpose ; no bare retention can possibly account for ideas re-appearing when once they have ceased to exist. But further explanatory assistance can be invoked from the other law already discussed, that of span or constant output. For this constancy of output accounts for the ideas being produced in consciousness at all, whereas the associations show why they are of one kind rather than of another ; differently expressed, the constant output implies the generating of a certain amount of energy, whereas the associations supply this energy with paths of least resistance.

Problems arising. This law of dispositions that we have now to consider calls up numerous problems of the highest interest, both theoretical and practical. One large group of these concerns the relation of such disposition-forming to *g.*

---

[1] *The Nature of Intelligence,* etc., p. 132.

Does a person's g (or " intelligence ") consist in his aptitude to acquire dispositions ?

The direct advocacy of such a theorem appears to have been comparatively infrequent. But doctrines that seem to imply it have enjoyed, and still enjoy, a very wide currency indeed. Here may be included, for instance, all those writings which straightly assert that intelligence consists in " the capacity to learn " ; for " learning "—when the term is thus used without any saving qualifications—cannot but largely consist in the forming of dispositions (see ch. ii. pp. 19-20). Another instance is afforded by those statements which, adopting a physiological terminology, depict intelligence as the property of the brain to preserve " traces " or " engrams " of its experience ; for these must, in great measure at least, be the physical rendering of what have psychologically been called dispositions.

A further instance can seemingly be derived from the doctrine that tests of intelligence measure a person's ability to establish mental " bonds " ; for these, as often interpreted at any rate, would appear to mean little more than associative connections. And here, finally, must be placed those authors who maintain that the higher powers of intelligence fail to be called into play by the ordinary tests ; these latter, they say, are limited to unfamiliar operations on unfamiliar material in brief periods of time ; to reach the higher powers, they urge us to go rather to the achievements of long periods with material that has become thoroughly familiar. For all such prolonged operations are really made up of brief ones, and all the said familiarity must needs derive from the establishment of dispositions.

Furthermore, we have in the present chapter to encounter once again the great problem as to the existence of a unitary faculty. In the speech of " the plain man " at any rate, such a faculty seems to be definitely accepted ; for he habitually credits people with having in general " a good memory " (or a bad one). But, nevertheless, he is just as likely to use upon occasion language implying the opposite doctrine, that memory splits up into a large number of abilities independent of each other ; he may remark, for instance, that he has an excellent memory for faces but a poor one for names. Even with professed psychologists there appears to be a danger of thus falling into both these contradictory assumptions.

INDEPENDENCE BETWEEN DISPOSITIONS AND G

Isolated recurrence of ideas. Beginning with the first of the two groups of problems just outlined, we have to seek for facts that can show how retentivity—in the sense of the power to establish dispositions and cause reproductions—is related in general to g. But among the reproductions must be distinguished at least three marked types. The first consists in an isolated and casual recurrence of an idea. Another is supplied by any of those systematically connected propositions that make up a person's disposable " information," general or scholastic. The third derives from the still more systematically inter-linked reproductions that enter into his remembrance of his own past.

The first type, that of reproducing isolated ideas, may be found abundantly even in such tests as are in the main eductive ; the two kinds of process are conglomerated. None the less, they can still be sharply distinguished ; there is a simple way of doing so ; in every genuine eduction, the required response is intrinsically determined by what has been given to start with, so that whatever constituent in the response has *not* been thus determined must needs be credited to reproduction. This fact may be illustrated by the following interesting contrast due to Perera [1] :

(1) Mainly eductive :

" Snow is to White as Coal is to——."

Here, the ideas given to start with (Snow, White, and Coal) completely determine the response, " Black." This response

---

[1] *The Qualitative Analysis of Intelligence Tests*, 1922 (thesis to be seen in the Library of the University of London).

is wholly self-evident ; it could be effected by a visitor from Mars (provided, of course, that he had the starting ideas). The process is therefore essentially eductive.

(2) Mainly reproductive :

" White is to Snow as Black is to——."

Here, the ideas given to start with do not determine any response completely, beyond the bare idea of " a-black-thing." No detailed response is wholly self-evident ; the visitor from Mars, however great his *g*, might quite well be baffled. The evoking of a correct response (as " ink," or " coal," or " tar ") requires therefore not only some eduction (to get to the general idea of " a-black-thing "), but also some reproduction (to get to such a particular idea as " ink ").

As regards such isolated reproductions, the most enlightening research seems to be that which was recently contributed by Hamid and has been already quoted in chapter xii. (p. 204). From this work we have already learnt several important differences between good and bad tests of *g*. But still more fundamental in this respect would appear to be the difference which separates reproduction from eduction. The author illustrates the two by the following pair of Analogies :

(1) Mainly eductive :

" Blacksmith is to Horseshoe as Builder is to
Design Survey *Dwelling* Painting

(2) Largely reproductive :

" Duet is to Orchestra Playing as Partners are to
Whist Company Business Finance."

In (1) the operation is based throughout upon words that may fairly be assumed as well known to all the subjects under test, so that only the superimposed eductions are " critical " in the sense of supplying a process that some subjects can accomplish but not others (see p. 207). In (2), on the other hand, there is obviously needed some previous acquaintance with the game of whist, an experience far from being universal. As result of the testing, the bright subjects succeeded much better than the dull at the mainly eductive operation, but showed little if any advantage at the one that is so largely reproductive. And very similar seems to be the tendency everywhere ; on the whole, the bright subjects surpassed the dull four times more often in the eductive than in the reproductive tests. Hamid finally concludes that

" Eduction and not Reproduction is the only reliable basis of a successful test." [1]

General Information. Turning to the second type of reproduction, that to which the name of information is usually applied, and beginning with the general as opposed to the scholastic kind, this has been investigated in a recent work of McCrae.[2] Here use was made of the Binet series as revised by Burt and supplemented by Terman. The sub-tests making up the series were sorted by McCrae according as they seemed to involve more essentially eduction or reproduction. Then the whole series was applied to children of two special sorts. The one consisted of the so-called mentally defective ; these had enjoyed the full ordinary amount of time at school. The other sort were defective physically instead of mentally, and to such a degree that their amount of schooling had been greatly curtailed. Finally, McCrae ascertained the success of these two sorts of children with both the eductive and the reproductive sub-tests as compared with their success with the whole series ; the latter or total success, of course, constituted what is called their " mental age."

As an example may be cited the sub-test for 8-year-old normal children, which consisted in having to recognize coins. Here McCrae decided that " there is clearly nothing of noegenesis (eduction)," but only reproduction. And in point of fact, the physically defective who on the whole series reached the mental age of eight did no better at this particular sub-test than did the mentally defective who

[1] *Brit. J. Psychol.* xvi. 1925, p. 115.
[2] *Loc. cit.* p. 163.

reached the same mental age ; just 54 per cent. of both sorts succeeded in recognizing the coins as required of them. Very different were the results obtained from another of the sub-tests for the same age, where such questions had to be answered as : In what way are wood and coal alike ? This McCrae judged to involve eduction ; it was passed by 60 per cent. of the physically defective, but only 20 per cent. of the mentally defective (again taking in both cases only those whose mental age was eight).

In order to get a numerical valuation of the whole tendency to agreement between his psychological analysis and the subsequently obtained actual results of testing, the sub-tests were divided into four classes according to the degree that they had been rated by him as eductive, and then they were similarly divided according to the actually shown superiority of the physically over the mentally defective. The grade of correspondence between the two classifications is shown in the following table of the frequencies with which the two differ by 0, 1, 2, or 3 places :

Mental age.	Frequency of deviation by 0 to 3 places respectively.			
	0	1	2	3
VII.	5		3	
VIII.	6			1
IX.	3	2	1	
X.	4			2
XI.	4	1		
XII.	4	2		2
Totals	26	5	4	5

Thus 26 out of the 40 cases agreed exactly. To obtain a measure of the agreement altogether, McCrae calculated from the above data Yule's Q or coefficient of association. This came to no less than ·89. The author concludes :

" It would seem then tolerably clear that we have, in these two noegenetic principles of cognition, the most accurate theoretical criterion of the value of mental tests, and the most trustworthy standard according to which any new scales of tests may be built."

School information. So far, our discussion has referred only to the general kind of information which is picked up casually in life rather than the special kind which is systematically taught in schools. The latter kind—unlike the former—has in all tests of " intelligence " been sedulously avoided. But McCrae's work included this also, particularly as represented in the tests of Burt for Mental Arithmetic, Spelling and Reading. How far do such tests as these involve g ?

To ascertain this, McCrae compared the pool of these scholastic tests with a series devised expressly to measure g (the Oral tests mentioned on p. 202). Between the one and the other, for 47 *physically* defective youths, the correlation came to the surprisingly high value of ·83.

From such a result one might be led to suppose that the constructors of tests have hitherto been doing just what they ought not to have done, and not doing what they ought to have done ! For the general information which has been welcomed by them turns out to measure the intelligence very badly indeed ; whereas the school information which they have scrupulously rejected appears here to measure it quite well.

Nor is the superiority of the scholastic tests hard to explain. In the first place, as so excellently constructed by Burt, they to a large extent do not require information at all, but eduction ; for instance his Mental problems and his Comprehension of Reading are mainly eductive. And in the second place, even what does depend upon bare reproduction at the time of testing may nevertheless have depended on eduction at the time of being originally learnt. This last fact, no doubt, applies also to the non-scholastic kind of information ; but this latter is gained so casually as to depend on the haphazard of different persons' diverse previous experiences ; herein, it contrasts with the scholastic kind, which is taught to all the children in much the same manner.

There are, however, some less favourable aspects of the scholastic information as a measure of g. In general, school progress is very greatly influenced by emotional and conative conditions, as also by state of health ; the mere change to a more sympathetic teacher, or the removal of some minor bodily ailment, may make a child spring from the lower to the upper end of his class ; only tests of non-scholastic character avoid this gravely confusing influence. Again, the scholastic tests become grossly misleading when applied to children that have been educated in different manners ; they may have served fairly well to compare the subjects of McCrae with one another, but they would have been useless to compare them with any other subjects whose schooling had been normal ; this was proved by the fact that the mental age of these youths was only a year behind normal according to the non-scholastic tests of g, but over three years behind according to the scholastic tests.[1]

On the whole, then, the scholastic tests do not appear to have manifested any correlation with g except in so far as they involved eduction, either at the actual testing, or during the antecedent learning. Up to the present point, there has been nothing to indicate that g has any correlation with pure retentivity.

Ability to memorize. On the other hand, the cases that have been examined by us were scarcely such as to bring any correlation of this sort, even if it should exist, very clearly to view. The dispositions which were at issue had been formed in some unknown manner and at some unknown time previously to the experiments. For decisive evidence, we need instead dispositions that are formed in the actual course of the experiment itself ; and this is supplied by tests of ability to memorize.

The earliest data of this description would seem to have

[1] It seems probable that the correlation just mentioned of ·83 was unduly swollen by the special nature of the subjects. But to explain the grounds for this surmise would take us too far afield.

been those of Krueger and the present writer, who found that the memorizing of lists of numbers had a correlation with g not appreciably above zero.

Further light was thrown on the matter by the first investigation of Abelson.[1] Here nine tests were employed, which included three for memorizing respectively Sentences, Commissions, and Objects. When these three tests were ranked along with the other six according to their correlation with g, the first two were top of all, but the third was bottom of all. Such high positions for the first two, however, must be discounted by the fact that all the six non-memory tests were what would now be regarded as very poor measures of g. The later research of the same author took in such good tests of g as Opposites and Absurdities, and to these the memorizing of Sentences did show itself to be distinctly inferior, although it remained superior to all his other nine tests. He also tried this time the memorizing of Form ; but this came out very low indeed.

Next may be mentioned the results of Carey (*loc. cit.* p. 174). Here, verbal memories were tested of three sorts ; those of Sentences, Association (between words and number) and Unconnected Words. The correlations of these with estimates of intelligence had (for two school classes) the following low values :

Sentences.	Association.	Words.
·33	·20	·14

Another interesting investigation has been that of King and Homan, who applied memory tests to 64 children in elementary schools, 72 in high schools, and 110 college students.[2] Throughout, the material consisted of prose passages. But the conditions were systematically varied ; in respect of quantity, they were short (1-$1\frac{1}{2}$ minutes), medium (2-3 minutes), and long (4-6 minutes) ; in respect of quality, they were historical, descriptive, and narrative ; in respect of time interval, the testing was done in part immediately

[1] *Brit. J. Psych.* iv. 1911.
[2] *Journ. Educ. Psych.* iv. 1918.

after memorizing, and in part after a delay of 1-2 days. For the high school group, there were further tests, including some known to involve much g; also estimates were obtained of scholastic ability. The significance of all this otherwise unique work, unfortunately, is almost destroyed by want of regard for attenuation (appendix, p. i); we are compelled to accept all the correlations at their face values, which may be widely erroneous. Taking them in this way, their most obvious feature is a striking uniformity despite all the changes of condition; throughout, the memory correlates with the measures of g to an amount close upon ·30. So far as can be judged by comparison with other experiments, these values must be regarded as considerably smaller than those obtained for tests which are essentially eductive.

On the whole, then, all the preceding investigations (together with many others that could be quoted in support) indicate that the memorizing even of sentences and passages has only a medium correlation with g. And in proportion as the material to be learnt becomes either unrelated or sensory—so that the influence of eduction whilst learning diminishes—the correlation with g dwindles down towards the point of disappearance.

Adaptability to new situations. Another line for comparing the influences of reproduction and eduction is by way of the much used concept of "adaptability to new situations" (see ch. ii. p. 18).

Under this equivocal phrase most psychologists would at any rate include the already mentioned experiments of Strasheim, where the subject had to find an object in a series of mazes which, although built upon a common underlying principle, differed more or less widely in appearance (ch. xii. p. 215). As to the manner in which such a situation was met by bright and dull children respectively, the main conclusion of the author was as follows:

"With few exceptions they (the "dull" children) are able to memorize the correct paths in the five principal mazes as quickly as the 'bright'; but in the later mazes (*i.e.* those constituting the test) they continually come to grief, and their false move is always due to the influence of reproduction. In the later stages this tendency became even more noticeable. . . . Wherever the ' reversed Mazes ' were presented, the old-dull, almost without exception, went straight to the familiar spot, to the path which has been correct, when the Maze was in its ordinary position."

To sum up, he says :

" The great difference between the ' dull ' and the ' bright ' testees was that the former relied mainly upon reproduction, while the latter made use of eduction."[1]

Still more unhesitatingly may a further experiment by the same investigator be accepted as testing adaptibility to new situations ; in fact, it had been expressly devised for this very purpose. Throughout the test the choice had to be made between two persons by lot ; but such lot had to be decided under ever increasing unfamiliarity of circumstances.

First of all, the subject was provided with an original experience—as a basis of comparison—by the following story, which was read out to him :

" One day some boys wanted to play football, and so Tom and Dick, the two biggest boys, were asked to pick sides. As they had no money with which to toss for first pick, they had to find another way. One saw some pieces of paper on the ground, took two, and made one piece shorter than the other. He then held the two pieces in his hand with only the tops sticking out, so that his friend could not see which piece was the longer. He then said to his friend : ' If you draw the longer one, you shall have first pick.' "

Then followed a situation which deviated from the original experience in smallest degree :

" The next day after school the same boys decided to have a game of football. Tom and Dick, the two

---

[1] This corroborates Goddard, that the subnormal person is a " creature of habit."

biggest boys, wanted to pick sides, but no one had any money to toss for first pick. So they looked about for something else and saw some pieces of paper lying on the ground. Show me what the boys did to find out who was to have first pick."

After nine situations of gradually increasing unfamiliarity, this character reached its culminating point in the tenth :

" During the last war two English sailors were captured by the Germans. As it was summer and the water was quite warm they decided to escape by swimming. As soon as it was dark, therefore, they undressed and got into the water. When they were near the land they heard shouts and saw a boat coming along. The one said to the other, ' Look here, if one swims back to the boat and keeps it busy, the other can escape.' So they decided to toss to see who would go back. Of course they had no money, so they had to find another way."

After a minute examination of all the responses throughout the series, Strasheim summarizes the results as follows :

" *General Conclusions.*

The outstanding feature that emerges is the truth of the contention that " intelligence " must be taken to include all the processes derived from all three (qualitative) principles, and in particular that the ' two non-experiential principles most conspicuously deserve the name of intelligence.' [1] Again and again we have seen that, when any process of an eductive character is demanded, it is those testees that have been termed ' dull ' by their teachers, that have failed lamentably. And our results also seem to show clearly that ' the immediate cause of error consists in replacing the belief derived from the noegenetic principles by that which comes from the quantitative ones, especially in the form of associative reproduction.' "

[1] The author is here quoting from *The Nature of Intelligence*, etc., p. 352.

For this view as to the origin of all error, much corroborative evidence has already been cited in the present chapter ; and more can be derived from the further results of the same investigators (including Hamid), for which no space could here be allotted. But much more still has since been gathered by two later investigations now in mid course, those of Laycock and Bradley. The view about the origin of error seems to be passing beyond the stage of mere suggestion into that of positive demonstration. Should this last stage be definitely attained, its effect upon psychology would seem to be momentous.

Needed measure of pure retentivity. To complete and clinch all the preceding results, it would be very advantageous to obtain a measure of pure retentivity with all other influences eliminated.

For this purpose, the oldest and best known procedure is that of " saving " due to Ebbinghaus, whereby a comparison is effected between the number of repetitions required to memorize anything and the number required to re-memorize it at some later date. But up to the present, the application of this procedure to our problem seems not to have been attempted.

Another feasible procedure is afforded by the " memory ratio " of T. V. Moore ; here, the amount of anything that can be remembered immediately after cognizing it is compared with the amount that can be recalled subsequently.[1] Guillet, applying this method to 169 female students, found that the retentivity for a prose passage had only the insignificant correlation of ·11 with general school standing.[2]

There is a further procedure which also necessitates testing both the original cognition and the subsequent recall ; but this time the influence of the original cognition is eliminated by means of Yule's partial coefficients. This has been tried out by the writer on 178 university students, with the result of showing a correlation of the pure memory with g of little over zero.

[1] *Psych. Mon.* 1919, xxvii.   Whole No. 118.

[2] *Journ. Educ. Psychol.* 1917, viii.

A kindred line, but one along which investigations have been more numerous, is that of the correlations between ability and improvability. But most of the work done in this way has suffered from the correlations having only been obtained between ability and improvability in the self-same performance; whereas to throw light upon the connection with g, we need correlations between performances that are different. More serious still is the fact that the improvement subjected to investigation has usually derived equivocally from two disparate sources; first, there is the bare retentivity which we are here considering; and then, there is such improvement as derives from change in mode of operation, and therefore is not explicable by retentivity at all, but solely by eduction.

Another possible way of investigating the matter is by comparing, as regards the correlations with g, practised with unpractised subjects; this has been done by Burt, Peterson, Thorndike, and Woodworth. But here, as Slocombe has shown, so many influences are in play, that the interpretation of the results becomes difficult. Interesting to note, however, is that from this kind of research Perrin goes so far as to assert that

" capacity for improvement may be taken as an indication of inferior, not superior, ability." [1]

If in any research all the difficulties appear to have been even tolerably overcome, it is pre-eminently that of Woodrow.[2] He worked with 42 normal children averaging 9 years and 37 " defective " ones averaging 14 years, the two groups having been carefully selected as making equal scores with the Binet-Stanford tests. Both were then tested further in various ways : sorting five lengths of sticks, sorting coloured pegs, cancelling letters, cancelling geometrical forms, and sorting wads. In all these, be it noted, there is little room for advantageous change in mode of operation, so that any improvement made by practice must be credited to reten-

[1] *Psych. Rev.* 1919, xxvii. [2] *Journ. Educ. Psych.* 1917, viii.

tivity. Next, both groups of children were practised for eight minutes on 13 days at sorting wads. The question then was as to whether or not the effect of practice would improve the normal children more than the defective. Actually, the two groups improved to just about the same extent ; with both, there was considerable improvement in the performance actually practised (sorting wads), and some little improvement in most of the other performances, especially those that were most like the performance practised. Of the more intelligent children showing greater retentivity, there was no sign.

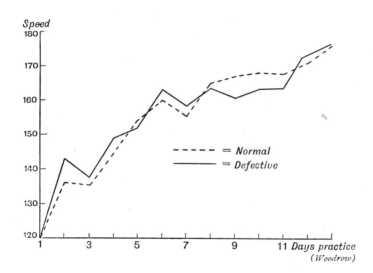

On the whole, then—just as in the earlier sections of this chapter—all the available evidence indicates that g is exclusively involved in eduction and not at all in bare retention.

FACULTIES AND GROUP FACTORS

Small group factor throughout memorizing. Let us now pass over to a different problem. To what extent does the retentivity of dispositions engender faculties, in the sense of broad functional unities or broad group factors ? Historically, it will be remembered, this was the sphere within which broad factors first revealed their existence at all (see p. 81).

To begin with, does there exist any factor of retentivity pure and simple ; that is to say, a unitary function broad enough to cover its entire domain ? That no such factor is at any rate present in high degree seems to have been implied already. For to some extent retentivity enters into cognitive operations of all kinds. If, then, it throughout constitutes a functional unity, it must be a second universal factor alongside of g. But such existence of two large universal factors would be in contradiction with the zero values of the tetrad differences as established in ch. x. and elsewhere.

We will turn, then, to a more restricted field, and one where the influence of retentivity is more dominant, so that any factor engendered by it will have a correspondingly greater magnitude and be the more easily detectible. Such a field is supplied by the tests that have been made of memorizing.

In order to find some indication as to whether any factor extends throughout this, we must select two operations which, whilst still lying within it, are otherwise as far apart as possible. Such purpose may be served by comparing memory for language with that for sensory qualities. Both of these were examined with exceptional thoroughness in the research of Carey ; language (see page 279) was represented by sentences, association of words with number, and unconnected words ; part of the sensory qualities were visual and represented by shades of yellow, size of angles, variety of patterns, and groups of colours ; the other part was auditory and represented by musical pitch, rate of ticking of a metronome, and musical phrases. The results show that a common factor does link together even such widely different manifestations of retentivity as the memorizing of language and that of sensory quality.[1]   But on the other hand, the amount of this factor proved to be very small ; the specific correlation between verbal and visual memory comes only to ·11 ; that between verbal and auditory memory is ·19.

Theoretically, there are several explanations possible. One is that the whole brain of the individual undergoes many influences in common, which might confer upon it some common tendency in respect of retention (or otherwise). A more superficial derivation of the common factor would be from some method of procedure by the subjects which is common to the memorizing even of the most diverse material. The point awaits further research.

Group factor in sensory memories.   Let us next compare together some retentive abilities that are not so extremely unlike each other.   We will take two that are both of sensory nature, although appertaining to different sensory organs.   Carey's work, as we have just seen, furnished several tests of both visual and auditory memory.   Is there any common factor extending from the one kind over to the other ?   The result of the experiments was to show that such a memory factor, common to both visual and auditory memorizing, is not only present but amounts to the considerable value of ·32.[2]   This issue for the two kinds of sensory memories is all the more remarkable by its contrast with the perfectly analogous comparison for the sensory

---

[1] This may be seen from the following four tetrads :

		Verb. mem. (pool).	Oppo- sites.				Verb. mem. (pool).	Sen- tences.
Vis. mem. (pool)	-	·28	·48		Vis. mem. (pool)	-	·28	·31
Sentences	- -	·34	·70		Opposites -	-	·31	·70
Aud. mem. (pool)	-	·33	·46		Aud. mem. (pool)		·33	·22
Sentences	- -	·34	·70		Opposites -	-	·34	·70

The tetrad differences amount respectively to +·053, +·100, +·070, and +·163, with a p.e. of about ·03.

[2] Tetrad difference = ·216, with a p.e. of only ·03.

					Vis. mem.	Sentences.
Aud. mem.	-	-	-	-	·44	·22
Opposites	-	-	-	-	·42	·70

discriminations ; for the latter, such a group factor was previously shown *not* to exist (ch. xiii. p. 235).

Group factor in verbal memories. Next, let us examine retentive abilities that resemble each other by reason of lying within the sphere of verbal remembrance, although in other respects as unlike as possible. For this purpose may be taken memory for sentences and that for lists of disconnected words. For relevant evidence we may turn to the work of Abelson. Actually, there is specific correlation this time to the amount of ·44.[1]

Similar evidence is offered by the work of Carothers, both for recall and especially for recognition.[2]

Group factor in non-verbal symbolic memories. For another important field, we may turn from verbal to non-verbal symbols. These can be exemplified by the original observations of Krueger and the present writer on the old work of Oehrn. This time, there would seem to exist a group factor much larger still.[3]

The influence of formal characters. There remain to be mentioned certain characters of a more formal nature than those considered by us so far.

Particularly important among these are the " imme-

[1]

					Mem. sen- tences.	Dis- crim. length
Mem. words	-	-	-	-	·50	·21
Crossing out rings	-	-	-	·15	·39

Tetrad difference = ·159 with a p.e. of ·03. See *loc. cit.* p. 174.

[2]

	Recall.				Recognition.	
	Memory pas- sages.	Com- pletion.			Memory pas- sages.	Com- pletion.
Mem. words -	- ·35	·21	Mem. words	- -	·26	·02
Opposites -	- ·19	·34	Opposites -	- -	·15	·34

The tetrad difference for Recall is ·079 and for Recognition ·129, with a p.e. of about ·03.

[3]

			Memory of syllabus.	Speed of writing.
Memory of Digits	-	-	·76	·00
Accuracy of adding	-	-	·00	·69

The tetrad difference comes to no less than ·50, which is probably significant even with the very small number of subjects (9).

diate" and the "delayed" kinds of remembrance; the former indicates that the testing is done immediately after the cognizing; the latter, that some lapse of time is allowed to intervene. These two kinds of remembrance certainly serve widely different purposes in life. Do they accordingly tend to constitute separate faculties, in the sense that each or both give rise to group factors?

The best available evidence appears to be that brought by G. Gates, who tested about 240 children in remembrance of both kinds, also partly with meaningful material and partly with meaningless. The issue is to indicate that neither the immediate nor the delayed possesses any group factor. And the results of Kitson so far as they go — unfortunately, not all the needful correlations are given — agree very well.[1]

Another interesting bisection of memory is into recall and recognition. Does either or both of these afford any group factor? Bearing on this point is the work of Carothers (*loc. cit.* p. 219). The results show that in neither case does any group factor exist.[2] And in good accord so far as the published correlations go (again several of the needful correlations are missing) appear to be the results obtained by Mulhall Achilles.[3]

CONCLUSION

The preceding inquiry about group factors—which, had space allowed, could have been pursued into far greater detail—places the power of retaining in a curious contrast with that of educing. The case of retention is much

---

[1] *Psych. Mon. Suppl.* xxiii. Whole No. 89, 1917.

[2]

	Recall passages.	Recog. passages.
Recall words - - - -	·35	·22
Recog. words - - - -	·28	·26

Tetrad difference = ·03 with a p.e. of ·03.

[3] *Archives of Psychology*, 1920, No. 44.

more what might naturally have been expected *a priori* ; for in general, the degree of functional unity corresponds fairly well with the degree of apparent likeness. When two kinds of memory resemble each other only in the bare fact of both involving retentivity, the correlation arising from this cause is little if at all above zero. In proportion as the likeness between them is augmented by resemblance of material—for instance, by both being sensory, or by both being verbal—the correlation becomes more and more marked. With eduction, on the other hand, all this is quite otherwise. The correlation arising from it can be very large even between operations that are extremely unlike (see ch. xi.). And the correlations, large or small, which exist between extremely unlike operations are no whit increased by virtue of introducing resemblance between them—until this resemblance becomes very close indeed.

In such manner is afforded from another angle a striking corroboration of the result reached in the earlier part of this chapter ; this is that the *g* manifested in eduction has nothing in common with the retentivity manifested in acquiring dispositions. And an explanation is at once afforded by the theory that the *g* measures something of the nature of an energy. For certainly *this* can have no power of retention. But nothing could be more natural, on the other hand, than that such a power should be possessed by the *engines*.

CHAPTER XVII

LAW OF INERTIA. " PERSEVERATION "

PRESENT STAGE OF INQUIRY

Formulation of the law. At the beginning of the previous chapter, the manifestations of retentivity were expressed in two laws, of which the first, that of " dispositions," was taken as the theme for discussion. We will now turn to the second, which has been called the law of lag or inertia and formulated as follows : *cognitive processes always both begin and cease more gradually than their (apparent) causes.*[1]

Significance for individual differences. On comparing these two laws, the difference might superficially seem to be a mere splitting of hairs. How, it might be asked, shall such an after " lag " of a process—especially when subconscious—be distinguished from the after " disposition " ? In truth, the difference between the two appears ever wider and deeper the more profoundly it is examined. For the lag involves nothing less than that which in the doctrine of " types "—amid all the obscurities, inconsistencies, and even follies that so often disfigured this doctrine—has from the earliest ages remained steadily persistent and has even

---

[1] *Nature of Intelligence*, etc., p. 133.

become increasingly definite. By this second law we are transported back to all the romantic psychologies set forth in chapter ix. As we there saw, the lag or inertia is essentially a generalization which combines—as supplementary to each other—two concepts that have put forward extraordinarily large claims, the " perseveration " of G. E. Müller and the " secondary function " of Heymans with his school. It constitutes the solid core of such copious and dramatic writings as those of Beneke, Gross, and Jung. It also wheels into general line the prolific suggestions of Meumann and the acute observations of W. Stern.

Nor has this doctrine been confined to the psychology of cognition. Everywhere the perseveration, secondary function, introversion, or however else it may be entitled, has been taken to include also the feelings, impulses, and will. The perseverator has been assumed to be stable in his emotions and steadfast in his purposes ; usually, indeed, a vast system of further traits of character has been attributed to him.

Reception by modern psychologists. All this stimulating literature, however, has met with a curious response. If it be truly as depicted, such perseveration ought forthwith to be made a foundation pillar for the whole science of individual differences. But if false, it ought to be attacked, destroyed, and obliterated, as the most pernicious of fallacies. Instead of taking either course, most psychologists would seem to make a strange compromise ; they accept this momentous doctrine without demanding any evidence for it, and then they proceed to psychologize without paying any regard to it ! In respect of " intelligence " they have measured individuals by millions, collating the results with all the information obtainable elsewhere, and enthusiastically deducing fundamental applications to education, industry, and society. But in respect of perseveration, have they thus measured and treated one single person ? Far from it, they seem not even to have cared to inquire whether such a character admits of being measured at all ; or, what comes to nearly the same thing, whether he who perseverates in one kind of operation may be expected to do so correspondingly in others.

EXPERIMENTAL EVIDENCE

The Dutch school. From this facile attitude of the great majority of psychologists, we will turn to the very small band of those who—unheeded, it would seem, by the others—have taken up the less alluring part of laborious investigation.

Pioneers in this field have been the Dutch school, who were the first to devise and employ for this trait of perseveration some definite and serviceable tests. This was brilliantly achieved in 1906 by Wiersma.[1]

Of his tests, one made use of a revolving colour-disc, which had two sectors, red and green respectively, so balanced in hue, saturation, and size that on the disc revolving with sufficient speed the colours fused to grey. Such fusion is well known to be due to the fact of the colour-sensations persisting for some brief time after the colour-rays themselves have ceased to impinge upon the retinal nerve. This persistence was attributed to the secondary function, perseveration or lag. It admitted of being measured by the slowness of the rate of revolution that for any individual just sufficed to produce the fusion. A second and analogous test was obtained from the phenomenon known as light adaptation. When a person is taken from a brightly lighted room into the darkness, he gradually becomes able to perceive fainter and fainter lights, until at last he reaches his maximum power in this respect. The time that he needs for this was taken by Wiersma as a further measure of the secondary function. The third and last test was again of rather similar kind, but now tactile instead of visual. A comparatively strong electric current was passed through the subject's hand, so as to render this temporarily insensitive to very weak currents. His secondary function was then measured

[1] *Journ. f. Psychol. u. Neur.* viii. 1906.

by the time which the hand needed in order to regain its full normal sensitivity.

All three tests were applied to 9 normal persons, 11 maniacs and 18 melancholiacs. The average results were as follows :

State of Subject.	Maniac.	Normal.	Melan-cholic.
Number of revolutions per second needed to produce fusion - -	27·2	15·7	12·2
Seconds needed for adaptation to darkness - - - -	33·5	102·9	233·2
Seconds needed for recovering sensitivity to weak currents -	0	39·6	205·5

Thus, in all three tests the melancholiacs showed much more secondary function than did the normal subjects, but the maniacs did just the reverse. The natural inference was drawn, that this secondary function or perseveration becomes increased all round by the state of melancholia, but diminished all round by that of mania. To this extent, then, it would constitute a functional unity or group factor.

But there are some objections possible. One is that in all three tests the kind of activity involved was closely similar, so that the generalization to activity of all kinds must be regarded as precarious. More serious still, perhaps, is the danger of arguing from cases of insanity ; for this might easily introduce conditions not appreciably influential in normal health ; there may even be felt some general distrust towards accepting results at all that are founded only upon the statements of the insane.

To some slight extent these objections were obviated in a subsequent research by Heymans and Brugmans in 1913.[1] They submitted 15 students to 6 tests of perseveration, which were as follows :

(1) Fusion of colours as before ; (2) light adaptation as before ; (3) limen for flicker ; (4) limen for sound after a

[1] *Zeit. f. Psych.* vii. 1913.

loud noise; (5) pronunciation of difficult words; and (6) motor perseveration, where 5 letters were first written 40 times in one direction and then 20 times in the reverse direction.

There were also several tests of each of the following : Intellect, Memory, Imagination, and Concentration.

As the chief result, the six perseveration tests showed an average inter-correlation of ·28, whilst the pool of all six had the following correlations with the pools of the other faculties :

Intellect.	Imagination.	Memory.	Concentration.
·14	− ·02	·03	− ·18

But what conclusion can be drawn ? Not much, it is to be feared. For no measurements had been obtained of attenuation (see p. 57), and consequently such correlations are equivocal. One might perhaps feel tempted to argue that at any rate the perseveration tests correlate higher with each other than with the intellect, and to infer that this fact indicates a group factor additional to any participation of g. But such inferences are very fallacious when made without using the definite formulae constructed for the purpose. Let us try out the matter in the same way as before. We get the tetrad :

	Perseveration$_a$.	g_a.
Perseveration$_b$ - - -	·29	·11
g_b - - - -	·11	·73

The tetrad difference does indeed have the high-looking value of ·20 ; but even this becomes insignificant on comparing it with the p.e., which is ·13.[1] The reason for the latter being so large, of course, is the very small number of subjects, 15 only.

Wynn Jones. The definite evidence so far lacking, however, that perseveration normally constitutes any functional unity or group factor, was eventually supplied by Wynn Jones. His research was already far advanced at the time

[1] The reader may be reminded that an experimental value should be at least three times larger than its probable error before it can be taken even as suggestive, and it must be five times greater before its evidence can be deemed conclusive (see pp. 140-141).

when the preceding experiments were published, but its final completion was much delayed (owing to disturbance by the war). It formed part of a larger investigation, which included various other aspects of ability all in charge of different investigators, viz. : Aveling (suggestion), Burt (g), Carey (motor dexterity), Flugel (oscillation of mental efficiency, also blood pressure and pulse), and the present writer (general arrangement). In addition, character estimates were begun, but these had subsequently to be abandoned (owing to the said disturbance).

The main group of subjects consisted of 77 children, about 12 years of age. All were submitted to the following four tests of perseveration [1] :

(1) Writing an S, first repeatedly in the usual way, and then as it would appear in a mirror.

(2) Writing digits, first in the usual way, and then making the stroke backwards.

(3) Mirror drawing.

(4) First copying prose in the usual way, and then doing so without dotting the i's or crossing the t's.[2]

The result was that the perseveration tests showed an average positive inter-correlation of ·492, the entire table being as follows :

	1	2	3	4
1. Mirror-wise S - -	—	·455	·340	·560
2. Back-stroke digits -	·455	—	·520	·515
3. Mirror drawing - -	·340	·520	—	·465
4. " i t " - - -	·560	·515	·465	—

Applying the same criterion as always hitherto, there ensues the following tetrad :

	Perseveration$_a$.	g_a.
Perseveration$_b$ - -	·642	·296
g_b - - - -	·296	·711

[1] Five others were used with some of the children, but were discontinued for the remainder.

[2] In the case of these first three tests a coefficient was calculated to show how much the habitual movement disturbed the non-habitual one.

The tetrad difference $= \cdot399$ with a p.e. of $\cdot048$, so that this time it is far beyond what can be credited to mere sampling. The specific correlation between the two perseveration values must be taken as no less than $\cdot6$.[1] Now at last, then, the evidence for some group factor or factors pervading these tests of perseveration leaves nothing to be desired.

But this conclusiveness is only as to whether such a factor exists, not yet as to whether it essentially consists in the perseveration that we are considering. However, we seem at least able to discard the two alternative explanations that lie nearest to hand. One is that the group factor derives from mere ordinary overlap owing to excessive resemblance between the operations involved. Against this is the fact that actually the resemblance appears to be far less than that which experience has shown to be needful for overlap of this sort (see all the preceding chapters of Part II.); moreover, between the pair of tests where such resemblance seems to be highest (the first and the third), the correlation in point of fact happens to be lowest. The other alternative explanation is that the inter-correlation between the tests comes from the fact of all consisting in motor dexterities. To guard against this had been the main reason why the research was extended to some tests of motor dexterity other than perseverative. These were :

(1) Speed of making dots in small rings.
(2) Accuracy in so doing.
(3) Speed in copying foreign letters of the alphabet.
(4) Accuracy in so doing.
(5) Dexterity with balls.

The inter-correlation proved to be throughout very small, averaging only $\cdot086$. Nothing of this diminutive size could possibly account for—or, even by being eliminated, sensibly diminish—the correlations shown in the foregoing table.

Provisionally at any rate, then, the doctrine that perseveration possesses functional unity, and therefore supplies a broad group factor, would appear to hold the field. This

[1] For method of calculating this, see appendix, pp. xxi-xxiii.

factor is the main constituent in all that is common to the four tests, although accompanied in these by a small admixture of g (taken reversely, since the correlation is minus)

Lankes. The next work to consider is that which was executed about the same time by Lankes.[1] One distinctive feature of this was the number, variety, and systematic conception of the criteria of perseveration (indeed, from these had been taken many of the tests used by Wynn Jones). They were made to comprise the following three cases :

" (1) The persistent after-effect of a sensory experience, *i.e.* the continuance, more or less prolonged, of the physiological and psychical impression beyond the real duration of the external stimulation.

" (2) The spontaneous recurrence to consciousness of an experience, without a fresh corresponding stimulation, after it has for a time been out of the mind.

" (3) The continuance, subconscious or even completely unconscious and purely physiological, of the effect of a past experience " as manifested by " the degree of hindrance which the perseverating effect of a past mental activity causes to a new one of the same kind."

To effect this purpose, one test consisted in the Natural Rate of Tapping. The subject was told " simply to move the finger, each subject at his own rate, just as he feels it natural to himself at the time."

Then came Letter-Writing. The subject wrote as rapidly as possible six letters (for example, tuvwxy) many times in their alphabetical order, and then a few times in the reverse order.

The third test was that of Cancellation. This was the ordinary test of that name, but first one letter was used, then another different one, and lastly the original one again.

The fourth was done with Colour Discs in the same way as by Wiersma, but with many technical improvements.

[1] *Brit. J. Psych.* vii. 1914.

The fifth consisted in Drawings, which the subject saw and very soon afterwards tried to describe. Half of these were exhibited each in succession for six seconds. The other half were exhibited alternately in pairs, first the left one for two seconds, then the right one for the same time, then the left one again, etc., the whole exposure of the two pictures lasting twelve seconds as in the case of the first half.

The sixth was constructed of Narratives. A passage of prose was read two or three times to the subject, who then had to answer questions about it. Immediately afterwards another passage was read once, the subjects being then questioned about this alone.

The seventh was called Associative Reaction. " The subjects had no other task than to react with the very first word that came to their mind on seeing the stimulus word and to be as fast as possible. The lists of stimulus words were so arranged that several words recurred repeatedly at different intervals."

Last came the Essays. " Twenty-five very difficult ' problems ' or themes were selected, to be treated one after another, five at each sitting, allowing for some of them four minutes' time, for others only forty seconds."

As measure of perseveration was taken : in the first test, the slowness of chosen rate ; in the fourth, the slowness of revolution that sufficed to fuse the sectors ; in the remainder, a coefficient showing the disturbance caused by rapid change to an activity of similar kind.

In addition to all these tests the subjects had to fill in the following interrogatory :

(1) Do you often notice a tune, line of poetry, phrase, problem, etc., coming back to your mind again without your intending it ? How often (about) a week ? At what time of day more frequently ?

(2) Are your dreams more commonly about some past experience or events ? Or rather about things scarcely ever thought of before ?

(3) When something is to be done or imminent, *e.g.* a task,

an examination, etc., does it often come to your mind during the days preceding it ?

(4) When writing an essay, or working out a problem, do you find it easy to interrupt it ? Or do you feel a strong tendency first to finish it in spite of fatigue ?

(5) When you have to interrupt it, does your attention easily pass on to other things ? Or do the thoughts of the essay or problem keep coming back to your mind ?

(6) On taking it up again after the interruption, do the former thoughts readily come again ? Or have you almost to begin anew ?

(7) When unexpectedly addressed or asked a question which you know well enough, but have not been thinking of at the time, can you answer readily and quickly at once ?

(8) Which would you like better, to go on in the same familiar occupation, place, companionship, etc., or to have frequent change ?

(9) Do you, after leaving (for a longer time or for good) a place, room, occupation, etc., feel, as it were, homesick after it ?

(10) (a) When you have once begun something, or done it a few times (gone away, played a game), do you feel a tendency to stick to it, to do it again and again, though you have no longer any reason for it ? (b) Or even against reason ?

(11) When stepping off a train before it has completely stopped, or sitting in a train when it starts or stops, do you feel a considerable shock ? Or do you scarcely notice any shock at all ?

(12) (a) Do you, after a long railway journey or sea voyage, seem to hear the noise and feel the motion of the train or ship for some time ? (b) Have you ever noticed it recurring in your dreams ?

Subjects for some preliminary experiments were 33 university teachers and students, mostly in the department of psychology under the direction of the present writer. For the final experiments, the subjects were 47 students in a

Training College. And here came in the second distinctive feature of this research. For this last group of students were among those who had been previously submitted by Webb to an exceptionally thorough estimate of character (see p. 345). By this means it was hoped to ascertain at last the truth or otherwise of the old belief that perseveration affects not only the cognitive processes but also the most important character-qualities.

Passing on to the results of this research, the following were the correlations :

	1	2	3	4	5	6	7	8	9
1. Tapping - -	—	·26	·07	·39	·23	·21	·24	·14	·09
2. Letter-writing -	·26	—	·31	·27	·26	·40	·39	·16	·29
3. Cancellation - -	·07	·31	—	·40	·16	·16	−·05	·02	·51
4. Colour discs -	·39	·27	·40	—	·50	·11	−·05	·12	·29
5. Drawings - -	·23	·26	·16	·50	—	·32	·26	·24	·12
6. Narrative - -	·21	·40	·16	·11	·32	—	·18	·21	·26
7. Assoc. reaction -	·24	·39	−·05	−·05	·26	·18	—	·02	·11
8. Essays - - -	·14	·16	·02	·12	·24	·21	·02	—	·18
9. Interrogatory -	·09	·29	·51	·29	·12	·26	·11	·18	—

From this table may be taken at once the answer to our first great question, namely, as to whether these mental activities, so systematically representing perseveration in each of its chief forms, are really inter-correlated. The answer is decidedly affirmative. Although the values are small (which may be due to attenuation), they are almost all positive and none are significantly negative. Nor is this fact explicable by g ; for the tests had been carefully designed so as to eliminate this ; in any case, it could hardly be expected to play any part in such a test as, for instance, the chosen rate of tapping. Furthermore, the correlations do not appear to be traceable to the mere ordinary overlap through resemblance, any more than was the case in the preceding work ; in point of fact, the greatest resemblance would seem to be between tests 6 and 8, and yet these have only about the average amount of inter-correlation.

But turning to the other great question, namely, as to whether not only the cognitive processes but also the character-qualities are positively inter-correlated, the answer of the research is surprising. There proves to be a correlation indeed, but a negative one! Its value is − ·26, and on being corrected for attenuation it rises to − ·40. The true value, then, must be either negative or at any rate not markedly positive, as had always been assumed before.

How shall this fact be explained? Lankes himself suggests that

> " the self, with persons used to act morally, from higher motives of reason and principle, not according to merely natural bent and inclination . . . can modify, and directly counteract, its own nervous system and its innate tendency towards perseveration or the opposite."

At bottom not very different, perhaps, is the following solution. We grant to Wiersma that perseveration tends to increase along the line maniac-normal-melancholic. But there also exists another tendency, which is for *self-control to be greatest with normal persons*. Accordingly, on passing from maniacs to normal persons, we find that both perseveration and self-control increase ; to this extent, these two traits are positively correlated. But on proceeding from the normal person to the melancholiac, only the perseveration increases, whilst the self-control decreases again ; to this extent, the two traits are correlated negatively. Along the entire line maniac-normal-melancholic, then, the correlation between the two traits may easily be zero, or even possibly incline towards being negative.

Bernstein. The last investigation for us to consider is that of Bernstein with 130 children.[1] Here, the perseveration had ten tests. In using so many, there was no longer any aim at covering the whole field of perseveration, but rather at obtaining an effective measurement by means of a large pool. Five of the tests were taken over from Lankes and Wynn Jones ; these consisted of Tapping, Mirror-wise drawn S's, Backwards drawn digits, Reversely ordered Letters, and the " *i t* " test. Another was the re-writing of

[1] *Loc. cit.* p. 252.

six letters mirror-wise. In another, the subjects drew a series of triangles, first with apex upwards, then with it downwards, and finally with it upwards and downwards alternatively. In the next test, the subject copied a passage, and in so doing had to reverse all the capital and the small letters (*e.g.* he was shown " The Duke Drew his sword," and had to write " tHE dUKE dREW HIS SWORD "). In the next, he had to reproduce four rows of simple geometrical patterns, replacing every horizontal line by a vertical one, and *vice versa*. In the remaining test, he had to copy a passage of prose, and in so doing to write an a after every e (*e.g.* " redeemer " became " readeaeamear "). In all cases, except the Tapping, the operations were done at full speed, the measure of perseveration was obtained by subtracting the score made in a habitual operation from that made in one so modified that the habit would tend to lead astray.

In addition to all the tests, long and careful observations were made of the perseveration exhibited by the children in their ordinary school work ; in particular, note was taken of the differences displayed by them in the ease with which they started any fresh lesson.

" Some would become immersed almost at once in the task, whilst others would take an appreciable time in settling down to work. . . . Those showing least adaptability to new work, taking an inordinate time to settle down to any task and perhaps finding themselves compelled to rush through a great deal of work in the last few minutes in order to produce a tolerable output were classed as the highest perseverators ; those at the other extreme, who never appeared to experience any difficulty in starting and who quickly adapted themselves to any change imposed in the work, were classed as non-perseverators."

Further, as already mentioned, very extensive and systematically varied tests were made of *g*.

With regard to the results, we may begin with the intercorrelations of the perseveration tests with one another.

These correlations, owing to the shortness of each separate test, were much lower than in the work of Wynn Jones ; but still they were positive for every single test on an average, as shown in the following table :

	1	2	3	4	5	6	7	8	9	10
1.	—	−·033	·285	·176	·058	−·017	·124	·163	·063	−·145
2.	−·033	—	·067	·337	·233	·151	·223	−·023	·082	·234
3.	·285	·067	—	·289	·157	·057	·049	·219	·155	−·031
4.	·176	·337	·289	—	·221	−·029	·219	·286	·215	·050
5.	·058	·233	·157	·221	—	·019	·088	·074	·134	−·021
6.	−·017	·151	·057	−·029	·019	—	·027	·030	·102	·016
7.	·124	·223	·049	·219	·088	·027	—	·158	·014	·100
8.	·163	−·023	·219	·286	·074	−·030	·158	—	·167	·052
9.	·063	·082	·155	·215	·134	·102	·014	·167	—	·103
10.	−·145	·234	−·031	·050	−·021	·016	·100	·052	·103	—

From these unpromisingly low correlations of the tests with each other, let us turn to their respective correlations with the personal estimates of perseveration in ordinary school life. The latter correlations alone really matter for our present purpose, All sorts of objections could be made out, or explanations suggested, about the correlations of the tests among themselves. But their correlations with the estimates cannot possibly be explained in any other way than by genuine perseveration. And in point of fact such correlations not only occur, but are comparatively high, having the following amounts.

1	2	3	4	5	6	7	8	9	10
·265	·390	·185	·395	·360	·205	·445	·220	·230	·095

And the correlation of the pool of the tests with the estimates, rises to no less than ·51. Moreover, none of these values are appreciably reduced on eliminating the influence of g, since the correlation of the tests with g is throughout negligibly small. Seeing that values no greater than this ·51 frequently occur between the most approved tests of g and the estimates of " intelligence " (see p. 188), the hope seems allowable that the measuring of perseveration (even by groups) has now entered upon a stage comparable with the present measuring of g itself.

To this the central result of Bernstein's research may be added important further elucidation in detail. One great point is as to whether the perseveration constitutes only a single factor (as *g* does, or a conglomerate of several, as " maturity " does, see pp. 142-143). So far, we have carefully left this question open. But a criterion to answer it is supplied, as always, by the frequency distribution of the tetrad differences. Now in the table of correlations given above, the actually observed median value of the said differences comes to ·014, whilst the theoretical probable error of sampling is ·013. This excellent agreement indicates that, in general, the whole of the correlations derive from *only one* factor.

Another point of much interest, chiefly for practical purposes, is as to what the precise conditions are under which the perseveration of one activity impedes the execution of any subsequent one. A not unnatural expectation would have been that the perseverating person should be hampered in the " haste " as compared with the " leisure " tests of *g* (for description of these, see p. 252). But the actual results, on suitable statistical treatment, show no such thing.[1] A further plausible expectation would have been that the perseverator should succeed worse in the " mixed " than in the " ordered " tests of *g*. But this, too, is decisively denied by the actual results.[2] On the whole, then, it would seem that the perseveration only produces interference in special cases. One of these is when the antecedent and the subsequent activities are mutually conflicting ; for example, the writing of an S in the usual way conflicts with writing it

[1] A value was got for each subject by deducting his score for the leisure tests from that for the haste ones, after reducing both to comparable units. This value, which may be written as *H-L*, showed itself to be quite uncorrelated with the perseveration.

[2] In the ordered arrangement, each kind of test was given completely in turn ; that is to say, first the four lengths of the Completion, then the four of the Directions, and so on ; moreover, the different lengths were given successively from shortest to longest. In the mixed arrangement, on the other hand, every kind and length of test was mixed up randomly. A value was obtained analogously to the preceding *H-L*, that is, an *M-O*. But this, too, was quite uncorrelated with the perseveration.

mirror-wise. And another case is when each of the two activities covers a very extensive field, so that to switch from the one over to the other becomes a correspondingly elaborate operation ; this probably occurs when a child shifts from lesson to lesson.

CONCLUSION

In this chapter, we have been examining the greatest of all the faculties, if by this may be signified the one which has been the most lavish of promises for individual psychology. It is also among the greatest—only second to " intelligence "—in the sense that whilst all the other asserted faculties have proved to be baseless, this perseveration now shows itself to be at any rate a *half truth*. For there does appear to exist, as a unitarily functioning factor varying in degree from one individual to another, a tendency for mental processes to have a certain lag or inertia and in this meaning to " perseverate."

The other and false half of the faculty, as this has hitherto been depicted, comes from confusing such a lag of activity with steadfastness of purpose. These two, far from being identical, would seem even to be somewhat opposed. On this matter, then, the copious literature, past and present, has been leading psychology into the gravest of errors. Equally at fault, though much less harmful—it may be added—is the further confusion sometimes made between the lag of an activity and disposition to repeat it, or the remembrance of it having happened.

From a theoretical standpoint, the difficult problem is raised as to how this second universal factor stands in relation to g. The two, as we have seen, vary independently of each other. Provisionally—it is here suggested—they may be taken to deal really with different aspects of the same thing, the mental energy ; as g measures its quantity, so the perseveration may express its degree of inertia. And herewith an explanation may be afforded of the seeming paradox, that the persistence involved in perseveration is so widely unlike that involved in dispositions; for naturally enough, the power of switching the energy from one to another system of neurones has nothing to do with the susceptibility of these neurones to retain engrams after wards.

Turning to the practical standpoint, the prospect here is extraordinarily hopeful. When once the pack of modern investigators can be called off the many false scents of illusory faculties to this genuine trail ; when the perseveration, already measurable even by groups, has been evaluated for persons of diverse age, sex, character, and social status ; when the connection has been traced out which it bears to success in different branches of education and varieties of vocation—then perhaps psychological science will have made a second advance not much less in magnitude than that which is being achieved with respect to " intelligence."

CHAPTER XVIII

LAW OF FATIGUE

NATURE OF THE PROBLEM

Formulation of the law. The next quantitative law is that of fatigue ; according to this, *the occurrence of any cognitive event produces a tendency opposed to its occurrence afterwards.* Evidently, this law acts in the contrary direction to that of retentivity. But such an antithesis has many parallels elsewhere in science, as, for example, in the mutual attraction and at the same time repulsion between atoms. The total resultant, of course, is that prescribed by the composition of forces according to their respective intensities.

The main questions arising here are analogous to those which derive from the other quantitative laws. What is the relation of this fatigue to g ? To what extent does it constitute any functional unity or group factor ? What light does it throw on the hypothesis of energy and engines ?

These questions have been invested with re-doubled interest by the writings of James, W. McDougall, and Claparède (see ch. viii. pp. 134-135). Take, for example, the quoted heroism of Colonel Baird Smith. When he suffered no loss of vigour from all his efforts and sufferings, was this due to a general absence of fatigability on his part ? Or to an extra supply of energy ? Or what ?

Special difficulties involved. The investigation of the topic is unfortunately beset with many special difficulties. One arises from the distinction which has to be made between the " objective " and the " subjective " kinds of fatigue, the former consisting in an absolute loss of ability for some operation or operations, whereas the latter essentially derives from a loss of inclination for it. The objective kind cannot, but the subjective kind can, be banished by emotion or overcome by will.

Another though less radical difficulty about fatigue springs from the oppositeness of its effects to those of retentivity. Since the manifestations of objective fatigue are in general much less prominent than those of retentivity, they are more seriously obscured in the compound effect of the two.

A further difficulty lies in the peculiar course taken by fatigue in its development. Recent investigation has shown that, on eliminating irrelevant influences, a person's efficiency at any continuous work diminishes very rapidly for a period of about two minutes,[1] but then undergoes very little diminution for hours, until finally there is an abrupt drop down to entire impotence.[2] But during all the time that so little diminution is manifested, a longer and longer rest becomes necessary in order to regain the full efficiency of the beginning [3] ; fatigue was really occurring all the time, but in such wise as to remain latent. The whole course of events has an extraordinary likeness to the usage of a cell in an electrical accumulator.

Yet another difficulty lies in the usual confusion between generality of two different kinds. By the first of these is

[1] G. Phillips, *Mental Fatigue, Records of the Education Society*, No. 40, Sydney.

[2] Thorndike, *Journ. Educ. Psych.* ii. 1911 ; Arai, Columbia Univers. *Contr. to Educ.* No. 54, 1912.

[3] Phillips, *ibidem.*

meant that the individual most susceptible to fatigue for any specific operation is so for others also. But by the second kind is meant, instead, that the fatigue caused by any specific operation makes itself felt in others also ; it is "transferred" to these. This second kind of generality does not strictly belong to the domain of individual differences ; but some brief account of the leading facts about it would seem to be an indispensable preliminary to considering this domain itself.

EVIDENCE AS TO FATIGUE BEING TRANSFERRED

The earlier investigations. In much of the earlier work on fatigue, the question as to whether it is general in the sense of being transferred to different operations was not raised at all. The answer was simply taken for granted ; but sometimes in the affirmative and sometimes in the negative ; often, contradictorily, in both at once. For instance, such a transfer was implicitly affirmed in the custom of testing fatigue by its effect on test operations unlike that from which the fatigue had been derived. On the other hand, the very person who used such tests would nevertheless, upon occasion, not hesitate to assume that change in occupation acts as a rest ; and hereby the transfer is implicitly denied.[1]

Eventually, however, there came to the problem several very capable investigators. But to review their work would take us too far afield, with small profit [2] ; for so great were the difficulties to be overcome, that for a long time the conclusions reached were far from convincing.

First experiment of Phillips. Here, we will only quote what seems to be the most cogent of these investigations [3] ; it is the previously mentioned research of Phillips.

[1] For the analogous problem involved in "formal training," see ch. iii. p. 36.

[2] A summary survey of it is given by Phillips.

[3] For further reference may be specially mentioned the researches done under the supervision of C. S. Myers.

In one of his experiments the fatigue-producing work was broken up into periods lasting one to four minutes, between which pauses were interposed that also lasted one to four minutes. The total amount of work each time lasted twelve minutes; it consisted, either of multiplication, or of cancellation, or of both sandwiched. The chief point at issue for our problem was as to whether the time spent in multiplication acted as a rest for the cancellation, and *vice versa*.

The answer of the experiment was negative. The fatigue caused by the multiplication made itself felt quite as much in subsequent cancellation as in subsequent multiplication itself. Otherwise expressed, the fatigue generated in this way was not specific but wholly general.

Second experiment of Phillips. In another part of this research, the subjects were 42 children, $11\frac{1}{2}$ to $13\frac{1}{2}$ years old. The work to produce fatigue consisted in multiplication, cancellation, memorizing 3-figure numbers, and rather strenuous physical drill. It lasted in each case 90 minutes.

The tests of fatigue were multiplication, cancellation, memorizing, dotting test (McDougall's apparatus), tapping, "spots" (the subject had to observe the spots in a group shown for one-tenth of a second), and an "alphabet" test (the letters were spread out before the subject, who had to pick them out as rapidly as possible in proper order).

First of all, a long preliminary practice was given, in order to eliminate the disturbing occurrence of practice during the main experiment. For this purpose, the tests were performed on alternate days for over three weeks. Such a general preparation was regarded as of vital importance for the whole research.

The main experiment lasted six days. The first and the last were only for control; on these, the subjects were tested twice, with an intervening 90 minutes' rest. On the other four days, the tests were similar, but the intervening 90 minutes were occupied by the fatigue-producing work.

At the end of each spell of the continuous or fatigue-producing work, the subjects were required to give their estimates of their own state of fatigue ; the following scale of values was used : " very tired," " tired," " fairly tired," " slightly tired," and " not tired at all."

Of the results obtained, the most important for our present purposes are contained in the following table. The effect of fatigue was calculated in two ways : (*a*) the loss of efficiency from the beginning to the end of the continuous work ; and (*b*) the loss from the initial to the final test. The table shows the size of (*b*) as a percentage of (*a*).

LOSS OF EFFICIENCY SHOWN IN THE TESTS, EXPRESSED AS A PERCENTAGE OF THE LOSS IN THE CONTINUOUS WORK.

Tests.	After continuous multiplication.	After continuous cancellation.
Multiplication - -	43	25
Spots - - - -	—	11
Memory - - -	40	54
Cancellation - - -	5	76
Tapping - - -	4	− 2
Alphabet - - -	1	10
Dotting - - -	20	45

To illustrate this table, take the top left hand figure. Here the continuous work and the tests were of the same kind, both consisting in multiplication. We see, then, that only 43 per cent. of the fatigue exhibited in the continuous work remained apparent in just the same kind of operation started immediately afterwards and regarded as a " test." Somewhat higher is the amount remaining apparent in the analogous case where both the continuous work and the tests consist of cancellation ; the percentage is 76 ; but even so, nearly a quarter of the fatigue displayed in the continuous work vanishes abruptly on starting the test. If we turn to the other cases, where the continuous work and the tests consist of different operations, there is to be seen a still greater dissipation of fatigue ; but some small amount always remains.

In this way, the fatigue manifested after 90 minutes of continuous work would seem to fall into three portions. First, there is a large share (24 per cent. to 57 per cent.) which forthwith vanishes as the subject proceeds to just the same kind of operation, but now rendered more interesting by being regarded as a test. Such fatigue so lightly dissipated can only be of the subjective sort. Second comes the portion of the fatigue which resists the excitement of being tested, but yields to a change in the kind of operation used for testing ; this in the case of fatigue by multiplication amounts to 18 per cent (43 minus 25) ; in that of fatigue by cancellation it comes to no less than 71 per cent. (76 minus 5). Such fatigue seems to be of the objective kind, but it is still specific in the sense of not being transferred to unlike operations. Third and last is the remaining portion of the fatigue, that which yields neither to excitement nor to change ; it amounts in the case of multiplication to 25 per cent., and in that of cancellation to 5 per cent. ; it is objective, and also general in the sense of transferable.

To sum up the matter from the present standpoint of transfer, subjective fatigue is wholly specific, whilst objective fatigue is partly specific and partly general.

EVIDENCE AS TO INDIVIDUAL DIFFERENCES

General subjective fatigue. Let us now look at the question of generality from the other standpoint, that of individual differences. Does the person who is most fatigable by one kind of operation tend to be so by other kinds ? And how does the subjective fatigue compare with the objective in such respects ?

On these very important matters there would seem to have been no considerable research previous to the just mentioned experiment of Phillips. This, however, does supply much information.

In respect of the subjective fatigue, this can be fairly well inferred from the subjects' estimates of their feelings of

tiredness. Such estimates were obtained for the four
fatigue-producing operations (see p. 311), and proved to be
inter-correlated as follows :

Tests.	1	2	3	4
1. Multiplication - -	—	·87	·30	·27
2. Cancellation - -	·87	—	·41	·07
3. Memorizing - -	·30	·41	—	− ·06
4. Physical drill - -	·27	·07	− ·06	—

Not only do these values tend obviously to be positive, but
their tetrad differences are of just about the size that should
be expected from the sampling errors alone (median tetrad
difference = ·06 with a p.e. of the same value). It would
appear, then, that subjective fatigue, although not a general
factor in respect of transfer, is so in respect of individual
differences. The person who experiences a tired feeling for
any kind of prolonged continuous work—and therefore usually
slackens in it—is likely to do the same for other kinds also.

On looking at the inequalities in the table, one is tempted
to add that this correspondence is greater between different
kinds of mental work than between mental and physical.
But this inference might be premature ; for the unequal
degrees of correlation may perhaps be explained by inequality
in the degrees of fatigue, this too being greater for the mental
than for the physical operations. The average values are
given below.

AVERAGE INTENSITY OF FATIGUE FELT AFTER EACH KIND OF
CONTINUOUS WORK (90 MINUTES).

Multiplica-tion.	Cancella-tion.	Memoriz-ing.	Physical Drill.
3·6	3·6	2·7	1·8

General objective fatigue. Turning to the fatigue of
objective nature, good evidence for this can only be obtained
from the loss of efficiency in the final test as compared with
the initial one. Such losses supply four tables of correlations, one for each of the four kinds of fatigue-producing
operations, namely, Multiplication, Cancellation, Memorizing,

and Physical Drill. The following table for Multiplication may be regarded as typical :

LOSS IN DIFFERENT TESTS AFTER FATIGUE BY MULTIPLICATON.

Tests.	1	2	3	4	5	6	7
1. Multiplication -	—	·06	·21	·29	− ·11	·35	− ·11
2. Spots - - -	·06	—	·44	·11	·17	·00	− ·24
3. Memory - -	·21	·44	—	− ·02	− ·26	− ·10	− ·10
4. Cancellation	·29	·11	− ·02	—	− ·14	− ·09	− ·06
5. Tapping - -	− ·11	·17	− ·26	− ·14	—	− ·16	− ·02
6. Alphabet - -	·35	·00	·10	− ·09	− ·16	—	− ·02
7. Dotting - -	− ·11	− ·24	− ·10	− ·06	− ·32	− ·02	—

The average of all 84 coefficients in the four tables is − ·02 ; moreover, the general distribution, positive and negative, is approximately what should be expected simply from sampling errors alone. We must conclude that the true correlations are close upon zero.[1] Thus objective fatigue, although quite general in respect of transfer, is quite specific in that of individual differences. Otherwise expressed, such normal persons as were here tested do not differ appreciably from each other in general objective fatigability.

Specific objective fatigue. So far the sailing has been plain enough. But now we encounter some results of Phillips which are much harder to interpret. The preceding correlations were between loss of efficiency in different tests after the same fatiguing operation. But there can also be calculated the loss for the same test after different fatiguing operations. This supplies the remarkable table on p. 316.

Since every one of these is positive, they can hardly be ascribed to mere sampling errors. Moreover, though they are small as they stand, on correction for attenuation the average rises to ·69.

If we accept this result, the sole possible meaning seems

[1] It must be admitted that here a large influence could have been exerted by attenuation (see appendix, p. i). For although each test alone had a very high reliability (av. = ·90), still the loss in the final test as compared with the initial test had a very low one (av. = ·28). Yet even such very low reliabilities as this fail to account for 84 coefficients averaging − ·02. Also these values may be contrasted with the very different ones quoted below.

to be that the person who is most easily fatigable for multi-plication by one kind of work is so also for multiplication (but not for other operations) by further kinds of work. Similarly as regards fatigability for cancellation, etc. Thus, although fatigue (objective) has above proved not to affect any individual in special degree for his operations all round, it now does show itself to affect him specially for certain particular operations (these being always the same, whatever may have been the operation by which the fatigue was produced). In other words, he has for these particular operations a chronic liability to fatigue. The important bearings of this on industry are sufficiently obvious.

Nature of test.	Average correlation between the fatigue caused in the same test by different fatiguing operations.
Multiplication - -	+ ·26
Spots - - -	+ ·34
Memory - -	+ ·47
Cancellation - - -	+ ·13
Tapping - -	+ ·39
Dotting - -	+ ·16
Total average -	+ ·28

Correlation of fatigability with ability and improvability. There remains the great question as to whether fatigability is correlated with either g or s.

This is a point upon which previous research had scarcely touched. The Kraepelin school—to whose pioneering study of fatigue we owe such a deep debt—had indeed put forward one notable suggestion; it was that fatigability at any performance is proportional to improvability at it; but on this matter there appears to have been less than the usual care of this school to secure adequate evidence.[1] Later came the valuable investigation of Wimms, who found that fatigability had no correlation at all with improvability, and

[1] Cron and Kraepelin, *Psychol. Arbeiten*, 1897, ii.; Lindley, *ibidem*, 1900, iii.

had even a negative correlation with retentivity. But among other considerations rendering this conclusion precarious is that only twelve subjects were used.

Proceeding to the more trustworthy results of Phillips, we find the following very definite indications :

| Nature of test. | Correlation of fatigability with | |
	Abilities.	Improvabilities.[1]
Multiplication -	+ ·06	+ ·01
Spots - - -	+ ·14	− ·04
Memory -	+ ·36	+ ·19
Cancellation - -	+ ·09	+ ·09
Tapping - -	− ·05	+ ·09
Alphabet - -	− ·10	− ·09
Dotting - -	+ ·35	+ ·16

Thus, fatigability shows very small correlations with the abilities ; the highest is less than four times the probable error (·10), whilst two are actually minus. We can infer that it has little correlation with the s's which enter into these abilities respectively, and none with g which enters into them all. With the improvabilities the correlations are even smaller.

CONCLUSION

As evidenced in these experiments, fatigue is a very complex and puzzling affair.

Our first main conclusion has been about the " subjective " kind, in the sense of that loss of efficiency which is only derived from tired feelings, and which may be banished by interest or overcome by will. Fatigue of this kind is not general in respect of being transferred from one sort of operation to another ; on the contrary, such change is very effective in banishing it. But it is general as an individual difference ; that is to say, those persons who get it in

[1] " Improvability " is a very difficult concept. Here, it simply indicates the increase of score obtainable by practice.

marked degree from one sort of operation are likely to get it correspondingly from other sorts. As regards theoretical interpretation, this subjective fatigue belongs to the domain of conation, and therefore appertains to a later chapter (xx.).

The other main conclusion has been about the " objective " fatigue in the sense of absolute loss of ability. In respect of transfer, this has proved to be partly general and partly specific ; that is to say, it to some extent persists after changing the sort of operations, but to some extent does not do so. But in respect of individual differences, it has not shown itself to be general at all. The person who manifested the greatest transfer of fatigue to one sort of operation did not tend to do so to other sorts.

On the theoretical side, this last finding seems to negate the view that fatigue—to the extent manifested in these experiments—can be attributed to decrease in the supply of the general psycho-physiological energy. All the observations would appear to be explicable by assuming that the transfer is due to the fact of certain toxins—wherever generated—being carried by the blood throughout the nervous system, and by further supposing that these toxins act selectively, so as to attack some systems of neurones with some persons but others with others.

If this be so, then such fatigue—like the retentivity of dispositions considered in chapter xvi.—primarily concerns not the energy but the engines.

CHAPTER XIX

OSCILLATIONS IN EFFICIENCY

THE PHENOMENON OF OSCILLATION

Lapses from consciousness. We may now conveniently turn to a phenomenon which may be described as oscillation of cognitive efficiency, and which probably has an intimate connection with the topic of the preceding chapter, fatigue.

Its earliest exactly observed manifestations seem to have been derived from very faint sensory stimuli ; the effect of such stimulation soon lapses from consciousness, then revives, then lapses again, and so on indefinitely. The simplest experiment is to place a watch just within hearing and to note how it thereafter becomes alternately inaudible and then audible again. Another classical experiment is that of Masson's disc. On a disc of white cardboard is fixed a patch of black paper so small that the disc, on being rapidly revolved, has an only just noticeable grey ring. This latter will then be found to come and go in the same way as the sound of the watch does. Similarly, a very light weight placed on the skin will be alternately noticeable and unnoticeable.

319

Rivalry. Another well known display of the oscillation consists in the " rivalry " which occurs between two mutually exclusive visual perceptions. An instance is where differently coloured stimuli fall upon corresponding points of the two retinas ; to experience this, a stereoscope may be so used that the one eye sees a red postage stamp and the other eye a green one of the same design. Then, whichever colour may appear in consciousness first, it will after a time give place to the other, and so on alternately. Another instance is that of ambiguous perspectives, as exemplified by the figure in chapter viii. p. 114, which may be perceived either as a chamber or as a boss. Here again, the two appearances will succeed each other in endless alternation. Even with a drawing expressly designed to favour the one perspective, this may still be sometimes displaced by the other if the subject carefully fixates the main outline ; the following figure is an illustration of this :

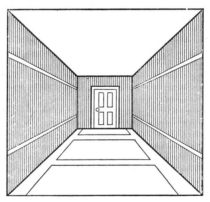

The whole phenomenon has been most thoroughly investigated by Flugel, from whose work the preceding figures and results are taken.[1]

Fluctuations in mental output. Yet a third typical manifestation is supplied by the fluctuations which always occur in any person's continuous output of mental work, even when this is so devised as to remain of approximately constant difficulty. A well known apparatus especially serving this end is the Dotting Machine of W. McDougall.[1] Among other ingenious instruments for the same purpose are those of Kehr,[2] and McComas.[3] But almost any kind of continuous work can be arranged so as to manifest the same phenomenon. In all cases alike, the output will throughout exhibit fluctuations that cannot be attributed to the nature of the work, but only to the worker himself.

Alleged fluctuations in longer periods. By many writers the fluctuations which we have been considering are taken to belong to a system which includes others of longer and longer duration. Many analogies are familiar in the sphere of physics ; for instance, the temperature at any place may exhibit variations from minute to minute, these being super-posed upon larger ones from hour to hour, and these latter again upon other still larger from season to season. Much the same occurs in many economical variations also, such as those in prices, transport, revenue, etc.

The point has become very important—and has even aroused keen disputes—with reference to successive measurements of a person's " I.Q." (see p. 61). Such measurements always turn out to be more or less discrepant, and by one party this fact has been portrayed as disastrous, but by the other party as negligible. What seems to have escaped the notice of both parties alike is that these variations really derive from the operation of measuring, not from the g itself which is measured. As regards the latter, recent experiments of Slocombe have shown that with children 11-12 years of age the relative amounts of g present no appreciable change at any rate up to periods of three months. This matter will be considered in more detail later on (ch. xxi.).

Uniformities of duration and recurrence. A feature that has been studied with especial interest about this pheno-

---

[1] For a description of it, see Burt, *Brit. Journ. Psych.* 1909, iii. p. 153.
[2] *Zeit. f. ang. Psych.* 1916, xi.　　　[3] *Journ. Exper. Psych.* 1922, v.

menon of oscillation—whether in the lapses, rivalries, or continuous output—is the tendency of both duration and recurrence to display certain uniformities.

Thus, several experimenters—notably Billings [1]—have brought evidence to show that any simple and monotonous mental process conducted with maximal effort has always a duration of somewhere near two seconds.

Again, the period of recurrence has been reported by the great majority of experimenters to have a constant length. But as to what this length is, there has been a curious disagreement ; by some, it has been put as low as 2-3 seconds ; by others, it has been said to be over ten times as long. The recent and apparently much more accurate work of Philpott, however, would appear to indicate that no such constancy of period exists at all ; instead, there is a series of periods increasing in length proportionally to the logarithm of the time. [2] And consonant with this has been some work of Gemelli and Galli. [3]

Controversy about origin. In order to explain the oscillation, some authorities have had recourse to an asserted fatigue and recovery of the sensory or muscular organ involved ; for example, the *tensor tympani* of the ear, or the accommodation muscles of the eye.

But others have brought forward reasons for believing that the phenomenon is—at least, in part—of more central physiological origin. Thus, Wiersma has pointed out that all the different senses give manifestations remarkably alike, a fact that seems to harmonize better with the central view. Pace has gone so far as to show that the visual oscillation continue unabated even after the accommodation muscles have been temporarily paralyzed by homoatropine.

INDIVIDUAL DIFFERENCES

Under abnormal conditions. Let us turn, now, to that aspect of the oscillation which specially interests us at

[1] *Psych. Rev.* 1914, xxi.   [2] Not yet published.
[3] *Archivio Italiano di Psicologia*, 1920.

present, namely, its differences with different individuals. How, if at all, does this phenomenon vary quantitatively or qualitatively from one person to another ? Does such variation run independently for each single kind of mental activity ? Or does it divide up into broad functions, as one for the lapses, another for the rivalry, and yet another for the fluctuations of output ? Or do the lines of division fall otherwise, as perhaps into one function for all operations of sight, a second for those of hearing, another for touch, and yet another for abstract thought ? Or, finally, does the oscillation constitute a general factor in operations of every kind, so that he who is most liable to it in one will tend to be so in all others ?

The first of these possibilities, that of independent variations for each different kind of activity, would conform well with the doctrine that the phenomenon is of peripheral origin, sensory or motor. Whereas the last possibility, according to which each individual shows the same characteristics in all activities however unlike, would lend support to the rival doctrine that the origin of the phenomenon is central.

The earliest definite evidence bearing on these questions seems to have been gathered from abnormal conditions, such as those produced by fatigue, drugs, or neurotic states. Thus, Wiersma found that the lapses of perception with faint stimuli were uniformly augmented for all three senses— sight, hearing, and touch—both by fatigue and by alcohol. Bromide had an equally uniform but reversed effect for all three.

Pointing in the same direction is the report of Kehr, that fluctuations in a long series of reaction-times were greatly increased by the so-called " shell-shock " ; for the effect of this can hardly be other than central. On the next page are typical curves taken from such a patient and from a normal person respectively.[1]

Hull, too, using his ingenious " index of fluctuation,"

[1] *Zeit. f. ang. Psych.* 1916. xi.

found this to be much smaller with normal persons than with those who were insane or mentally defective.

So far as they go, all these observations seem to side with the view that the oscillation has a central origin and constitutes a unitary function.

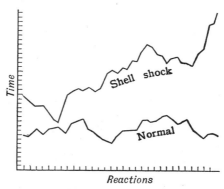

Reactions

Under normal conditions. With regard to normal conditions, unfortunately, the available information is still meagre. In fact, no investigation seriously illuminating the point would seem to have as yet been published. However, much of the required information is obtainable from some as yet unpublished investigations of Flugel (as mentioned on p. 320) and of Philpott. In the former of these, about 80 children, aged about 12 years, were measured as to the magnitude of their fluctuations in eight different sorts of mental work, as follows :

(1) Fours : Crossing out groups of 4 figures from among groups of 3, 4 and 5 figures.

(2) IX. : The usual " cancellation " test in which the letters i and x were to be crossed out.

(3) Words 1 : ⎰ Crossing out the "part" from pairs of
(4) Words 2 : ⎱ words, each pair containing a "whole and a part."

(5) Circles 1 : ⎱ Crossing through circles arranged in irre-
(6) Circles 2 : ⎰ gular rows.

(7) Subtraction 1 : ⎰ From a series of pairs of digits,
(8) Subtraction 2 : ⎱ marking those pairs where the difference between the digits amounted to three.

From these tests of oscillation there resulted the following table of correlations :

	1	2	3	4	5	6	7	8
1	—	·430	·190	·135	·085	·325	·000	·225
2	·430	—	·025	·035	·330	·320	·220	·355
3	·190	·025	—	·035	·020	·055	·170	·110
4	·135	·035	·035	—	·045	·140	·180	·405
5	·085	·330	·020	·045	—	·415	·300	·415
6	·325	·320	·055	·140	·415	—	·255	·440
7	·000	·220	·170	·180	·300	·255	—	·215
8	·225	·355	·110	·405	·415	·440	·215	—

At once arresting about these values is that, although very low, yet every one of them is positive. Another interesting feature is that the correlations between closely similar tests (as the two Words, the two Circles, and the two Subtractions) are not in general any higher than between two different tests.

The next step is to see whether these correlations can possibly be explained by g. Since the children had already been tested in the latter respect (by Burt, see p. 296), we can once more construct a crucial tetrad :

	Oscillation$_a$.	g_a.
Oscillation$_b$ - - -	·57	− ·18
g_b - - - -	− ·18	·75

The tetrad difference comes to ·39, which is about nine times greater than its probable error. We may conclude that whatever makes the different oscillations correlate with each other is at any rate certainly not g.

A similar comparison may be made between oscillation and perseveration, and the tetrad proves to be very similar :

	Oscillation$_a$.	Perseveration$_a$.
Oscillation$_b$ - - -	·57	− ·15
Perseveration$_b$ - -	− ·15	·59

Here the tetrad difference amounts to ·30, which is about eight times greater than its probable error. Accordingly, perseveration also must be rejected as a possible origin of the correlations displayed by the oscillations. Instead, then, this origin must be sought in something not hitherto encountered by us.

There remains to examine whether this new general influence can be reduced to any functional unity (as occurs with g), or involves several different group factors (as seems to be the case with "maturity," see ch. x. p. 142). The criterion between these two alternatives is supplied, as always, by seeing whether the frequency distribution of the actually observed tetrad differences does or does not conform with the theoretical values to be expected from the sampling errors alone. In point of fact, the two distributions agree admirably ; the observed median comes to ·032 and the theoretical probable error to ·031. The evidence, then, is as cogently affirmative as it could be ; the oscillation does possess functional unity.

To all the preceding facts, the work of Philpott would seem to add the important information, that the individual differences here at issue do not lie in the duration of the oscillation, and therefore can only lie in their *amplitude*.

CONCLUSION

Significance for theory. Here in oscillation, then, we have come upon a new single and universal factor, a third in addition to g and perseveration. To account for it, one might not unnaturally turn to those writers who have all along been attributing the phenomenon to a central and therefore presumably single influence. But as to the nature of this advocated central influence, and the reason for its producing oscillation, few of these writers have even attempted any explanation—beyond giving to it the not very illuminating title of "attention" or "apperception." Other authors, indeed, have with all desirable definiteness attributed the oscillation to some rhythmic character in the circulation of the blood. But this view would appear to be decisively contradicted by Philpott's and Flugel's recent very elaborate measurements of the actual oscillatory periods (see p. 322).

The only hypothesis which seems capable of reconciling all the facts observed hitherto is that this new universal factor derives from fatigue, the latter affecting the same psycho-physiological energy as has already been so greatly needed to explain many other phenomena. Unusually hard work, we may suppose, produces an increased consumption of this energy, and thereupon a corresponding increase in its recuperation. Physiology offers numerous analogies ; an example is the origin of the heart beat at the sino-auricular node, which Bayliss and Starling explain as follows :

> " We must suppose that these nodes discharge when they have stored up something to a sufficiently high degree, and that, after a discharge, they are incapable of further discharge until a fresh quantity has been formed." [1]

This view seems in excellent accord with the fact that the oscillations are much more marked in persons suffering from neurasthenia. It agrees very well, too, with the experimental result, that the oscillation does not extend over periods longer than a single spell of work. Furthermore, such an account of the way in which fatigue is manifested by the general energy furnishes the needed complement to the preceding chapter, where an account was given of how fatigue is manifested by the specific engines.

Accepting this view, the energy must be regarded as varying from individual to individual in three dimensions. First of all, it has a certain maximum of quantity, which is measured by g. In the second place, it has a certain degree of inertia, which is shown in slowness of shifting from one system of engines to another. And lastly, it has a certain facility of recuperation after effortful expenditure.

[1] *Principles of General Physiology*, Bayliss, 1924, p. 681.

Significance for practice. Of what importance, it may next be asked, is this third universal factor for practical purposes? Only the future can reply. Even more than in the case of perseveration, we have here encountered a new land of unknown magnitude.

To make further scientific advance, the first progressive step must be to perfect the technique of measuring. As at present constituted, the tests cannot be made reliable except at the price of excessive time.

Then can follow the ascertainment of how the oscillation varies for the same individual under varied conditions, such as those of age, health, occupation and surroundings. Along this line, there may perhaps be a rich harvest to be reaped, especially by education and by industry.

Finally, there is the great task of determining how this tendency to oscillate correlates with sex, race, social stratum, parentage, and above all with vocational success. Let, for example, the following curve represent the course of the cognitive efficiency of any individual whose oscillations are of great amplitude

Suppose, first, that he devotes himself to inventing aeroplanes. In that case, his success will depend upon his highest points, a, a, a ; as for his depths, b, b, b, no great harm will be done if here he be reduced to the point of paralysis. But suppose, instead, that his vocation is to *fly* aeroplanes, and that just when some sudden peril arises he happens to be down at one of the b's !

CHAPTER XX

LAW OF CONATION. *W* AND *C*.

THE TOPIC

Formulation of the law. The law now to be considered has been expressed in the following formula : *The intensity of cognition can be controlled by conation.*[1]

In these words an attempt has been made, not so much to include all that is true, as rather to exclude all that may possibly be untrue. The fact that such influence of conation upon cognition really occurs does not appear open to reason-

---

[1] *The Nature of Intelligence*, etc., p. 347.

able doubt. But so soon as we try to go further, fundamental difficulties are encountered, which seem to have hitherto scarcely received even notice ; much less, definite solution.

Thus, no inquiry appears to have ever been made as to whether the direct influence of conation is restricted to the clarifying of the items already present in the cognitive field, or also governs the transition to new items. Nor does any serious interest seem to have been taken as to whether the conative influence is always primarily enhansive, or may also be primarily inhibitive. Small effort has been made even to ascertain whether additional influence should be credited to the affective states, or instead these latter only act by way of instigating the conation.[1]

Hitherto, it would seem, the two great centres for investigating the phenomena of conation—those of Ach and Michotte—have been fully occupied in demonstrating its real existence and its general nature. But recently a new light has begun to dawn on the topic with the rise of the school of Aveling. By means of the researches done under his direction, the conative activity—besides being distinguished from pure " volition " [2]—has now been shown capable of quantitative estimation, both directly by means of introspection, and even indirectly by means of physical measurements. Moreover, the rule of law—so lately established for the sphere of cognition—is beginning to be extended over that of conation also. Aveling formulates the primary qualitative law as follows :

" All living organisms evolved to the perceptual level (or level of sensory apprehension) tend to strive in a

---

[1] Conspicuous among those who have *not* failed to notice the importance of the whole matter may be cited Claparède, as instanced in his *Comment diagnostiquer les Aptitudes chez les Écoliers*, 1924, p. 34.

[2] For this most remarkable distinction established by Aveling between, on the one hand " conation " in the sense of striving, and on the other hand " volition " in the sense of resolving, see his communication in *Brit. J. Psych.* 1926, xvi. Also, his paper at the Intern. Congress for Psychology, 1926. Corroboration was at once supplied by the work of Stevanović on Judgment in *Brit. J. Psych. Mon. Suppl.* 1927.

more or less definite and pre-determined manner towards specific ends, or goals of action, when excited by the presentation of a stimulus coordinated with such a tendency." [1]

Problems for the study of individual differences. Arising out of this matter are many questions which, so long as still unanswered, gravely obstruct the psychology of individual differences, and not seldom set the psychologists by the ears when submitting these abilities to test.

For example, how much does the success of anybody at a test of cognition really depend, not upon his cognitive ability in itself, but rather upon his conation to cognize? In particular, how far does his passing a mental test depend upon his conative and emotional attitude towards the very situation of being tested? Many persons, it has been suggested, fail to put forth anything like their highest powers.

" Additional incentive, such as hunger, or filial devotion, might change notably the relative positions." [2]

Again, to what extent does the effecting of any particular cognitive operation which enters into a test depend upon the degree that this appeals to some specially strong instinct in the testee? Or, contrariwise, might not some strong innate bias—for instance, an exaltation of the *ego*—tend to lead the cogniser astray? And allied to this question is the fear sometimes expressed, lest all tests of " intelligence " may be invalidated by the disturbing effects of the Freudian complexes which the words used may happen to touch off.

Once more, are there any definite facts to indicate whether those authors are right who maintain that only such cognition as is of purposive nature deserves the title of " intelligence."

And here, too, have to be faced a swarm of difficulties arising out of the concept of " attention." Is there any

[1] *Brit. J. Psych.* 1926, p. 345.
[2] H. L. Hollingworth, *Psych. Rev.* xxi. 1914.

truth in the statement that ability to cognize is really the same thing as ability to attend ?

Yet again, the present topic gives occasion to discuss the often advocated doctrine, that the intelligence of different individuals varies not only in quantity but also in quality. Is it true that one person is " profound," another " original," whilst a third possesses " common sense," and so forth ?

INFLUENCE OF EFFORT

" **Physiological limit** " **of operation.** Turning to the available definite facts bearing on the matter, we may begin with the most fundamental question of all. How great is the influence exercised upon a person's cognitive operations by the intensity of the effort he makes ? This question probes very deeply indeed ; it is almost equivalent to suggesting that perhaps the g may really be not of cognitive nature, but conative only. For both theory and practice, such a conclusion would be revolutionary.

Among the reported facts bearing on this question may be counted some experiments where persons even after lifelong practice at some operation, have nevertheless, on a sufficiently strong motive being supplied, surpassed what had previously been regarded as their ultimate " physiological limit."

A typical instance is afforded by the research of Aschaffenburg, who made four thoroughly experienced type-setters work under his supervision for $1\frac{1}{4}$ hours on four successive days. The average number of letters and spaces set by them in the first quarter of an hour each day showed a continual improvement, as follows :

Day.	Number set.
1	575
2	593
3	633
4	675

Thus, in spite of previous practice for many years, the type-setters still continue to make large further improvements. But unfortunately the possible grounds for such improvement are so complex as almost to defy reliable analysis. Not improbably, the most potent factor consisted merely in the overcoming of a deeply rooted *habit*, that of working at a rate which could be maintained with comfort and accuracy for the whole day. Such evidence, then, is far from being decisive in any direction.

Experimental variation of incentive. Another interesting kind of experiment has been supplied by Courtis.[1] This consisted in comparing the handwriting of a child done under three conditions : (*a*) in the usual way ; (*b*) with the addition of a personal appeal from the teacher that the child should do his best ; and (*c*) with the promise of a dime if he outdid his previous scores in both rate and quality. As result, the variation of conditions showed surprisingly little effect. The dime did, indeed, produce a greater rate than the personal appeal, together with the same quality. But still better scores on the whole were sometimes achieved *without either* of these additional incentives. In fact, such differences as occurred seemed to have been little more than mere random variations.

Other experimental variation of incentives had been tried about ten years earlier by the present writer in collaboration with several teachers,[2] but here using the ordinary tests of *g*. In half of the experiments, the children were told to work as hard as they possibly could ; in the other half, they were directed *not* to work particularly hard. Unfortunately, the research was interrupted before completion, and many of the original documents have been lost ; one rather unexpected result, however, was established. It was that, whether the tests were done with great or with little effort, the inter-correlations turned out to be in every case just about the same.

An inquiry on similar lines is now being re-undertaken by Wild, with both children and students ; although it is not yet finished, certain results have emerged already :

[1] *Loc. cit.* p. 207.　　　　[2] See p. 186.

(1) Some operations do, and others do not, need a considerable amount of effort to be executed at all.

(2) The operations needing such effort often coincide with those which are highly saturated with g (*e.g.* the test of Inferences, see ch. xii. p. 202). But there are notable exceptions; for instance, not much effort is needed even for such a good test of g as Opposites. The amount of effort needed increases chiefly as the task becomes more complex.

(3) *Very* great effort—such as is produced by a prize of money—tends only to increase speed at the expense of accuracy.

(4) Even when the great effort is specially aimed at improving the accuracy, the effect is generally small and may even be adverse. The latter paradoxical result seems to arise, partly from the fact of mental energy which should go to the cognition being diverted to the effort (see pp. 106-109), and partly from some ensuing emotional disturbance. It has some analogy with the bad effect of " pressing " in games of dexterity.

(5) In general, conation produces its effect mainly by directing the mental energy to the relevant processes. When once this much has been achieved, the desired cognition ensues without effort. This result is in full agreement with the results of Aveling and Stevanović.

The results of these experimental variations suggest, then, that—with the notable exception of the cases where only speed, not quality, has to be taken into account—a person's success at any cognitive operation is unexpectedly far from being completely dependent upon the degree of effort which he puts forth.

Individual differences in degree of exertion. Whilst on the present topic, the following incident may be not uninstructive. In a paper of Garnett, the view had seemed to be expressed that the normal procedure for dealing with a mental problem of exceptional difficulty is to master it by means of an intense exertion. But with the present writer, such a course had been found to produce, not any solution, but solely a headache ! For intensity he substitutes repetition ; he looks at the problem with an intentional *lack* of effort, and then soon puts it aside again ; after this has been repeated often enough, the solution begins to emerge as gradually and with as little effort as do the outlines of an approaching ship. Now, on these two curious extremes of procedure being explained to a class of students, and on their being asked which of the two (if either) they themselves adopted, it appeared *that about half worked in the one way and half in the other.*

On the whole, the view that the general cognitive superiority of one individual over another derives mainly from greater intensity of effort would not appear to be supported by any of the available evidence. A certain amount of effort is, indeed, normally required ; but by no means more, it would seem, than can readily be elicited in all normal testing.

INFLUENCE OF ATTITUDE TOWARDS MENTAL TESTS

Evidence from observation of demeanour. To be distinguished from the view just discussed—that the efficiency of a person's cognition in general depends on his intensity of conation—is a narrower but for practical purposes even more damaging doctrine ; this is that his success at mental tests in particular depends upon his conative and emotional attitude specially towards these.

The doctrine takes three chief lines. One consists in maintaining that those persons do best at the tests who, by reason of their general character, have the strongest impulses or will to succeed at them. The second line is that the success depends in dominant degree upon freedom from nervousness. And thirdly, it has been said that the effect of tests may be greatly disturbed by the Freudian complexes that they arouse unconsciously.

To some extent this doctrine is opposed by the same arguments as before, namely, those used where the subjects tested received different incentives. But further evidence covering a wider ground can be obtained by a study of the subjects' personal demeanour.

Now, in certain cases, the view we are considering does appear to have some amount of foundation. The most striking instance that has come within the notice of the present writer occurred in the course of testing a group of adults who were under treatment for various psychoses, such as hysteria and neurasthenia. Some of these patients whilst doing the tests could actually be heard to make a running fire of comments upon them—mostly unfavourable !—that could scarcely fail to have a distracting effect upon the performances. In lesser degree, a similar tendency seems to be noticeable in many adults, especially among those who . are apprehensive that the result of the testing may not be to their credit. And even among children there are a few —generally among the clever ones—who appear to suffer from a disadvantageous attitude ; they are always wasting their energies in looking out for some " catch." Furthermore, occasionally observation does indicate that a child submitted to an individual test (not a group one) is suffering from a nervousness likely to affect his performance.

On the other hand, all such disturbances seem to be unexpectedly rare. In general, competent experimenters report unanimously that normal children display a wonderful interest and zeal. And even in the exceptional cases, the disturbance would not seem to be beyond the control of the skilled tester ; mental, like physical testing, is not fool-proof, but an art.

Evidence from discrepancies between tests and estimates. There is another source of evidence, and one which in many respects is still more cogent ; it consists in comparing on the one hand the verdict of the tests, and on the other hand the " intelligence " as estimated by teachers or companions. For if any of the above mentioned traits of character—insufficient volitional control, nervous temperament, or susceptibility to complexes—really do handicap people in the execution of tests as compared with the performances of ordinary life, then such traits ought to predominate in those persons whose rank in the tests is markedly lower than in the estimates.

Now, for many years careful note has been taken in the laboratory of the present writer concerning all cases where the tests of g and the estimates of intelligence were exceptionally discrepant. Once, and once only, has such a discrepancy been explicable by emotional disturbance. It occurred when testing the officers at the British Naval Staff College. These were 16 in number, and estimates of their " general intelligence " had been most carefully formed by eight instructors, with the following results :

Order by test.	Order estimated by Instructors.		
	Variation for different instructors.		Compound order.
1	1	to 5	2
2	8	,, 13	9
3	3	,, 7	3
4	4	,, 16	5
5	1	,, 3	1
6	6	,, 14	10
7	2	,, 13	11
8	1	,, 7	4
9	5	,, 10	9
10	8	,, 14	10
11	4	,, 10	11
12	12	,, 15	14
13	14	,, 16	13
14	11	,, 15	15
15	9	,, 15	15
16	3	,, 8	6

As will be seen, in 12 out of the 16 cases, the order as given by the test falls actually within the limits of the estimates by the instructors. There are only two discrepancies at all large, the officers who by the test were 2 and 16 respectively. On the present writer asking if any explanation could be found for these two cases, a reply was received that on re-considering the case of 2, the verdict given by the test seemed after all to be more correct than the estimates formed by the instructors. But as regards the case of " 16," the comparatively low ranking by the test still seemed to be mistaken. Subsequently a further communication was received reporting the discovery that on the very day of the testing this officer who was 16th had received calamitous news from home.

With this single and natural exception, experience has throughout shown that lack of control and nervousness tend to be reported of those persons who fare, not worse, but *better* at the tests than in the estimates. The following are typical cases of this kind, as observed more than a decade ago :

" He is childish, highly nervous and easily moved to tears. He shows little practical ability, often forgets what he is told when sent on an errand. Often finds some difficulty in getting off to sleep."

" She is usually disappointing at examinations. The child says she gets upset and nervous when the examination takes place. This is probably true, as she seems to be of a very highly strung temperament."

" The girl is cunning and underhand, scatterbrained and unstable and incapable of sustaining attention. She is frivolous minded and will never take anything seriously." [1]

Since that time similar results have been obtained from persons of all ages, all social strata, and all grades of g.

Nor has investigation any more tended to indicate that failure at the tests may derive from the nervous state induced by touching off complexes. During the last three years particular care has been given to this matter in respect of the tests given by the present writer to all newly matriculated students at his college. An expert in psycho-analytical treatment has been investigating all the chief discrepancies between the results of the test and success of academic career.

[1] Abelson, *loc. cit* p. 191.

But although originally expecting that complexes would play an important part in such comparative failure at the tests, he actually found no definite evidence of any such thing.

On the whole, the truth would appear to be that insufficiency of will power, nervous temperament, and susceptibility to complexes do handicap people in the prolonged, familiar, and monotonous occupations of ordinary life, but have no such effect in the brief, novel, and interesting performances constituting the tests.

INFLUENCE OF INSTINCTS AND INTERESTS

A biological standpoint. Next to be examined is conative and emotional influence of still narrower scope. Already we have considered such influence upon cognition in general, and also upon any systematic test-series. Yet to examine is the influence exercised upon any single specific operation. Does not every actual activity—it may be, and indeed has been, asked—constitute one single whole response to a single whole situation ? And in such a response, how can cognition, conation, or emotion ever possibly be separated from each other ? Is not even the taking of one apart from another an idle feat of mere abstraction ? Could not such verbiage be advantageously replaced by resolving all behaviour into its really fundamental biological elements ; that is to say, into certain definite situations with their appropriate responses, these being either instinctive, or at least acquired out of the instincts ?

Wundt's " heterogony of purposes." Any such view must here be rejected in favour of the profounder biological conception expressed by Wundt as the heterogony of purposes :

" The purposes attained reach further than the motives or purpose-ideas from which they have originated. . . . Not the result that was originally willed, but that which was finally attained, constitutes the basis of further motive-series." [1]

As here indicated, the purpose becomes parted from the

[1] *Physiologische Psychologie*, 6th ed. iii. p. 765.

situation and response of the present moment ; it ranges further and further in advance of these.   In time, any single purpose can be served by the most varied responses.   Conversely, any single response can be brought into the service of most varied purposes.   When, for example, a person is tested with the Analogy, " Back is to Front as Past is to——? " and he answers " Future," of which of the instincts shall such a situation and response be thought to constitute an essentially appropriate manifestation ? That of feeding ?   Or of fighting ?   Or of mating ?   Each suggestion seems more ridiculous than the other.

Acquired group factors.   Nevertheless, whilst decisively rejecting any such absolute and principial view—the biology of the penny-in-the-slot description—there do appear to occur certain particular cases where a class of mental activities may be specially connected with some particular conative tendency.

Here may be recalled the recent research of McFarlane.   On considering this, we found that a remarkably broad group factor in mechanical ability could most plausibly be explained as due to individual differences from a very early age in the instinct to play with mechanical toys (ch. xiii. pp. 229-230).

So far, however, no analogous broad factor has presented itself elsewhere.   Most of all, perhaps, it might have been expected in the sphere of music, where not only innate instinct but also environmental encouragement are incomparably more favourable for some individuals than for others. And yet just here the existence of connection between *elements* has been disproved ; the abilities to appreciate, for instance, the relations of pitch, loudness, and rhythm have extremely low inter-correlations ; no more, in fact, than must be attributed to g alone.[1]

Acquired specific factors.   A further interesting conative influence has been suggested by another research ; but this time the apparent effect is less broad ; it tends to produce specific rather than group factors.

[1] See the fine series of investigation conducted by Seashore and his school.

This has been due to Franzen, who aimed at explaining the individually varying success of children with the different branches of study at school, such as Latin, English, Mathematics, etc. He arrived at the surprising conclusion that, when adequate measures are taken to oblige the pupils to work as hard as they can at all the different branches, the correlations between these increase so greatly as to indicate that none of these depend at bottom upon any specific ability in any degree, but solely upon g.[1]

On the whole, it would appear that the influence of instincts and interests upon cognitive ability has an unexpectedly restricted scope. In certain exceptional cases, however, such an influence is so strikingly suggested as to urge the pressing need for at least further investigation.

INFLUENCE OF "ATTENTION"

Advocacy by Burt, Woodrow, and Garnett. The foregoing considerations have prepared the way for examining one of the most important theories that have been advanced to account for g. It is that which ascribes individual differences of ability to inequalities in power of " attention."

So long ago as 1909 this view received some remarkable experimental support from Burt. He concluded as follows :

" The test which correlates most with all the other tests, and consequently heads the hierarchy, is the Dotting test. The Dotting test was specially devised to measure power of sustained effort of maximal concentration, in short to test Voluntary Attention. The inference is that the power of Voluntary Attention is the capacity, common to all the functions tested, which enters into the processes involved. The hypothesis that Attention is the essential factor in Intelligence is already a well-known one. In view of it, before the hierarchies were drawn up, the tests were arranged in order according to the degree in which Attention might be expected to be required in the successful performance

[1] Teachers' College, *Columbia Univ. Contr. to Educ.* No. 125, 1922.

of the tasks. Such arrangements were obtained from interrogations of the boys, and independently from three psychologists. The average arrangement is as follows : Dotting, Spot Pattern, Memory, Mirror, Alphabet, Sorting, Sound, Lines, Touch, Weight, Dealing, Tapping. This corresponds closely with the order of the various correlations with Intelligence, and nearly as closely with the orders given by the hierarchies." [1]

Subsequently, an investigation of exceptional originality was devoted to this problem by Woodrow. He tested " simple " reaction time to touch, sound, and light ; also " choice " reaction time, where the two alternative stimuli consisted in a sudden increase or decrease of light, whilst the responses were made by the two hands respectively. Each of these kinds of reaction time was tried : (a) with a regular preparatory interval of two seconds, and (b) with irregular preparatory intervals. There were 12 subjects, of whom some were adults practised in such reactions, some were unpractised adults, and some were children. In the whole investigation, no less than 19,350 reaction times were measured. The results were as follows :

Subject.	Excess reaction time for irregular as compared with regular preparatory signal, in thousandths of a second.			
	Touch.	Sound.	Light.	Choice.
Practised - -	42	48	51	68
Practised - -	45	40	52	63
Practised - -	45	55	71	91
Unpractised - -	52	55	61	85
Unpractised - -	64	65	79	135
Unpractised - -	59	66	77	116
Child - - -	85	82	96	143
Practised - -	87	94	97	160
Child - - -	90	104	123	174
Child - - -	97	115	131	—
Child - - -	124	143	147	206
Young child (8) -	147	175	181	—

[1] *Loc. cit.* p. 174.

Here, even the disturbing influences of varying practice and age cannot explain away the astonishingly high correlations between the four columns ; these correlations are, in fact, close upon perfection.   Such a result is attributed by the author to the factor of " pure attention." [1]

Yet a third advocacy much too important to be omitted even in this brief sketch is that of Garnett, who takes g to measure " capacity to concentrate attention." [2]   His method of arriving at this result was by means of a new and very valuable statistical procedure, which will be considered in the next section of this chapter.

Experiments in inattention.   Now, one difficulty about all this support of the theory of attention is to reconcile it with the following research done by Koch and Habrich (under the direction of Bühler) on the ability to cognize *without* attention.[3]   Here, two groups of symbols were exhibited for three seconds, and the subject was instructed to discover which of the symbols occurred in both groups.[4]   Introspection shows that when performing this task the common elements stand out prominently in full " attention," whereas the remainder are hardly detectible in consciousness at all. Next, however (without re-exhibiting the symbols), the subjects were called upon to do a secondary operation ; they were asked to describe the other elements which had *not* been common to the two groups, and which therefore had never been perceived attentively.   The subjects came from eight classes in a school, nine being picked out of each class as clever, eight as medium, and nine as stupid.   Koch treated boys in this way; Habrich, girls.   The resulting scores were as follows :

Operation.	Boys.			Girls.		
	Clever.	Medium.	Stupid.	Clever.	Medium.	Stupid.
Primary - -	777	712	585	851	714	516
Secondary - -	950	899	751	560	455	415

[1] *Brit. Journ. Psych.* 1919, ix.   [2] *Journ. Exper. Psych.* 1916, i.
[3] *Zeit. f. ang. Psych.* 1913, vii. ; 1914, ix.
[4] This procedure was originally due to Grünbaum.

Evidently, the clever children surpass the stupid, not only in the primary operation, but no less so in the secondary one ; and this happens for both sexes, despite the contrast between these in other respects.

Thus, whether the operation is performed attentively or inattentively, with high or with low degree of consciousness, with the focus or with the fringe of the mental energy, with or without expressly directed effort—all this would seem to make no difference in the dependence of the cognition upon g.

Equivocality of the term. The way out of the difficulty appears to lie in recognizing that the term " attention " is very equivocal (see ch. vii. p. 89). One well known way of defining it is as

" simply conation so far as it requires for its satisfaction fuller cognisance of its object." [1]

Here " attention " would seem to be nearly synonymous with " effort." And that g measures this would seem to have been decisively contradicted by the earlier part of the chapter.

Another widely accepted version of attention is as :

" the bringing of something to the focus of consciousness and the holding it there." [2]

But to suppose that attention in this sense will fit g seems to be contradicted by the work of Koch and Habrich.

In much the same way many other versions of " attention " can be discarded. But there remains one where this is no longer the case. It is the defining of the term as

" the application of intellectual energy." [3]

For now at last the view that g measures attention enters into excellent agreement with every fact so far encountered by us. Moreover, such an interpretation of the word seems

[1] Stout, *Manual of Psychology*, 1913.
[2] Lloyd Morgan, *Introduction to Comparative Psychology*, 1894.
[3] Maher, *Psychology*, 1911.

not inconsistent with the researches and writings of Burt, of Woodrow, and perhaps even of Garnett.

INFLUENCE OF GENERAL CHARACTER

Procedure of Webb. The remaining influence of conation upon cognition to be considered in this chapter may be thrown together as that of general " character." What exactly this word is here meant to signify will become clear as we go on.

Our source of information will be mainly the work of Webb, since this appears to stand up to the present time without rival.[1] His principal subjects were 200 students with an average age of 21 years. These were submitted to tests of g as described on p. 203. But the leading characteristic of the research was the extreme care given to, and exceptionally favourable opportunities for, very diversified and systematic mental estimates. The students were divided into groups of 20, each of which was kept for several months under the continual observation of two prefects (students themselves). At the start, these prefects studied the subjects in whatever way seemed best to themselves and summed up the result for each subject in the form of a general character sketch. They were then supplied with a schedule of all the traits to be investigated specially, and they had to mark each subject for each trait on a scale running from $+3$ to -3.

Elaborate precautions were taken to eliminate or minimize all sources of error. The subjects were divided by the prefects into the groups in such a way, that no prefect had to deal with any subject towards whom he had any particular strong feeling, either of friendship or of enmity. Each prefect took pains to work in complete independence of his colleague. Each added to his assessments of each trait a precise description of what he understood by the terms used. The subjects themselves were kept in entire ignorance

[1] *Loc. cit.* p. 181.

that they were under observation. The present writer can add his own testimony that these prefects—inspired by their personal relations to Dr. Webb—undertook and maintained their observational duties with veritable scientific enthusiasm.

In .addition, some of the tests and estimates were also obtained for 140 boys aged about 12. But with these, of course, no such peculiarly felicitous arrangement for observation was possible. However, besides all the generally approved precautions, the further step was taken of selecting schools that had at least two masters for each class, in order to obtain two tolerably independent estimates (any attempt to obtain independence between a class master and the headmaster was rejected as not really feasible).

Correlation between different kinds of " intelligence.", Now, among the mental traits estimated were four that appeared to represent " intelligence " of different kinds ; they were respectively Profoundness of Apprehension, Quickness of Apprehension, Common Sense, and Originality of Ideas. These, together with the test of g and the records of scholastic examinations, produced for the students the following inter-correlations (corrected for attenuation).

	1	2	3	4	5	6
1. Test of g - - -	—	·67	·56	·53	·29	·47
2. Examinations - -	·67	—	·65	·25	·52	·57
3. Estimated profoundness	·56	·65	—	·96	1·00	·88
4. Estimated quickness -	·53	·25	·96	—	·81	1·00
5. Estimated common sense	·29	·52	1·00	·81	—	·81
6. Estimated originality -	·47	·57	·88	1·00	·81	—

Here, although all six correlated values purport to be measurements of some or other aspect of intelligence, there is not even a rough approximation to satisfying the criterion of tetrad differences. For instance, one of these is

$$·53 \times ·52 - ·29 \times ·25 = ·20 ;$$
another is $\quad 1·00 \times ·67 - ·29 \times ·65 = ·48.$

The former is about five times and the latter about sixteen

times its probable error. Consequently, there must be some large group factor or factors in play.

Webb's theorem of W. To ascertain the nature of any such influence, Webb began by noticing that two of the traits just quoted, the Profoundness and the Quickness, although very highly correlated with each other, nevertheless presented some remarkable discrepancies in their correlations with other traits. The Profoundness correlated in especially high degree with the following :

1. Perseverance, as opposed to wilful changeability.
2. Perseverance in the face of obstacles.
3. Kindness on principle.
4. Trustworthiness.
5. Conscientiousness.

The Quickness, on the other hand, showed relatively high correlation with the following :

6. Readiness to become angry.
7. Eagerness for admiration.
8. Bodily activity in pursuit of pleasures (games, etc.).

Thereupon, the author proceeded to examine how these eight traits were correlated with one another. The following is the table for the students, after correcting for attenuation and eliminating the influence of g (by Yule's formula, see p. 156). It may be added that the results for the boys were quite similar :

	1	2	3	4	5	6	7	8
1	—	·92	·58	·74	·68	− ·45	− ·55	− ·08
2	·92	—	·46	·52	·50	− ·29	− ·45	·07
3	·58	·46	—	1·00	·95	− ·85	− ·61	·11
4	·74	·52	1·00	—	1·00	− ·78	− ·78	·13
5	·68	·50	·95	1·00	—	− ·78	− ·74	− ·26
6	− ·45	− ·29	− ·85	− ·78	− ·78	—	·93	·36
7	− ·55	− ·45	− ·61	− ·78	− ·74	·93	—	·37
8	− ·08	·07	·11	− ·13	− ·26	·36	·37	—

Next, the correlations were calculated between each column in this table, showing an average of ·94 ; and this value, approximating as it does to unity, was taken to indicate that the whole of the correlation in the table derives from one and the same factor.[1]

Having thus established that such a new general factor exists, the author's next step was to discover for it some valid psychological explanation. With this in view, he remarked that all the eight traits could be subsumed under one or other of the following : (a) moral qualities and deeper social virtues (3, 4, 5) ; (b) persistence of motives (1, 2) ; (c) instability of emotions (6) ; and (d) the lighter side of sociality (7, 8). Thence he argued as follows :

> " The nature of our general factor must obviously be sought in these four headings. . . . We therefore venture to suggest (tentatively and with much desire for further evidence) that the nature of the second factor, whose generality would appear to extend so widely in character, is in some close relation to ' persistence of motives.' This conception may be understood to mean *consistency of action resulting from* volition or will."

For this general character-factor, he proposes the symbol of *w*.

Correlation of " Profoundness " and " Common Sense." Assisted by this far-reaching theorem of *w*, let us return to the problem of analyzing the six kinds of intelligence whose inter-correlations so decidedly failed to be explicable by any single common factor. We will begin with a pair of them, Profoundness of Apprehension and Soundness of Common Sense.

Let us consider what these terms were intended to signify.

---

[1] This criterion of incolumnar correlation has, indeed, now been superseded by that of tetrad differences. But here—indeed almost everywhere when properly applied—the two lead to concordant results (see ch. x.).

The conclusion of Webb was in the following year supported by the finding of Burt, that the correlations between different emotional tendencies " suggest the presence of a general factor " (*Proc. Brit. Ass.,* 1915). Quite recently, Webb has been further corroborated by Allen's work on Temperamental Tests (see thesis in Library of the University of London).

Here are some of the explanations given as regards the Profoundness :

> " The subjects grasp not only the new truth or problem, but its relationship to other truths and problems at the same time." " The grasping an idea fully, turning it over, and viewing it from every point of view." " Having grasped a point, the +men (*i.e.* those rated highly for this trait) see its bearing on the subject and associate it readily with other information on the same subject."

As regards the Common Sense :

> " When he spoke or acted, he did so in a sensible way." " General reasonableness." " The degree to which he possesses a good, sound, reliable, and balanced judgment." " Advice and assistance always practical and to be relied on."

As thus understood, Profoundness would hardly appear to be an ability of any special kind, but rather a conative attitude, one which utilizes all abilities to best advantage. Moreover, it is a conative attitude remarkably like the *w* which we have just seen. Nothing of this sort, however, seems to enter into the portrayal of Common Sense ; this figures as a cognitive ability pure and simple.

From all these explanations which the judges give of what they are judging, let us turn to the actual correlations which their judgments produce. Very different is the story told. Between the Profoundness and the Common Sense—despite their being descriptively so unlike each other—the correlation really reaches the extraordinary value of 1·00. And still more striking is the agreement between the two as regards their respective correlations with all the *other* traits, as shown in columns 1 and 2 below ; between these two columns themselves, the correlation is well-nigh perfect.[1]

---

[1] For a full appreciation of these other traits, reference must be made to the definitions given of them by the judges. (See Webb's paper.)

CORRELATIONS OF THE SIX COGNITIVE TRAITS WITH ALL THE OTHERS.

		Pro-found-ness.	Com-mon sense.	Quick-ness.	Origi-nality.	Ex-ams.	Test of g.
		1	2	3	4	5	6
Selected to prove W.	1. Perseverance v. chang.	·75	·71	·40	·48	·39	·34
	2. Perseverance v. obstacles	·72	·77	·59	·69	·41	·28
	3. Kindness on principle	·69	·79	·46	·47	·17	·23
	4. Trustworthiness	·66	·57	·40	·46	·31	·28
	5. Conscientiousness	·66	·64	·24	·43	·19	·22
	6. Readiness to become angry	− ·39	− ·53	− ·01	− ·09	·07	·00
	7. Eagerness for admiration	− ·29	− ·37	·19	− ·07	·17	·10
	8. Bod. act. for pleasure	·02	− ·04	− ·16	·17	− ·16	− ·19
Emotions.	9. Cheerfulness	·26	·34	·59	·58	·11	·34
	10. Oscillation of mood	− ·48	− ·51	− ·38	− ·36	− ·30	− ·39
	11. Occasional great depression	− ·17	− ·40	− ·43	− ·48	− ·12	− ·31
	12. Quick recovery from anger	·24	·48	·21	·18	·07	·09
	13. Occasional great anger	− ·18	− ·30	·06	·14	·06	− ·01
	14. Aesthetic feeling	·71	·76	·55	·64	·46	·46
	15. Sense of humour	·49	·45	·85	·79	·18	− ·17
Self-regard.	16. Desire to excel	·63	·61	·42	·54	·62	·39
	17. Desire to impose will on others	− ·13	− ·25	·19	− ·05	·08	·13
	18. Belief in own powers	·27	·16	·38	·36	·46	·35
	19. Esteem of self	− ·05	− ·20	·17	·27	·25	·11
	20. Offensive self-esteem	− ·28	− ·49	·10	·13	·07	·22
Social tendencies.	21. Love of large gatherings	− ·16	− ·12	·42	·44	− ·08	·30
	22. Love of intimate circles	·64	·55	·22	·31	·33	·35
	23. Kindness on impulse	·19	·37	·21	·30	− ·07	− ·19
	24. Corporate spirit	·32	·38	·40	·45	·21	·03
	25. Interest in religion	·54	·52	·03	·18	·22	·28
	26. Suggestibility	− ·09	·10	− ·22	− ·30	− ·04	·02
	27. Desire to be liked	·13	·02	·38	·20	·07	·07
	28. Wideness of influence	·77	·69	·66	·70	·21	·11
	29. Intensity of influence	·88	·74	·87	·86	·35	·39
	30. Tact	·32	·35	·40	·45	·00	− ·02
Activity.	31. Work on study	·74	·67	·30	·40	·78	·60
	32. Work on pleasure	·01	·02	·27	·11	− ·16	− ·15
	33. Bod. act. in business	·34	·21	·34	·54	·19	·13
	34. Far-sightedness	·75	·67	·27	·36	·59	·45
	35. Pure-mindedness	·47	·54	·11	·15	·24	·15
	36. Rapid mental work	·84	·70	·96	·94	·81	·54
	37. Bodily physique	·01	·04	·15	·17	·09	− ·07
General.	38. Excellent est. by prefects	·62	·53	·15	·26	·60	·37
	39. Character est. by staff	·77	·88	·50	·55	·43	·36
	40. Strength of will	·75	·95	·61	·69	·67	·29
	41. Excitability	− ·29	− ·47	·23	− ·09	− ·10	·23

Accordingly, the Common Sense—quite as much as the Profoundness—shows a striking affinity to all the traits involving w. For instance, both abilities alike have high positive correlation with Kindness on Principle, Trust-worthiness, Conscientiousness, as also with the cognate Interest in Religion, Farsightedness, Pure-mindedness, and Love of Intimate Circles. Still in agreement, both alike have markedly negative correlations with Readiness to become Angry, Oscillation of Mood, Eagerness for Admiration, and Offensive Self-esteem. Incidentally, we may note that, despite this negative correlation with Self-esteem, there is a high positive correlation with Desire to Excel. Moreover, the tendency of the " Profound " students to suspend their judgment does not prevent them from having the power " to think rapidly and get through their work expeditiously " (36 in the table).

So far, all the correlations that Profoundness and Common Sense have with the other traits are forthwith explicable as due to a combination of g with w. And most of the remaining chief features about these two can, on a little more reflection, be explained in like manner. An instance is the fact that both correlate highly with Work on Study. In part, this can be ascribed to w, since the latter would naturally help its possessors to sacrifice the present comfort of idleness for the future benefits of good education ; and as for the other part, it can easily be explained by g, since school study—like all activity—brings most satisfaction to those who excel at it. Another case worth noticing is the surprisingly high correlation of both Profoundness and Common Sense with Aesthetic Feeling. If this latter were really a " feeling " at all, the correlation would be mysterious indeed. But this is far from being the truth. It is described by the judges in such terms as the following :

> " Love of the beautiful because it appealed to their finer nature and to their finer emotion." " If he loves Art and all that is clean and pure for its own sake, then he has the true aesthetic feeling."

As thus interpreted, this so-called feeling most certainly involves both w and g.

There remains, however, among the emotions one whose correlation with Profoundness and Common Sense does create difficulties ; this is Humour. On superficial regard, one might be tempted to explain this correlation on the ground that humour involves much g. But Webb's other results contradict this.

On the whole, then, what were designated by the prefects as Profoundness and Common Sense appear to be in very large measure reducible to a combination of g with w. But there remains an appreciable unexplained residue, which is particularly noticeable in the correlations with Humour.

Consideration of " Quickness " and " Originality." We will take next for examination the further pair of traits " Quickness of Apprehension " and " Originality of Ideas." The former is described in such terms as the following :

> " The +men saw the point at once." " Alacrity in understanding new material." " Taking in circumstances at a glance and judging accordingly."

With this may be contrasted " Originality " :

> " The +men had many ' happy thoughts,' but I estimated the *originality* of the ideas, not their *value.*" " The +men could suggest solutions to all kinds of difficulties." " The number of new ideas, strange fancies, novel aspects of situations, which occurred to him, and the speed with which they came into his mind."

There is thus a great difference indicated between the two traits, namely, in that the " quick " person is he who understands others speedily, whereas the " original " man is he who speedily creates novel ideas of his own. Despite this radical difference in the description, however, the actual estimates proved to have an almost perfect inter-correlation (+1·00, as correlated for attenuation) ; and they agree no less well in respect of correlation with all the other traits. That is to say, every subject found by the judges to be quick at understanding others was in about exactly the same degree found by them to be original for himself ; probably no one could be more surprised at this result than were the judges themselves.

Proceeding, then, to consider the characteristics of this single Quickness-Originality trait, the most important perhaps is that, although not correlating with w qualities so highly as did the previous pair, still they do so to a very considerable degree. Here again, then, w and g are largely involved.

As regards several other traits, however, Quickness and Originality show a marked deviation from the former pair. Most conspicuous in this respect is Humour, with which they correlate to a surprising degree ($+\cdot85$ and $+\cdot79$). Very notable also are their high correlations with Cheerfulness, Love of Large Gatherings, Tact, and above all with Capacity for Rapid Mental Work ($\cdot96$ and $+\cdot94$). Interesting further are their exceptionally *low* correlations with Interest in Religion and with Pure-mindedness. All these cases indicate that the Quickness and Originality contain, over and above the w and g, some very important further ingredient.

Consideration of g and examinational ability. These two traits form yet a third pair that are remarkably akin to each other. Their inter-correlation is $\cdot67$, and also they present much agreement in their respective correlations with the other traits.

In general, these correlations with the other traits are chiefly remarkable for their lowness ; this is especially the case with g. Such a neutrality, as Webb points out, indicates the " purity of g as a mental content."

Among the few exceptions to such behaviour of g, the most striking is its high correlation with the amount of work devoted to studies ($+\cdot60$). At first sight, this result might be taken to imply that previous studiousness had proved helpful towards doing the tests of g. But against this surmise is the fact of still higher correlations with Studiousness being shown by all the other five cognitive traits, including especially the Common Sense ($+\cdot67$), where any such explanation seems impossible. We appear compelled, then, to fall back upon the same double explanation of the studiousness as before ; a satisfaction in study derived from success at it, this success being due to superior g ; and a tendency to take pains in the present for the sake of gains in the future, this tendency being bestowed by w.[1]

Not quite so easily disposed of are the quite appreciable correlations of g, positively with Cheerfulness (+ ·34), negatively with Emotional Oscillation (– ·39) and with Liability to Depression (– ·31). The most plausible explanation seems to be that advanced by Webb, namely, that they are all manifestations of mental vigour and therefore agree with the hypothesis of mental energy.

Turning next to Examinational Ability, the chief correlations of this are with Desire to Excel (+ ·62), Strength of Will (+ ·67), Far-sightedness (+ ·59) and Perseverance in the face of Obstacles (+ ·41). The connection of all these with examinational success is obvious enough ; moreover, they are clearly characteristic of w.

On the whole, then, the six cognitive traits which we have been examining are in large measure traceable partly to g and partly to w. But there evidently exists an important remainder—most conspicuous in respect of Quickness, Originality, and Humour—that fails to be reducible to these two factors.

Third factor of Garnett "c." The experimental results of Webb were subsequently submitted to a masterly and most valuable further mathematical analysis by Garnett. The latter demonstrated that all this remainder not explicable by g or w could be comprised in a third unitary factor, c, independent of the other two.[2] And he was even able to calculate the correlations of this new factor with all the traits investigated by Webb. The results are as follows :

---

[1] For further light on the relation between work and w, see the research of Allen quoted on p. 348.

[2] *Brit. J. Psych.* 1919, ix.

Correlation with
third factor c.

General tendency to be cheerful	·97
Oscillation of mood	− ·05
Occasional general depression	− ·57
Readiness to become angry	·15
Quick recovery from anger	·33
Occasional great anger	− ·18
Aesthetic feeling	·39
Sense of humour	·98
Desire to excel	·46
Desire to impose will on others	·58
Eagerness for admiration	·18
Belief in own powers	·32
Esteem of self	·30
Offensive self-esteem	·12
Love of large gatherings	·85
Love of intimate circles	·01
Kindness on impulse	·50
Kindness on principle	·40
Corporate spirit	·68
Trustworthiness	·07
Conscientiousness	− ·05
Interest in religion	− ·39
Suggestibility	− ·29
Desire to be liked	·56
Wideness of influence	·67
Intensity of influence	·84
Tact	·60
Work on study	− ·01
Work on pleasure	·31
Bodily activity in business	·64
Far-sightedness	− ·07
Perseverance in the face of obstacles	·39
Perseverance as opposed to wilful changeability	− ·06
Quickness of apprehension	·95
Profoundness of apprehension	·59
Soundness of common sense	·51
Originality of ideas	·88
Pure-mindedness	− ·45
Rapid mental work	·59
Bodily physique	·16
Excellence of character, estimated by prefects	·33
Do. do. do. staff	·02
Examinational ability	·30
Athletics	·27
Strength of will	·41
Excitability	·22

Now, the author himself suggests that this new factor might perhaps be describable as "cleverness." But the existence of any unitary power of such a nature seems to have been disproved by the masterly analysis of Hargreaves (*loc. cit.* p. 187). A better explanation is supplied by the apparent kinship of the new factor to one that has been established already, namely, mental inertia (ch. xvii.). For a low degree of this latter, just as well as a high degree of any cleverness, will tend to make a person appear quick of apprehension in the sense of rapidly "understanding new material," or original in the sense of "seeing novel aspects of situations." And furthermore, low degree of inertia will also explain much for which cleverness can give no account whatever; above all, we have the extraordinarily high correlation of this new factor with Cheerfulness, the value of this being $+ \cdot 97$ or almost perfect unity. For there seems not the least reason why all clever people should be cheerful; such a proposition would contradict daily experience. But as regards the non-perseverators, on the other hand, freedom from melancholy (as also from inhibitions) has already been found most strikingly characteristic (ch. xvii.).

Thus the two lines of research—on the one hand that of Lankes, Wynn Jones, and Bernstein, and on the other that of Webb and Garnett—meet finally in mutual corroboration. "Perseveration" and c may be taken, pending further evidence, as only the opposite aspects of one and the same thing.

Trustworthiness of estimates. Finally, a word may be said about a not unnatural objection, namely, that the estimates of character—despite all Webb's precautions—must nevertheless remain affected by large errors. And in this statement there is unquestionably much truth; under the best of conditions realized hitherto, the estimates can scarcely escape being very fallible. Still, before this fallibility can be admitted as a valid objection to our present results, it must be shown to have such a nature as is likely to engender these. And this appears not to be the case.

The chief errors in estimating traits of character are—so far as hitherto established—of only two kinds ; first, the random ones ; and then, the bias of a judge for or against any individual all round. By neither of these kinds of error do our foregoing results seem to be seriously affected.

Moreover, before discarding such systematic investigations as that of Webb, we have to think whether there is anything better to take their place. From the language used by most of the objectors, preference should be given to the estimates or other observations that arise " naturally " in the ordinary course of life. But why should these be rated so highly ? Take, for instance, the research of Flanders, where 47 men of a large express company were selected under the direction of the superintendent, the only restriction to his freedom of choice being that he should not pick anyone who had not been in the employ of the company for at least a year and that he should be able to give the desired information with confidence.[1] The selected men were then classified, each by three of his superiors independently, in seven traits. The result was to show the following " reliability coefficients " (see p. 189) for the estimates made of the same trait by different judges :

Speed of work.	Accuracy of work.	All-round efficiency.	Intelligence.	Dependability.	Co-operativeness.	Loyalty.
·46	·53	·33	·37	·16	·22	·18

The highest of all these values is lower than even the average of those obtained by Webb !

Another investigation relevant to the present matter is that of Magson, which included not only estimates formed on prolonged acquaintance (at least a year) but also those based upon a single interview.[2] The subjects were 149 men students in Training Colleges for teachers. 91 judges took part in the work ; they were all adults and were chosen from many different professions and businesses.

[1] *Journ. Appl. Psych.* 1918, ii.
[2] *Brit. J. Psych.* 1916, *Mon. Suppl.* ix.

One result of this work was to show that the estimates of " intelligence " gained from a single interview—although expressed with great confidence—were really almost valueless ; for on being compared with those formed of the same trait on prolonged acquaintance, the correlation was only ·22. The correlation with quickness of apprehension and with profoundness of apprehension, both formed on prolonged acquaintance, was only ·13 and ·04 respectively. As for the tests, the correlation of this with the estimates made on an interview was only ·15, whereas with those which were made on prolonged acquaintance, it rose to ·54.[1] The reason why this latter value was not higher still was reported as being that such mature estimates are greatly swayed by the general mental attitude of the judge towards the subject.[2] From the whole work, we seem forced to conclude that neither long nor short acquaintance in ordinary life is in the least likely to secure estimates of traits that can even equal, much less surpass, those obtained by a more systematic procedure. And any person who opposes Webb's great array of results on the ground of his own few personal uncontrolled observations would indeed be straining at the gnat whilst swallowing the camel.

CONCLUSIONS

To summarize the chief results of this chapter, the earlier portion had a negative issue. We saw that the value obtained for an individual's g was not—when measured properly—dependent to any appreciable extent upon his intensity of effort. This conclusion held good whether we regarded the effort as a general mental function, or as a special attitude towards the mental tests, or even as a concentration of " attention " if the latter term be understood according to the most common definitions of it.

On the positive side, there have been various indications

---

[1] This is as high as the correlation between the estimates made on prolonged acquaintance by different observers. See p. 189.

[2] Compare the illuminating work of Thorndike on " halo."

supporting the hypothesis that g measures something of the nature of an energy (and in *this* sense, favouring the theory of " attention ").

Further, we have examined what are usually regarded as different types or kinds of general ability ; in particular, " profoundness," " quickness," " common sense," and " originality." What the world means by all these, and even by plain " intelligence " itself—especially in the case of adults—certainly does appear to mean much over and above g. But this surplus is in part reducible to freedom from the inertia discussed in chs. vii. and xvii. To this obverse aspect of inertia we may, with Garnett, give the name of c. The remainder is really not cognitive at all, but conative ; it is the trait measured by w, and describable as purposive consistency, or even as self-control. And in this manner our inquiry, which started with no higher aim than cognition, has actually led us up to what would seem to be the most fundamental truth on the other side of the personality, that of character.

CHAPTER XXI

INFLUENCE OF AGE

EFFECT OF GROWTH ON *G*

Formulation of fifth law. There is one more quantitative law of knowledge besides the four that we have been so far considering (span, retention, fatigue, and conation). It has been called that of " primordial potencies," and formulated as follows : *Every manifestation of the preceding four quantitative principles is superposed upon, as its ultimate basis, certain primordial but variable individual potencies.*[1] Thus it is in a way even more fundamental than the other four, since it descends deeper into the regions of the purely physiological. It falls into several heads, of which the most important seems to be Age, Health, Sex, and Heredity. The influence of age is chiefly exerted during two periods, those of youth and of senescence respectively. We will begin with the former, and particularly with its bearings upon *g*.

---

[1] *Nature of Intelligence*, etc., p. 136.

Age at which *g* becomes adult. The first great problem here is to determine the curve along which *g* increases as the person grows older. And since *g* is that which comes to more or less approximate measurement in the usual tests of " general intelligence," it is also that which furnishes the real significance of the so-called " mental age " (rather than that of the " I.Q.," see p. 61). About the growth of this *g*, several questions have lately excited a lively interest ; and none more so than that of the age at which it reaches its zenith, so that as regards " intelligence " the person may then be regarded as fully grown-up. The age for attaining to this point, as reported by the great majority of investigators, has been unexpectedly young ; some estimates have gone so low as 13 years, and very few have exceeded 16. But even the latter figure has been roundly denounced by many writers—including one or two professed psychologists— as flying in the face of " common sense." [1]

It is at any rate certain that investigation of this problem lies beset with great difficulties. The path which most naturally suggests itself—and has been most usually attempted—consists in testing numerous persons of different ages and then seeing at what age all noticeable average improvement ceases. But here the objection at once arises, that the groups for the different ages are rarely, if ever, properly comparable with each other. If, for instance, two school classes are compared, the children in the higher class, besides being older, have also been specially selected as more advanced in their studies ; their superior *g* may then really depend, not upon their age, but upon the selection.

To avoid this obstacle, other investigators have instead compared the scores made by the self-same subjects tested and re-tested at varying ages. But thereby is created a new difficulty ; for in each later test the subject profits by

---

[1] Among the chief contributors to the topic have been Baldwin, Ballard, Brooks, Burt, Cobb, Dearborn, Kuhlmann, Porteus, Terman, Thorndike, and Woodrow.

the practice afforded in the earlier ones ; and to such advantage may, really be due any improvement that ensues.

This obstacle, also, has been circumvented, notably by Thorndike.[1] He tested a group of children at two successive years of age, averaging about 16 and 17 respectively ; the result was an improvement of about 23 per cent. And his ingenious procedure enabled him to separate this amount into two nearly equal parts, of which the one appeared due to the practice, but the other to derive genuinely from the difference in age. Here, however, a new difficulty arrives on the scene. The author reports (without further detail) that he employed " a composite of recognized group tests of intelligence." But often such " recognized " tests depend largely upon information ; and *this* indubitably will increase with the schooling enjoyed from 16 to 17 years of age ; indeed, information may increase up to any age whatever.

The problem appears, in fact, to be really insoluble until the distinction is introduced between retention on the one hand and eduction on the other. Only the latter, never the former, as we have seen, is involved in the genuine g (see especially ch. xiv.). And only when the critical processes in the tests are restricted to this eduction is there any hope of really determining the point where g attains to its maturity.

Taking this and the preceding considerations into account, there appear to have been two investigations which easily outstrip all others in significance for the present purpose. One is that of Burt into the development of reasoning.[2] Here,

> " An endeavour was made to construct examples illustrating all the more important types of logical fallacies and inferential principles ; and at the same time to avoid any problem depending for its solution upon specific information outside the scope of the children tested."

[1] *J. Educ. Psych.* 1923, xiv.   [2] *Journ. Exper. Pedag.* 1919, v.

As a result, the average scores for each age from the 7th to the 14th showed continual improvement, as follows :

Age	7	8	9	10	11	12	13	14
Average score	5·0	11·0	17·2	23·2	30·0	34·1	39·1	44·7

The other outstanding research was that of Ballard.[1] He selected the well-known test of Absurdities. The subjects had to detect what is absurd in such statements as, for example, the following :

" A man who bought a dog that had been advertised complained to the seller that the dog's legs were too short. The seller replied : ' They are long enough to reach the ground, aren't they ? What more do you want ? ' "

Of such statements 34 were used with about 2,000 children, and the following were the average scores :

Age	11	12	13	14	15	16	17
Average score	13·1	14·4	15·1	17·4	18·5	18·9	18·9

Evidently the result is quite concordant with that of Burt so far as the latter goes, namely, in that improvement continues up to 14 years. But it supplies the additional information that by the 15th or 16th year such improvement is no longer to be seen.

But now comes the difficulty mentioned before, namely, that the children of different ages have undergone selection and therefore are not legitimately comparable. Ballard enters into this troublesome point with unequalled thoroughness ; he shows that it is here capable of accounting for certain irregularities in the progression of values. Notably, the rather steep rise from 13 to 14 is definitely traceable to selection of both intellectual and social kind. But in no way could such a thing account for the cessation of growth at 16 ; the said selection must necessarily tend to make the point of cessation appear higher, not lower, than it really is.

There still remains the other difficulty ; this is, that

[1] *Brit. J. Psych.* 1921, xii.

perhaps the greater success at the more advanced ages depends in some degree—despite all efforts to the contrary —upon the education received during the later years. But this influence, again, could only tend to make the apparent point of maturation unduly high. On both counts, then, the evidence indicates that the growth of g certainly does not continue to any appreciable amount after the ages of 15 or 16, and perhaps even ceases some years earlier. A person is thus adult in respect of g long before he is so in respect of physical stature. And if such a conclusion is really opposed to the verdict of " common sense," why then it seems time that this verdict should be revised.[1]

The cases of inferior and of superior persons. So far, we have been considering children of the usual type, neither exceptionally clever nor excessively stupid. The question arises, then, as to whether and how these extreme strata behave differently.

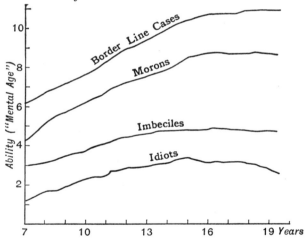

As regards the lower extreme, an interesting investigation is due to Kuhlmann, who examined 639 " feeble-minded "

---

[1] A parallel question—including the difficulty of obtaining comparable samples—exists also about the growth in size of brain. For instance, Scanmore (as quoted by Woodrow) puts the limits of this at 15 years, but Porteus at 25 !

children five times each, at intervals of two years, using the Binet-Stanford scale.[1] The result is shown in the figure on page 364; evidently, the lower the mental grade the *sooner* all improvement ceases. In fact, children of this sort are inclined to grow *worse* rather than better in later years.

As regards the upper extreme, valuable information has been supplied by Bird Baldwin, who re-tested 143 children at varying intervals of time.[2] From the results, he puts together two curves ; the one for average children whose mean I.Q. is about 100 ; the other for superior children with a mean I.Q. of 120.

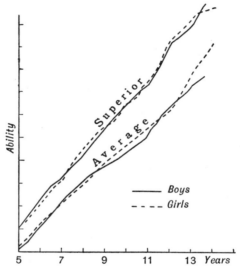

As is at once seen, the boys and girls who are best at five years of age show not the least compensating tendency to cease improving soonest.

Possibility of change in a child's standing. An even more vital problem—especially for practical purposes—is whether a child who ranks low in g at one time of life can reasonably hope for betterment later on. Popular opinion, at any rate, takes the more charitable view and cherishes a hope that children who have previously failed to distinguish themselves may yet some time turn out to be " late-bloomers."

The question may be brought into a concrete form by supposing that a number of children are tested twice with a more or less lengthy interval. How nearly will the second set of measurements agree with the first ? Many researches have been devoted to this point. As criterion of the agreement they have taken, either (a) the correlation between the two sets of tests, or else (b) the average closeness of the two sets of I.Q.'s (see p. 61). The outcome has been much controversy, some of the investigators asserting the discrepancies to be large, whilst others contend that they are small. But in truth, the actual results of the different experiments have been quite as near to each other as was to be expected from the varying conditions of testing. On the whole, the average discrepancy between two successive carefully made testings with the Binet-Stanford series would appear to have been about 5 per cent. on the I.Q. scale.

All this work, however, has suffered from two serious disadvantages, both due to employing a test-scale of this description. For when it is applied after an interval of time, the parts of it in actual use are partly the same as before but partly different. In so far as they are the same, there intervenes the disturbing effect of practice. And in so far as they differ, this fact alone may possibly account for the observed discrepancy.

To escape all such disturbances it was that some very elaborate experiments have recently been devised and executed by Slocombe.[1] Numerous tests, varying in both form and material, were applied by him to 240 children of ages 11-12 at intervals varying from zero up to two months. By means of a very elaborate experimental arrangement, all these different intervals were put upon an equal footing as regards all other influences. The significance of the procedure was that, if the relative abilities of the children

[1] *Brit. J. Psych.* 1926, xvii.

underwent any change, this should manifest itself in the fact of the correlations between different tests decreasing for the larger intervals. Actually nothing of the sort happened. The correlations between different tests with an interval of three months were just as high as without any interval at all. The conclusion emerged that throughout the three months, at any rate, the relative amount of g possessed by the children had remained quite constant. And on considering the case of still longer intervals, the author concluded that here also no real departure from such constancy had been established by any of the previous researches, the appearance to the contrary being always traceable to some inadequacy of experimental technique.

If once, then, a child of eleven years or so has had his relative amount of g measured in a really accurate manner, the hope of teachers and parents that he will ever rise to a much higher standing as a late-bloomer would seem to be illusory.

All this, of course, does not apply to pathological cases, where the removal of some disturbing influence—even adenoids—may quite well produce a marked betterment. Reversely, any supervention or aggravation of a pathological influence may have a very harmful effect. In such manner, probably, may be explained the very few instances where children do seem to have made large changes on being re-tested.[1]

EFFECT OF GROWTH ON S

Irregularity of experimental results. The foregoing problems about the growth of g must obviously reappear in some form or other about the growth of each s. But the difficulties of investigation appear to be far greater still.

In the case of abstract eduction, the s is generally hard to observe on account of its being masked by the dominant influence of g. And in the case of the opposite extreme, that of motor ability where g has its least influence, here

[1] See Wallin, *J. Educ. Psych.* 1921, xii.

confusion arises from the late development of the peripheral muscular apparatus.

Much more favourable might seem to be the field offered by sensory perception, since *g* has here fairly small influence and the peripheral organs reach their final development very early in life. But this time one is baffled by the wide discrepancy in the experimental results. For even in such an elementary performance as the discrimination of colours, the improvement was found by Gilbert with 1,200 children to continue up to the 16th or 17th year, as shown below.[1]

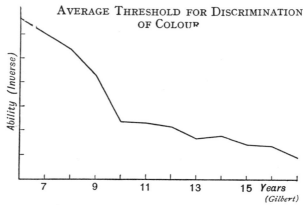

AVERAGE THRESHOLD FOR DISCRIMINATION OF COLOUR

Ability (Inverse)

7   9   11   13   15 *Years*

(Gilbert)

Whereas for the seemingly far more advanced performance of drawing, Childs with 2,177 children found all appreciable improvement to cease at about nine or ten years.[2]

So, too, with regard to such pictorial tests as that of Completion. Here, Davey finds progress to cease at or about nine years of age (*loc. cit.* p. 212). But Healy finds it to continue up to 15 or 16 years.[3]

If we turn to memory, which might also seem to afford a very favourable sphere for observation, the discrepancies are no less astonishingly large. Pohlmann, for instance, has made a most elaborate and careful investigation of memory for words and numbers ; he came to the conclusion

---

[1] *Studies from Yale Psychological Labor.* 1894, ii.

[2] *Journ. Educ. Psych.* 1915. vi.   [3] *Journ. Appl. Psych.* 1923, xiv.

that such ability increases at least up to the 20th year.[1] But Chamberlain, on the other hand, found that memory for objects had no appreciable increase after as low an age as about 11 ; indeed, very little even after about nine. Moreover, he demonstrated ingeniously that no appreciable part was played in the test by differences of interest.[2] But on turning to the research of Mulhall, we find that as regards memory for both words and forms the improvement with age is still continuing at 14 and even 15.[3]

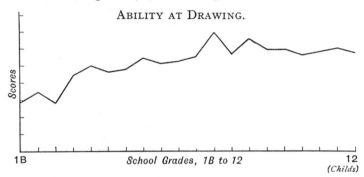

ABILITY AT DRAWING.

Scores

1 B   *School Grades, 1B to 12*   12
(Childs)

Strangest of all, perhaps, are the results obtained by one and the same investigator on the same children with the same tests. Wolley and Fischer, for instance, from the experimental investigation of about 700 normal children by annual re-tests arrived at the following growth for the " simpler functions " of perception : [4]

YEARLY IMPROVEMENT, IN TERMS OF STANDARD DEVIATION.

Age.	Boys.	Girls.
14-15	·723	·776
15-16	·097	·005
16-17	·146	·195
17-18	·408	:440

[1] *Beiträge z. Lehre vom Gedächtnis*, 1906.
[2] *Psych. Rev.* 1915, xxii.   [3] *Journ. Educ. Psych.* 1917, xiii.
[4] *Psych. Rev. Monogr. Suppl.* Whole No. 77, 1914.   *Journ. Educ. Psych.* 1915, vi.

Here, we have a very large improvement from 14 to 15 years ; little or none from 15 to 16 ; a moderate amount from 16 to 17 ; and a large increase again from 17 to 18. Who shall make anything intelligible of this ? (the curves of Pohlmann are, as a matter of fact, no less unintelligible in detail).

Explanation by analysis of *s.* To obtain any light upon all this irregularity in the growth of *s*, let us recall what we have already seen as to its general constitution. For this, too, has shown itself to be unexpectedly irregular. Part of it has appeared to derive only from the influence of the sensory and motor apparatus (p. 217). A further part, but probably not important for our present purposes, is the specific fatigability (p. 313). A large part, apparently, comes from the power to retain impressions ; for this, as we have seen, belongs altogether to *s*, not at all to *g* (ch. xvi.). But there is still another and yet more per-plexing constituent ; this consists in the manifold mental procedures possible for performing one and the same task. To such variations of procedure had to be attributed the fact that two operations, substantially the same and merely presented to the subject from a slightly different angle, nevertheless made for him two functionally quite different tests (p. 240). In the main, such varying procedures appear to be only matters of habit ; but their differences from one individual to another depend not so much on variations in power to retain as on the haphazard of previous experi-ence. What, if anything, remains in *s* additional to the foregoing constituents ? Nothing appears to be known.

The preceding considerations suggest that in the growth of specific ability there may be an aspect which is primarily not so much quantitative as qualitative. At different ages, varying methods of procedure may become adopted ; there may even occur from age to age certain sequences of pro-cedure prescribed by logical or psychological necessity. This recalls to mind the interesting theories that have been propounded by Claparède, Dewey, Hobhouse, Nunn,

Thorndike, and della Valle among others. But the truths contained in all these theories can and must be reduced to special cases of one and the same ultimate system of laws ; those, namely, which have been guiding us all along. All knowing must inevitably start from experiencing ; it must grow further, in the first place by cognizing relations of increasingly high order, and in the second place by educing correlates of greater and greater complexity. Throughout, every item must needs move by the path from utter obscurity towards increasing clearness. In each instance, too, eduction must inevitably precede reproduction. All these necessities, of course, cannot fail to produce differences of quality in the specific abilities of persons who are at different stages of growth. But to enter into such matters here would carry the present volume far beyond its scope.

Among the practical consequences of this complicated and still obscure nature of *s* is the extreme difficulty of measuring *specific aptitudes*. For any total ability of any person at any stage of growth, a good measurement can be obtained without any difficulty whatever ; so much is afforded by the corresponding " test of achievement." And after ascertaining this, together with the person's *g*, one can easily deduce his *s* as a whole (see app. p. xviii.). But for both theoretical and practical purposes, we require to eliminate from this whole *s* all that is merely due to some more or less accidental and changeable habit of procedure. And for this kind of inquiry, so needful for education, industry, and even medicine, there seems to be so far scarcely a beginning.

INFLUENCE OF OLD AGE

Influence suggested by tests of American Army. Analogous to the question of the rise in ability is that of its eventual fall. This might, perhaps, be thought of immeasurably smaller importance. And so it doubtless would be, if the fall were confined to those last flickerings of life characterizing the " senile " stage. But some evidence has been put forward of much more tragical import ; according to this, no sooner does the growth reach its highest point than it forthwith begins to descend again ; the suggestion arises that a man becomes too old for his best work, not at 70 or even at 50, but already at 30. Some alarming consequences appear to be suggested ; the boy or girl on quitting school, instead of as now proceeding to work his or her way up in the world, would everywhere—in business, army, navy, law, church, university, and government itself—straightway assume supreme command, but thenceforward, as gradually as may be, plane downwards. Youth is indeed coming to its own !

And the evidence bearing such threats of social topsy-turvydom consists in nothing less solid than the tests applied to the American Army. Here are the median scores of 15,385 white officers for different ages up to 60.

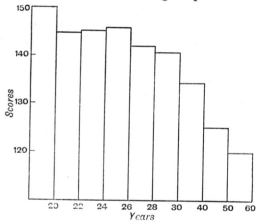

Curiously, however, the official account of this testing expressly declines to draw what seems to be such a near lying conclusion. The continual lowering of the scores, it is declared,

" cannot be said, on the basis of the present information, to point to a decrease of intelligence with age."

But as to how this conclusion may thus be evaded, no hint is given.

Still there certainly are a number of considerations that present themselves upon a little thought. In the first place, the differences are really much less formidable than they seem to be from the table, this having apparently been constructed so as to give them the greatest possible prominence. In particular, the differences from age to age are negligibly small as compared with those between persons belonging to the same age ; this is shown by means of the correlation between score and age, which only comes to the insignificant amount of about − ·15. In the next place, there is the old objection that the samples for the different ages are not properly comparable with each other. For instance, there may have existed some tendency for the more intelligent men to leave military service at a younger age, or else to be restrained from subsequently rejoining for the war by more important civilian duties. Yet again, there may have been some tendency of the older men to undergo the testing in a more carping mood and therefore less whole-heartedly (see p. 336).

But before indulging in any such surmises, the first task appears to be that of psychological analysis. Were the older men inferior in g, or only in some of the s's involved ? Was their unsuccessfulness scattered over all the eight sub-tests, or instead confined to certain of these. Did they fail in both accuracy and speed, or only in the latter ? How much of the information required by the tests was of the kind that is chiefly learnt at school and afterwards innocuously fades into oblivion ? Nothing is told us.

Evidence of subsequent experiments. In default of all such information we must turn for any genuine light on the matter to subsequent researches. One was supplied by Beeson in 1920.[1] The Stanford-Binet tests were applied by him to ten men and ten women averaging 75 years of age. Of especial interest, to begin with, is the description of their general attitude. At first they inclined to be suspicious ; later on, they became garrulous about other things ;

[1] *Journ. Appl. Psych.* iv.

at no time did they display any interest in the work to be done. As for the actual results, they failed very badly at the copying of designs from memory ; none of them passed this test, although it had been designed for ten-year-old children. Also every one failed to repeat seven digits. But on the other hand, they did on the whole quite well at the test of vocabulary :

"Eight out of the 20 subjects passed the superior vocabulary tests out of 75 words, all but one of these defining 80 words or more."

Much more elaborate, however, was the work done in the same year by Foster and Taylor.[1] Here, the 20 tests of Yerkes were applied to 316 children aged 10-19, 315 men aged 20-29, and 106 persons aged 50-84 ; all were "normal." The surprising result was that, in the great majority of the tests, even the oldest subjects showed no failing whatever. In certain tests, notably those depending on linguistic power, age seemed throughout to be even an advantage ; the 50-84 subjects did somewhat better than the 20-29, and these again better than the 10-19. Where the old people did fail was, just as with Beeson, in the power of memorizing, especially percepts. Now, all this accords excellently with our previous finding that retentivity is independent of g. It also agrees with the experience of ordinary life that old people complain—and with manifest justice—of their increasingly weak remembrance for recent experiences. Indeed, the figures just quoted suggest that some loss of this kind is already beginning so early as the age of 20. And quite possibly future investigation, on making adequate measurements of pure retentivity, will find that this diminishing occurs even from infancy onwards. Such a life-long deterioration would only be analogous, after all, to the diminishing elasticity of the lenses in the eyes ; this decrease does not become noticed until late in life (when it produces inconvenient failure of sight for near objects), but nevertheless really commences in babyhood.

[1] *Journ. Appl. Psych.* 1920, iv.

CONCLUSIONS

As a general summary of the chapter, g increases from birth—at first rapidly, then more and more slowly—until somewhere not later than 15-16 years (and perhaps much earlier) its growth definitely ceases. Thereafter, it normally retains this maximum level unaltered right up to the end of life (or, at least, to the onset of senility). The lines for different individuals run parallel to each other ; that is to say, whoever is ahead of another at some early age (11 years, or perhaps still younger) will normally retain this advantage for the rest of his days.

For the s's, the life-history cannot be traced on such simple lines, since these s's themselves are far from simple. At the core of each is what may properly be called a pure innate specific aptitude ; but up to now this has only shown itself to comprise three parts, depending respectively on the peripheral apparatus (sensory and motor), the retentivity, and the fatigability. In so far as the growth involves the sensory apparatus, the main development may be much earlier than that of g ; in so far as muscular efficiency is involved, it will be considerably later ; in so far as retentivity is concerned, it will tend to degenerate for a large portion (and perhaps the whole) of life, but rapidly and noticeably in old age. The effects of age upon fatigability have here been omitted, for want of precise data.

Over and above such pure aptitude, the s's contain further constituents upon which age acts in a highly irregular manner. In some directions, especially that of information, improvement may occur up to any time of life, however advanced ; in other directions, especially that of more or less accidentally formed habits of procedure, either improvement or deterioration may occur at any period.

CHAPTER XXII

HEREDITY AND SEX

DIFFERENCES OF RACE

The white races. Next, we have to consider how far ability, either the g or the s, is inbred rather than acquired. The question appears to be cardinal for all human improvement. This is at present everywhere blocked by the rivalry between two plans of procedure. Any serious enterprise to better man by means of more effective breeding always breaks against the opposition of those who seek, instead, for betterment by means of more effective training. Conversely, all great efforts to improve human beings by way of training are thwarted through the apathy of those who hold the sole feasible road to be that of stricter breeding. As for the bearings of the matter upon education, industry, and society in general, these have been too often stressed to need any further urging here.

Proceeding to consider the fundamental facts that appear

to have been established, a commencement may be made by comparing together the chief white nations. Prominent for this purpose stands the record of the Alpha tests as applied to the American Army " white draft," which included recruits from many different countries. These latter manifested notable variations from each other ; the order of merit (as calculated by freedom from low grade of " intelligence ") was reported in the official account of the testing to be as follows :

1. England	5. Germany	9. Norway	13. Greece
2. Holland	6. Sweden	10. Austria	14. Russia
3. Denmark	7. Canada	11. Ireland	15. Italy
4. Scotland	8. Belgium	12. Turkey	16. Poland

The results of the same tests have been interestingly expressed by Brigham in the percentages of each nationality that exceed the average native white American.[1] These are :

England	63	Denmark	48	Belgium	35	Greece	21
Scotland	59	Canada	47	Austria	28	Russia	19
Holland	58	Sweden	42	Ireland	26	Italy	14
Germany	49	Norway	37	Turkey	25	Poland	12

Not very dissimilar is the following record obtained subsequently in a very different manner by G. Brown. He applied the Binet-Stanford tests in American schools to 913 children whose parents had been born in foreign countries.[2] The following were the results :

Country.	Number of cases.	Median I.Q.
Norway - -	34	103
England - -	90	102
Germany - -	67	102
Sweden - -	187	102
Austria - -	28	99
France - -	199	95
Finland - -	226	90
Slovakia - -	31	86
Italy - -	51	77

[1] *A Study of American Intelligence*, 1923, Princeton University.
[2] *Journ. Educ. Research*, 1922, v.

On a still larger scale, including no less than 10,000 pupils, was the work of Berry at Detroit in 1922.[1] According to the result of " intelligence " tests, all these children were divided into three groups. The percentages falling into the top group for the children of foreign parentage were as follows :

England - - - 29·8	Russia - - - - 15·4
Canada - - - 29·6	Poland - - - - 9·0
United States - - 28·7	Italy - - - - 6·1
Germany - - - 25·2	Remaining countries,
Various countries other	pooled - - - 16·1
than those mentioned 16·1	

Interesting also are the following percentages supplied by the different countries towards the group of " gifted " children, so laboriously collected by Terman and his collaborators. Only those are given here which exceed 1 per cent.

English.	German.	Scotch.	Irish.	Swedish.	Italian.	Welsh.	Austrian.
30·7	15·7	11·3	9·6	2·5	1·4	1·4	1·3 %

But all these results, we must at once add, require to be interpreted with great caution. Those of Terman—he himself points this out—are almost meaningless as they now stand ; we need still to know how large these percentages in the constitution of the group are as compared with those in the general population whence the group was taken. Here, even such comparative values as are quoted above from the work of Brown do not afford much light, seeing that large variations may be expected in different states. This fundamental objection does not, indeed, affect any of the other results quoted above; but even these suffer from the fact that they only represent the class of persons from each nation that happened to be living in the United States, and this may be far from adequately representing the whole nation. Moreover, some of the foreign nations may have been handicapped by the fact of the tests being largely

[1] *Journ. Educ. Research*, 1922, vi.

linguistic. Against this surmise, however, is the following observation by Brown :

"It was found that after a pupil had attended an American school for one or two years, he tested as high by employing the English language as by using his native tongue. . . . In all cases, however, in which there was any doubt as to a pupil's ability to understand English sufficiently well to pass a test, he was given the test in his native language."

The records show, too, that some of the countries that speak English are surpassed by several who do not. Be all this as it may, the general conclusion emphasised by nearly every investigator is that, as regards "intelligence," the Germanic stock has on the average a marked advantage over the South European. And this result would seem to have had vitally important practical consequences in shaping the recent very stringent American Laws as to admission of immigrants.

The coloured races. A much easier task would seem to be the comparing of the white races with the coloured. For no great difficulty is said to attend the selecting of samples of persons wherein the two are in respect of education approximately equal.

As typical of the research done along this path may be taken that of S. L. Pressey and Teter, who applied ten tests to 120 coloured American children of ages 10-14 and compared the results with those obtained from 2,000 white American children.[1] On the average of all the tests, the coloured were about two years behind the white ; their inferiority extended through all ten tests, but it was most marked in just those which are known to be most saturated with g. Similar results ensued on comparing white with coloured college students, as was done by Derrick.[2] And soon afterwards, an investigation of Arlitt not only confirmed the older results, but contributed the interesting

[1] *Journ. Appl. Psych.* 1919.   [2] *Journ. Appl. Psych.* 1920.

addition that the superiority of the whites only begins after the fifth or sixth year of life.

On the other hand, however, the objection has been raised that, although the coloured and the white children may have been equal in respect of the education received at school, they may still have been very unequal in respect of that received at home and in social intercourse.[1]

There has also been comparison attempted between many other coloured races, including especially Chinese, Japanese, Red Indians, and Hindoos. To quote the results obtained would exceed our present limits. But certainly the conclusions to be drawn as regards the influence of heredity are even less decisive here than in the cases considered above.

On the whole, there has been found a large body of evidence that races do differ from one another, at any rate in respect of g. And there have been some indications—as yet hardly decisive—that such differences persist even when the members of the respective races are living in the same environment, educational and otherwise; to this extent, then, the cause would appear fairly traceable to inheritance. Nevertheless such racial differences, even if truly existing, are indubitably very small as compared with those that exist between individuals belonging to one and the same race. Proof of the influence of heredity in the former case can then, after all, carry us but a small way towards estimating its scope in the latter.

DIFFERENCES OF FAMILY

Influence of parentage. Another and more fruitful sphere for investigating mental inheritance is obtained by turning from the race to the family. How far does a person's ability tend to correspond with that of his parents and other near kindred ?

[1] For some further interesting comparisons between the " intelligence " of coloured and white Americans respectively, see the investigations of Murchison (Pedag. Semin. 1925).

Among the earliest works that have brought this question from the quicksands of dogmatic assertion to the firm ground of definite measurements has been that of Burt.[1] His tests were applied to two schools of sharply contrasting grades. The one was a " superior elementary school " frequented by boys of the so-called lower middle class ; they were mostly the sons of local tradesmen. The other was a high class " preparatory school," where the boys in nearly every case were sons of men who had attained to intellectual eminence. In most respects, the two schools appeared to be on about an equal footing ; notably, the all-round education given at the school for the middle class children was said to be at least as good as at the other. Nevertheless, the performances of this school with the tests proved to be decidedly inferior, a result that strongly suggested some inferiority of mental inheritance. Still, over and above the small number of children tested (only 43 altogether) there remains the objection that the sons of eminent men may have had better education or more stimulating intercourse at home.

A later investigation with far more numerous children (548) of ages 10-14 was carried out by S. L. Pressey and Ralston.[2] The scores for the Pressey tests of " general intelligence " were compared with the vocations of the fathers, and showed a great superiority for those vocations which are commonly taken to be of higher status.

Vocation.	Average test-score.
1. Professional (teacher, lawyer, doctor, minister, editor) - - - - - - - - -	85
2. Executive (independent business man, foreman) -	68
3. Artisan (electrician, engineer, skilled workman) -	41
4. Labourer (section hand, factory operator, unskilled labourer) - - - - - - - -	39

Next year, L. Pressey applied the best four of these same tests to 357 children of much younger age, 6-8, since here

[1] *Loc. cit.* p. 174.   [2] *Journ. Appl. Psych.* 1919, iii.

the author supposed that previous instruction would be much less influential, and therefore that innate ability would be more so. The actual results, however, were just about the same as before.[1] Later, the Pressey tests were applied by Book to no less than 5,748 children in high school senior classes ; once more, quite analogous results were obtained.[2]

More recently, still, Haggerty and Nash applied other tests (those of Haggerty himself and of Miller) to 8,688 children of grades iii. to vii. (about 9-14 years). When the results were grouped according to the vocation of the parents, the median I.Q.'s proved to be as follows : [3]

Pro- fessional.	Busi- ness.	Skilled worker.	Semi- skilled.	Farmer.	Unskilled worker.
116	107	98	95	91	89

And all the preceding results have been emphatically corroborated by those which Terman got for his " gifted " children.

Indisputable as the fact may be, however, that the differences of ability shown by children correspond in large measure with the status of their parents, there remains much to be desired in most of the evidence that such differences derive from original aptitude. For beyond doubt, the children of the professional classes on the one hand, and those of the labourers on the other have, in general, undergone very unlike environmental influences, both at home and elsewhere.

The case of twins. Much of this difficulty, it has been thought, may be evaded by a consideration of the mental similarity between twins. For these are not in general influenced by community of environment much more than are other brothers or sisters nearly like each other in age. And yet the twins notoriously present a far greater resemblance to one another in all qualities both mental and physical.

[1] *Journ. Appl. Psych.* 1919, iii.

[2] *The Intelligence of High School Seniors,* 1922.

[3] *Journ. Educ. Psych.* 1924, xv.

To Thorndike, in particular, is due the credit for having put this matter upon an experimental basis. He submitted 50 pairs of twins to several mental tests, with the following correlations as result [1] :

Opposites.	Multiplication problems.	Spelling.	Addition problems.	Cancellation.
·90	·84	·75	·80	·70

These values are much higher than have ever been reported from other fraternal pairs. The surplus, then, would seem to be of innate origin. Notable, too, is the fact that the rank of these values for the different tests has an excellent correspondence with their usual ranking in respect of saturation with *g*. And these results have quite recently been corroborated by a still more extensive investigation of Merriman.[2]

But this time, a new difficulty arises. The excessive likeness between the twins can scarcely, indeed, be attributed to the community of environment after birth. But still it may possibly have arisen from community of pre-natal uterine conditions, and thus not be hereditary after all.

Quantitative theories of inheritance. Another way in which an endeavour has been made to demonstrate mental heredity involves still greater quantitative exactitude. The first step here is to lay down *a priori* the magnitude that correlations should attain between persons of varying degrees of kinship. And then follows an empirical examination as to whether such a magnitude really occurs.

Thus, one theoretical school has adopted the doctrine that all correlations between brothers and sisters, in respect of any trait mental or physical, should always approximate to ·5. And very extensive numerical results have been published which purport to show that such a value does actually ensue. But unfortunately, this statistical edifice would appear to have rested upon an insecure psychological foundation. It is undermined by the fact that estimates of

[1] *Archives of Phil., Psych. and Scient. Meth.* 1905.
[2] *Psych. Mon.* xxxiii. 1924.

mental traits have usually a large admixture of error. For this produces a correspondingly large " attenuation " of the correlations in respect of any mental trait (see p. 57), so that the values of such correlations as actually observed must necessarily fall far below the true values. But no such fall in value will, as a rule, affect the correlations in respect of physical traits. If, then, the actually observed correlations for the mental and the physical traits really did approximate to one and the same value—·5 or otherwise—the true correlations would necessarily have very different values ! It may be added that the correlations of the mental estimates are affected by many other gross disturbances over and above that of attenuation, so that any alleged constancy of value claimed for them can only be viewed with grave suspicion.[1]

Seeing what formidable difficulties beset even the comparatively simple task of verifying such a crude rule as that of a constant correlation of ·5 between brothers or sisters taken in mass, courage indeed must be needed when undertaking to find quantitative confirmation for all the niceties of the more scientific biology that has been based upon the re-discovered work of Mendel. Here come into play the intricate complications of similar and dissimilar gametes, blended and alternative inheritance, heterozygotes and homozygotes, simple and compound allelomorphs, dominance and recession, mixo-variation and idio-variation. Nevertheless even here, such excellent pioneering work as that of Heymans and Wiersma,[2] of Davenport and his pupils,[3] of Bühler,[4] and of Peters [5] are full at any rate of promise.

[1] See the criticisms made by the present writer as long ago as 1904 (*Brit. J. Psych.* xv. pp. 96-99). Since then, a member of this statistical school itself has found that the estimation of " intelligence " made by one teacher has a correlation no higher than ·5 with another teacher's estimation of *the self-same children* (Waite, *Biometrika*, 1912, viii).

[2] *Zeit. f. Psychol.* 1906-1912.

[3] See especially Davenport's *Inheritance of Temperament*, published by the Carnegie Institution of Washington, No. 236, in 1918.

[4] *Die geistige Entwicklung des Kindes*, 1922.

[5] *Vererbung geistiger Eigenschaften*, 1922.

Intensive case analysis. For the present, however, we seem impelled to have recourse to work that is less extensive and more intensive, less statistical and more psychological.

Of interest in this direction has been the research of Gruhle, who found that among the youths sent to a reformatory institution 10 cases could be attributed exclusively to the influence of environment, 22 exclusively to that of original nature, and 72 to a mixture of the two.[1] Somewhat different has been the issue of the recent fine work of Burt on juvenile delinquency ; for this viciousness he traced back to hereditary as compared with environmental influence in the ratio of only about 2 : 3.[2]

Up to now, however, such intensive investigation of the influence attributable to heredity and to environment respectively seems to have been concerned only with character, and not yet to have touched our present theme, which is ability.

DIFFERENCES OF ENVIRONMENT

Evidence from amount of schooling. So far, we have been considering the chief influences—race and family—by which differences of ability might be inherited. We may now approach the same problem from its obverse side, examining the chief influences by which the differences might be acquired. Foremost here comes the amount of education which the children receive. The question as to the part played by this has recently been made more acute by the following conclusion of Gordon :

"From the results obtained among children who get most of their education at school and very little at home, it is very evident that the mental tests do not measure their native ability apart from schooling."[3]

[1] *Vererbung und Erziehung, Archiv für Pädagogik,* 1914.

[2] *The Young Delinquent,* 1925, p. 603.

[3] *Educational Pamphlets,* Board of Education (British), No. 44, 1923.

This conclusion and the evidence brought in its support have excited considerable notice, and have even been taken to involve a general condemnation of all tests except those of scholastic achievement.

Still, even if Gordon's work could be unreservedly accepted, it would have little bearing on tests constructed in a more scientific manner than those employed by him (those of Binet). They ought, as we have seen, to be based as purely as possible upon eductive processes (see ch. xv. and elsewhere).

Moreover, there are indications that the author has overstated his case. His principal evidence consisted in finding that those children who had enjoyed very little education at school failed just as much at the tests of so-called intelligence as they did at tests of scholastic achievement. But this finding was contradicted by the subsequent research of McCrae (see p. 201); such children were now shown to be the very large amount of two years better at the tests of intelligence than at the scholastic ones.

More cogent, indeed, seems to be the testimony offered by Berry in just the opposite direction. On examining the records of the very numerous children who had been divided into three classes according to their success at tests of g, he found that those in the lower classes had been to school just as regularly as those in the higher. He concluded that:

" Intelligence is a much more important factor in determining the amount of work done (in the test) than is a high percentage of attendance."

Evidence from experimental teaching. Another line along which to approach the same question is by influencing the education experimentally. An interesting instance of this has been supplied by Remer [1]; he gave special instruction two to three hours daily for a whole year to a girl of eight who had shown an I.Q. of only 75. But at the end of the

[1] *Journ. Educ. Psych.* 1922, xiii.

time a re-test showed this I.Q. to have remained unaltered.

A still more important experimental control of education
has been that of Franzen.[1] He had been struck by the fact
of the current instruction at school being only adapted for
the middle children in a class. In order to give every child
an opportunity of doing his best, he very carefully divided
them into classes according to their ability, and then made
every effort to push on any children who did not do as well
in any school subject as might have been expected from their
I.Q.'s. The result of thus equalising the environmental
opportunities of the children was not to decrease, but to
increase, the individual differences between them. A
further and peculiarly interesting result was that now their
ability for school work had become almost exactly corresponding with the tests of g. He concluded that ability is
always due to one and the same general factor.

Here may also be quoted the enforced seclusion of a 15-
year-old boy, as reported by Foster.[2] The case was specially
studied in view of the not infrequent objection, that a child
cannot be expected to do as well at the tests as other children of his own age when he has passed his life on a lonely
farm without playmates. The present boy seems to have
had extremely little schooling, or even society of any kind.
Nor did he so much as receive instruction from his parents.
Most of the day he slept, or read a few religious books.
His ignorance of the world about him was astounding.
Nevertheless, on being submitted to the Binet-Stanford
test, he came out just at age.

Evidence of partial correlations. With all this conflict of
opinion about the relative influences of school work and of
heredity upon " intelligence " as measured by mental tests,
much interest must attach to the theorem of Burt wherein
he has sought to apportion these two influences in an
exact quantitative manner by means of " partial " corre-

[1] Teachers Coll. Columbia Univ. *Contr. to Educ.* No. 125, 1922.

[2] *Journ. Appl. Psych.* 1919, iii.

lations.[1] Employing these, he arrives at the conclusion that as regards success with the Binet-Simon scale,

" one-ninth is attributable to age, one-third to intellectual development, and over one-half to school attainment. School attainment is thus the preponderant contributor."

Now, such an employment of partial correlations is certainly in accordance with the usage of them now prevalent among psychologists. But in general, this usage itself is open to serious criticism.[2] Even so, however, it may yet upon occasion lead to results of no little importance.[3] This line of enquiry, deserves then, some further examination.

DIFFERENCE OF SEX

In respect of g. In addition to heredity, there is at least one other great influence of innate kind, namely, sex. That this plays a dominant role in the determination of character has rarely, if ever, been seriously denied. How far does it also govern cognitive ability ?

Among the pioneering experimental researches along this path may be specially mentioned those of Thompson,[4] Thorndike,[5] and Burt.[6] Of the recent and more elaborate work, particular mention must be made of the investigations of Terman,[7] as also of Pressey and Pressey.[8] The results of

---

[1] *Mental and Scholastic Tests*, 1920, p. 183.

[2] The present writer for his part has always regarded usage of this kind as being to a large extent fallacious, and had indeed long been waiting for leisure to make a publication on the subject. But in this he has now been anticipated by Holzinger and Freeman (*Journ. Educ. Psych.* 1925, xvi. ; 1926, xvii.).

[3] For instance, the work done with partial correlations by Truman Kelley would seem to be among the most interesting contributions to mental testing that have been yet made (*Educational Guidance*, Teachers' Coll., Columbia Univ., *Contributions to Education*, No. 71, 1914).

[4] Univ. Chicago, *Contrib. Philos.* 1903.

[5] *Educational Psychology*, 1910, note to p. 20.   [6] *J. Exper. Pedag.* 1911.

[7] Stanford Revision of the Binet-Simon Scale, 1917.

[8] *Journ. Appl. Psych.* 1918.

the former with respect to g are summarized in the following
pair of curves:

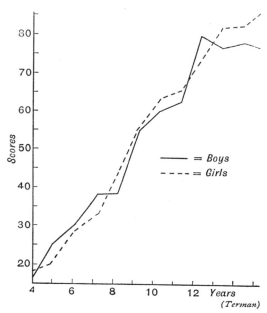

(*Terman*)

The two sexes cross and re-cross in a way and to an extent
that—even if significant at all—is at any rate so small as to
be negligible for most purposes. Even the seeming inferiority of the boys about 14 is attributed by the author to the
mere fact that more of them than of the girls had been pro-
moted to the high school.

On the other hand, the same author's investigation of the
" gifted " children did appear to show a notable superiority
on the male side, since they contained 55 per cent. of boys
as opposed to only 45 per cent. of girls. This naturally
suggests the historical fact that eminent men have been
far more numerous than eminent women, even in such
domains as music or poetry, where women seem to
suffer from no great disadvantage. One explanation
which has been offered is that females, though equal to

males on an average, tend less to either extreme, good or bad.[1]

In respect of s. Much less simple have, here again, been the results with respect to specific ability. The best proven superiorities on the female side have been discrimination of colour (Thompson) and that of neighbouring points on the skin (Burt), both of which powers seem to be rooted in pure physiology. But there has also been a strikingly uniform advantage shown by females in the memorizing of prose passages.[2] On the other side, Woolley and Fischer report that boys are " enormously superior " at the Puzzle Box test ; and this accords with the already quoted advantage of boys in the educing of spatial relations and correlates (p. 229). But, as mentioned, the evidence of this difference being really innate is still dubious.

Here may also be cited the comparison made by Burt between the two sexes in respect of reasoning power. On the whole, the two showed themselves to be just about level. But nevertheless, the following qualitative differences were observed :

" Girls excel in patient and persevering analysis, in attention to minutiae and details, in jumping to presumptive conclusions, in constructing concrete hypotheses or picturing definite situations by the aid of the imagination, and, above all, in rapidly extracting the meaning of printed statements and in formulating their solutions in words."

" Boys tend to be more methodical in their thought processes, and more critical of their own conclusions ; they are less wordy and less diffuse ; they appear less prone to commit logical fallacies, and more resistant to the suggestions embodied in phrase and form of statement."[3]

---

[1] Yet in another work, that just quoted, the same author denies that the variation among boys for these tests is greater than among girls. These two results are difficult to reconcile.

[2] Pyle, *J. Educ. Psych.* 1911, ii.   [3] *Journ. of Exper. Pedagog*, 1919, v.

All this, in so far as it is not traceable to traits of character rather than of cognition, may perhaps arise from a greater tendency of the male sex to perseveration (ch. xvii.).

REVIEW OF THE PROBLEM

Summary of evidence. In examining how far ability is innate, we began with the influence of nationality and race. Here we found some indications of difference, especially in respect of g ; but it appeared to be at any rate very small as compared with that which exists within one and the same race. We turned to the dependence of ability on parentage. Even here, the available evidence left much to be desired ; to disentangle the effects of heredity from those of environment turned out to be a task of great difficulty. So far as could be judged, however, the effects of heredity upon g are very large indeed. To a more limited extent, even s seems to be influenced in the same manner.

Next, the question of inheritance was approached from its reverse aspect ; we examined how far ability could be traced to any specific effect of education. The issue was to corroborate the previous results, in that at any rate the usual differences of education between children of the same social status have but small influence upon g, however much they may have upon s.

Lastly, we examined the other great innate influence, that of sex. It showed itself—here in the domain of cognition— to have comparatively small effects.

Harmony with earlier conclusions. But now, finally, we may attempt another line of consideration, one that seems to illuminate the topic in a more profound manner. We will compare, that is to say, these empirical observations with the chief theorems established in earlier parts of the present volume.

To begin with, any resolving of g into an effect of education seems hard to reconcile with the conclusion which we reached about its growth. For this arrives, as we saw, at its highest point about or before 15-16 years of age ; whereas education certainly may continue for many years later.

Still more decisive would appear to be the conclusion attained (ch. xv.) that g is involved in all eduction but in no retention. For in so far as a process is purely eductive, it is essentially *new* ; hence a person's success at it cannot possibly be due to his having done it before ; to this extent, the influence of education would seem to be absolutely eliminated.[1]

On the whole, the most reasonable conclusion for the present appears to be that education has a dominant influence upon individual differences in respect of s, but normally it has little if any in respect of g. Still the question is, no doubt, in great need of further more exact investigation. And the most hopeful course would seem to lie in grasping and utilizing the profound distinction between eductive and reproductive processes.[2]

[1] A very different question, naturally, is that as to how far a purely eductive operation can be obtained in actual practice. Moreover, even a test that is almost purely eductive for one class of subjects may become largely reproductive when applied to another class. Suppose, for instance, that the test consisted in asking whether " go " and " depart " are nearly alike or very different. For normal children of eight years the "critical" part of the operation (see pp. 207, 274) would be almost entirely eductive. But for children only six years old, it might introduce considerable difficulty in reproducing the sense of the word " depart."

[2] Unfortunately, the recent book of Truman Kelley on *The Influence of Nurture upon Native Differences* arrived too late to be incorporated in the present chapter. But it can at once be signalled as extraordinarily original and deserving of study by everyone interested in the subject.

CHAPTER XXIII

MIND AND BODY

MENTAL COMPARED WITH PHYSICAL TRAITS.
The Case of Adults.   The Case of Children.
PATHOLOGICAL INFLUENCES.
Effect of Cerebral Injury on g.   Effect of Cerebral Injury on s.   Effect
of Ill-health.
PHYSIOLOGY OF THE BRAIN.
Localization of Function.   Psycho-physiological Mechanics.

MENTAL COMPARED WITH PHYSICAL TRAITS

The case of adults. What relation do all the mental differences that we have seen bear to the bodily differences of the same individuals ?

Most readily perceived and easily measured are such conspicuous bodily traits as height, weight, size of head, girth of chest, etc. But the numerous investigations made in these respects upon adults—at least upon such homogeneous groups as university students—have had an almost unanimously negative issue ; the correlations between the mental and the physical measurements have turned out to be little above zero.

The recent results of Naccarati, however, are more promising.[1] With 221 college students he found that an ordinary test of " general intelligence "—that is, an approximate measure of g—manifested correlation as follows : With height, it had only the insignificant amount of ·04, the p.e. being ·045 ; but with weight, the value, though still small,

[1] *Archives of Psych.* 1921, No. 45.

393

namely – ·18, was at any rate four times its p.e. ; and with the ratio of height to weight the correlation rose to ·23, which is five times the p.e.   Working with another group of students, this time unfortunately only 75 in number, the following very notable correlations were found : With volume of trunk, – ·36 ; with the "morphologic index" (ratio of length to volume of trunk) + ·36.   The author advances the view, that men fall into two types which possess great anthropological importance.   The one is called by him " microsplanchnic," and derives from over secretion of the thryoid and pituary glands together with under secretion of the genital glands.   On the bodily side, such a hyper-thyroid person tends to have :

"wide palpebral fissures, large pupils, glistening eyes, long eye lashes, thick moist shining hair ; well deve-loped and healthy teeth and nails, hand and fingers long and thin, this being part of the general tendency of the hyperthyroid to grow in length rather than in width ; .... digestion and assimilation irregular and defective, a condition which renders the hyperthyroids very cautious in the selection and use of food."

Mentally, on the other hand,

" the hyperthyroids do not indulge in athletic exercises and take little interest in the practical side of life, but conversely acquire a great transport for its aesthetic side.   Therefore, the hyperthyroids love indoor games, music, poetry, arts in general, theatre, reading, and works of the nature of scientific research.   Also their minds, not unlike their bodies, tend to preserve the characteristics of youth, so they are rather prone to day-dreaming and to being absent-minded.   Being in-telligent, they possess lively ideation, prompt perception, easy imagination, strong memory, and shrewd critique ; but lack of concentration and unsteady will power may hinder their learning capacity."

" The intelligence of the hyperthyroid possesses more intensity than duration, it acts as a stored energy which can be better employed as explosive material. Occupations which require long, patient application and too much concentration are not fit for the bright but exhaustible hyperthyroid."

In the reverse type of "macrosplanchics," there is said to be an excessive secretion of the antagonistic group of hormones, that is to say, those which promote the development of the visceral system. Consequently, all the preceding traits are replaced by their reverse.

Now, should any such a view receive substantial confirmation, the conditions of case suggest that the secretions of the thryoid glands contribute towards the psycho-physical energy underlying g. The converse fact has long been established, namely, that when the thyroid excretion is deficient, the " intelligence " also becomes defective.

The case of children. Contrasting with the very low correlations usually obtained from adults are the very considerable values got with younger persons.

Baldwin, for instance, found for 49 normal children, after eliminating the influence of age by Yule's formula, a correlation between g and height amounting to ·52.[1] In good agreement was Terman's investigation of 623 " gifted " children; for these distinctly surpassed a control group of ordinary children in all such measurements as height, weight, grip, arm span, width of shoulders, and width of hips.[2] Similar, too, was the result obtained by Doll with 477 mentally defective subjects ranging from 5 to 40 years.[3] On eliminating the influence of age, the " intelligence " as tested showed the following correlations :

	Stand. height.	Sitting height.	Weight.	Right grip.	Left grip.	Vital capacity.
Boys	·39	·47	·34	·69	·67	·63
Girls	·31	·41	·23	·62	·61	·64

Taken together, the researches seem to indicate that g goes markedly with greater bodily size (especially height)

[1] *Loc. cit.* p. 156. [2] *Loc. cit.* p. 197.
[3] Publ. of Training School at Vineland, No. 8.

in the case of children, but little if at all in that of adults. The suggestion becomes plausible, that the more intelligent children are at the same time physically more mature than the common run. And this is supported by Terman's further report that the gifted boys are slightly earlier than usual in respect of the development of pubic hair, as are the gifted girls in respect of the commencement of menstruation. But too wide a generalization in this matter is discouraged by the finding of Freeman and Carter, that the correlations of g with maturity in another respect, namely, the ossification of the carpal bones, is negligibly small (on eliminating age, it is only ·09). Such a disagreement between the different manifestations of maturity are concordant with a work of A. I. Gates, which indicated that maturity in different respects proceeds with a considerable degree of mutual independence.[1]

PATHOLOGICAL INFLUENCES

Effect of cerebral injury on g. Another approach to the problem of the relation between mind and body is by way of pathology. How does mental ability become affected when the bodily state falls into disorder ?

To throw some light upon this matter was the aim of a research instituted by Dr. Hart in collaboration with the present writer.[2] The cases to be studied were taken as presenting a diversity of mental troubles, including precox, general paralysis, epilepsy, primary dementia, paranoia, maniac-depression, psychasthenia, imbecility, and alcoholic hallucinosis. For comparison, we tested in exactly the same manner 33 normal persons from different strata of society. The testing embraced 18 sorts of cognitive activity, comprising instances of sensory perception, memorizing, association, together with the wealth, discrimination, and synthesis of ideas (at that time, the analysis of cognitive activity into eduction and reproduction had not yet been effected).

[1] See p. 143.   [2] *Loc. cit.* p. 81.

From such a great diversity in the nature of the disorders —which certainly derived from cerebral affections that varied greatly in both kind and site—there might have been expected a corresponding diversity in the kind of damage done to cognitive power. And many writers do describe the damage as consisting in special more or less isolated defects. Instead of any such thing, however, the definite experiments and measurements showed that in every case the most obvious cognitive injury was always of the same kind, namely, universal. In every instance, too, all abilities were impaired in proportion to their respective saturations with g ; the correlation between the impairment of ability and the saturation with g came to no less than ·87, an amount which, on being corrected for attenuation, could not fall appreciably short of unity.

Thus in each case the main damage may reasonably be attributed to a diminution of the general energy, this latter being derived from the whole cortex (or still wider area) and lessened by injury to any considerable part of it.

Effect of cerebral injury on s. In addition to such impairment of g, does injury to the brain produce any specially harmful effect on s ? So far as the experience of the present writer goes (in English and German asylums and nerve-clinics) there exists only one kind of harm that occurs frequently. This consists in a loss of retentivity for recent impressions, or, as it might better be described, a loss of capacity for new retentions. It ought not to be confused with the weakness of " memory," which is so often reported in patients as if it were something specific, when in truth it is no more than the most easily detectible manifestation of an impairment which really extends to all other cognitive power. Inability to remember may, indeed, come from loss of retentivity ; but it may also derive from loss of g (see ch. xvi.).

Among the few investigators who have had success in isolating pure retentivity may be mentioned T. Moore.[1] By employing his " memory ratio " and using a statistical pro-

[1] *Psych. Monogr.* 1919, xxvii.

cedure substantially equivalent to that of tetrad differences, he demonstrated a great diminution of retentivity in many patients, especially those suffering from senile dementia and the Korsakoff ailment.

In good agreement has been the work of Wechsler on Korsakoff patients.[1] These showed themselves able to remember a list of words or digits, *immediately* after hearing them, almost or quite as well as normal persons. But on increasing the time interval, or on making the remembrance so difficult as to require several repetitions, the patients broke down altogether. All this is quite concordant with our finding in ch. xvi. that retentivity and g are mutually independent, also with our result in ch. xxi. that retentivity diminishes with age, although g remains unaffected thereby.

As for damage to s other than such loss of retentivity, far the most prominent in recent pathological investigation has been that due to superficial wounds of the brain. Particularly interesting have been the reports of this kind furnished by Head, Fuchs, Poppelreuter, Goldstein, and Gelb. For example, the two last named investigators found that a patient suffering from a superficial wound in the back of the brain was unable to perceive whether a line was bent or not ; and yet his visual acuity was quite up to the average standard. Want of space forbids us to discuss such cases in detail ; but in general, they may be said to have concerned either perception or language ; they have consisted in impaired ability to educe or to reproduce some particular kinds of relations or correlates.

Effect of ill-health. The bodily affections just discussed were for the most part of an extremely grave nature. We have still to inquire, then, about the effect of ordinary ill-health.

One relevant research was carried out by Dawson (not yet published). Certain children had become incapable of doing their school work satisfactorily, on account of having fallen into a state of mal-nutrition. Nevertheless, on tests

[1] *Psychiatric Bulletin*, Oct. 1917.

of *g* being applied to them, their performances proved to be quite up to the normal standard. The suggestion seemed to be that the lack of nutrition produces not so much a decrease of ability as an increase of fatigability. Such preservation of mental power would agree well with the known physiological fact that in starvation the most important organs—above all, the brain—are the last to suffer.

There is some other evidence, however, which tends more to support the old maxim, *mens sana in corpore sano*. The gifted children of Terman, for instance, showed on an average nearly 30 per cent. less " general weakness " than ordinary children. They also suffered less from " nervousness " and from headaches. Turning to the other extreme, mentally defective children are notoriously susceptible to illness of nearly every sort.[1]

Very important, too, would seem to be the following research of Sandwick.[2] Here 423 students were submitted to an intelligence test, and then the highest 40 as also the lowest 40 were made to undergo a very exhaustive medical examination. The proportion of each group reported as suffering in the various respects examined is given in the table on the following page.

The results are startling, especially the bottom one showing that 52 per cent. of the highest 40 were free from all defects, whereas *none* of the lowest 40 were so. Doubt only remains as to the relation of cause and effect. Do the bodily ailments produce the lowering of *g* ? Or are the two ills only outward manifestations of some more deeply seated weakness ?

A still more recent work bearing on the same point is that of McCrae.[3] He tested two groups of children, both being of the kind called physically defective. But one group had been undergoing special treatment consisting, it seems, in heliotherapy and graduated exposure to open air. After three months of this treatment their metabolism had increased some 20 per cent. Now, this second group obtained a considerably higher average score in the tests of *g* ; and

[1] *Loc. cit.* p. 197.   [2] *Journ. Educ. Research*, 1920.   [3] Not yet published.

since no other explanation was forthcoming, the improvement was attributed to the increased metabolism. This, too, would be in good accord with the hypothesis of a general psychophysical energy.

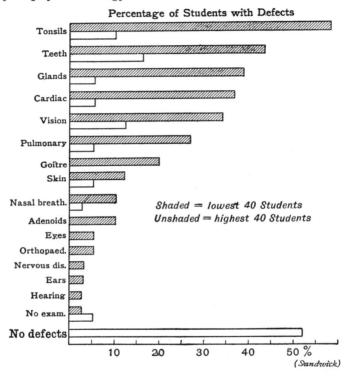

Percentage of Students with Defects

Shaded = *lowest* 40 Students
Unshaded = *highest* 40 Students

10   20   30   40   50 %
(*Sandwick*)

PHYSIOLOGY OF THE BRAIN

Localization of function. Interesting as may be all these observations and speculations, they can scarcely be said to penetrate very deeply into the main problem. The site of most obvious connection between body and mind is to be sought mainly at least in the brain, and particularly in its cortex. To the functioning of this, then, it is that investigation must be intensively directed.

Unfortunately, this is just the region where physiology is

at present most backward. Even in the most up-to-date text-books, a very small number of pages are given to it, and these themselves are chiefly filled with anatomy, psychology, or mere hypothesis, instead of definite physiological facts.

Of all the questions arising here, perhaps none has excited such a long and spirited controversy as that which asks whether the brain functions as a single whole or as a multitude of more or less independent parts. At the one pole stood Flourens, who believed himself to have demonstrated by crucial experiments that the whole surface of the cerebral hemisphere is mutually equivalent, so that any portion can be functionally replaced by any other portion. But at the other extreme have been Munk and Flechsig who—each in his special fashion, the one basing his verdict on extirpation, the other on myelogenesis—concluded that the cortex is divided up into a large number of sharply distinct regions, each of which possesses a function of its own. The great majority of physiologists have adopted some intermediate position, but so diversely conceived that there have been almost as many different teachings as teachers. Nor, perhaps, need this be wondered at. The problem of cerebral localization consists essentially in ascertaining the correspondence between the physiological regions on the one hand and the psychological functions on the other. But these earlier disputants had naïvely assumed that, for solving this problem, scientific investigation was needed only on the physiological side ; the other or psychological correspondent was taken as sufficiently supplied by " common sense."

A great step forward, then, would appear to have been achieved when the technique of physiological and that of psychological experimentation were combined together. Along this path it is that Fuchs, Goldstein, Gelb, Poppelreuter, and Head have reaped their precious harvest. By the same means, Shepherd was able to show that the removal of particular motor areas of the cortex destroys permanently certain motor habits, but does not preclude these habits from being re-acquired. Such a result agrees well enough with the suggestion which has already arisen in the present volume on purely psychological grounds, that retentivity is subserved by the localized " engines " underlying s rather than by the general " energy " that subserves g.

Peculiarly fruitful and promising has been the utilization of the same combined procedure in the study of " conditioned reflexes " by Pavlov and his pupils, especially Anrep. Here, some stimuli instinctively evoking some particular reaction—chiefly used have been the sight and smell of food which cause a flow of saliva—are given together with some second and arbitrary stimulus having no such instinctive reaction. The result of doing this sufficiently often is that the arbitrary stimulus acquires the property of evoking the reaction even when the natural stimulus for this is withheld. The effects of the natural and the arbitrary stimuli have been called respectively " unconditioned " and " conditioned " reflexes. By such means a dog has been taught in a year to react to a musical note of 800 vibrations per second whilst ignoring any other note as much as 12 vibrations either above or below this. Similarly, it has been taught to react to a metronome beating at the rate of 100 per minute, whilst taking no notice of one of 104. Further, a great variety of psychological and physiological influences have been introduced (such as longer training, lapse of training, extirpation, and drugs) to see how these modify the reaction previously established.

Research along these lines has already supplied far more precise evidence than ever obtained before concerning the localization of functions. At the same time, it has no less certainly corroborated the view that—within definite limits—the function exercised by one locality can, on this being destroyed, be taken over by another.

Even the study of these conditioned reflexes, however, if it is to reap anything like all its great potentialities, will be obliged to work in much more intimate collaboration with psychology. The latter alone is capable of prescribing the kinds of arbitrary stimuli that can render the experiments of greatest scientific value. For instance, more important than any such reacting to absolute musical pitches would be the reacting to *relations* between these. Indeed, there seems to be no escape from eventually introducing the whole psychology of relations and correlates that has been supporting us throughout the present volume. Some time or other, too, such questions will have to be raised, as whether and why the animal which succeeds best at discriminating notes does so also at discriminating rates. And herewith an analysis of function may be achieved ; the ability may reveal, not only a localized factor, but also a general one ; our *s* and *g* may reappear here again. In this manner, after having rendered full justice to the standpoint of Munk, the conditioned reflexes may reveal an element of truth in that also of Flourens.

Psycho-physiological mechanics. The final word on the physiological side of the problem, however, must needs come from the most profound and detailed direct study of the human brain in its purely physical and chemical aspects.

The whole cerebral cortex, like the rest of the nervous system, consists of immensely numerous neurons ; and each of these is made up of three parts, a cell-body, fibres, and an enclosing membrane. Many anatomists have made large claims for the functional significance of the cell-body ; this, they have shown, displays a certain amount of regular variation from one cortical area to another ; striking instances are the large pyramidal cells in the pre-central convolution and the two granular layers in the region of the *fissura calcarina*. But the physiologists, for their part, seem to be short-circuiting such claims by evidence that the cell-bodies—apart from their merely nutritive influence—do nothing but supply a meeting place for, and some reinforcement to, the impulses propagated along the fibres. On turning to these latter, however, they seem always to perform only one and the same extremely simple office ; they act as conductors for a negative electric wave. To subserve the mental functions, then, there would seem to be nothing left but the membranes, especially at the place where two neurons meet ; to these, accordingly, the greatest importance has been attached ; in particular, they have been supposed to be permeable to one of the ions into which an electrolyte is dissociated, but not permeable to its oppositely charged fellow-ion, so that in this way the membrane supports a double electric layer.

On turning to consider how far these physical concepts and facts have gone towards explaining the psychological phenomena, we do not find—and could scarcely hope for—any marked success in the respect of the three qualitative laws of mind ; even those who believe that " matter " as commonly conceived really exists, can hardly be sanguine enough to suppose that any such concept is ever going to account for the occurrence of knowledge. Nor does the situation seem more favourable with respect to one even of the quantitative laws, that of conation ; for matter, as such, is the very antithesis to conation or purposiveness. But about the other four quantitative laws the prospect brightens. With three of them—retentivity (chs. xvi. and xvii.), fatigue (chs. xviii. and xix.), and primordial potency (chs. xxi. and xxii.)—the neural mechanism seems to be rich in explanatory possibilities ; and hereby a long advance is made towards accounting for our specific factor in mental ability, s. As regards the remaining principle, that of span (chs. viii. and xv.), this too would seem, generally speaking, to lie well within the possibility of some material explanation ; but on the other hand, it altogether fails to be accounted for by the particular mechanism as just described, a mere agglomerate of cell-bodies, fibres, and membranes. And together with this failure to explain the law of span goes also—as one might have expected—a similar inability to explain any of the three characters found by us to be mentally universal, g, perseveration, or oscillation.

Proceeding, then, farther afield in the search for some material counterpart to the law of span, the most natural suggestion is to look for this in the physiological concept of "inhibition." But here, the present state of science is, for our purpose, disappointing. Literature, research, and theory are, indeed, abundant ; but all the views at present most strongly advocated—whether that of nutrition, adsorption, physical interference, or synaptic block—are restricted in their scope to what may be called specific antagonism ; that is to say, one particular kind of process tends to hinder some other particular kind. Although such specific antagonism does indeed exist mentally also (for instance, in binocular vision and reversible perspective), it has nothing whatever to do with the mental law of span ; so far as *this* goes, no kind of activity has any sort of personal hostility to any other kind ; instead, there is merely a limitation to the simultaneous total quantity of all kinds (see pp. 113-114).

From this radical objection only one theory of inhibition escapes ; it is the very one which we have already seen (ch. ix.) to have had a very large number of pre-eminent advocates from at least as early as the time of Malebranche. Here, the nervous system is assumed to possess an "energy" in limited amount. Hence, to apply it in any direction is necessarily to drain it from all others ; no explanation could be simpler or more complete.

Nevertheless, physiologists have brought many arguments against it, and, it would seem, with latterly increasing emphasis. Now, some at least of these counter-arguments have certainly gone astray. For instance, it has been urged that an individual may be palpably deficient in mental energy and nevertheless have a full amount of the physiological energy as determined by burning his brain and spinal cord in a calorimeter.[1] But waiving the rather speculative nature of this assertion, surely there is no need to suppose that the entire amount of the energy subserves the conscious processes. Much more plausible seems the view that

[1] Adrian, *Brit. J. Psych.* 1923, xiv.

this service is performed by some *peculiar kind or configuration* of energy.

There are also, however, some other arguments against the energetic theory which do appear to be serious, though not so entirely conclusive as is often supposed. One is that any transfer of energy is definitely opposed to the known nature of the excitatory process in nerve, since each neuron acts as a separate train of gunpowder, producing and consuming its own energy on its own premises (this energy being, too, of infinitesimally minute quantity). But here, even from the purely physico-chemical standpoint, doubt may be felt about the closeness of similarity between the two cases. Each particle of gunpowder explodes quite regardless of the particle lying next beyond it in the train, and *a fortiori* the explosion passes along any single train regardless of further trains that may prolong this. But no such mutual independence appears to have been demonstrated for the successive constituents in a chain of neurons. Furthermore, the very concepts of "producing," "consuming," and transferring energy appear to admit of widely differing interpretations. Fundamentally, there can be neither production nor consumption locally at all, but *solely* transfer. And the manner in which this happens would seem to be still unknown.

Another commonly urged objection is that the transfer of general energy would at any rate fail to explain the inhibition in certain cases, and would therefore involve an undesirable multiplicity of explanations. But to this the reply may be made, that the psychological phenomena themselves cogently indicate inhibition of two radically unlike kinds, namely, general and specific respectively (see ch. vii. pp. 113-114). That these two should have unlike physiological explanations is but natural.

Most important of all, however, is the objection, supported by the great authority of A. V. Hill, that the usage of the term "energy" to explain mental phenomena will lead to confusion with its usage in physics, and will make people think that they understand a thing which they most certainly do not. This seems to the present writer a very real danger indeed. For his part, he is keenly alive to the fact that the energy invoked to explain mental span is of an extremely hypothetical nature. As a concept, it is incomparably less definite than that of the physical energy which serves the physiologist so well. And as for the relation between the two things, this is for the present buried in complete obscurity.

In short, although there seem to be grounds for hoping that a material energy of the kind required by psychologists will some day actually be discovered—whereby physiology will achieve the greatest of all its triumphs—still there is no reason why such energy should have more than a broad analogy to anything of the kind that has been suggested hitherto. Consider, for comparison, how far off the modern concept of electricity is from the old two fluids of Symmer ; yet, by virtue of certain analogies, his view is still to this day found sufficiently near the truth to afford the most convenient concept for the purpose of instructing children. For our present purpose, promising ideas are being put forward already, notably by Head and Myers.[1] The latter writes quite definitely :

" I see no reason why we should not identify central nervous energy with mental energy."

Employing more general terms, the best account so far published of physiological energetics is such as might have been *expressly constructed for dealing with the law of span.* For instance, replace the word " vital " by " mental " in the following summary by W. M. Bayliss and A. V. Hill :

" The phenomena peculiarly characteristic of vital changes are those associated with the actual process of transfer or transformation of energy. . . . The ' struggle for existence ' is for the possession of free energy." [2]

[1] Inter. Congr. for Psychology, 1923.

[2] *Principles of General Physiology*, by Bayliss, ch. ii. revised by A. V. Hill.

Should, however, the rigorous physiologist refuse to be comforted by such broad indications and decline to rely on pious hopes for the future; should he insist on the fact that no energy of the particular kind or configuration here needed has ever actually been discovered; then the answer can only be that certainly *no other* physiological explanation has been found for the mental facts here at issue. And even should the worst arrive and the required physiological explanation remain to the end undiscoverable, the mental facts will none the less remain facts still. If they are such as to be best explained by the concept of an underlying energy, then this concept will have to undergo that which after all is only what has long been demanded by many of the best psychologists—it will have to be regarded as purely mental. Both by history and otherwise, the concept of energy belongs at least as much to the science of mind as to that of matter.

CHAPTER XXIV

CARDINAL CONCLUSIONS

PREPARATORY DESTRUCTIVE CRITICISM

On looking back at the ground traversed in this volume, one almost fears the temerity of having attempted such a vast extent—nothing less than the entire system of fundamental theorems for a large branch of science. Scores of times, only a few curt lines could be spared to report some proposition that had been achieved by long years of labour and was so wide-reaching as to deserve a book for itself. Nevertheless, to conclude, we must here make a still further effort of condensation, in order to concentrate emphasis upon certain results of dominant importance.

The earlier chapters were in the main destructive only. Before any new building could be possible, the ground had to be cleared of many deep-rooted fallacies. One of the most pernicious theoretically was found to be the current usage of the word "intelligence" without any definite idea behind it. Another, that does even greater mischief in practice, was the irrepressible tendency to assume that terms like "attention," "combination," "analysis," "range of association," "co-ordination of hand and eye," and so forth represent so many functional unities or behaviour units. Alongside of these two great impediments to the advance of science has been the pseudo-explanation of the tests of a person's "intelligence" as measuring a "level," "average," or "sample" of his abilities, whereas really no such measurement is conceivably possible—or, in truth, has ever genuinely been attempted.

A CRITERION OF ALL THEORIES

Next, on the other or constructive side, there first followed, not the advancing of any particular theory, but instead the development of a criterion by which to adjudicate upon all theories whatever. This was such as to admit of quantitative gradation ; it did not necessarily condemn any theory at all ; it indicated, rather, *in what degree* the rival theories possess each some modicum of truth.

USE OF QUALITATIVE LAWS

Then this criterion has been applied throughout the whole domain of cognitive activity, thereby affording due satisfaction to those critics who have hitherto quite properly reproached the testers of "intelligence" with failure to show the real scope of their tests, or even to prove that these are anything more than insignificant stunts.

The possibility of such a general survey of cognition has come from the recently developed doctrine of "noegenesis," according to which all knowing originates in three fundamental laws with corresponding processes—the awareness of one's own experience, the eduction of relations, and that of correlates.[1] Each of these, again, admits of sub-classification in an exhaustive manner, so that no considerable field of cognition need be overlooked. For such further subdivision, the most useful concepts have been (a) the different classes of relation that are cognizable, (b) the different kinds of fundaments that can enter into these relations, and (c) the varying kinds and degrees of complexity in which such relations and fundaments can be conjoined.

USE OF QUANTITATIVE LAWS

Besides these three qualitative laws, employment has also been made of the five quantitative ones. These latter, as much as the former, have served here to map out the entire domain of ability and thus render the whole of it amenable to systematic investigation. These five laws are respectively those of Span, Retentivity (two kinds, inertia and dispositions), Fatigue, Conation, and Primordial Potencies (including such influences as those of age, sex, heredity, and health).

DISCOVERY OF G

First and foremost among the results of all these investigations has been a Copernican revolution in point of view. We have not—as all others—set out from an ill-defined mental entity the "intelligence," and then sought to obtain a quantitative value characterising this. Instead, we have started from a perfectly defined quantitative value " g," and then have demonstrated what mental entity or entities this really characterises. The g proved to be a factor which enters into the measurements of ability of all kinds, and which is throughout constant for any individual, although varying greatly for different individuals. It showed itself to be involved invariably and exclusively in all operations of eductive nature, whatever might be the class of relation or the sort of fundaments at issue. It was found to be equally concerned with each of the two general

[1] See *The Nature of Intelligence*, etc., 1923, by the present writer.

dimensions of ability, Clearness and Speed. It also applied in similar manner to both the dimensions of span, which are Intensity and Extensity. But it revealed a surprisingly complete independence of all manifestations of Retentivity. Whether there is any advantage in attaching to this *g*, the old mishandled label of " intelligence," seems at least dubious.

DISCOVERY OF GENERAL INERTIA (C)

Only second in importance to the establishment of *g* has been that of another factor as also possessing functional unity or acting as a behaviour unit. This consists in the first kind of retentivity (see above), and may be called general mental inertia or lag ; another convenient name for it, especially when present to excess, is perseveration. Comparative freedom from it, which with Garnet we may call *c*, has proved to be the main ground on which persons become reputed for " quickness " or for " originality." It would seem to have an extraordinary importance — hitherto almost wholly overlooked — for education, medicine, and industry.

DISCOVERY OF GENERAL OSCILLATION

Yet a third cognitive functional unity has been discovered ; it appertains to the oscillations of mental efficiency (these being probably manifestations of fatigue). Here again is a behaviour-unit with seemingly rich opportunities for practical application.

REJECTION OF DISPOSITIONS

As for the second kind of Retentivity, or the tendency to retain dispositions, this has shown itself *not* to possess any such functional unity (though commonly assumed to do so). Normally, the individual whose dispositions are quickly formed and lastingly retained for one kind of mental operation has little or no general superiority for other kinds.

DISCOVERY OF W

Still another great functional unity has revealed its existence ; this, although not in itself of cognitive nature, yet has a dominating influence upon all exercise or even estimation of cognitive ability. On trying to express it by any current name, perhaps the least unsatisfactory — though still seriously misleading — would be " self-control." It has shown itself to be chiefly responsible for the fact of one person's ability seeming to be more " profound " or more inclined to " common sense " than that of persons otherwise equally capable.

Altogether, then, there are four factors with claims to the character of universality. But only one of them, g, is of such a nature as to manifest appreciable individual differences in the ordinary tests of " intelligence."

CORRELATIONS AND CONSTITUTION OF S

Since the g is only a " factor " in measurements of ability, we can infer that such measurements contain also some further constituent or factor. This has been designated as s.

The first class of leading characteristics about it concern its correlations. Now, under all conditions it is wholly uncorrelated with g. Further—with certain exceptions (chiefly those introduced by the already mentioned inertia, oscillation, and w)—every s is independent of every other one, unless the two operations are closely similar. But this fact at once demolishes all the supposed functional faculties (such as that of " attention ") together with all the " profiles " into which these faculties have been systematised. At the same time is also shown the ineffectiveness of most of the current industrial tests of " specific abilities " ; for any such test to be really valid, it must *very closely* resemble the actual industrial operation at issue.

The second class of characteristics of this s refer to its constitution. This has proved to be very complex. The chief constituents seem to derive from any sensory or motor apparatus that happens to come into play, or else from some influence of retentivity.

HYPOTHESES OF ENERGY, ENGINES, AND ENGINEER

So far, we have carefully restricted ourselves to the bare facts that have been definitely ascertained. In particular, we have introduced no hypothesis as to the essential nature of what is measured by g. For anything we have urged, it might consist in any of the alternatives specified in ch. vi. Indeed, save for some particular and cogent evidence to the contrary, it might even have been some mathematical function of a large number of elements distributed by " chance." And we are under no absolute necessity of going beyond these actually established facts. But for scientific ends, there is much advantage in doing so. For the purpose of building up an intelligible whole, and also for that of inspiring further investigation, there is urgent need of framing —however tentatively and provisionally—some or other explanatory hypothesis.

Now, out of all that have been suggested hitherto, one and only one appears to fit all the facts known at present. This is to regard g as measuring something analogous to an " energy " ; that is to say, it is some force capable of being transferred from one mental operation to another different one. Even on the physiological side, there are some grounds for hoping that some such energy will sooner or later be discovered in the nervous system, especially the cerebral cortex.

Moreover, both the other two cognitive universal factors that we have been able to establish can be regarded as further aspects of this same energy ; whilst g measures its quantity, the other two may represent its inertia and its oscillation.

But all energy needs to be supplemented by some engine or engines in which to operate. And such engines are obviously supplied by the nervous system, in so far as its function is localised. Incidentally, this leads to the suggestion that cerebral localization serves three main purposes, sensation, movement, and retention. Some of us may be inclined to take yet another step and think that, where energy and engines operate, there must furthermore exist an engineer. And this requirement also seems to be met, namely, in the conative law as expounded in ch. xix. and as specially manifested in *w*.

THE SCIENTIFICATION OF PSYCHOLOGY

Nevertheless, science is never final. All the preceding conclusions—and even more so, the minor ones mentioned earlier—will probably in the course of time suffer at least modification. The very formulation of them here will, it is hoped, serve to elicit further and still more searching inquiry.

In fact, our essential aim throughout has been to stimulate psychologists towards investigation of more fundamental and therefore more fruitful kind than is now customary. Our system of ultimate mental laws, together with the statistical criterion, did actually inspire by far the larger part of all the mass of research that has here been quoted. But over twenty years of arduous work were needed to do this. Had these efforts of a small band of investigators been seconded by the almost limitless resources—spiritual and material—of other psychological laboratories, the harvest garnered might by this time have been great indeed.

Besides thus inspiring research for facts, our aim has been to arrange these when ascertained into one orderly intelligible system. This should embrace, not only all individual differences of cognitive ability, but also the whole general psychology of cognition, as well as its linkage to that of conation. And actually in the preceding volume the entire wealth of experimentally ascertained facts—even such of these as had been discovered in ignorance of the said laws—does seem to have spontaneously fitted into such a unitary system without apparent remainder. In this way, it is hoped, a step has been achieved towards supplying psychology with a genuinely scientific foundation.

APPENDIX CONTENTS

APPENDIX

I. Proof of Divisibility into the Two Factors.

1. *Original criterion and proof.*—The commencement consisted in noting that, when any pair of abilities are to any extent correlated with each other, to this extent *they can be regarded as depending upon a common factor* (either simple or complex). Otherwise expressed, each of the abilities may be taken to involve two factors, the one common to both, the other specific to that ability alone. Let, for example, the pair be the discrimination of musical pitch and that of visual length. For brevity, let us call these a and b respectively. Each of these discriminations will have a specific factor, which we will call s_a and s_b respectively ; and they will also have a factor in common, say g. As a further step, we may regard a and b as two different measures of g, whilst s_a and s_b represent the random errors made in the two measurings.

Let now another pair of abilities be brought upon the scene ; for example, the power to succeed at school work and the trait which bears the name of " common sense." These two sorts of " intelligence " can, of course, be treated in just the same way as the two sorts of discrimination. If p denotes the one intelligence and q the other, whilst g' is whatever belongs to both, then p can be regarded as measuring g' with the error s_p and q as measuring it with the error s_q.

But at this stage of the argument, we can employ the formula that has been devised for the purpose of eliminating the " attenuating " effect of such random errors upon any correlation, and in this way we obtain the value of the correlation between g and g' themselves. The corrective formula, expressed generally for two measurements, is as follows :

$$r_{uv} = \frac{\left(r_{u_1v_1} \cdot r_{u_1v_2} \cdot r_{u_2v_1} \cdot r_{u_2v_2}\right)^{\frac{1}{4}}}{\left(r_{u_1u_2} \cdot r_{v_1v_2}\right)^{\frac{1}{2}}} , \dagger \tag{1}$$

* All this original proof of the divisibility into two factors will be found in a paper by the present writer in the *Am. J. Psych.* 1904, xv. pp. 268-272.

† It should be noted that the correction for attenuation only has, and only can have, the virtue of producing *on an average* the true amount of correlation. Hence, if this true amount is close on unity, the correction will in nearly half the cases produce values *greater than unity*, although no such amounts of correlation are actually possible. $r_{u_1u_2}$ and $r_{v_1v_2}$ have been called " reliability " coefficients.

i

where u and v are any variables, the subscripts 1 and 2 indicate the first and second measurements respectively, whilst r_{uv} is the desired corrected correlation

For our present purposes, then, all we have to do is to replace in the equation (1) the symbols u_1, u_2, v_1, v_2, u and v by a, b, p, q, g and g' respectively.

Now, the needful experiments and calculations were actually made, with the remarkable result that this correlation between g and g' proved to be almost perfect. That is to say, it was found that approximately,

$$r_{gg'} = 1 \cdot 00. \tag{2}$$

But since g and g' are thus correlated perfectly, they can have no specific factors relatively to one another. And in this way, the factor common to the two sensory discriminations showed itself to be functionally identical with that common to the two intelligences. Expressing the same fact in other words, we may say that the measurements of all four abilities proved to be divisible into two factors each, the one being common to all four, whilst the other was in each case specific and independent.

2. *Later forms of criterion and proof.*—In 1906, Krueger and the present writer used a proof of substantially the same nature as that given above. Their criterion also agreed, being immediately derivable from the above (1) and (2), since it was of the form :

$$\left(r_{ab} \cdot r_{pq}\right)^{\frac{1}{2}} = \left(r_{ap} \cdot r_{aq} \cdot r_{bp} \cdot r_{bq}\right)^{\frac{1}{4}} * \tag{3}$$

Shortly afterwards, however, one of us suggested that (3) could conveniently be converted into the following more lucid shape

$$\frac{r_{ap}}{r_{aq}} = \frac{r_{bp}}{r_{bq}}. \dagger \tag{4}$$

The proof of the convertibility (not previously published) is as follows. By assumption (3) holds good whichever of the four variables at issue are denoted by a, b, p and q respectively. We can therefore get another equation from (3) by interchanging in it b and p. Similarly, a third equation can be got from (3) by interchanging in it b and q. From these three equations, simple arithmetic leads to the equation (4).

For this new form, however, a new proof was devised. Objection had been raised to that given originally on the score of being " vague." But now (4) was directly derived from Yule's well-

* *Zeit. f. Psych.* 1906, xliv. p. 85.

† See Burt, *Brit. J. Psych.* 1909, iii. p. 159, footnote.

known formula for partial correlations. Let $r_{ap.g}$ denote the correlation that a would have with p if the influence of the general factor g were eliminated. Then, by Yule's formula,

$$r_{ap.g} = \frac{r_{ap} - r_{ag} \cdot r_{pg}}{(1 - r_{ag}^2)^{\frac{1}{2}}(1 - r_{pg}^2)^{\frac{1}{2}}}.$$

But by definition of r_{ap}, $r_{ap.g} = 0$, so that $r_{ap} = r_{ag} \cdot r_{pg}$, and similarly, $r_{bp} = r_{bg} \cdot r_{pg}$. Hence $r_{ag}/r_{bg} = r_{ap}/r_{bp}$, and in the same way $= r_{aq}/r_{bq}$, which gives us at once the above equation (4).*

Subsequently, the only change made in the criterion has been the obvious conversion of (4) into the more convenient " tetrad equation " (see p. 73), namely,

$$r_{ap}r_{bq} - r_{bp}r_{aq} = 0. \tag{5}$$

3. *Reversibility of proof.*—The preceding demonstration had been to the effect that, when every variable could be divided into the two factors g and s, then the criterion (in whichever of its forms) would necessarily be satisfied. There remained the far more difficult reverse problem, namely, as to whether, when the criterion was satisfied, then every variable would necessarily be divisible into the said two factors.

This problem was first solved, and affirmatively, by Garnett for the case of " normal " frequency distribution of the variables.†
Another solution, this time covering all frequency distributions whatsoever, so long as the number of variables is large, was given by the present writer.‡ Finally, a complete solution of the problem, including all manner of distribution and any number of variables, was given by the present writer, as follows : §

From (4) or (5) we may readily get

$$r_{xy} = \lambda_{xz}r_{yz}, \tag{6}$$

where λ_{xz} is constant whilst y takes all values except x or z.

Our question, then, is tantamount to asking whether, on assuming (6), each of the variables involved, say a, can be reduced to the form

$$a = f_a\eta + \delta_a, \tag{7}$$

where 1. f_a, f_b, etc., are constant for all particular values of a, b, etc.
2. η is an element common to all the variables.
3. δ_a, δ_b, etc., are uncorrelated with η,
4. δ_a, δ_b, etc., are uncorrelated with each other.

* Hart and Spearman, *Brit. J. Psych.* 1912, v. p. 58.
† *Proc. Royal Society*, A. lxxxxvi. 1919.   ‡ *Psych. Rev.* 1920, pp. 167-8.
§ *Proc. Royal Society*, A. ci. 1922.

Now, we can always write any of the variables, say a, so as to satisfy 1 and 2, giving to f_a and to η any values we please, so long as, and only so long as, $\delta_a = a - f_a\eta$.

But in order to fulfil the third condition, we must also have

$$0 = r_{(a - f_a\eta)(f_a\eta)}$$ which is equivalent to $0 = \sigma_a r_{a\eta} - f_a\sigma_\eta,$[†]

which $= r_{a\eta} - f_a$, if this time we choose the units so that

$$\sigma_a = \sigma_b = \ldots \sigma_\eta = 1.$$

Hence we can fulfil the third condition by, and only by, making $f_a = r_{a\eta}$.

In such manner, the first three conditions can be satisfied for any set of variables whatever. But there remains the fourth condition, which will be satisfied if, and only if, we also obtain

$$0 = r_{\delta_a\delta_b} = r_{(a - f_a\eta)(b - f_b\eta)}$$ and therefore

$$= r_{ab} - f_a r_{b\eta} - f_b r_{a\eta} + f_a f_b,$$[†] which, on replacing the f's by their values from (7)

$$= r_{ab} - r_{a\eta} r_{b\eta}. \tag{8}$$

This is effected easily in the case where the set of variables entering into the table of coefficients is very large. For then we need only choose for η the value of $\overset{x=z}{\underset{x=a}{S}}$, where the summation is over the said large number of variables, and there is a change of unit so as to make $\sigma_\eta = 1$. For now we get

$$r_{a\eta} = \frac{\sqrt{(m)}\,\bar{r}_{ax'}}{\sqrt{(1 + [m-1]\bar{r}_{x'x''})}},$$[†]

where $x' \neq x''$ denote any of the variables including a itself, whilst m is the number of these variables

$$= \frac{\bar{r}_{ax'}}{\sqrt{(\bar{r}_{x'x''})}}$$ approximately,

since m is by assumption very large.

Hence,　　　　　　$$r_{a\eta} r_{b\eta} = \frac{\bar{r}_{ax'}\bar{r}_{bx'}}{\bar{r}_{x'x''}}. \tag{9}$$

But by (6), if we let x and x^* exclude respectively a and b,

$$r_{ab} = \frac{r_{ax^*}r_{bx^*}}{r_{xx^*}} = \frac{r_{ax'}r_{bx^*}}{\bar{r}_{x'x''}} = \frac{\bar{r}_{ax'}\bar{r}_{bx} + \sigma_{r_{ax}}\sigma_{r_{bx}}r_{r_{ax}r_{bx}}}{\bar{r}_{x'x''}}. \tag{10}$$

Further, the numerator of $r_{r_{ax}r_{bx}}$ can be written as

$$\overline{(r_{ax} - \bar{r}_{ax})(r_{bx^*} - \bar{r}_{bx})},$$

which owing, to the largeness of m, approximates to the value

[†] Spearman, *Brit. J. Psych.* vol. v. p. 419.

it would have if x and x^* took all values quite independently of each other. And this is zero.

Again owing to the largeness of m, $\bar{r}_{ax'}$ and $\bar{r}_{bx'}$ approximate respectively to $\bar{r}_{ax}$ and $\bar{r}_{bx}$.

Accordingly, r_{ab} approximates to $\dfrac{\bar{r}_{ax'} \cdot \bar{r}_{bz'}}{\bar{r}_{x'x''}}$, which by (9)

$= r_{a\eta} r_{b\eta}$, so that $r_{\delta_a \delta_b} = 0$ and condition 4 is fulfilled as required. (11)

This not only corroborates the result obtained in the above-mentioned paper of Garnett, but dispenses with his particular assumption of "normal" frequency distributions, so that it extends the theorem to one of perfect generality, except that m must be very large.

In order to fulfil condition 4 freed even from *this* limitation, the constitution of η must be more complicated. Let us choose for it the value expressed in the following determinant

$$
\begin{vmatrix}
p\surd(S/M_i i) & p\mu_a a & p\mu_b b & . & p\mu_z z \\
-1 & \mu_a{}^2 - 1 & 0 & . & 0 \\
-1 & 0 & \mu_b{}^2 - 1 & . & 0 \\
. & . & . & . & . \\
-1 & 0 & 0 & . & \mu_z{}^2 - 1
\end{vmatrix},
$$

where $\mu_a \equiv 1/\surd(\lambda_{aq} r_{aq})$, λ having a meaning as in (6), so that μ_a retains the same value whatever variable may be taken as q,

$i \equiv$ *any new* variable uncorrelated with all the others $(\sigma = 1)$,†

$M_i \equiv$ the complementary minor of the first element ‡ in the first row,

$S \equiv$ the sum of such minors for all elements in the first row,

and p is such a value as will make $\sigma_\eta = 1$.

This gives us, expanding the determinant according to the elements of the first row,§

$$
r_a = \frac{\mu_a M_a + \mu_b M_b r_{ab} + \ldots + \mu_z M_z r_{az}}{\surd(\mu_a{}^2 M_a{}^2 + \ldots + \mu_z{}^2 M_z{}^2 + M_i S + 2S_x S_y[\mu_x \mu_y M_x M_y r_{xy}])}.
$$

† This is here assumed to be possible, at any rate if the present theorem is only applied to a finite number of variables. The case of an infinite number has already been demonstrated by (11).

‡ Of course, "element" is here no longer used with the same meaning as previously in this paper.

§ Spearman, *Brit. J. Psych.* vol. v. p. 419.

But by (6)

$$r_{xy} = \lambda_{xq} r_{yq} = \lambda_{yq} r_{xq} = \sqrt{(\lambda_{xq} r_{xq})} \sqrt{(\lambda_{yq} r_{yq})} = 1/\mu_x \, 1/\mu_y,$$

so that

$$r_{a\eta} = \frac{1}{\mu_a} \frac{(\mu_a^2 - 1)M_a + S'}{\sqrt{([\mu_a^2 - 1]M_a^2 + \ldots + [\mu_z^2 - 1]M_z^2 + M_i S + S'^2)}},$$

where $S' = S - M_i$.

But, on considering the determinant, clearly $(\mu_x^2 - 1)M_x = M_i$. Substituting M_i accordingly,

$$r_{a\eta} = \frac{1}{\mu_a} \frac{S}{\sqrt{(M_i S' + S'^2 + M_i S)}} = \frac{1}{\mu_a}. \qquad (12)$$

Consequently $r_{ab} - r_{a\eta} r_{b\eta}$ or $r_{\delta_a \delta_b} = 0$. And extending this result to all the other variables, all of them become actually reduced to the required form of $f_x \eta + \delta_x$, fulfilling all the required conditions.

4. *Freedom of criterion from influence of " attenuation."*—Not infrequently, the objection has been raised to the usage of the preceding criterion in one or other of its forms (3), (4) or (5), on the ground that the correlations concerned ought first to be corrected for " attenuation " before they can properly be submitted to the criterion at all.

But this is an error. If the criterion is passed by the correlations when they are corrected for attenuation, then it must also be passed when they are not so. And *vice versa*. This may be seen in the following manner. Suppose that the correlations as attenuated satisfy (4), so that

$$r_{ap}/r_{aq} = r_{bp}/r_{bq}.$$

On correcting for attenuation, r_{ap} becomes multiplied by

$$(1 + r_{a_1 a_2})^{\frac{1}{2}} (1 + r_{p_1 p_2})^{\frac{1}{2}} / 2r_{a_1 a_2}^{\frac{1}{2}} \cdot r_{p_1 p_2}^{\frac{1}{2}}.^{*}$$

But on making all such multiplications throughout any of the equations (3), (4) or (5), it remains eventually quite unchanged.

5. *Division otherwise than into g and s.*—The fact that any variable can be divided into the two factors g and s does not, of course, preclude it from being divisible in an infinity of other ways. Take the case particularly interesting us, where Thomson composed each variable by adding together very numerous independent factors, so that

$$V = v_1 + \ldots + v_N.$$

He so ingeniously arranged this composition that none of the v's were general factors, but any number of them could be

* Present writer, *Brit. J. Psych*, 1910, iii. p. 276.

" group " ones, and yet nevertheless the tetrad equation was almost perfectly satisfied.   But in every such case, as Garnett proceeded to show, the V could equally well be divided instead as follows :

$$V = g + s_v,$$

that is, just our general and specific factors.   The connection between the two manners of division is given by

$$g = \frac{1}{N^{\frac{1}{2}}}(v_1 + \dots + v_N).$$

It appears, then, that each of Thomson's v's had really introduced a little bit out of the g together with a little bit out of the s_v, these bits being on the whole (by the special arrangement of " chance ") so matched that each pair was independent of all the other pairs.*

On the other hand, although the division is always possible in different ways, this is inevitably at the price of introducing limiting conditions.   As a particularly important example of such limitations, let us consider the doctrine of " faculties." To fix our ideas, suppose one of these to be " Comprehension " and another to be " Invention."   If we take any two operations belonging to each of these, denoting them by the suffixes a and b, there ensues the following tetrad of correlations :

	Comprehension$_a$,	Invention$_a$,
Comprehension$_b$,	$r_{c_a c_b}$	$r_{c_b i_a}$
Invention$_b$,	$r_{c_a i_b}$	$r_{i_a i_b}$

Since by the doctrine of faculties Comprehension is a unitary function, it must contain a large group factor which greatly raises the value of the correlation between c_a and c_b.   The same happens as regards that between i_a and i_b.   On both grounds, the product $r_{c_a c_b} \cdot r_{i_a i_b}$ will—in conflict with the tetrad equation— tend to be greater than the product $r_{c_a i_b} \cdot r_{c_b i_a}$.

There is another particularly important limitation to the divisibility of the variables into factors.   It is that the division into general and specific factors all mutually independent can be effected *in one way only* ; in other words, it is unique.   For the proof of this momentous theorem, we have to thank Garnett.†

6. *Extension of* g *to cases of " overlap."*—The demonstrations given so far have confined themselves to establishing the presence of one and the same g throughout any set of variables whose s's

* See Garnett, *Brit. J. Psych.* 1920, **x**.
† *Brit. J. Psych.* 1920, **x**. pp. 252-253.

are mutually independent (so that the tetrad equation is satisfied). The problem, then, arises of ascertaining whether the existence of a common g can also be established between variables whose s's are not independent, but on the contrary overlap. Our consideration may be aided by the following figures.

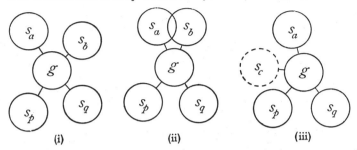

In Fig. (i) the linked pair of circles g and s_a jointly represent the ability a ; g and s_b jointly represent b ; and so on.

Here the specific factors do not overlap ; the tetrad equation holds good.

In Fig. (ii) the representation of the linked pairs of circles is as before.

But here the specific factors of a and b do overlap, so that the tetrad equation can no longer hold. How in this case—we are asking—can proof ever be furnished that either a or b contains the g which is common to p and q ?

This is done simply by finding out some further ability c which, taken conjointly with a, p, and q, does satisfy the tetrad equation. Such a case is illustrated in Fig. (iii).

When such a further ability can be found, this fact serves to demonstrate that the g which is common to.p and q is also shared by a. And a similar proceeding, of course, can show that this same g is shared by b also. Moreover, the facts represented in Figs. (ii) and (iii) respectively may quite well be derived from different investigations. After this fashion then, partly as in Fig. (i) and partly as in Fig. (iii), one and the same g may be shown to extend over any domain however large. In every ability within this domain, the g will always be independent of the accompanying s. But the different s's will only be mutually independent so long as the abilities containing them do not overlap.

II. Allowance for Errors of Sampling.

1. *Inter-columnar correlation.*—As an illustration of what this " inter-columnar correlation " means, we may turn to the table

of (imaginary) correlations given on p. 74. Let us select any two columns in this table, say the first and second, omitting in each the value which has no counterpart in the other. We get :

				Opposites.	Completion.
Memory	-	-	-	·60	·48
Discrimination	-	-		·30	·24
Cancellation	-	-		·30	·24

Between these two columns, evidently, the correlation can be calculated ; and, as may easily be seen, it is perfect ; the values in the one column always keep in the same proportion to those in the other. This correlation it is that has been termed " inter-columnar " and denoted by R_{xy}, where x and y symbolize any two columns (in our illustration, Opposites and Completion). The criterion to act as substitute for (3), (4) or (5) is, then,

$$R_{xy} = 1·00.* \tag{13}$$

Unfortunately, this substitute is not exact. In the first place, it may be satisfied perfectly when the true criterion is so imperfectly. Let, for example, the two columns of correlations in question be :

·10	·10
·20	·40
·30	·70

At a glance, one can see that (13) is perfectly satisfied, but not (4) or (5). A second and much more serious objection, however, is that (13) becomes altogether unusable whenever the correlations in either of the two columns compared have a small mean scatter compared with their probable errors. As an extreme case, let the columns be :

·20	·40
·20	·40
·20	·40

Obviously, both (4) and (5) are satisfied perfectly, but the inter-columnar correlation has no determinate value at all. As a result of this, (13) has the grave disadvantage of usually not being applicable to all the pairs of columns in a table of correlations, but only to a portion of them. And the consequences introduced by this selectiveness in usage are not easy to foretell.†

* Hart and Spearman, *Brit. J. Psych.* 1912.

† The precise relation between (13) and (4) has been demonstrated by Garnett (*Proc. R. Soc.*, A. 1919).

2. *Compensation of inter-columnar correlation for errors of sampling.*—The reason why this inter-columnar correlation was introduced and widely employed, despite this grave defect, lay in the fact that means had been found to make compensation in it for the effect of errors of sampling. Just this compensatory formula, however, has originated the most acute controversy about the theory of Two Factors. The objections of Thomson,* in particular, amounted in substance to asserting that the proof of the compensatory inter-columnar correlation treated as negligible a certain quantity which he for his part maintained to be far from being so. In reply to this, however, the present writer was able to show that almost identically the same compensatory formula could be reached by an entirely different proof which neglected nothing at all except—as is done throughout the theory of correlations—terms involving higher differentials.† But, of course, this reply did nothing to free this substitute criterion (13) from the above mentioned fault of being only applicable in a selective manner.

3. *Probable error of the tetrad difference.*—For this last reason, it was an immense advance when the whole usage of this inter-columnar correlation could be dropped—and thereby incidentally the quarrel about its compensation be short-circuited—by the discovery of the probable error of the tetrad difference which forms the left side of equation (5).

The full value for the squared standard deviation of the tetrad difference $r_{13}r_{24} - r_{23}r_{14}$ is as given by Holzinger and the present writer in the *Brit. J. Psych.* 1924, xv. p. 19, namely :

$$\frac{1}{N^{\frac{1}{2}}}\left[r^2_{13} + r^2_{14} + r^2_{23} + r^2_{24} - 2\left(r_{12}r_{13}r_{23} + r_{12}r_{14}r_{24} + r_{13}r_{14}r_{34} + r_{23}r_{24}r_{34}\right)\right.$$
$$\left. + 4r_{13}r_{14}r_{23}r_{24}\right].$$

To get the probable error from this, the usual convention has been adopted of taking the square root and then multiplying by ·6745.

But since the using of so many terms is laborious, there is need of something simpler that will, nevertheless, be sufficiently approximate for most practical purposes. Originally, a very simple formula indeed was proposed by us.‡ It was—

$$\text{p.e.} = \frac{1·349}{N^{\frac{1}{2}}}r(1 - r) \tag{14}$$

* *Essentials of Mental Measurements*, 1921, chs. ix. and x. For conclusive arguments against all his other objections, see Udny Yule (*Brit. J. Psych.* 1921, xii. p. 100) and Garnett (*Brain*, 1921, xliv. p. 332).

† *Brit. J. Psych.* 1923, xiii. p. 268. *Ibidem*, 1924, xv. p. 19.

‡ *Brit. J. Psych.* 1924, xv. p. 19.

where r denotes the mean of the correlations taken into account. The values given in this way, however, turned out to be often appreciably too small. We then proposed the following approximation.

$$\text{p.e.} = \frac{1 \cdot 349}{N^{\frac{1}{2}}} [r^2(\mathrm{I} - r)^2 + s^2]^{\frac{1}{2}} \qquad (15)$$

where s^2 is the mean squared deviation of all the r's from their mean.* But this was usually found to err somewhat in the opposite direction, that of giving too large values.†

A much closer approximation than either is given by the following :

$$\text{p.e.} = \frac{1 \cdot 349}{N^{\frac{1}{2}}} [r^2(\mathrm{I} - r_{12} - r_{34} + r^2) + (\mathrm{I} - 2r^2)s^2]^{\frac{1}{2}}. \qquad (16)$$

There is possible, however, quite a different procedure ; it is one which—although on some theoretical points still awaiting further elucidation—in practice at any rate appears to be far more convenient, and even more reliable, than (14), (15), or (16). Here, one single frequency distribution is made up of all the tetrad differences that arise from any number of variables. Its squared p.e. can easily be shown to equal the mean of the squared p.e.'s for all the tetrad differences taken separately ; and this mean has been proved to have approximately the following value, which has been used in the preceding volume.‡

$$\text{p.e.} = \frac{1 \cdot 349}{N^{\frac{1}{2}}} [r^2(\mathrm{I} - r)^2 + (\mathrm{I} - R)s^2]^{\frac{1}{2}}, \qquad (16\text{A})$$

where

$$R = 3r\frac{n-4}{n-2} - 2r^2\frac{n-6}{n-2}.$$

It should be noted that in this equation (as in all the previous ones), the p.e. is obtained by the usual convention that it $= \cdot 6745\sigma$. Sometimes, this will be appreciably inaccurate. Usually, however, it will be near enough for the present purpose of estimating the range of sampling errors, especially where (as here) the frequency distribution proves to be fairly " normal." See the distributions on pages 146 and 149, as also the lower one on page 154.

* *Ibidem*, 1925, xvi. p. 86.

† In arriving at (15), we had treated as negligibly small the terms of the form $d_{xy}d_{xz}$. But Prof. Truman Kelley has kindly suggested that they may be worth taking into account. This, accordingly, we have now done.

‡ The proof will be published shortly.

In order to exemplify these formulas for the p.e., let us take the following table of Bonser : *

	1	2	3	4	5
1. Mathematical judgment -	—	·485	·400	·397	·295
2. Controlled association -	·485	—	·397	·397	·247
3. Literary interpretation -	·400	·397	—	·335	·275
4. Selective judgment -	·397	·397	·335	—	·195
5. Spelling - - - -	·295	·247	·275	·195	—

Now, a tetrad consists of any four correlations which in such a table form a rectangle. The following are three examples :

	1	2		2	5		3	4
3.	·400	·397	1.	·485	·295	2.	·397	·397
4.	·397	·397	3.	·397	·275	5.	·275	·195

Each such tetrad supplies a tetrad difference, that is, the difference between the product of the top left value with the bottom right value and the product of the top right with bottom left value. In the above cases they are respectively :

$$·400 \times ·379 \sim ·397 \times ·397 = ·001,$$
$$·485 \times ·275 \sim ·295 \times ·397 = ·028$$
$$\text{and} \quad ·397 \times ·195 \sim ·397 \times ·275 = ·032.$$

The total number of different tetrad differences for n different variables is $3^n C_4$; and this for our table, comes to 15, since n, the number of variables, $=5$.

Let us first consider the case of a single tetrad difference taken alone, so that we employ the formula (16). This, with the left of the three examples given above, yields the following values :

$$r = (·400 + ·397 + ·397 + ·397)/4 = ·398,$$
$$s^2 = (·002^2 + ·001^2 + ·001^2 + ·001^2)/4,$$
$$\text{which is negligibly small,}$$
$$N = 757.$$

Putting these values into (16), there ensues, p.e. = ·012.

Next we will take an example of calculating the p.e. collectively for a whole table of correlations, and therefore using the formula (16A). In the table given above, the mean (*i.e.* r) is ·342 ; the mean squared deviation (*i.e.* s^2) is ·007 ; whilst n is 5.

Hence $R = 3 \times ·342 \times \dfrac{1}{3} - 2 \times ·342^2 \times \dfrac{-1}{3} = ·420$, so that

$$\text{p.e.} = \frac{1·349}{757^{\frac{1}{2}}} [·342^2 \times ·658^2 + (1 - ·420) \times ·007]^{\frac{1}{2}}$$

$$= ·011, \text{ or much the same as before.}$$

* *Brit. J. Psych.* 1912, v. p. 62.

If we were to neglect R here, we should get p.e. = ·012, or still very approximately the same.

III. Hypothesis of " Chance."

1. *Arbitrariness and artificiality of arrangement.*—The results reached by the three investigators (see p. 96) were strikingly divergent, especially with regard to the " inter-columnar correlation." According to Thomson, this in order to accord with the hypothesis of chance should be perfect. According to Garnett, it should on the contrary be zero. According to Spearman, it should have an intermediate value, equal to the correlation between the two variables from which the columns respectively derive.

The simple reason for this discord was that the three authors had conceived the influence of " chance " in different ways. Very great latitude is possible in this respect. All theories of chance are based upon conceiving certain different elementary events as having an equal probability (or at any rate some constant ratio of probability). And the consequences will greatly vary according to what events are taken to be equally probable.

Thus, to begin with, it is possible to take either the absolute or else the relative values of the elementary events as having equal probability of occurring ; Spearman took the relative version ; Garnett, the absolute one.

A much more important option is in respect of the degree of complication and artificiality introduced. Garnett and Spearman avoided these. They let the basal assumption of equal probabilities work out its course undisturbed by further subsidiary probabilities. But Thomson, on the contrary, introduced several of these subsidiary probabilities, whereby—in the opinion of the present writer—the whole arrangement became artificial to the highest degree. For instance, one of the cardinal rules in statistics is that the frequency of the deviations from the mean should be in inverse relation to their magnitude. But Thomson's arrangement was so constructed that the largest deviations became just as frequent as the smallest. There were many further peculiarities in the arrangement, some of which have already been indicated by Garnett (*Brit. J. Psych.*, 1919, ix.).

2. *Compatibility of " Chance " with the Two Factors.*—Over and above such latitude of arrangement, three main facts have emerged out of the discussion.

The first is that no derivation of mental abilities from any arrangement of chance can under any conditions make the slightest difference to the divisibility of the values into g and s ; this divisibility stands or falls solely with the fulfilment or not of the tetrad equation. Far from being opposed to the theory of g in general, this doctrine of chance is not even opposed to any particular interpretation of g (or of s), but at most brings supplementary details. Take, for example, the interpreting of g as a person's psycho-physical " energy." There is no obvious reason why this energy itself should not derive from a large number of elements distributed among individuals by " chance."

The second leading fact is that this hypothesis of chance, in all three variants, can actually satisfy the tetrad equation. If no further facts entered into the matter, the theory of chance would stand as one of the possible ways of explaining g. Its claims would have to be duly weighed in comparison with those of the rival interpretations.

The third fact, however, is that this hypothesis of chance only satisfied the tetrad equation in a very peculiar way. That is to say (as mentioned on pp. 96-97), it only becomes compatible with the existence of g in proportion as the value of this g for every individual tends to be the same.

IV. The Chief Values required in Practice.

1. *General analysis of a measurement.*—The general form of the analysis is already given on p. 75, footnote. It is as follows :

$$m_{ax} = r_{ag} \cdot g_x + r_{as_a} \cdot s_{ax}, \qquad (17)$$

where m_{ax} denotes the measurement obtained for any individual
  x in any ability (or other variable) a ;

g_x ,, his amount of g, the factor common to all the abilities ;

r_{ag} ,, the correlation between, on the one hand the whole measurement of a, and on the other hand the factor g which a shares with the remainder of the abilities,

whilst r_{as_a} ,, the correlation between the whole measurement of a and the factor s_a specific to a.

In a similar manner, we may get for any other abilities, c, d, etc.,

$$m_{bx} = r_{bg} \cdot g_x + r_{bs_b} \cdot s_{bx},$$

$$m_{cx} = r_{cg} \cdot g_x + r_{cs_c} \cdot s_{cx},$$

$$\cdot \quad \cdot \quad \cdot \quad \cdot$$

For any other individual y, there ensues analogously :

$$m_{ay} = r_{ag} \cdot g_y + r_{as_a} \cdot s_{ay},$$

$$m_{by} = r_{bg} \cdot g_y + r_{bs_b} \cdot s_{by},$$

$$\cdot \quad \cdot \quad \cdot \quad \cdot$$

These varied application of the formula (17) are given in order to illustrate the following points. First of all, g_x is always the same for the individual x, whatever may be the ability under consideration, a, b, c, etc. Contrariwise, his s_{ax}, s_{bx}, s_{cx}, vary from one ability to another independently both of each other and of the value of g_x. Turning to the individual y, he in a similar manner has for all his abilities the same constant factor g_y (which may differ to any degree from g_x) ; but his s_{ay}, s_{by}, s_{cy}, etc., vary in independence of each other and of all the other values. As for the r's, these vary for the different abilities a, b, c, etc., but, of course, do not vary for the different individuals.

The proof of (17) is obtained as follows. It has been shown already (I. 3), that we can write m_{ax} in the following form :

$$m_{ax} = r_{ag} \cdot g_x + s'_{ax}, \tag{18}$$

where m_{ax} and g_x have the same standard deviation. Hence

$$s'_{ax} = m_{ax} - r_{ag} \cdot g_x.$$

And as this holds good for all denotations of x, we get

$$s'_{ax} - \bar{s}_a' = (m_{ax} - \bar{m}_a) - r_{ag}(g_x - \bar{g}).$$

Squaring, summing for all individuals, and dividing by their number, we find that the standard deviation of $s_a' =$ to that of m_a multiplied by $(1 - r_{ag}^2)^{\frac{1}{2}}$. And this latter value will presently (IV. 3) be shown to be $= r_{as_a}$. This result enables us to write the s' in (18) as $r_{as_a} \cdot s_{ax}$, which at once gives (17).

Surprise may be felt that the measurement m_{ax}, even if truly enough a function of the two factors general and specific, should so simply consist of merely the *sum* of these added together. For instance, it might instead, and perhaps with greater plausibility, have been supposed to consist of the *product* of the two factors. Or it might have been any of an endless number of other and more complex functions of the two factors.

The answer to this question is that our proof has depended upon usage of Taylor's theorem, according to which all mathematical functions however complex can, in general, be expressed in the above simple additive form with some approximation. This theorem has supplied the main foundation for the whole theory of correlation, from the original work of Bravais onwards ; indeed, it is among the main props even of physics. For our present purposes we may conclude that, if the measurements of the abilities are really the simple additive functions of the two factors, then we must expect the tetrad equation to be satisfied *exactly* (so far as this point is concerned). Whereas if the measurements are any other functions of the factors, then we can only hope to find the tetrad equation satisfied more or less *approximately*.

2. *To find the correlation of a measurement with* g.—The preceding equation (17) has left us with a known quantity on the left and four unknown ones on the right. Of these four, the first to determine must necessarily be r_{ag}. The simplest solution of this is given below in (19). A far more exact determination is given in (20). An equally exact and more convenient, but not always feasible determination is given in (21)

The proof is as follows :

The correlation between s_a and s_b may be regarded as the partial correlation between a and b eliminating g, so that by Yule's theorem

$$r_{s_a s_b} = r_{ab \cdot g} = (r_{ab} - r_{ag} \cdot r_{bg})/(1 - r_{ag}^2)^{\frac{1}{2}}(1 - r_{bg}^2)^{\frac{1}{2}}.$$

But since this correlation by assumption $= 0$,

$$r_{ab} = r_{ag} \cdot r_{bg} ; \text{ similarly for any other ability } c,$$

$$r_{ac} = r_{ag} \cdot r_{cg},$$

$$r_{bc} = r_{bg} \cdot r_{cg}.$$

Multiplying the first of these equations by the second, dividing the product by the third, and taking roots on both sides,

$$r_{ag} = (r_{ab} \cdot r_{ac}/r_{bc})^{\frac{1}{2}}. \tag{19}$$

As an example, let a, b, and c denote respectively 2, 1, and 3 in the table of Bonser. This gives

$$r_{2g} = (\cdot485 \times \cdot397/\cdot400)^{\frac{1}{2}} = \cdot694.$$

Taking as b and c every other available pair, we get the further determinations of r_{ag} as ·696, ·638, ·697, ·597, and ·709. The usual and easiest way of treating such a set of determinations is to take their average, which $= \cdot668$.

But a shorter and yet a more reliable way than averaging is as follows :

$$r_{ag}^2 = \frac{r_{ab}r_{ac}}{r_{bc}} = \frac{r_{ab}r_{ad}}{r_{bd}} = \ldots = \frac{r_{ax}r_{ay}}{r_{xy}}$$

$$= \frac{r_{ab}r_{ac} + r_{ab}r_{ad} + \ldots + r_{ax}r_{ay} +}{r_{bc} + r_{bd} + \ldots + r_{xy}}, \tag{20}$$

where all the correlational coefficients thus introduced obey the tetrad equation (5).

If, as in our table, all the correlations throughout the table do this, we can reduce (20) to

$$r_{ag} = (A^2 - A')^{\frac{1}{2}}/(T - 2A)^{\frac{1}{2}}, \tag{21}$$

where A is the sum of the correlations between a and every other test, A' is the sum of the squares of these correlations, and T is the total of all the correlations in the whole table. In this way we get

$$r_{2g} = (1 \cdot 526^2 - \cdot 611)^{\frac{1}{2}}/(6 \cdot 846 - 2 \times 1 \cdot 526)^{\frac{1}{2}} = \cdot 718.$$

3. *To find the correlation of a measurement with a specific ability.*—The next step towards interpreting (17) consists in the determination of the value of r_{as_a}. This can be done as follows, resolving it into terms of r_{ag}, which we have just found.

By partial correlations,

$$r_{as_a \cdot g} = (r_{as_a} - r_{ag} \cdot r_{s_a g})/(1 - r^2_{ag})^{\frac{1}{2}} (1 - r^2_{s_a g})^{\frac{1}{2}}.$$

But by assumption $r_{as_a \cdot g} = 1$ and $r_{s_a g} = 0$, so that on substituting these values, there easily ensues,

$$r_{as_a} = (1 - r^2_{ag})^{\frac{1}{2}} \quad \text{and} \quad r_{ag} = (1 - r^2_{as_a})^{\frac{1}{2}} \tag{22}$$

4. *To measure a person's g.*—Lastly we arrive at the practically all-important problem of determining g_x and s_{ax}. The solution is as follows :

$$g_x = r_{ag} \cdot m_{ax}, \tag{23}$$

with a probable error of $\pm \cdot 6745 \, \sigma_a \, (1 - r^2_{ag})^{\frac{1}{2}}$, where σ_a is the standard deviation of a. The proof of (23) has been given in the *Eugenics Review*, 1924, p. 13. But it is at once evident from the general theory of correlations.

We thus see that the common practice of taking g_x as being simply m_{ax} suffers from errors of two kinds. In the first place, m_{ax} has a constant tendency to be too large (either on the plus or the minus side), since it needs to be multiplied by r_{ag}, which is always less than unity. And in the second place, it has the variable tendency indicated by its probable error. Neither of these errors, it seems safe to say, has ever been determined in all the current testing. For they both depend upon the values of r_{ag}, which itself cannot be determined until such loose concepts as " levels " and " samples of all abilities " are replaced by the exact theory of g.

To obtain a notion how such errors pan out in practice, let us suppose $r_{ag} = \cdot 50$. Then the acceptance of m_{ax} in place of g_x means that the value taken is twice as large as it ought to have been ! And besides this constant error in the measurement, there is a variable one as indicated by the above root quantity, which works out to $\cdot 87$. This means that the variable error to be expected from adopting m_{ax} as a valuation of the g of the individual x is no less than 87% of the magnitude to be expected from a pure guess. Can testing of this sort be taken seriously ?

5. *To measure a person's specific ability.*—This value is now easily obtainable by an equation analogous to (23), namely,

$$s_{ax} = r_{as_a} m_{ax},^*$$ (24)

with a probable error of $\cdot 6745\,\sigma_a(\mathrm{I} - r^2_{as_a})^{\frac{1}{2}}$, or more simply $\cdot 6745\,\sigma_a \cdot r_{ag}$.

Here again, the trying out of this formula by inserting various values for r_{ag} discloses that errors of very great magnitude are at issue. When (31A) is available, this value of g_x can be put into (17), whence s_{ax} may be obtained with any desired degree of accuracy.

6. *" Weighting," so as to make the best team of tests.*—For serious testing of g, evidently, we must above all things manage somehow to make the correlation between our measurement and g extremely high.

To effect this, there are two cardinal rules already announced in 1904.† The one is to adopt as measurement, not the result of any single test, but that of a *team* or *pool* of several diverse tests. For it has been shown that, in general, the sum of several variables tends to give larger correlations than most or all of the variables singly.‡ The other rule is that even each of the single tests should correlate as highly as possible with g.

But in addition, we urgently require to know how the single tests should be relatively " weighted " in their combination, as also the degree of correlation with g that can be achieved by weighting in the best possible manner.

When, as usual, the s's do not overlap, the formula for best possible weighting is as given below in (29). The amount of correlation thus obtained is given by (30).

The proof is as follows :

Let the weights to be given to the respective m's be denoted by w's with corresponding subscripts. Then, weighting in the usual way, the score for the whole team of, say, z tests will be proportional to

$$G_x = w_a \cdot m_{ax} + w_b \cdot m_{bx} + \ldots + w_z \cdot m_{zx}.$$ (25)

---

* A kindred but less reliable equation was given by the present writer in 1914, *Eugenics Review*, p. 14.

† Present writer, *Am. J. Psych.* xv.

‡ See Correlation of Sums and Differences, by present writer, *Brit. J. Psych.*

The problem is to discover what values to assign to the w's in order to make r_{tg} as large as possible, where t denotes the measurement supplied by the whole team.

By the formula for correlations of sums (present writer, *Brit. J. Psych.* v. 1913, p. 419),

$$r_{tg} = S(w_u \cdot r_{a_u g})/[S(w_u{}^2) + 2SS(w_u \cdot w_v \cdot r_{a_u a_v})]^{\frac{1}{2}}, \qquad (26)$$

where S indicates summing over all values of u, and SS over all different values for u and v.

The value on the right of the preceding equation will reach its maximum when its total differential, or that of its log, $= 0$. Differentiating, then, the term on the right of (26) with respect to w_u and equating the result to zero, there ensues after some arithmetic

$$\frac{r_{ag}}{w_a + r_{ag} \cdot S'(w_u \cdot r_{ug})} = \frac{S(w_u \cdot r_{ug})}{S(w_u{}^2) + 2SS(w_u \cdot w_v \cdot r_{ug} \cdot r_{vg})}, \qquad (27)$$

where S' indicates summing over all values except a.

But, by symmetry, the term on the left of (27) $=$ a similar term with a replaced by any other letter. In this way we get, with some arithmetic, quite generally,

$$w_u(1 - r_{ug}^2)/r_{ug} = w_v(1 - r_{vg}^2)/r_{vg}. \qquad (28)$$

That is to say, the weight w_u of any correlation r_{ug} has to be made proportional to

$$r_{ug}/(1 - r_{ug}^2). \qquad (29)$$

Let us proceed to ascertain what this ensuing maximum value of r_{tg} amounts to. We have by the formula for correlations of sums quoted above (remembering that all our test-scores have been reduced to equal standard deviations)

$$r_{tg} = S(w_u \cdot r_{ug})/[S(w_u{}^2) + 2SS(w_u \cdot w_v \cdot r_{ug} \cdot r_{vg})]^{\frac{1}{2}},$$

and simplified

$$= 1/(1 + 1/S)^{\frac{1}{2}}, \text{ where } S \text{ denotes } S(w_u \cdot r_{ug}) \qquad (30)$$

7. *To express the team measurement in absolute value.*—The preceding equations have shown us how the single tests should be weighted relatively to one another. But this will only serve to compare the different individuals submitted to this same team of tests ; it will be of no use towards comparing individuals thus tested with those who have been submitted to a different team of tests. For the latter purpose, the standard deviations for the different teams must be equalized (or at least shown to have some common unit).

The simplest and best plan is to make the standard deviation everywhere equal to unity. To do this, first make the standard deviation of each single test equal to unity ; so far, there is no difficulty. Then, by known formula, the mean square deviation of the team of test will be

$$S(w_u{}^2) + 2SS(w_u . w_v . r_{uv}).$$

Replacing, now, each w_u by $r_{ug}/(1 - r_{ug}^2)$ in accordance with (29), the preceding mean square deviation reduces with a little arithmetic to

$$S^2 + S.$$

Hence, finally, denoting the team measurement by t_x, we get

$$t_x = S[m_{ux} . r_{ug}/(1 - r_{ug}^2)] \div (S^2 + S)^{\frac{1}{2}}$$
$$= G_x \div (S^2 + S)^{\frac{1}{2}}. \tag{31}$$

Hence, using the usual regression equation,

$$g_x = r_{tg} . t_x$$
$$= G_x/(S + 1). \tag{31A}$$

8. *An example of the calculation.*—For the Bonser table, we have already found r_{2g} in iv. 2. We can similarly get r_{1g}, r_{3g}, r_{4g} and r_{5g}. Thereupon we can fill up the following scheme, which will supply all the values here required :

Test.	r_{ug}	$w_u = $ $r_{ug}/(1 - r_{ug}^2)$	$w_u . r_{ug}$	Scores (imaginary) of the individual x.	Scores × w_u
1	·701	1·401	·984	+ 1·3	+ 1·822
2	·672	1·224	·823	+ ·9	+ 1·102
3	·607	·952	·578	+ 1·2	+ 1·141
4	·550	·789	·437	+ 1·5	+ 1·182
5	·398	·471	·188	− ·1	− ·047
		$Z = 4·837$	$S = 3·010$		$G_x = + 5·200$

From these,

$$r_{tg} = 1/(1 + 1/S)^{\frac{1}{2}} = 1/(1 + 1/3·010)^{\frac{1}{2}} = ·866,$$
$$t_x = G_x/(S^2 + S)^{\frac{1}{2}} = 5·2/(3·010^2 + 3·010)^{\frac{1}{2}} = 1·807.$$

The preceding method is not theoretically inconsistent, of course, with weighting according to Yule's well-known regression for multiple correlations.

It seems hardly needful to remark that the above elaborate way of calculating t_x is not intended for application every time that any child is submitted to a test of g. It supplies, rather, a standard by which any briefer method actually employed can always be checked up.

9. *To get "reference values" for detecting specific correlation.*[*]—Let the two abilities to be examined for specific correlation be denoted by v and w, whilst the further available tests are $t_1, \ldots t_n$. The correlations of v and w with the t's are assumed to be given; also, the inter-correlations between the t's. In addition, we assume that all the said correlations may be taken to be exclusively due to g. A method is required of collecting the t's into two pools with the least possible arbitrariness.

When feasible, the most natural method is to take half the t's for the one pool and half for the other, choosing them in such a manner that the mean inter-correlation of the t's in one pool is equal to that in the other. We then get, using the theorem for correlations of sums : [†]

$$r_{(t_1+\ldots+t_{\frac{n}{2}})(t_{\frac{n}{2}+1}+\ldots+t_n)} = \frac{\frac{n}{2}\bar{r}_{t_x t_y}}{1+\left(\frac{n}{2}-1\right)\bar{r}_{t_x t_y}}, \tag{32}$$

$$r_{(t_1+\ldots+t_{\frac{n}{2}})v} = \frac{\left(\frac{n}{2}\right)^{\frac{1}{2}}\bar{r}_{t_x v}}{\left[1+\left(\frac{n}{2}-1\right)\bar{r}_{t_x t_y}\right]^{\frac{1}{2}}}, \tag{33}$$

$$r_{(t_{\frac{n}{2}+1}+\ldots+t_n)w} = \frac{\left(\frac{n}{2}\right)^{\frac{1}{2}}\bar{r}_{t_x w}}{\left[1+\left(\frac{n}{2}-1\right)\bar{r}_{t_x t_y}\right]^{\frac{1}{2}}}. \tag{34}$$

Whenever these two natural pools cannot be made, two others can be constructed instead, whose correlations with one another and also with v and w have the same values as shown in (32), (33) and (34). For suppose each t, say t_x, to be divided into two parts t'_x and t''_x such that for all denotations of x these two have the same mean square deviations, whilst the correlation between the two is equal to the mean correlation between all the $2n$

parts of the n t's. These two conditions can (with large populations) always be satisfied. There is no need, be it observed, to construct the parts *actually*. By virtue of these divisions we get at once,

$$\bar{r}_{t_x t_y} = \frac{2 r_{t_x^\times t_y^\times}}{1 + r'_{t_x t_x''}}, \text{ where } t^\times \text{ stands for either } t' \text{ or } t'', \tag{35}$$

$$\bar{r}_{t_x v} = \frac{2^{\frac{1}{2}} \bar{r}_{t_x^\times v}}{[1 + r'_{t_x t_x''}]^{\frac{1}{2}}}, \tag{36}$$

$$\bar{r}_{t_x w} = \frac{2^{\frac{1}{2}} r_{t_x^\times w}}{[1 + r'_{t_x t_x''}]^{\frac{1}{2}}}. \tag{37}$$

But, by employing these last three equations, we can get without difficulty the three of which we stand in need. That is to say, we find that the three correlations,

$$r_{(t_1' + \ldots + t_n')(t_1'' + \ldots + t_n'')}, \quad r_{(t_1' + \ldots + t_n')v} \quad \text{and} \quad r_{(t_1'' + \ldots + t_n'')w}$$

are equal respectively to the right-hand sides of the equations (32), (33) and (34).

The required pools are, then, $(t_1' + \ldots + t_n')$ and $(t_1'' + \ldots + t_n'')$.

As an example, we may take the experiments of Davey quoted on page 224. The tests to be examined for specific correlation were Inference and Likelihood, whilst there were six further tests to supply the two pools. Their mean correlation with Inference was ·353 ; with Likelihood, ·360 ; and with each other, ·445. There ensue, using (32), (33) and (34),

$$r_{g_a g_b} = \frac{3 \times \cdot 445}{1 + 2 \times \cdot 445} = \cdot 709,$$

$$r_{g_a i} = \frac{3^{\frac{1}{2}} \times \cdot 353}{(1 + 2 \times \cdot 445)^{\frac{1}{2}}} = \cdot 445,$$

and

$$r_{g_b l} = \frac{3^{\frac{1}{2}} \times \cdot 360}{(1 + 2 \times \cdot 445)^{\frac{1}{2}}} = \cdot 452.$$

10. *To find the value of a specific correlation.*—This is a value which has often been quoted in the preceding volume. Since it is the value which the correlation between a and b becomes when the influence of g is eliminated, it can be determined at once by the method of partial correlations, as follows :

$$r_{s_a s_b} = r_{ab \cdot g} = (r_{ab} - r_{ag} \cdot r_{bg})/(1 - r_{ag}^2)^{\frac{1}{2}} (1 - r_{bg}^2)^{\frac{1}{2}}. \tag{38}$$

Here r_{ab} is known immediately, whilst r_{ag} and r_{bg} are given by (19), (20), or (21). If the two latter values are determined reliably, the probable error of $r_{s_a s_b}$ becomes known, being equal to that of r_{ab}. In this way we get a substitute for the tetrad equation in

$$r_{s_\iota s_b} = 0. \tag{39}$$

For example, the specific correlation between 1 and 2 in Bonser's table

$$= (\cdot485 - \cdot701 - \cdot672)/(1 - \cdot701^2)^{\frac{1}{2}}(1 - \cdot672^2)^{\frac{1}{2}} = \cdot027,$$

whilst its p.e. for zero correlation

$$= \cdot6745/(757)^{\frac{1}{2}} = \cdot024,$$

or just about the same magnitude, so that the specific correlation is *not* significant.

INDEX

(Pages in the Appendix are denoted by *Roman* numerals.)